LOST AND FOUND

AN
AMY DEVLIN
MYSTERY

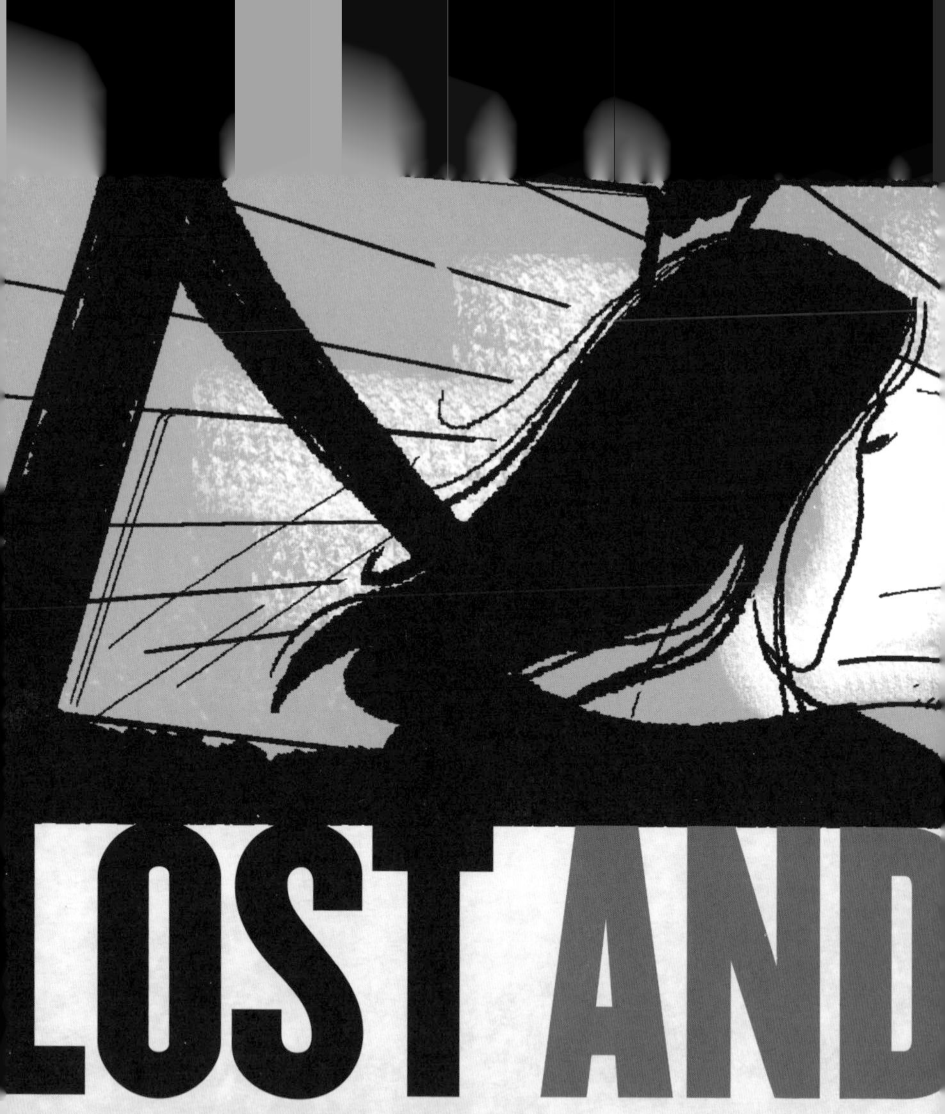

LOST AND

AN AMY DEVLIN MYSTERY

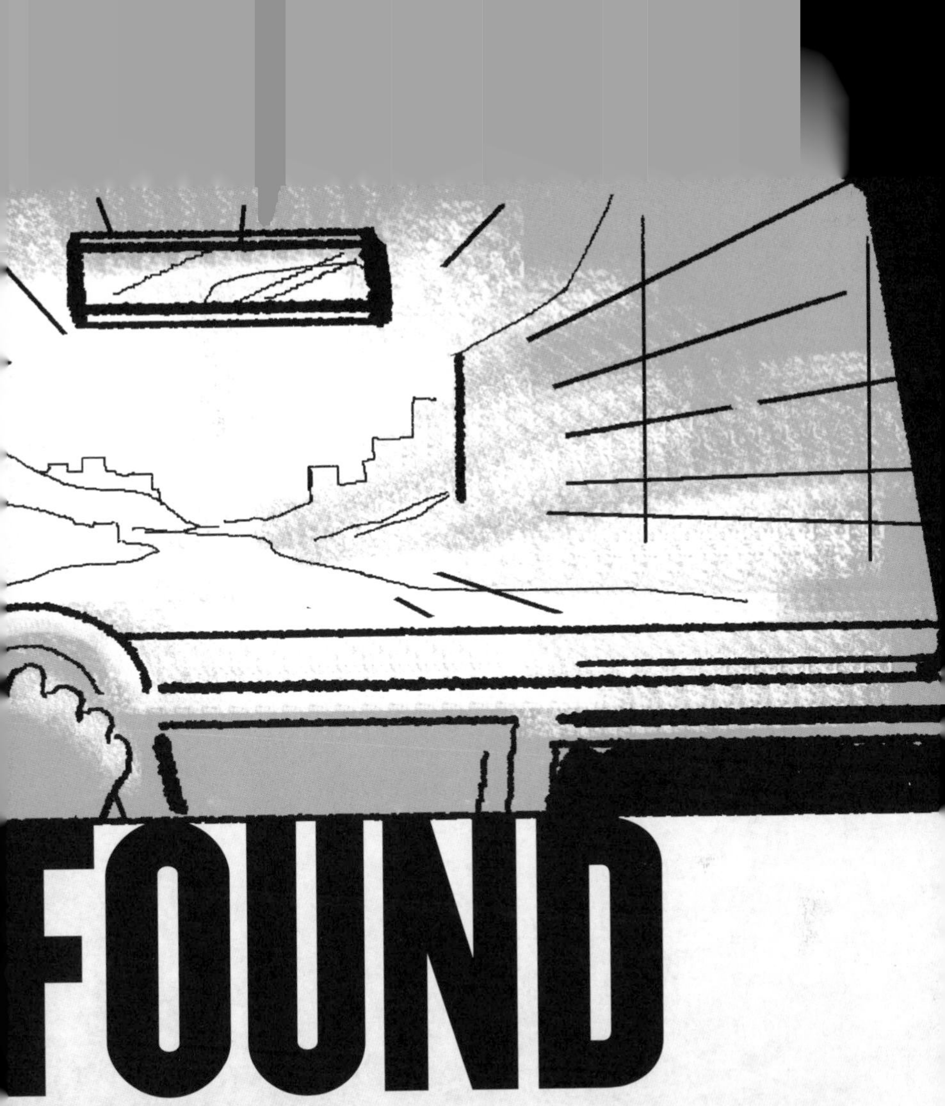

FOUND

WRITTEN BY CHRISTINA WEIR & NUNZIO DEFILIPPIS

ILLUSTRATED BY T.J. KIRSCH

LETTERED BY SHAWN DEPASQUALE
DESIGNED BY TROY LOOK
EDITED BY JILL BEATON

Published by Oni Press, Inc.
Joe Nozemack, publisher
James Lucas Jones, editor in chief
John Schork, director of publicity
Cheyenne Allott, director of sales
Troy Look, production manager
Jason Storey, senior graphic designer
Jill Beaton, editor
Charlie Chu, editor
Robin Herrera, administrative assistant

Oni Press, Inc.
1305 SE Martin Luther King Jr. Blvd.
Suite A
Portland, OR 97214

www.onipress.com
facebook.com/onipress
twitter.com/onipress
onipress.tumblr.com

First Edition: May 2014

ISBN 978-1-62010-017-2
eISBN 978-1-62010-055-4

Library of Congress Control Number: 2013956035

10 9 8 7 6 5 4 3 2 1

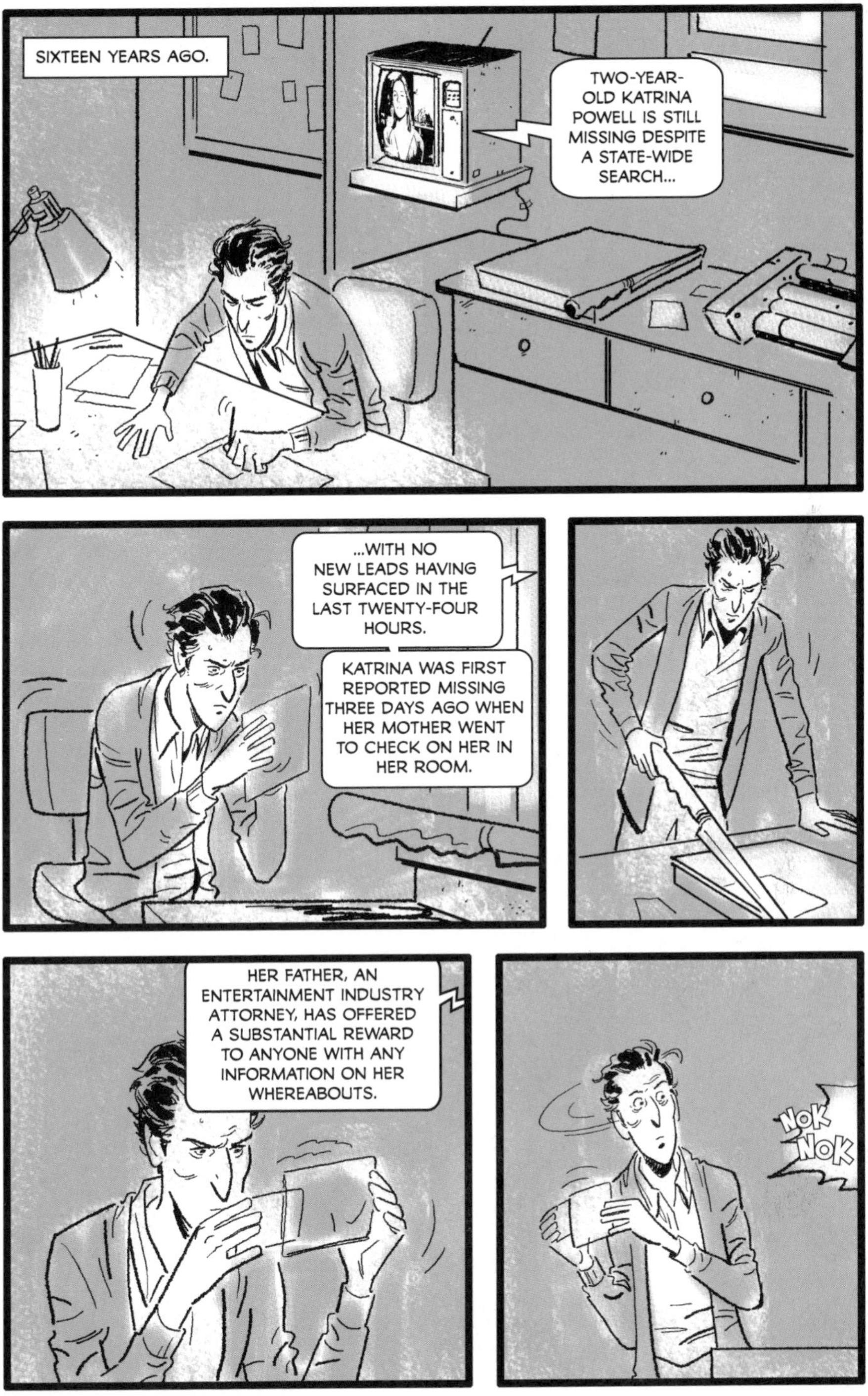
SIXTEEN YEARS AGO.
TWO-YEAR-OLD KATRINA POWELL IS STILL MISSING DESPITE A STATE-WIDE SEARCH...
...WITH NO NEW LEADS HAVING SURFACED IN THE LAST TWENTY-FOUR HOURS.
KATRINA WAS FIRST REPORTED MISSING THREE DAYS AGO WHEN HER MOTHER WENT TO CHECK ON HER IN HER ROOM.
HER FATHER, AN ENTERTAINMENT INDUSTRY ATTORNEY, HAS OFFERED A SUBSTANTIAL REWARD TO ANYONE WITH ANY INFORMATION ON HER WHEREABOUTS.
NOK NOK

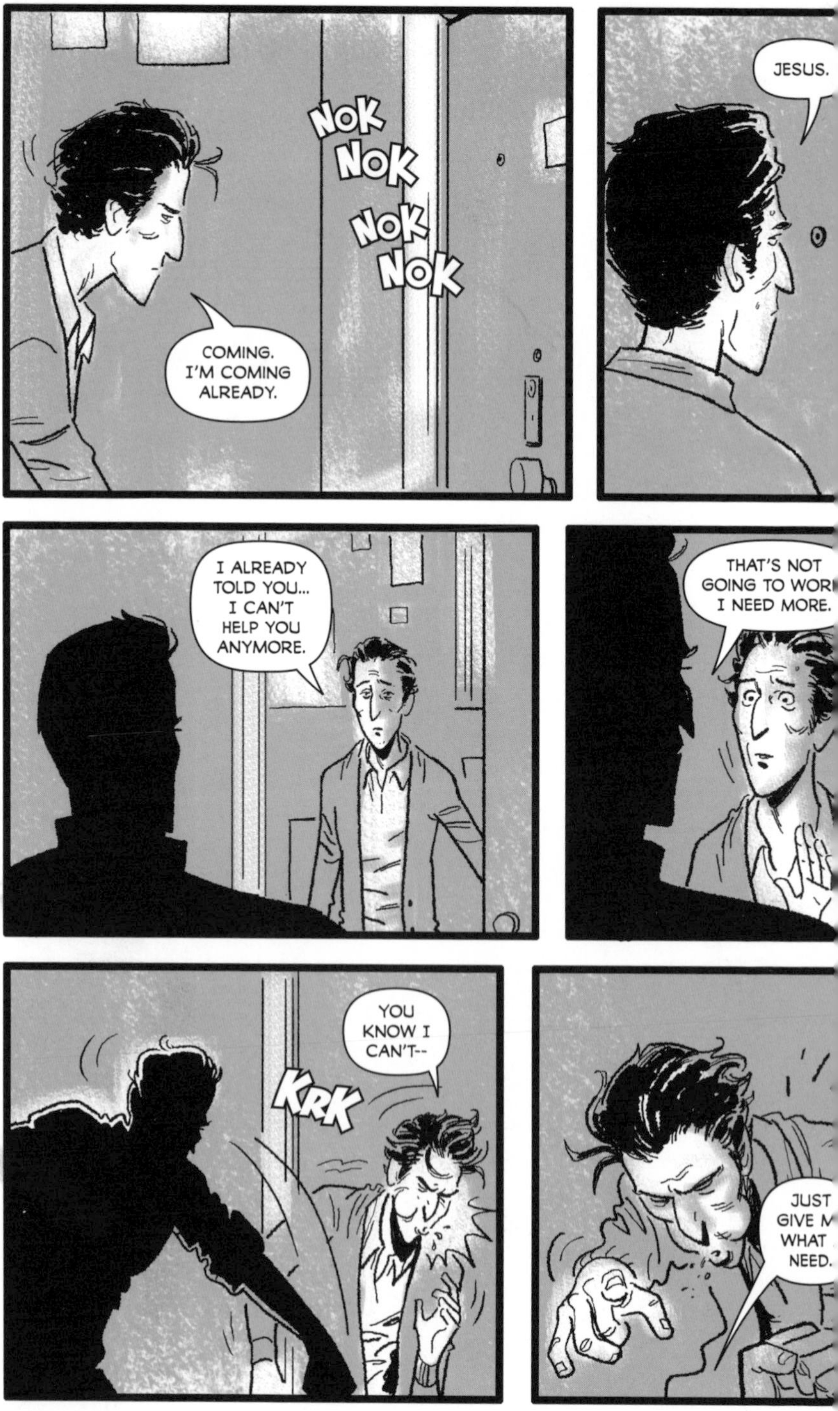
NOK NOK NOK NOK
COMING. I'M COMING ALREADY.
JESUS.
I ALREADY TOLD YOU... I CAN'T HELP YOU ANYMORE.
THAT'S NOT GOING TO WOR I NEED MORE.
YOU KNOW I CAN'T--
KRK
JUST GIVE M WHAT NEED.

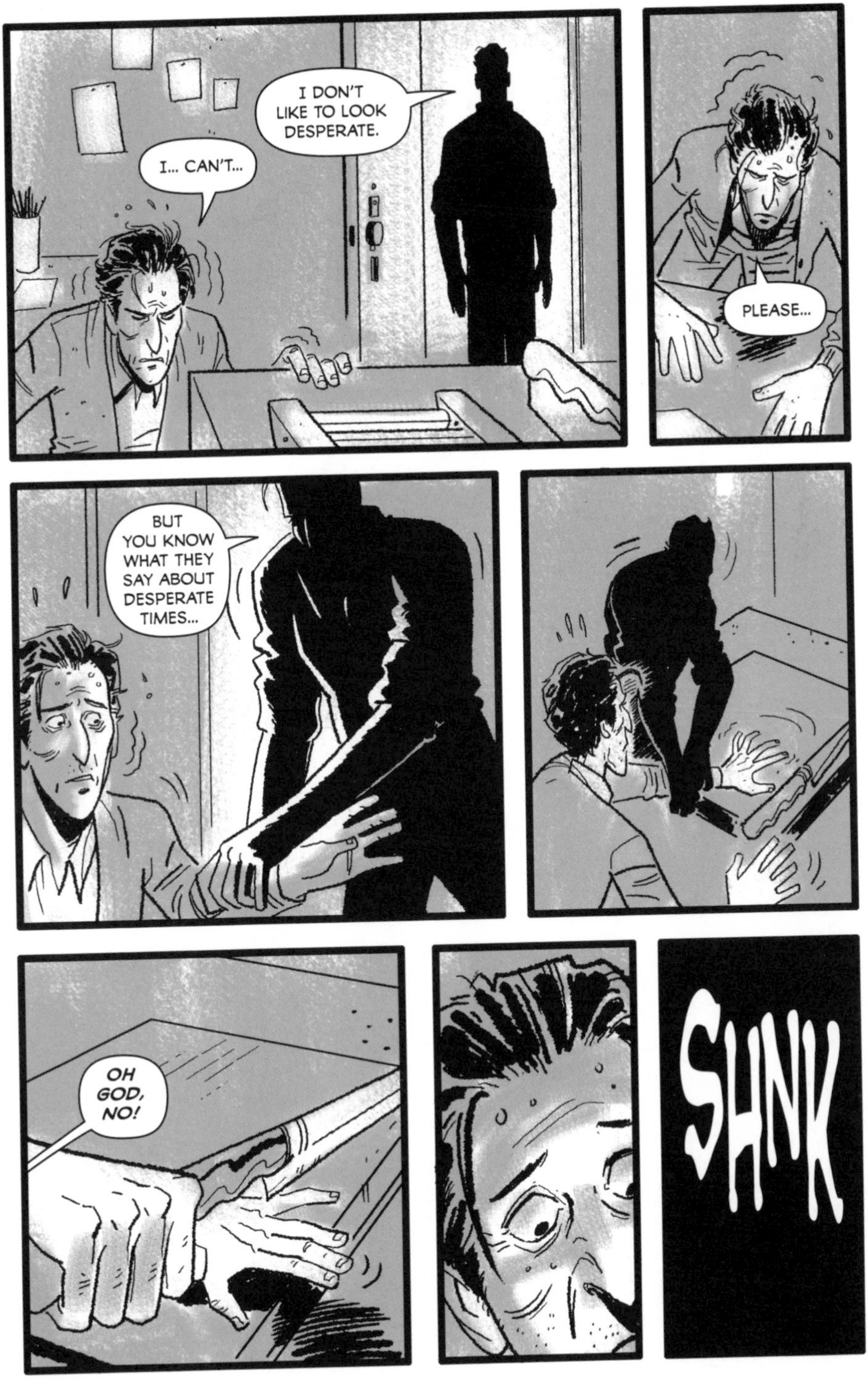
I... CAN'T...
I DON'T LIKE TO LOOK DESPERATE.
PLEASE...
BUT YOU KNOW WHAT THEY SAY ABOUT DESPERATE TIMES...
OH GOD, NO!
SHNK

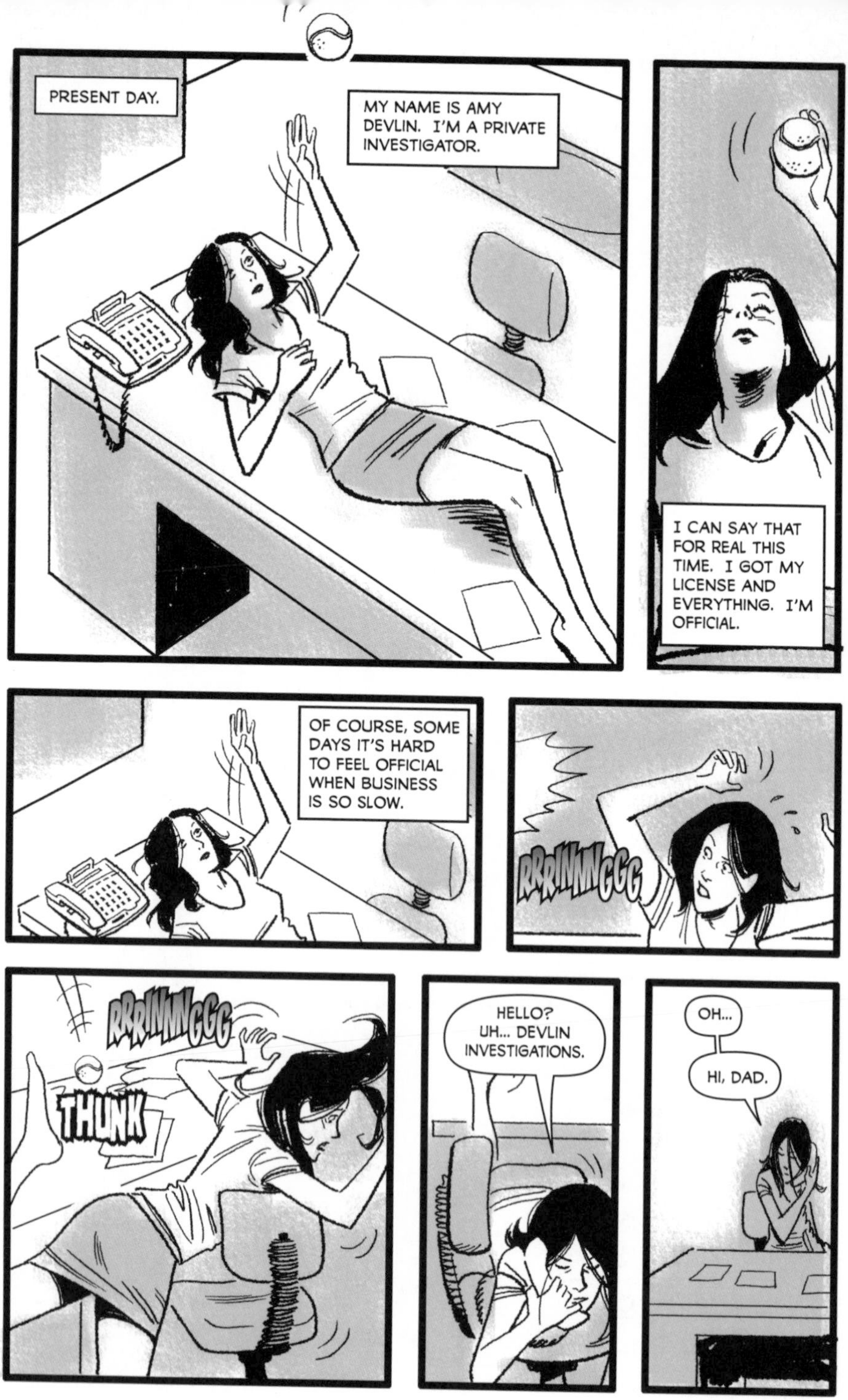
PRESENT DAY.
MY NAME IS AMY DEVLIN. I'M A PRIVATE INVESTIGATOR.
I CAN SAY THAT FOR REAL THIS TIME. I GOT MY LICENSE AND EVERYTHING. I'M OFFICIAL.
OF COURSE, SOME DAYS IT'S HARD TO FEEL OFFICIAL WHEN BUSINESS IS SO SLOW.
RRRINNNGGG
RRRINNNGGG
THUNK
HELLO? UH... DEVLIN INVESTIGATIONS.
OH...
HI, DAD.

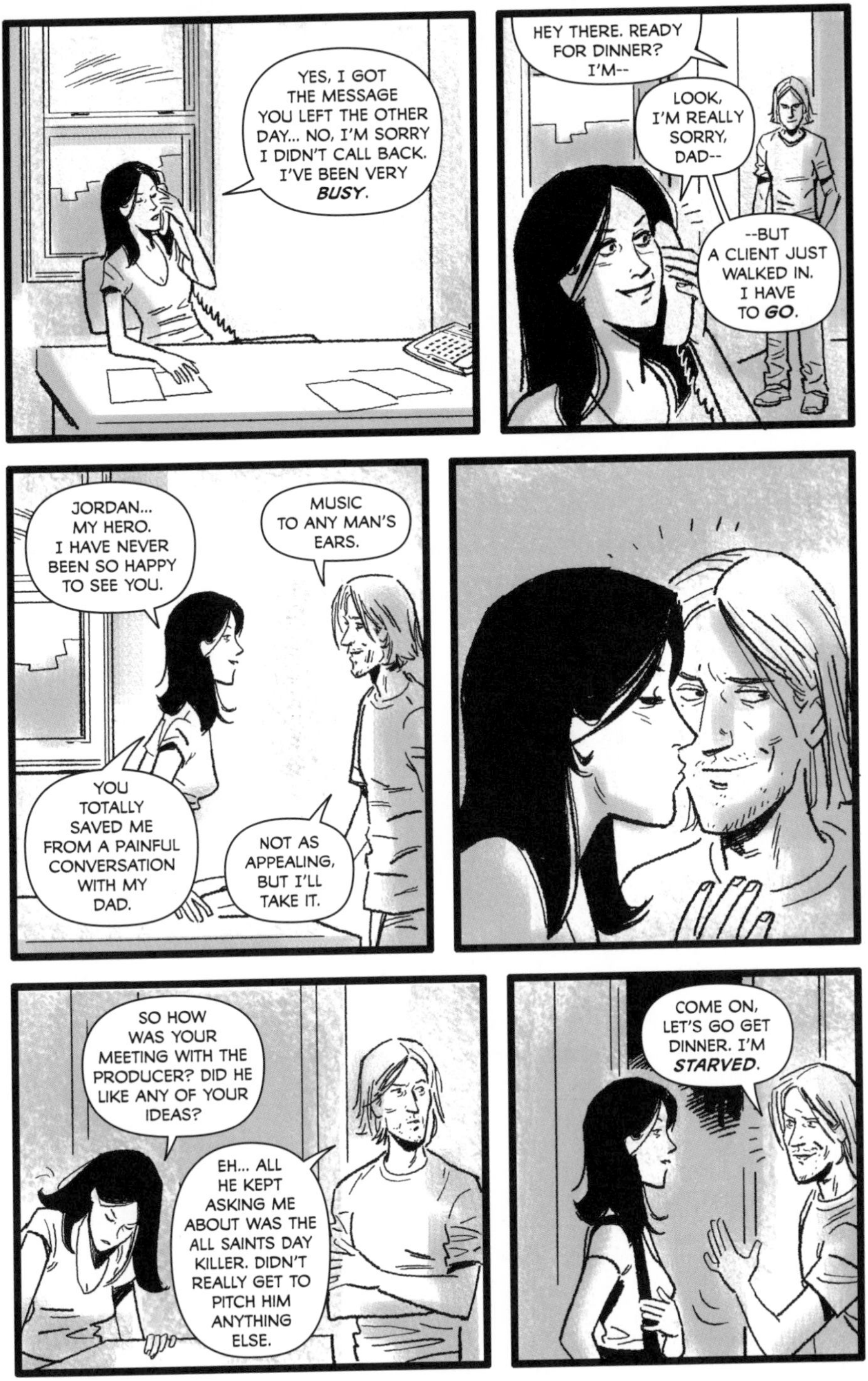
YES, I GOT THE MESSAGE YOU LEFT THE OTHER DAY... NO, I'M SORRY I DIDN'T CALL BACK. I'VE BEEN VERY *BUSY*.
HEY THERE. READY FOR DINNER? I'M--
LOOK, I'M REALLY SORRY, DAD--
--BUT A CLIENT JUST WALKED IN. I HAVE TO *GO*.
JORDAN... MY HERO. I HAVE NEVER BEEN SO HAPPY TO SEE YOU.
MUSIC TO ANY MAN'S EARS.
YOU TOTALLY SAVED ME FROM A PAINFUL CONVERSATION WITH MY DAD.
NOT AS APPEALING, BUT I'LL TAKE IT.
SO HOW WAS YOUR MEETING WITH THE PRODUCER? DID HE LIKE ANY OF YOUR IDEAS?
EH... ALL HE KEPT ASKING ME ABOUT WAS THE ALL SAINTS DAY KILLER. DIDN'T REALLY GET TO PITCH HIM ANYTHING ELSE.
COME ON, LET'S GO GET DINNER. I'M *STARVED*.

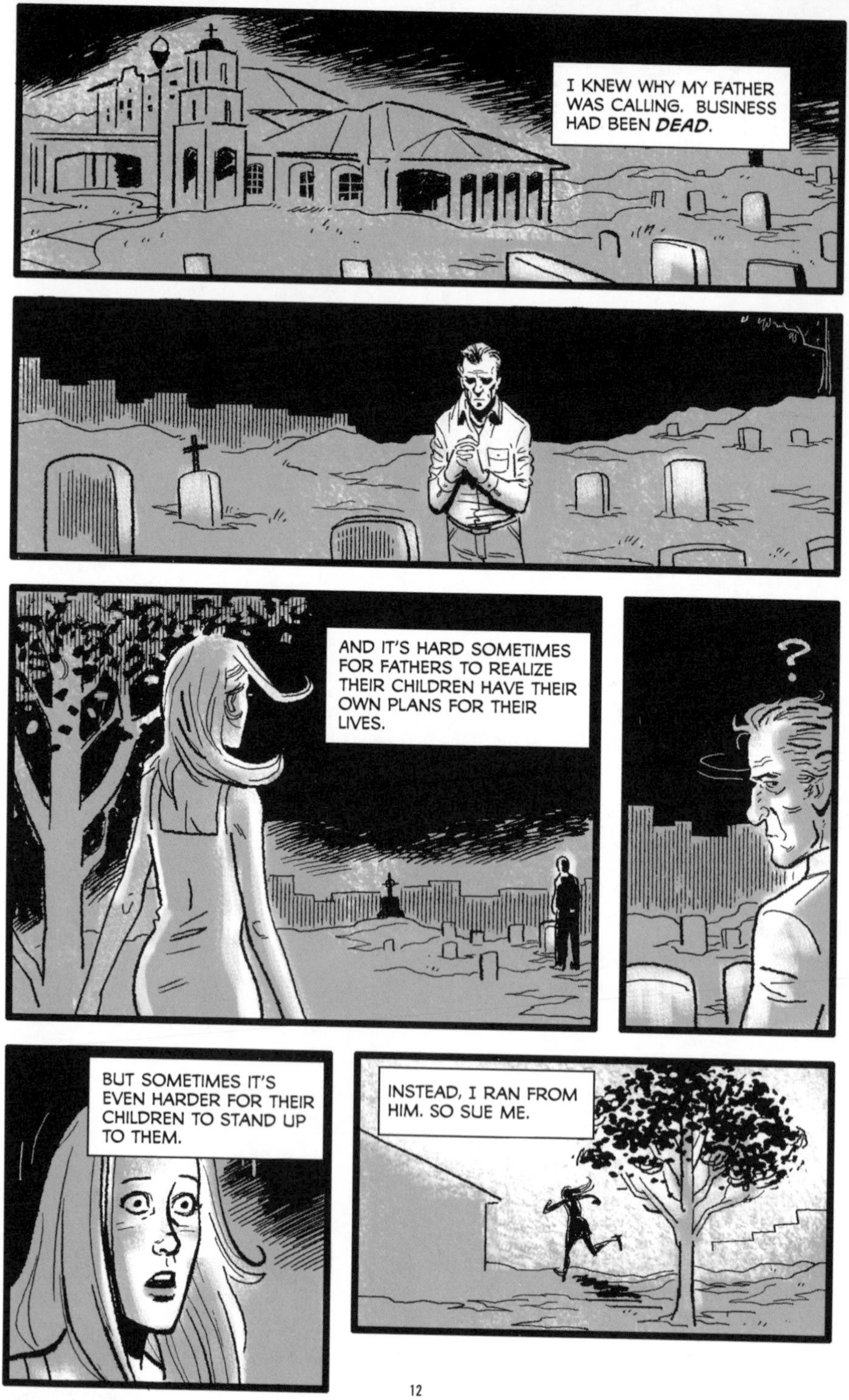
I KNEW WHY MY FATHER WAS CALLING. BUSINESS HAD BEEN *DEAD*.
AND IT'S HARD SOMETIMES FOR FATHERS TO REALIZE THEIR CHILDREN HAVE THEIR OWN PLANS FOR THEIR LIVES.
?
BUT SOMETIMES IT'S EVEN HARDER FOR THEIR CHILDREN TO STAND UP TO THEM.
INSTEAD, I RAN FROM HIM. SO SUE ME.

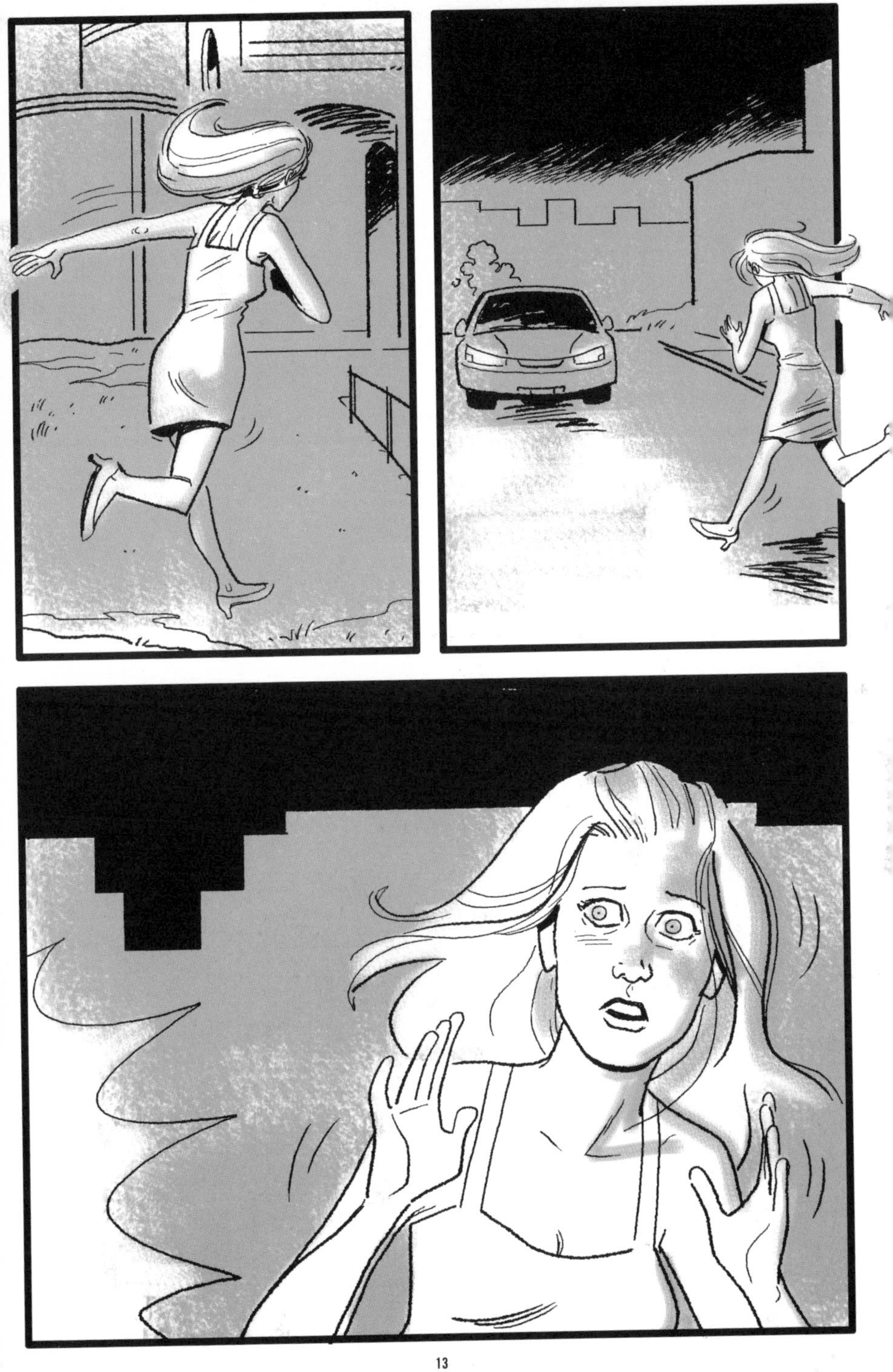

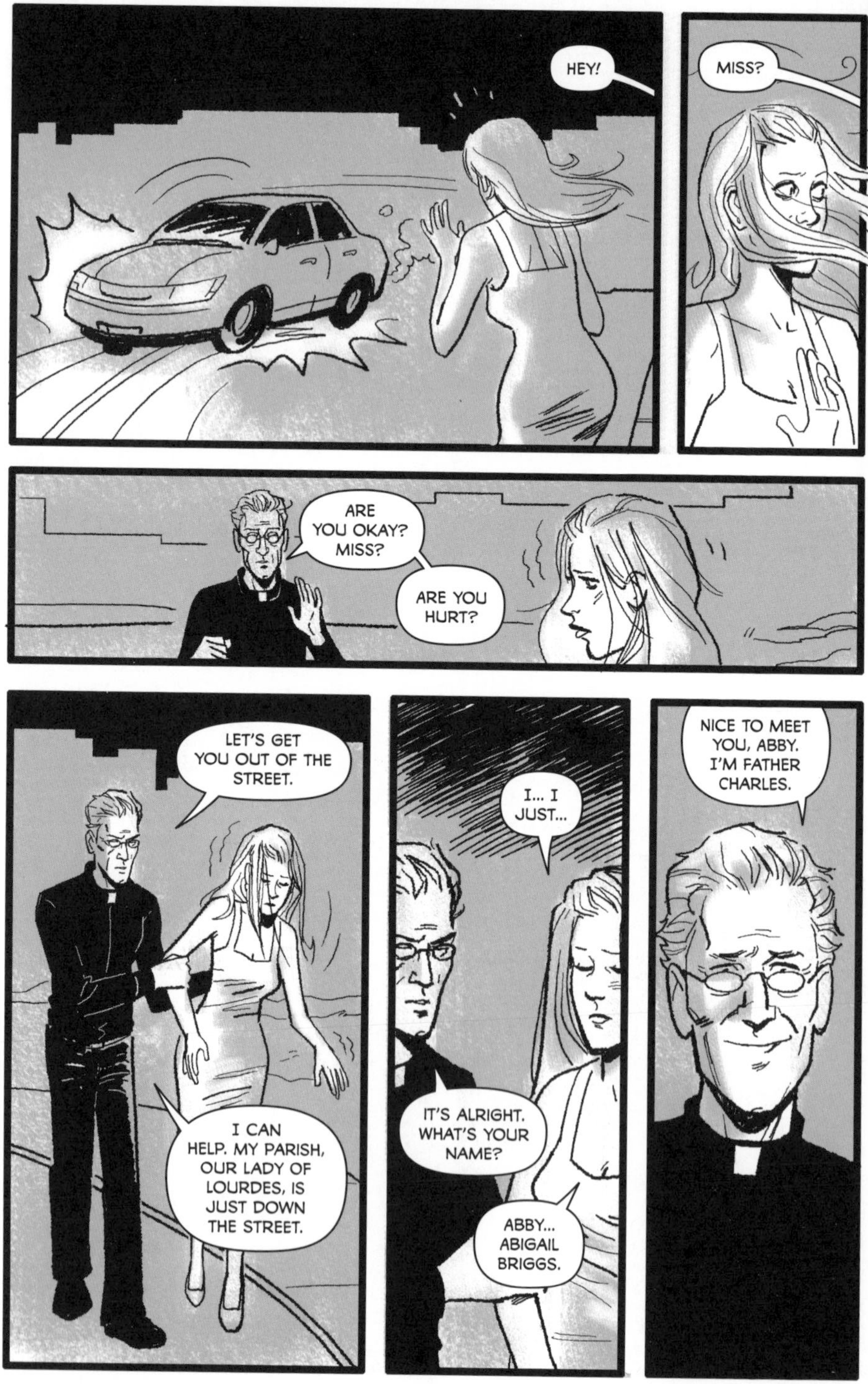
HEY!
MISS?
ARE YOU OKAY? MISS?
ARE YOU HURT?
LET'S GET YOU OUT OF THE STREET.
I CAN HELP. MY PARISH, OUR LADY OF LOURDES, IS JUST DOWN THE STREET.
I... I JUST...
IT'S ALRIGHT. WHAT'S YOUR NAME?
ABBY... ABIGAIL BRIGGS.
NICE TO MEET YOU, ABBY. I'M FATHER CHARLES.

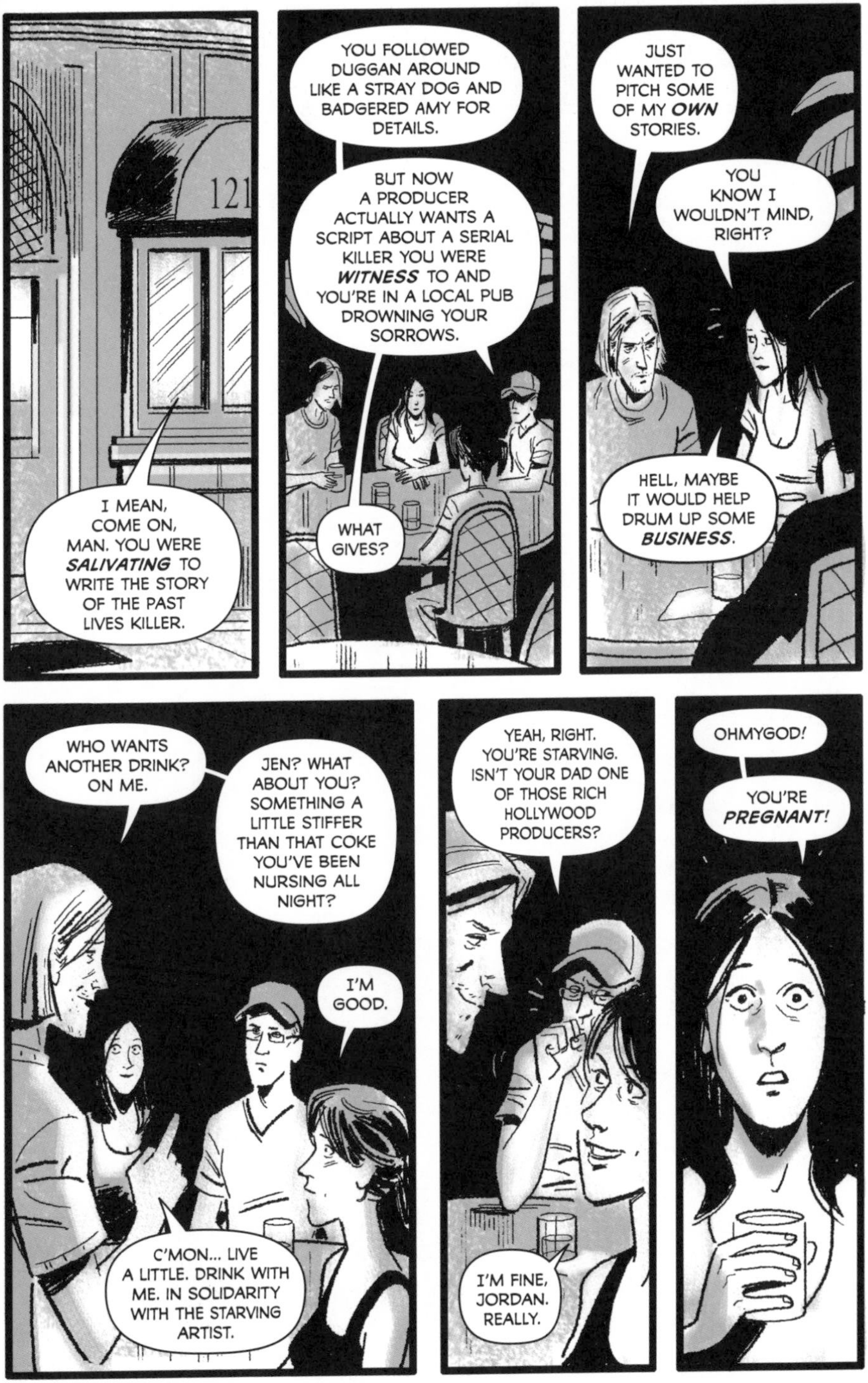
I MEAN, COME ON, MAN. YOU WERE *SALIVATING* TO WRITE THE STORY OF THE PAST LIVES KILLER.
YOU FOLLOWED DUGGAN AROUND LIKE A STRAY DOG AND BADGERED AMY FOR DETAILS.
BUT NOW A PRODUCER ACTUALLY WANTS A SCRIPT ABOUT A SERIAL KILLER YOU WERE *WITNESS* TO AND YOU'RE IN A LOCAL PUB DROWNING YOUR SORROWS.
WHAT GIVES?
JUST WANTED TO PITCH SOME OF MY *OWN* STORIES.
YOU KNOW I WOULDN'T MIND, RIGHT?
HELL, MAYBE IT WOULD HELP DRUM UP SOME *BUSINESS*.
WHO WANTS ANOTHER DRINK? ON ME.
JEN? WHAT ABOUT YOU? SOMETHING A LITTLE STIFFER THAN THAT COKE YOU'VE BEEN NURSING ALL NIGHT?
I'M GOOD.
C'MON... LIVE A LITTLE. DRINK WITH ME. IN SOLIDARITY WITH THE STARVING ARTIST.
YEAH, RIGHT. YOU'RE STARVING. ISN'T YOUR DAD ONE OF THOSE RICH HOLLYWOOD PRODUCERS?
I'M FINE, JORDAN. REALLY.
OHMYGOD!
YOU'RE *PREGNANT*!

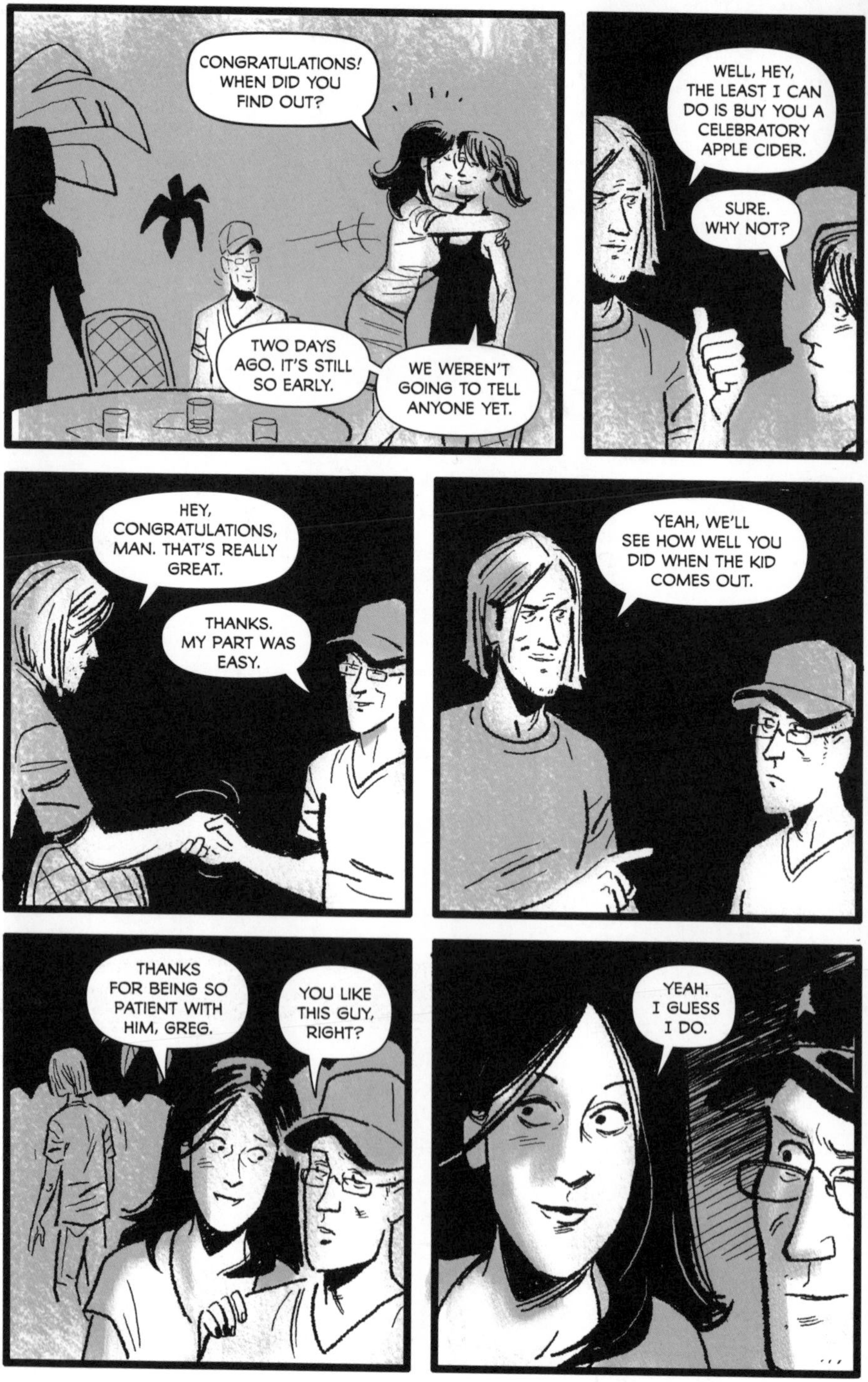
CONGRATULATIONS! WHEN DID YOU FIND OUT?
TWO DAYS AGO. IT'S STILL SO EARLY.
WE WEREN'T GOING TO TELL ANYONE YET.
WELL, HEY, THE LEAST I CAN DO IS BUY YOU A CELEBRATORY APPLE CIDER.
SURE. WHY NOT?
HEY, CONGRATULATIONS, MAN. THAT'S REALLY GREAT.
THANKS. MY PART WAS EASY.
YEAH, WE'LL SEE HOW WELL YOU DID WHEN THE KID COMES OUT.
THANKS FOR BEING SO PATIENT WITH HIM, GREG.
YOU LIKE THIS GUY, RIGHT?
YEAH. I GUESS I DO.

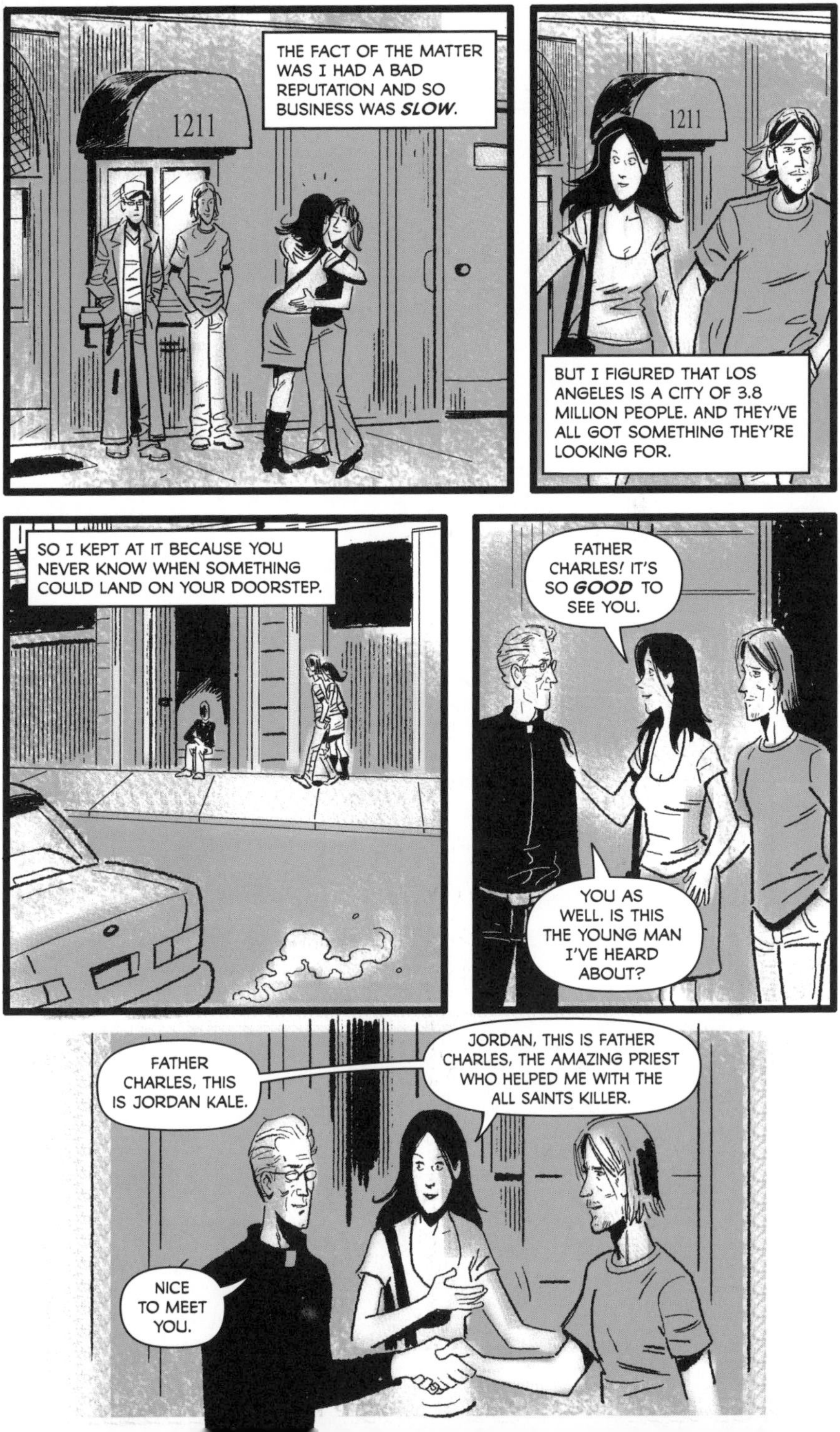
THE FACT OF THE MATTER WAS I HAD A BAD REPUTATION AND SO BUSINESS WAS *SLOW*.
1211
1211
BUT I FIGURED THAT LOS ANGELES IS A CITY OF 3.8 MILLION PEOPLE. AND THEY'VE ALL GOT SOMETHING THEY'RE LOOKING FOR.
SO I KEPT AT IT BECAUSE YOU NEVER KNOW WHEN SOMETHING COULD LAND ON YOUR DOORSTEP.
FATHER CHARLES! IT'S SO *GOOD* TO SEE YOU.
YOU AS WELL. IS THIS THE YOUNG MAN I'VE HEARD ABOUT?
JORDAN, THIS IS FATHER CHARLES, THE AMAZING PRIEST WHO HELPED ME WITH THE ALL SAINTS KILLER.
FATHER CHARLES, THIS IS JORDAN KALE.
NICE TO MEET YOU.

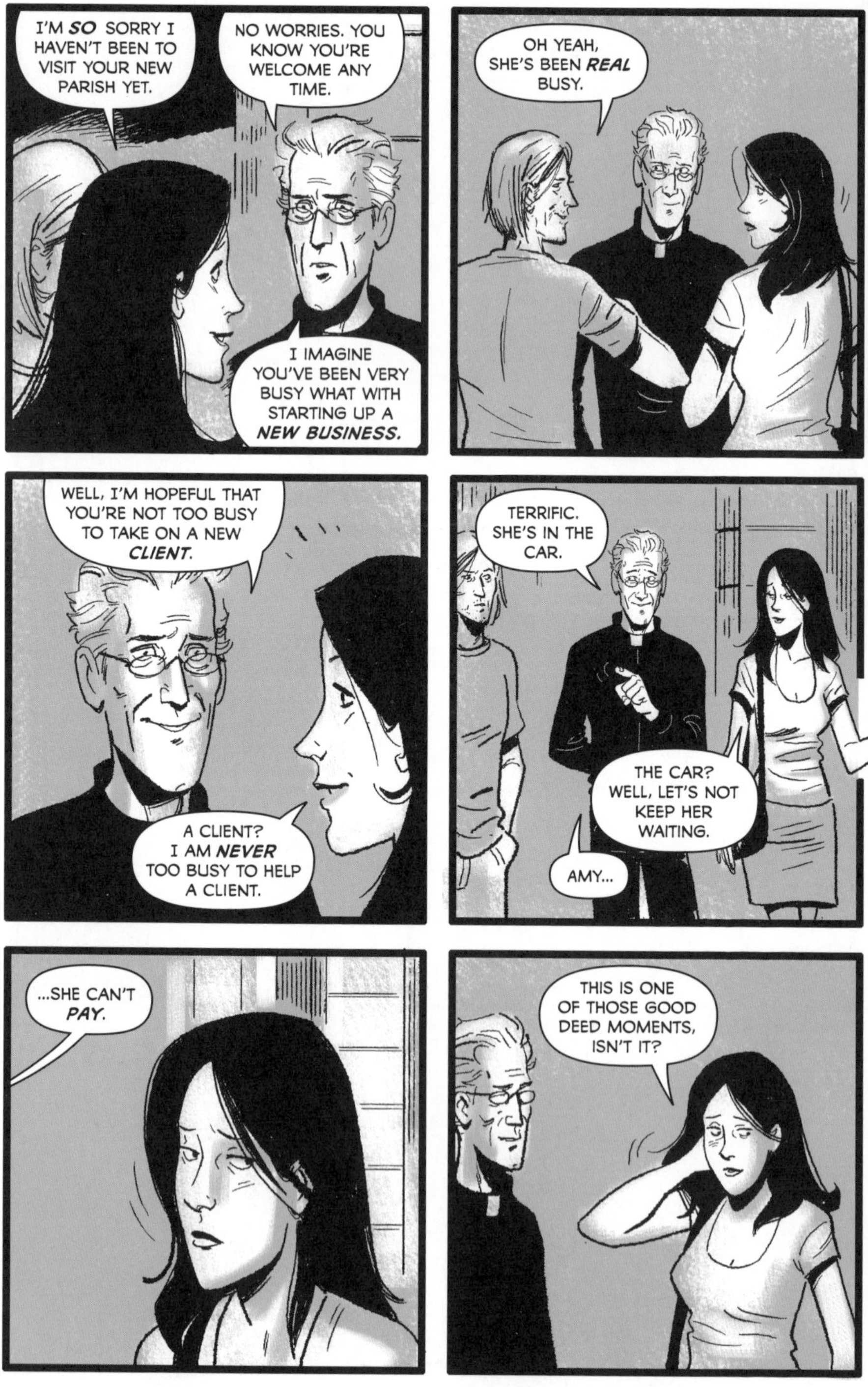
I'M SO SORRY I HAVEN'T BEEN TO VISIT YOUR NEW PARISH YET.
NO WORRIES. YOU KNOW YOU'RE WELCOME ANY TIME.
I IMAGINE YOU'VE BEEN VERY BUSY WHAT WITH STARTING UP A NEW BUSINESS.
OH YEAH, SHE'S BEEN REAL BUSY.
WELL, I'M HOPEFUL THAT YOU'RE NOT TOO BUSY TO TAKE ON A NEW CLIENT.
A CLIENT? I AM NEVER TOO BUSY TO HELP A CLIENT.
TERRIFIC. SHE'S IN THE CAR.
THE CAR? WELL, LET'S NOT KEEP HER WAITING.
AMY...
...SHE CAN'T PAY.
THIS IS ONE OF THOSE GOOD DEED MOMENTS, ISN'T IT?

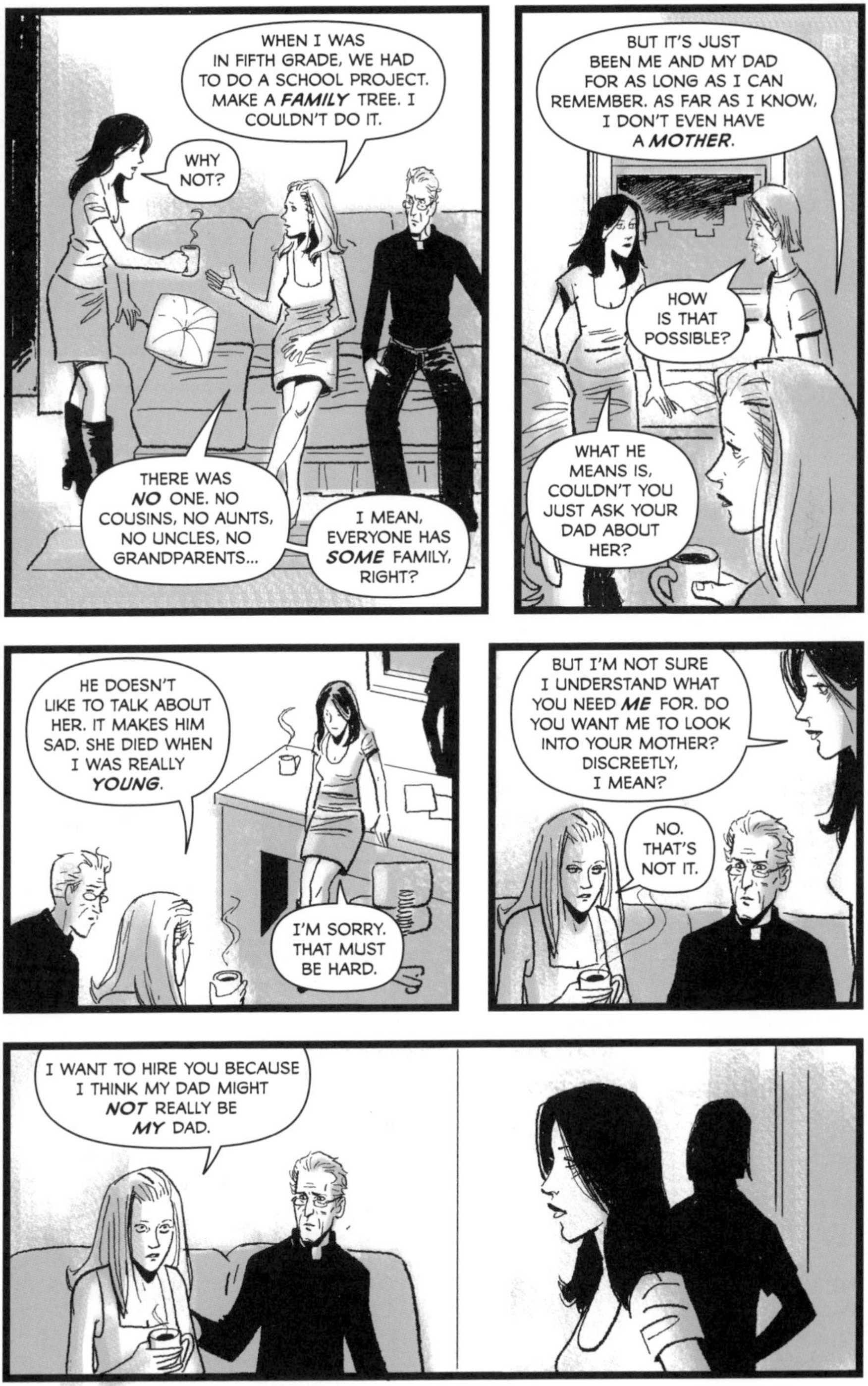
WHEN I WAS IN FIFTH GRADE, WE HAD TO DO A SCHOOL PROJECT. MAKE A FAMILY TREE. I COULDN'T DO IT.
WHY NOT?
THERE WAS NO ONE. NO COUSINS, NO AUNTS, NO UNCLES, NO GRANDPARENTS...
I MEAN, EVERYONE HAS SOME FAMILY, RIGHT?
BUT IT'S JUST BEEN ME AND MY DAD FOR AS LONG AS I CAN REMEMBER. AS FAR AS I KNOW, I DON'T EVEN HAVE A MOTHER.
HOW IS THAT POSSIBLE?
WHAT HE MEANS IS, COULDN'T YOU JUST ASK YOUR DAD ABOUT HER?
HE DOESN'T LIKE TO TALK ABOUT HER. IT MAKES HIM SAD. SHE DIED WHEN I WAS REALLY YOUNG.
I'M SORRY. THAT MUST BE HARD.
BUT I'M NOT SURE I UNDERSTAND WHAT YOU NEED ME FOR. DO YOU WANT ME TO LOOK INTO YOUR MOTHER? DISCREETLY, I MEAN?
NO. THAT'S NOT IT.
I WANT TO HIRE YOU BECAUSE I THINK MY DAD MIGHT NOT REALLY BE MY DAD.

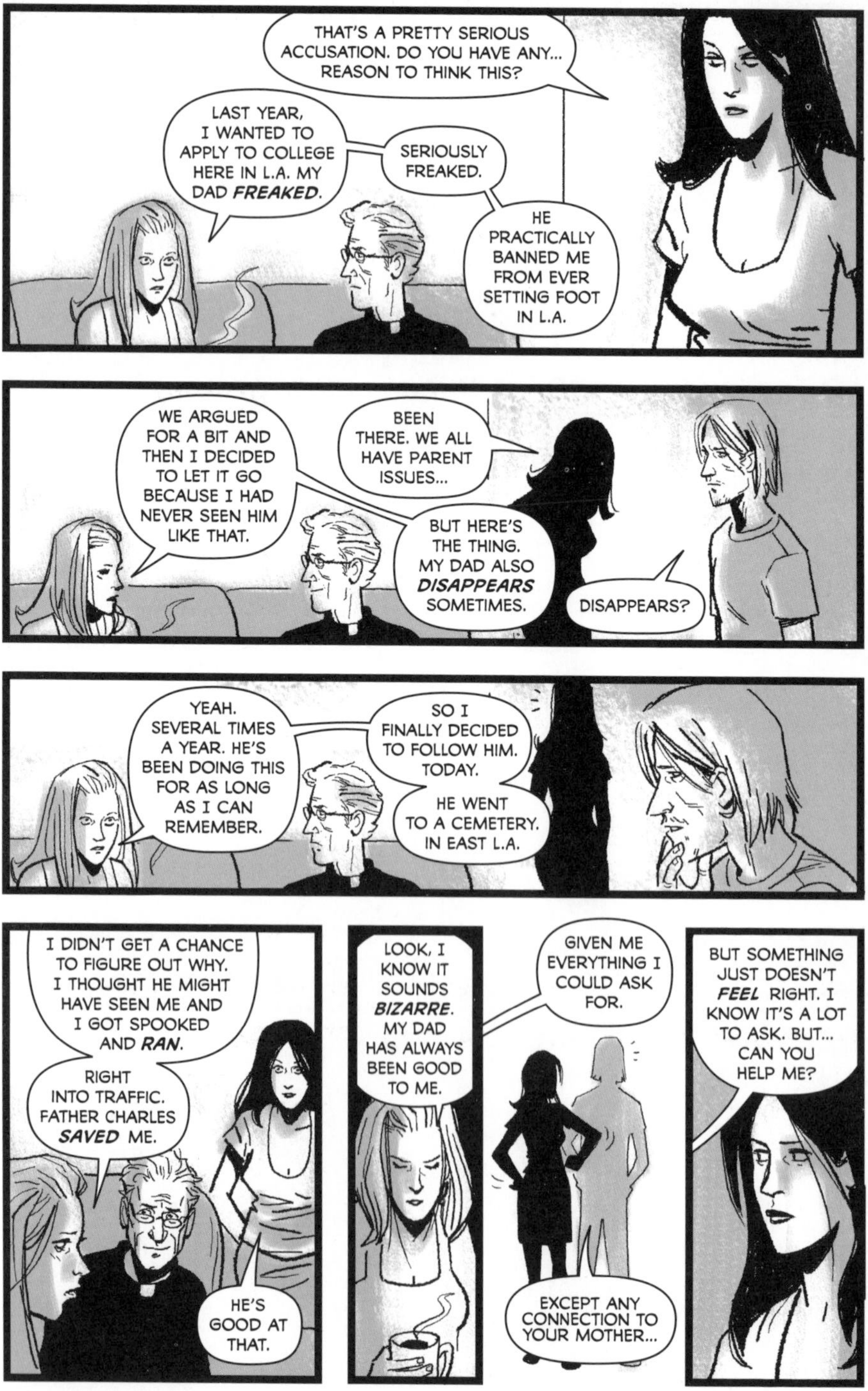
THAT'S A PRETTY SERIOUS ACCUSATION. DO YOU HAVE ANY... REASON TO THINK THIS?
LAST YEAR, I WANTED TO APPLY TO COLLEGE HERE IN L.A. MY DAD *FREAKED*.
SERIOUSLY FREAKED.
HE PRACTICALLY BANNED ME FROM EVER SETTING FOOT IN L.A.
WE ARGUED FOR A BIT AND THEN I DECIDED TO LET IT GO BECAUSE I HAD NEVER SEEN HIM LIKE THAT.
BEEN THERE. WE ALL HAVE PARENT ISSUES...
BUT HERE'S THE THING. MY DAD ALSO *DISAPPEARS* SOMETIMES.
DISAPPEARS?
YEAH. SEVERAL TIMES A YEAR. HE'S BEEN DOING THIS FOR AS LONG AS I CAN REMEMBER.
SO I FINALLY DECIDED TO FOLLOW HIM. TODAY.
HE WENT TO A CEMETERY. IN EAST L.A.
I DIDN'T GET A CHANCE TO FIGURE OUT WHY. I THOUGHT HE MIGHT HAVE SEEN ME AND I GOT SPOOKED AND *RAN*.
RIGHT INTO TRAFFIC. FATHER CHARLES *SAVED* ME.
HE'S GOOD AT THAT.
LOOK, I KNOW IT SOUNDS *BIZARRE*. MY DAD HAS ALWAYS BEEN GOOD TO ME.
GIVEN ME EVERYTHING I COULD ASK FOR.
EXCEPT ANY CONNECTION TO YOUR MOTHER...
BUT SOMETHING JUST DOESN'T *FEEL* RIGHT. I KNOW IT'S A LOT TO ASK. BUT... CAN YOU HELP ME?

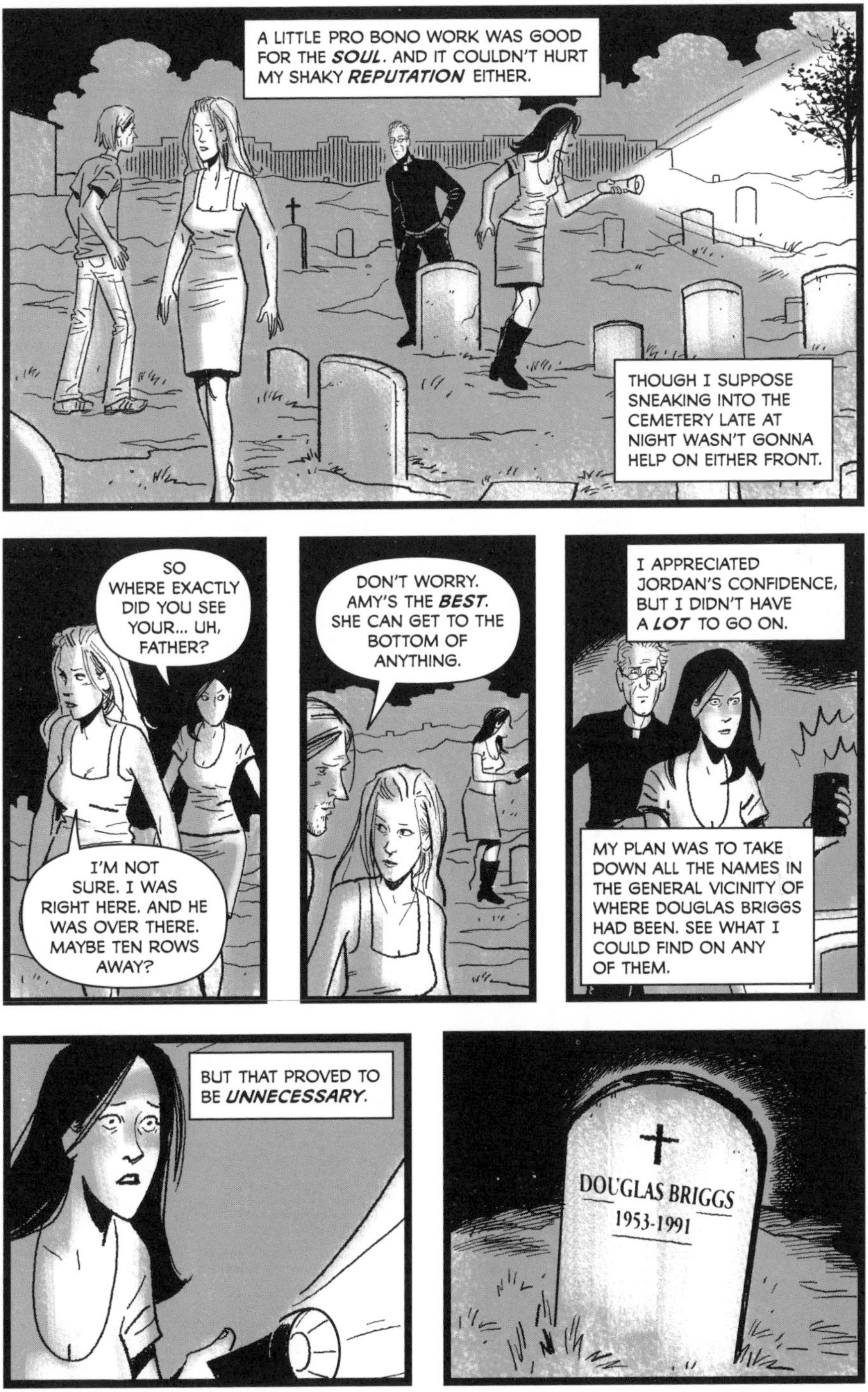
A LITTLE PRO BONO WORK WAS GOOD FOR THE *SOUL*. AND IT COULDN'T HURT MY SHAKY *REPUTATION* EITHER.
THOUGH I SUPPOSE SNEAKING INTO THE CEMETERY LATE AT NIGHT WASN'T GONNA HELP ON EITHER FRONT.
SO WHERE EXACTLY DID YOU SEE YOUR... UH, FATHER?
I'M NOT SURE. I WAS RIGHT HERE. AND HE WAS OVER THERE. MAYBE TEN ROWS AWAY?
DON'T WORRY. AMY'S THE *BEST*. SHE CAN GET TO THE BOTTOM OF ANYTHING.
I APPRECIATED JORDAN'S CONFIDENCE, BUT I DIDN'T HAVE A *LOT* TO GO ON.
MY PLAN WAS TO TAKE DOWN ALL THE NAMES IN THE GENERAL VICINITY OF WHERE DOUGLAS BRIGGS HAD BEEN. SEE WHAT I COULD FIND ON ANY OF THEM.
BUT THAT PROVED TO BE *UNNECESSARY*.
DOUGLAS BRIGGS
1953-1991

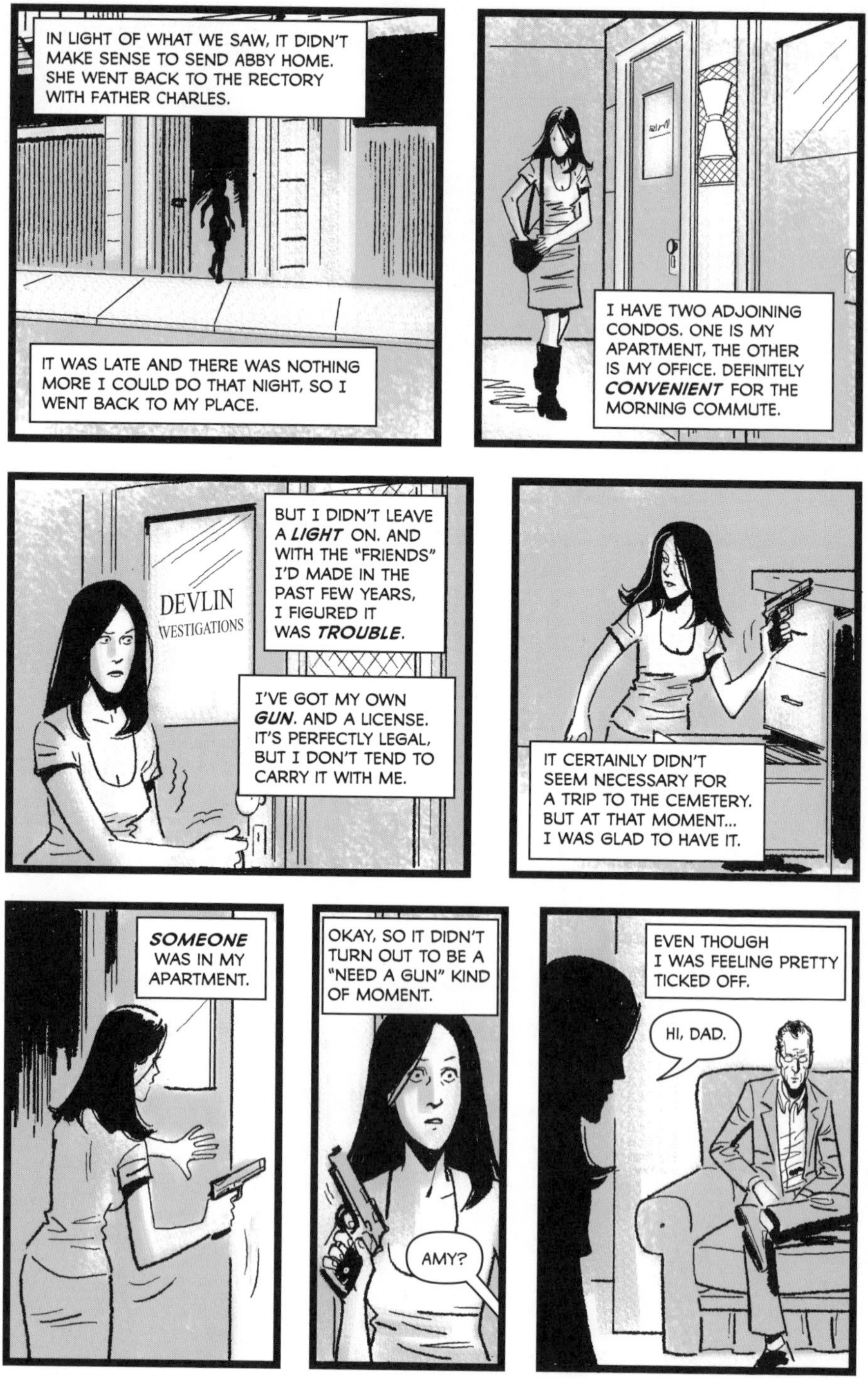
IN LIGHT OF WHAT WE SAW, IT DIDN'T MAKE SENSE TO SEND ABBY HOME. SHE WENT BACK TO THE RECTORY WITH FATHER CHARLES.
IT WAS LATE AND THERE WAS NOTHING MORE I COULD DO THAT NIGHT, SO I WENT BACK TO MY PLACE.
I HAVE TWO ADJOINING CONDOS. ONE IS MY APARTMENT, THE OTHER IS MY OFFICE. DEFINITELY CONVENIENT FOR THE MORNING COMMUTE.
DEVLIN
VESTIGATIONS
BUT I DIDN'T LEAVE A LIGHT ON. AND WITH THE "FRIENDS" I'D MADE IN THE PAST FEW YEARS, I FIGURED IT WAS TROUBLE.
I'VE GOT MY OWN GUN. AND A LICENSE. IT'S PERFECTLY LEGAL, BUT I DON'T TEND TO CARRY IT WITH ME.
IT CERTAINLY DIDN'T SEEM NECESSARY FOR A TRIP TO THE CEMETERY. BUT AT THAT MOMENT... I WAS GLAD TO HAVE IT.
SOMEONE WAS IN MY APARTMENT.
OKAY, SO IT DIDN'T TURN OUT TO BE A "NEED A GUN" KIND OF MOMENT.
AMY?
EVEN THOUGH I WAS FEELING PRETTY TICKED OFF.
HI, DAD.

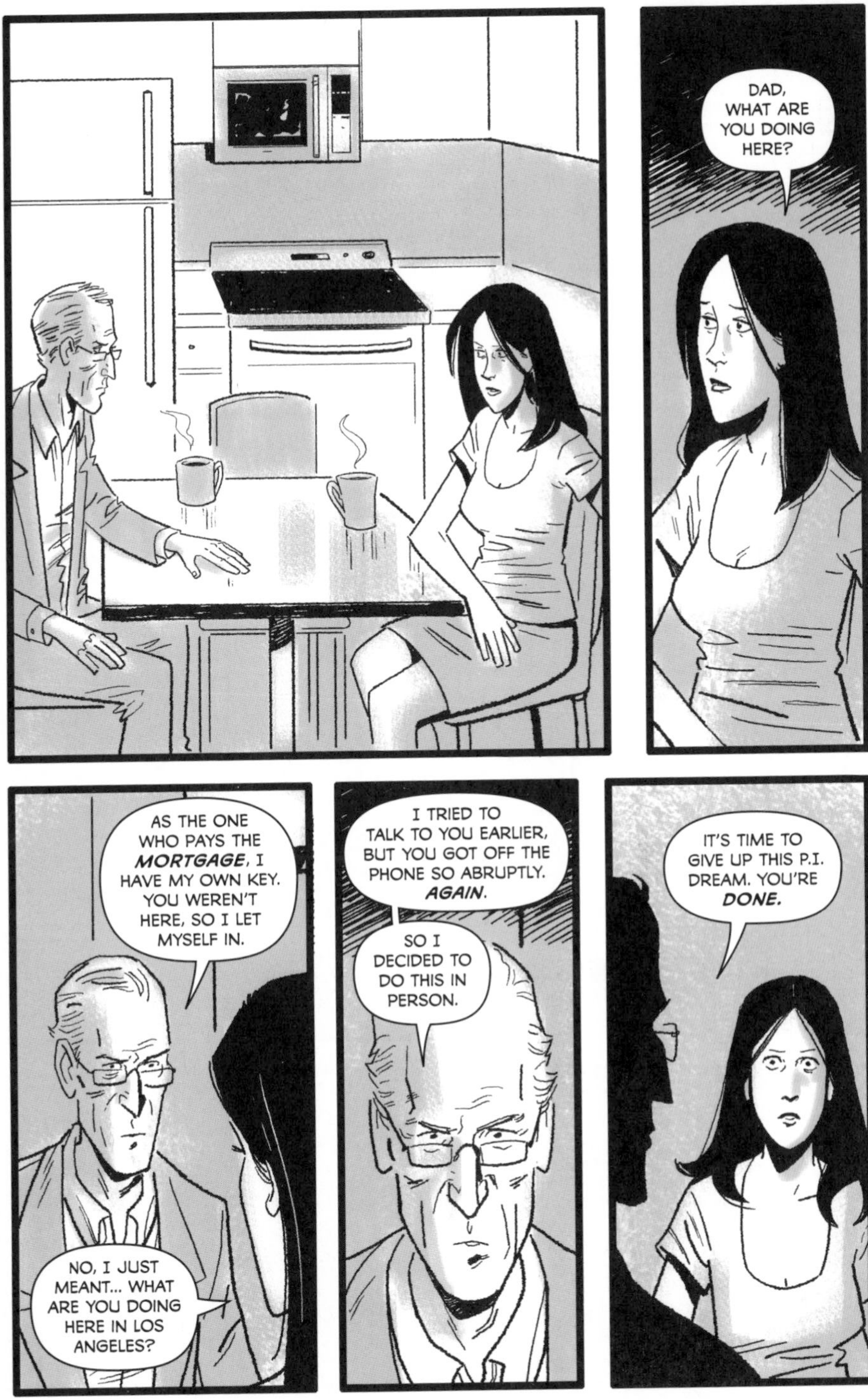
DAD, WHAT ARE YOU DOING HERE?
AS THE ONE WHO PAYS THE MORTGAGE, I HAVE MY OWN KEY. YOU WEREN'T HERE, SO I LET MYSELF IN.
NO, I JUST MEANT... WHAT ARE YOU DOING HERE IN LOS ANGELES?
I TRIED TO TALK TO YOU EARLIER, BUT YOU GOT OFF THE PHONE SO ABRUPTLY. AGAIN.
SO I DECIDED TO DO THIS IN PERSON.
IT'S TIME TO GIVE UP THIS P.I. DREAM. YOU'RE DONE.

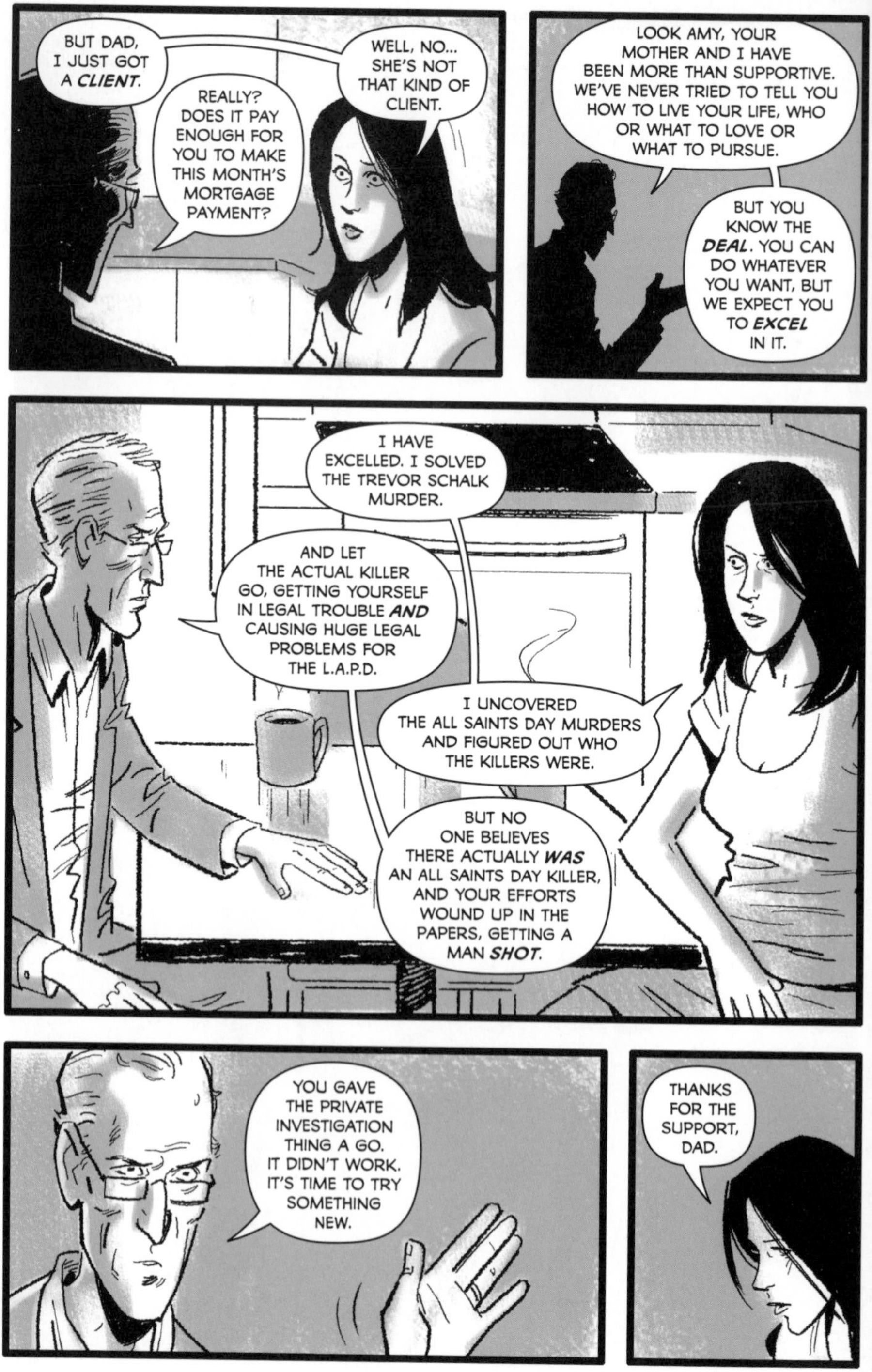

BUT DAD, I JUST GOT A *CLIENT*.
REALLY? DOES IT PAY ENOUGH FOR YOU TO MAKE THIS MONTH'S MORTGAGE PAYMENT?
WELL, NO... SHE'S NOT THAT KIND OF CLIENT.
LOOK AMY, YOUR MOTHER AND I HAVE BEEN MORE THAN SUPPORTIVE. WE'VE NEVER TRIED TO TELL YOU HOW TO LIVE YOUR LIFE, WHO OR WHAT TO LOVE OR WHAT TO PURSUE.
BUT YOU KNOW THE *DEAL*. YOU CAN DO WHATEVER YOU WANT, BUT WE EXPECT YOU TO *EXCEL* IN IT.
I HAVE EXCELLED. I SOLVED THE TREVOR SCHALK MURDER.
AND LET THE ACTUAL KILLER GO, GETTING YOURSELF IN LEGAL TROUBLE *AND* CAUSING HUGE LEGAL PROBLEMS FOR THE L.A.P.D.
I UNCOVERED THE ALL SAINTS DAY MURDERS AND FIGURED OUT WHO THE KILLERS WERE.
BUT NO ONE BELIEVES THERE ACTUALLY *WAS* AN ALL SAINTS DAY KILLER, AND YOUR EFFORTS WOUND UP IN THE PAPERS, GETTING A MAN *SHOT*.
YOU GAVE THE PRIVATE INVESTIGATION THING A GO. IT DIDN'T WORK. IT'S TIME TO TRY SOMETHING NEW.
THANKS FOR THE SUPPORT, DAD.

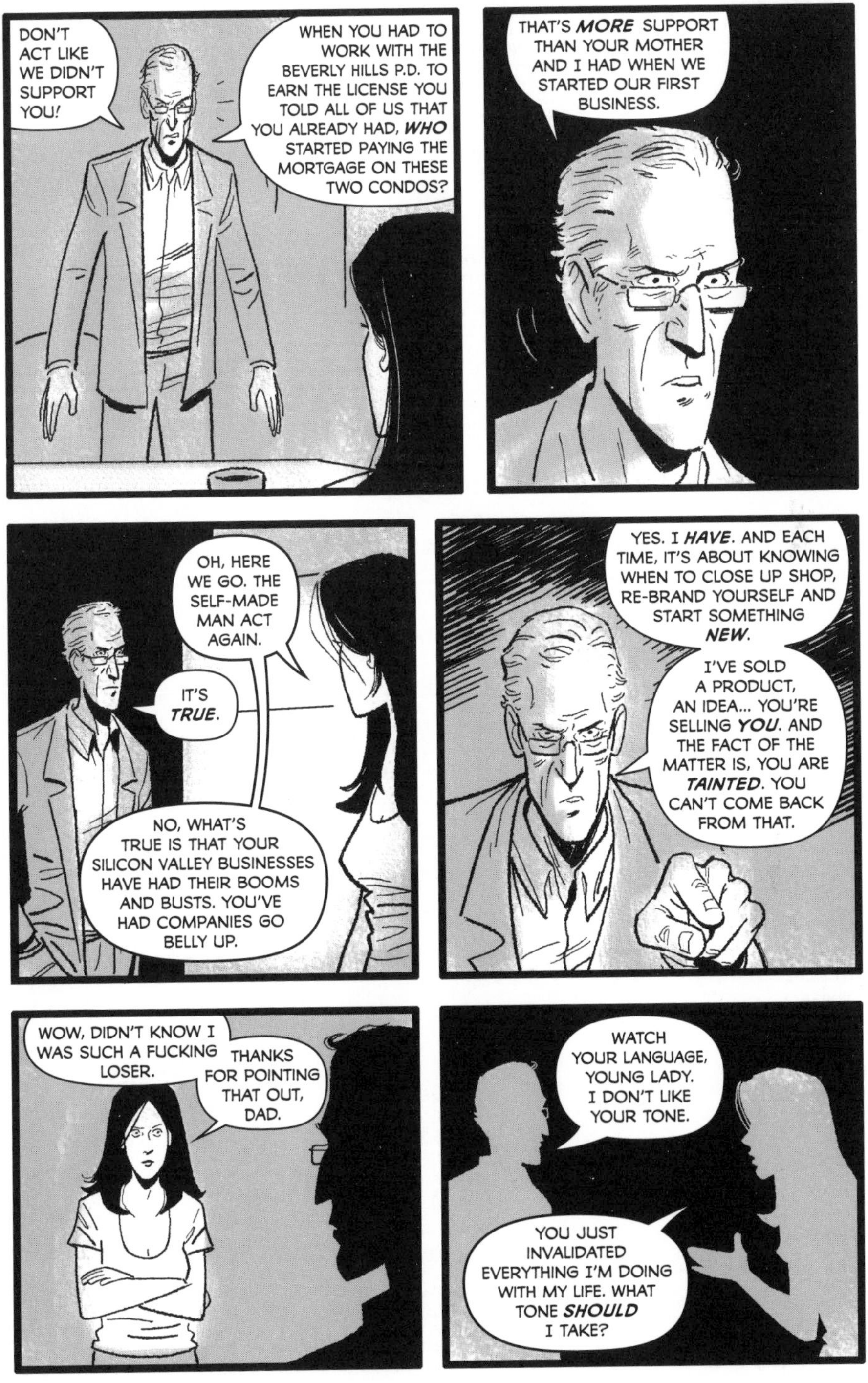
DON'T ACT LIKE WE DIDN'T SUPPORT YOU!
WHEN YOU HAD TO WORK WITH THE BEVERLY HILLS P.D. TO EARN THE LICENSE YOU TOLD ALL OF US THAT YOU ALREADY HAD, WHO STARTED PAYING THE MORTGAGE ON THESE TWO CONDOS?
THAT'S MORE SUPPORT THAN YOUR MOTHER AND I HAD WHEN WE STARTED OUR FIRST BUSINESS.
OH, HERE WE GO. THE SELF-MADE MAN ACT AGAIN.
IT'S TRUE.
NO, WHAT'S TRUE IS THAT YOUR SILICON VALLEY BUSINESSES HAVE HAD THEIR BOOMS AND BUSTS. YOU'VE HAD COMPANIES GO BELLY UP.
YES. I HAVE. AND EACH TIME, IT'S ABOUT KNOWING WHEN TO CLOSE UP SHOP, RE-BRAND YOURSELF AND START SOMETHING NEW.
I'VE SOLD A PRODUCT, AN IDEA... YOU'RE SELLING YOU. AND THE FACT OF THE MATTER IS, YOU ARE TAINTED. YOU CAN'T COME BACK FROM THAT.
WOW, DIDN'T KNOW I WAS SUCH A FUCKING LOSER.
THANKS FOR POINTING THAT OUT, DAD.
WATCH YOUR LANGUAGE, YOUNG LADY. I DON'T LIKE YOUR TONE.
YOU JUST INVALIDATED EVERYTHING I'M DOING WITH MY LIFE. WHAT TONE SHOULD I TAKE?

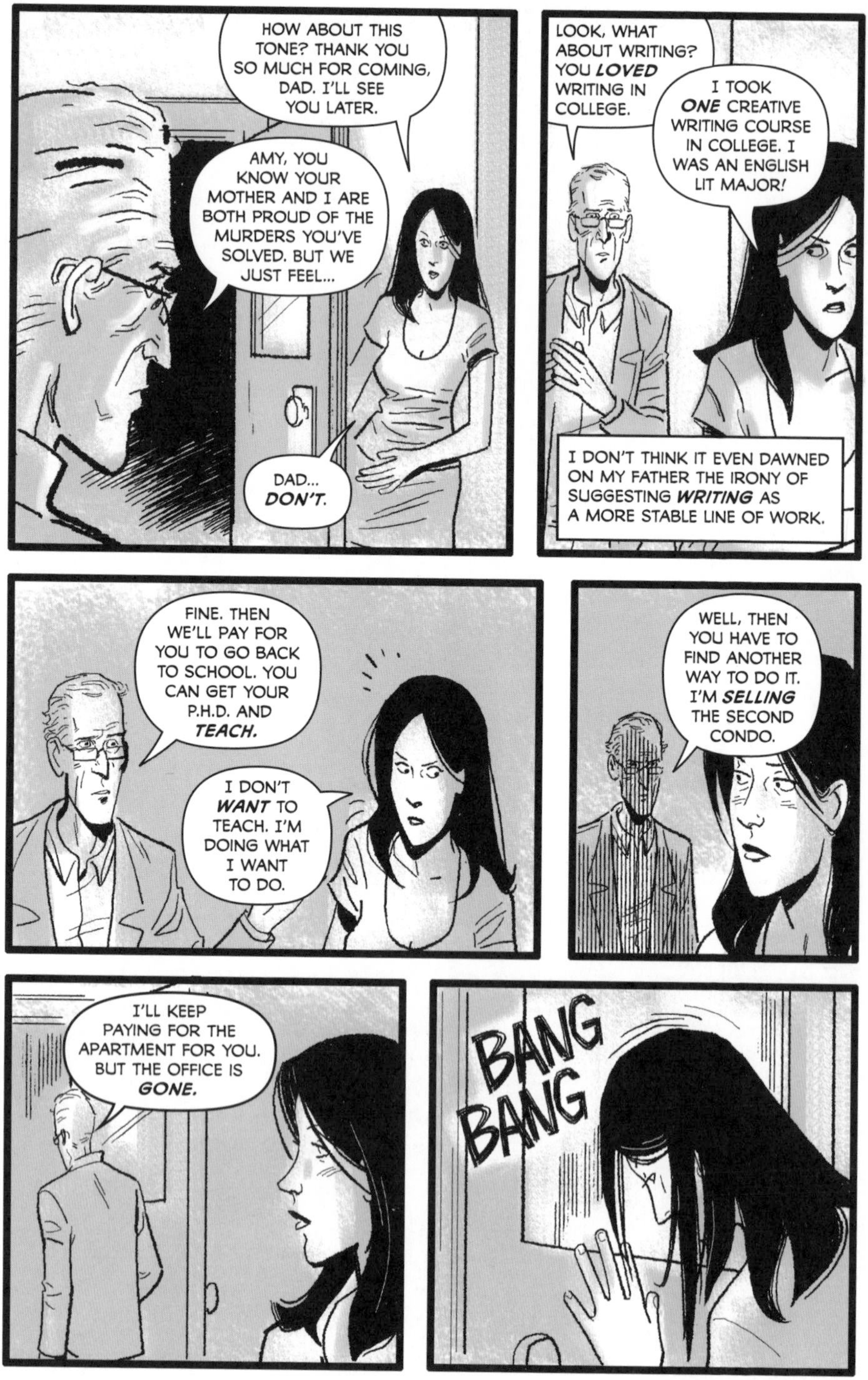
HOW ABOUT THIS TONE? THANK YOU SO MUCH FOR COMING, DAD. I'LL SEE YOU LATER.
AMY, YOU KNOW YOUR MOTHER AND I ARE BOTH PROUD OF THE MURDERS YOU'VE SOLVED. BUT WE JUST FEEL...
DAD... DON'T.
LOOK, WHAT ABOUT WRITING? YOU LOVED WRITING IN COLLEGE.
I TOOK ONE CREATIVE WRITING COURSE IN COLLEGE. I WAS AN ENGLISH LIT MAJOR!
I DON'T THINK IT EVEN DAWNED ON MY FATHER THE IRONY OF SUGGESTING WRITING AS A MORE STABLE LINE OF WORK.
FINE. THEN WE'LL PAY FOR YOU TO GO BACK TO SCHOOL. YOU CAN GET YOUR P.H.D. AND TEACH.
I DON'T WANT TO TEACH. I'M DOING WHAT I WANT TO DO.
WELL, THEN YOU HAVE TO FIND ANOTHER WAY TO DO IT. I'M SELLING THE SECOND CONDO.
I'LL KEEP PAYING FOR THE APARTMENT FOR YOU. BUT THE OFFICE IS GONE.
BANG
BANG

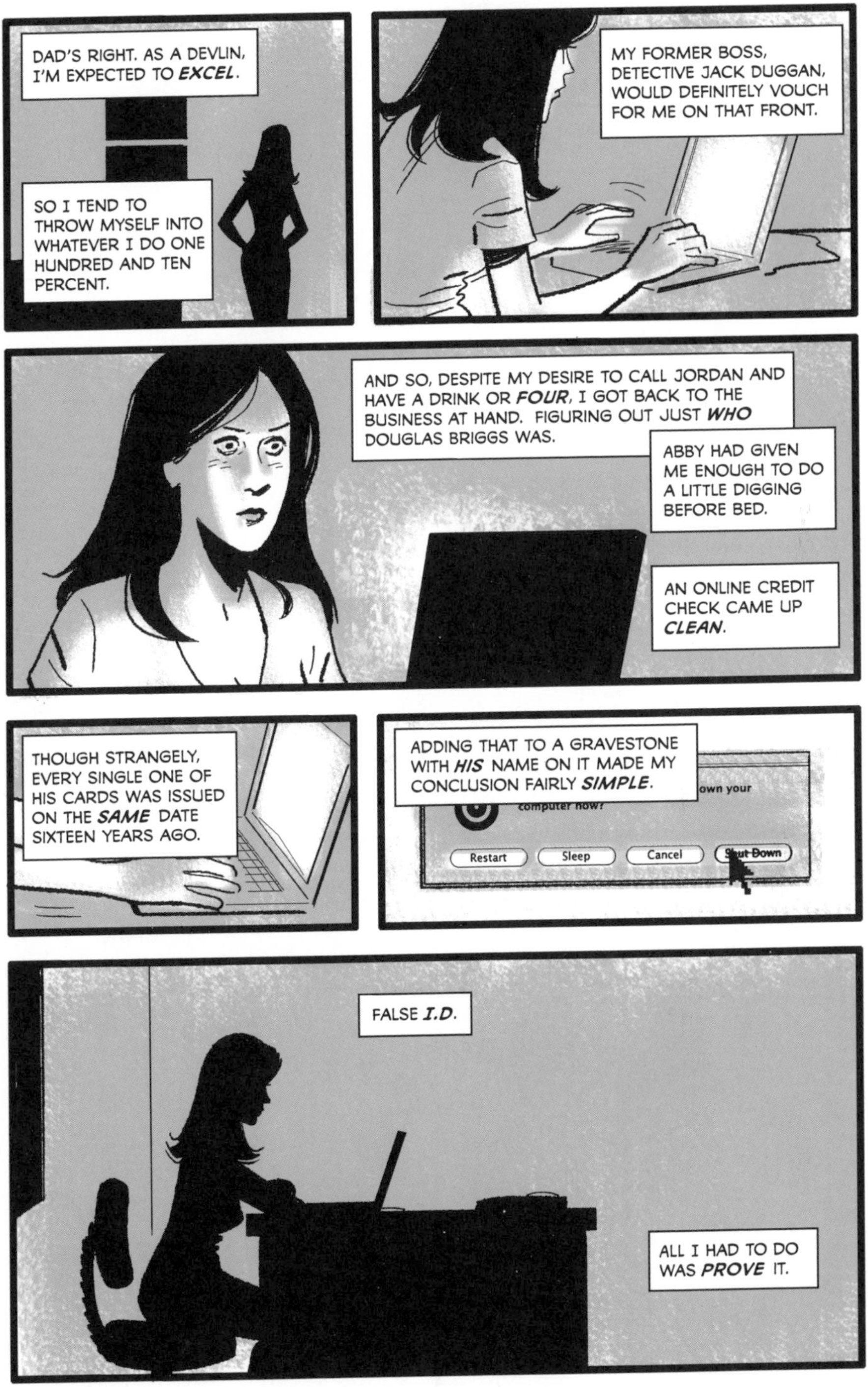
DAD'S RIGHT. AS A DEVLIN, I'M EXPECTED TO *EXCEL*.
SO I TEND TO THROW MYSELF INTO WHATEVER I DO ONE HUNDRED AND TEN PERCENT.
MY FORMER BOSS, DETECTIVE JACK DUGGAN, WOULD DEFINITELY VOUCH FOR ME ON THAT FRONT.
AND SO, DESPITE MY DESIRE TO CALL JORDAN AND HAVE A DRINK OR *FOUR*, I GOT BACK TO THE BUSINESS AT HAND. FIGURING OUT JUST *WHO* DOUGLAS BRIGGS WAS.
ABBY HAD GIVEN ME ENOUGH TO DO A LITTLE DIGGING BEFORE BED.
AN ONLINE CREDIT CHECK CAME UP *CLEAN*.
THOUGH STRANGELY, EVERY SINGLE ONE OF HIS CARDS WAS ISSUED ON THE *SAME* DATE SIXTEEN YEARS AGO.
ADDING THAT TO A GRAVESTONE WITH *HIS* NAME ON IT MADE MY CONCLUSION FAIRLY *SIMPLE*.
own your
computer now?
Restart
Sleep
Cancel
Shut Down
FALSE *I.D.*
ALL I HAD TO DO WAS *PROVE* IT.

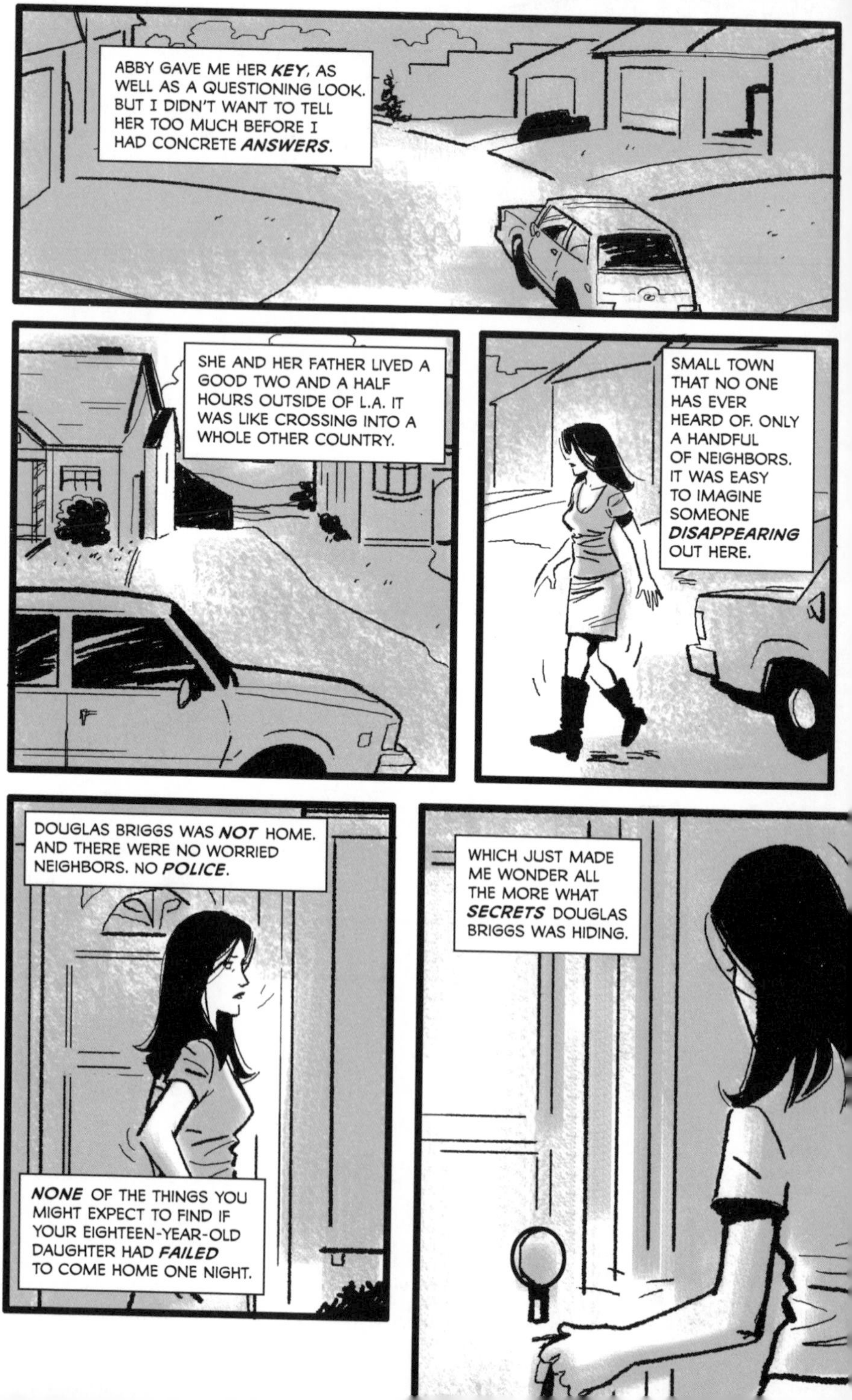
ABBY GAVE ME HER KEY, AS WELL AS A QUESTIONING LOOK. BUT I DIDN'T WANT TO TELL HER TOO MUCH BEFORE I HAD CONCRETE ANSWERS.
SHE AND HER FATHER LIVED A GOOD TWO AND A HALF HOURS OUTSIDE OF L.A. IT WAS LIKE CROSSING INTO A WHOLE OTHER COUNTRY.
SMALL TOWN THAT NO ONE HAS EVER HEARD OF. ONLY A HANDFUL OF NEIGHBORS. IT WAS EASY TO IMAGINE SOMEONE DISAPPEARING OUT HERE.
DOUGLAS BRIGGS WAS NOT HOME. AND THERE WERE NO WORRIED NEIGHBORS. NO POLICE.
NONE OF THE THINGS YOU MIGHT EXPECT TO FIND IF YOUR EIGHTEEN-YEAR-OLD DAUGHTER HAD FAILED TO COME HOME ONE NIGHT.
WHICH JUST MADE ME WONDER ALL THE MORE WHAT SECRETS DOUGLAS BRIGGS WAS HIDING.

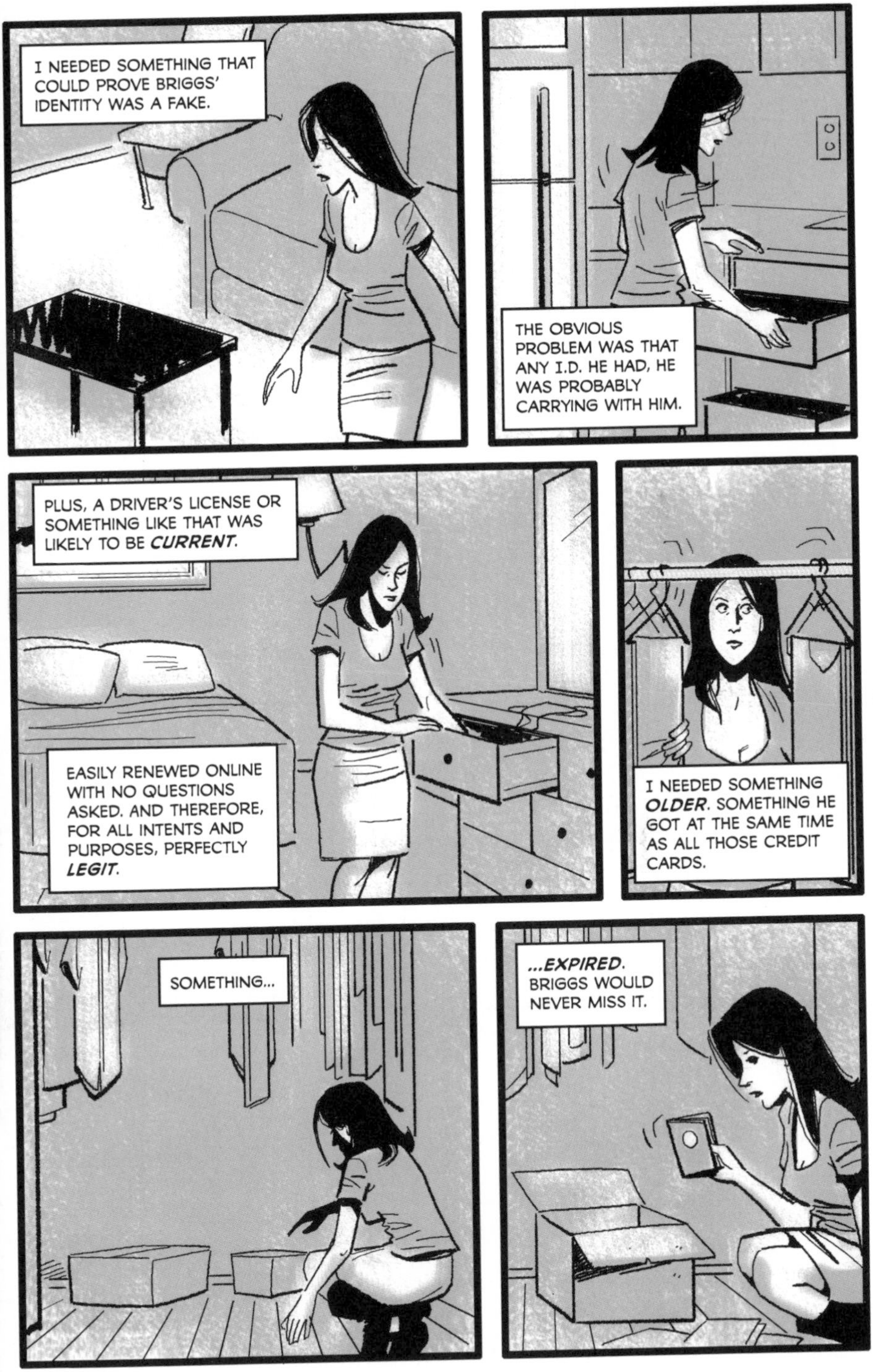
I NEEDED SOMETHING THAT COULD PROVE BRIGGS' IDENTITY WAS A FAKE.
THE OBVIOUS PROBLEM WAS THAT ANY I.D. HE HAD, HE WAS PROBABLY CARRYING WITH HIM.
PLUS, A DRIVER'S LICENSE OR SOMETHING LIKE THAT WAS LIKELY TO BE *CURRENT*.
EASILY RENEWED ONLINE WITH NO QUESTIONS ASKED. AND THEREFORE, FOR ALL INTENTS AND PURPOSES, PERFECTLY *LEGIT*.
I NEEDED SOMETHING *OLDER*. SOMETHING HE GOT AT THE SAME TIME AS ALL THOSE CREDIT CARDS.
SOMETHING...
...EXPIRED. BRIGGS WOULD NEVER MISS IT.

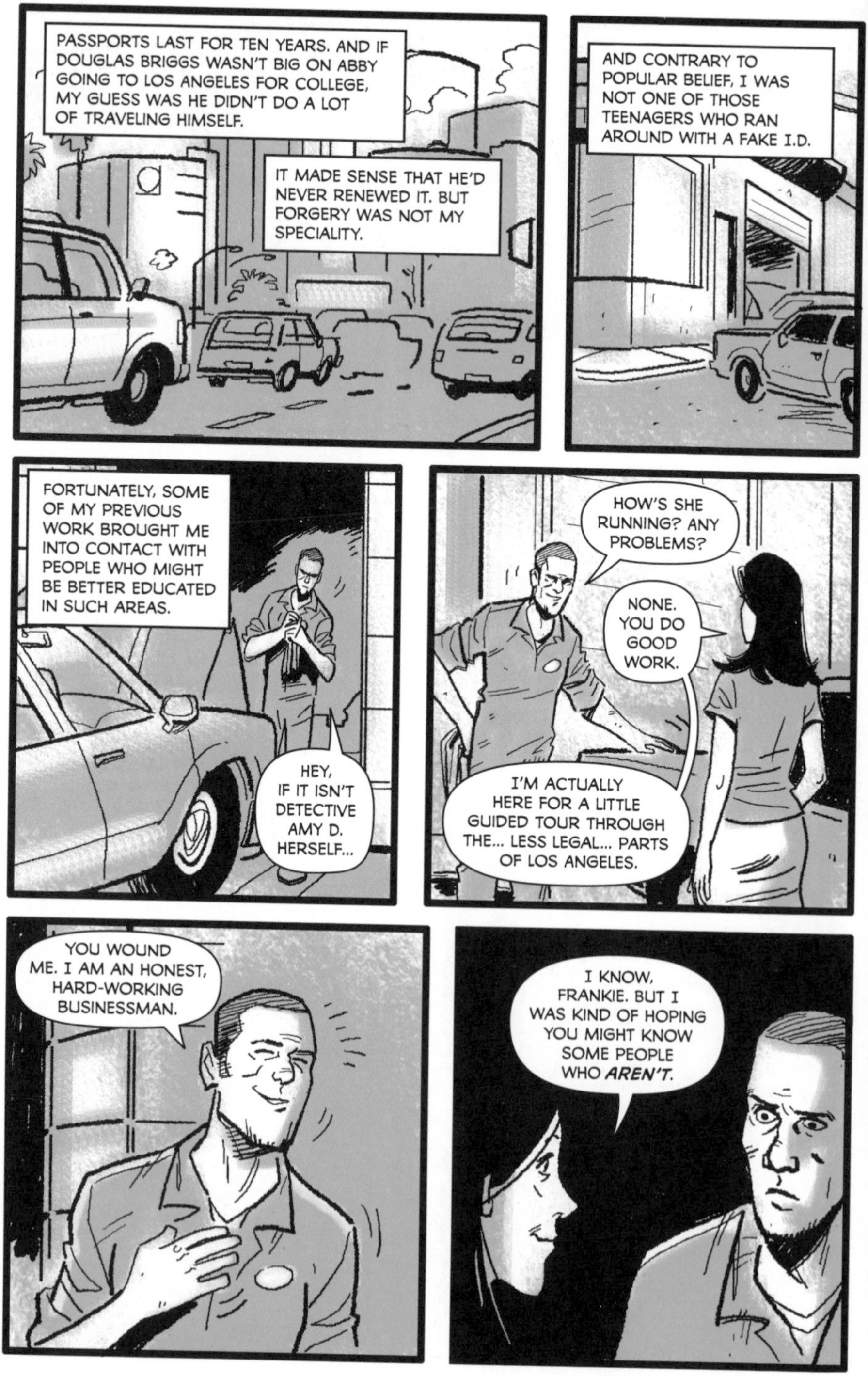
PASSPORTS LAST FOR TEN YEARS. AND IF DOUGLAS BRIGGS WASN'T BIG ON ABBY GOING TO LOS ANGELES FOR COLLEGE, MY GUESS WAS HE DIDN'T DO A LOT OF TRAVELING HIMSELF.
IT MADE SENSE THAT HE'D NEVER RENEWED IT. BUT FORGERY WAS NOT MY SPECIALITY.
AND CONTRARY TO POPULAR BELIEF, I WAS NOT ONE OF THOSE TEENAGERS WHO RAN AROUND WITH A FAKE I.D.
FORTUNATELY, SOME OF MY PREVIOUS WORK BROUGHT ME INTO CONTACT WITH PEOPLE WHO MIGHT BE BETTER EDUCATED IN SUCH AREAS.
HEY, IF IT ISN'T DETECTIVE AMY D. HERSELF...
HOW'S SHE RUNNING? ANY PROBLEMS?
NONE. YOU DO GOOD WORK.
I'M ACTUALLY HERE FOR A LITTLE GUIDED TOUR THROUGH THE... LESS LEGAL... PARTS OF LOS ANGELES.
YOU WOUND ME. I AM AN HONEST, HARD-WORKING BUSINESSMAN.
I KNOW, FRANKIE. BUT I WAS KIND OF HOPING YOU MIGHT KNOW SOME PEOPLE WHO ***AREN'T***.

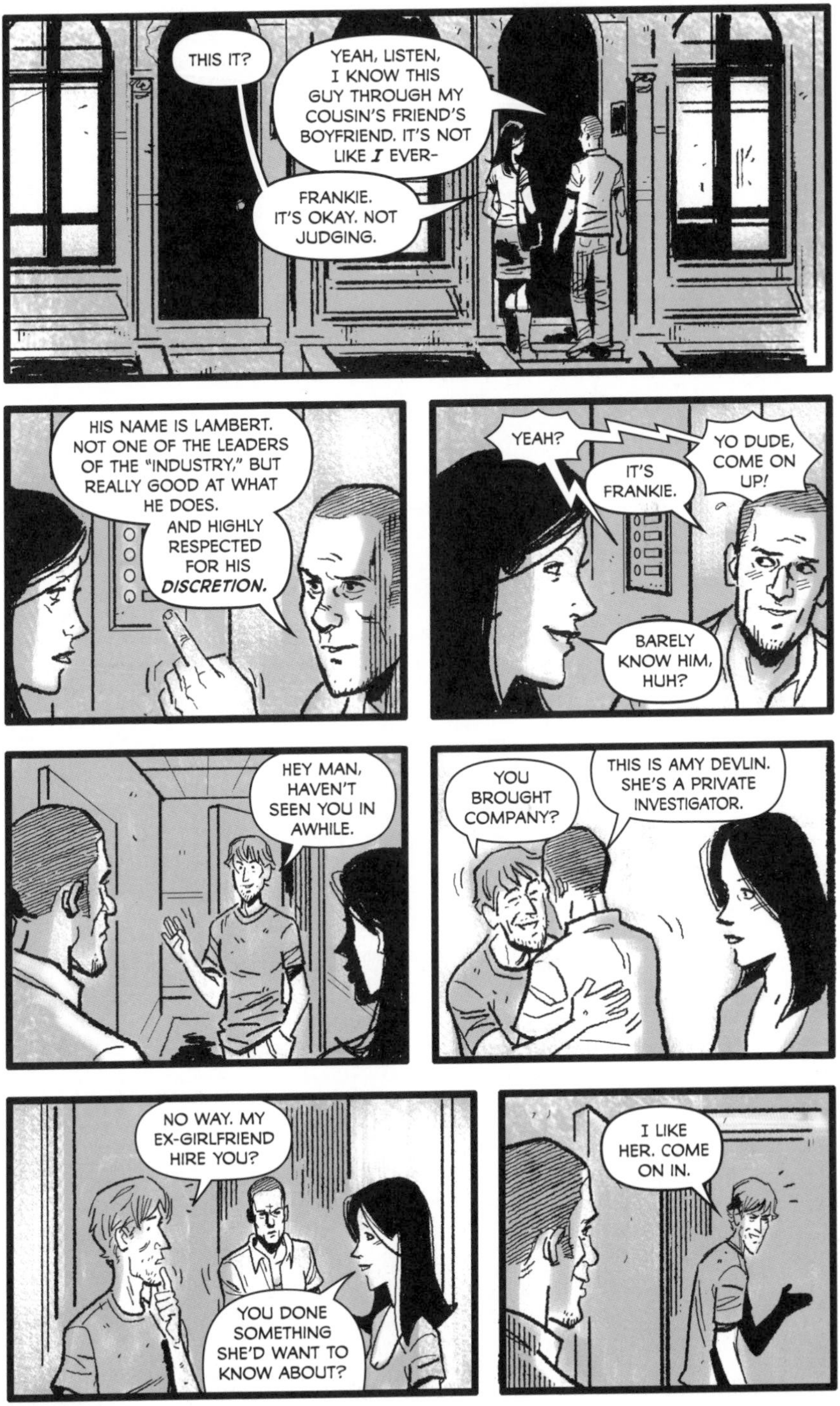
THIS IT?
YEAH, LISTEN, I KNOW THIS GUY THROUGH MY COUSIN'S FRIEND'S BOYFRIEND. IT'S NOT LIKE *I* EVER-
FRANKIE. IT'S OKAY. NOT JUDGING.
HIS NAME IS LAMBERT. NOT ONE OF THE LEADERS OF THE "INDUSTRY," BUT REALLY GOOD AT WHAT HE DOES.
AND HIGHLY RESPECTED FOR HIS *DISCRETION.*
YEAH?
IT'S FRANKIE.
YO DUDE, COME ON UP!
BARELY KNOW HIM, HUH?
HEY MAN, HAVEN'T SEEN YOU IN AWHILE.
YOU BROUGHT COMPANY?
THIS IS AMY DEVLIN. SHE'S A PRIVATE INVESTIGATOR.
NO WAY. MY EX-GIRLFRIEND HIRE YOU?
YOU DONE SOMETHING SHE'D WANT TO KNOW ABOUT?
I LIKE HER. COME ON IN.

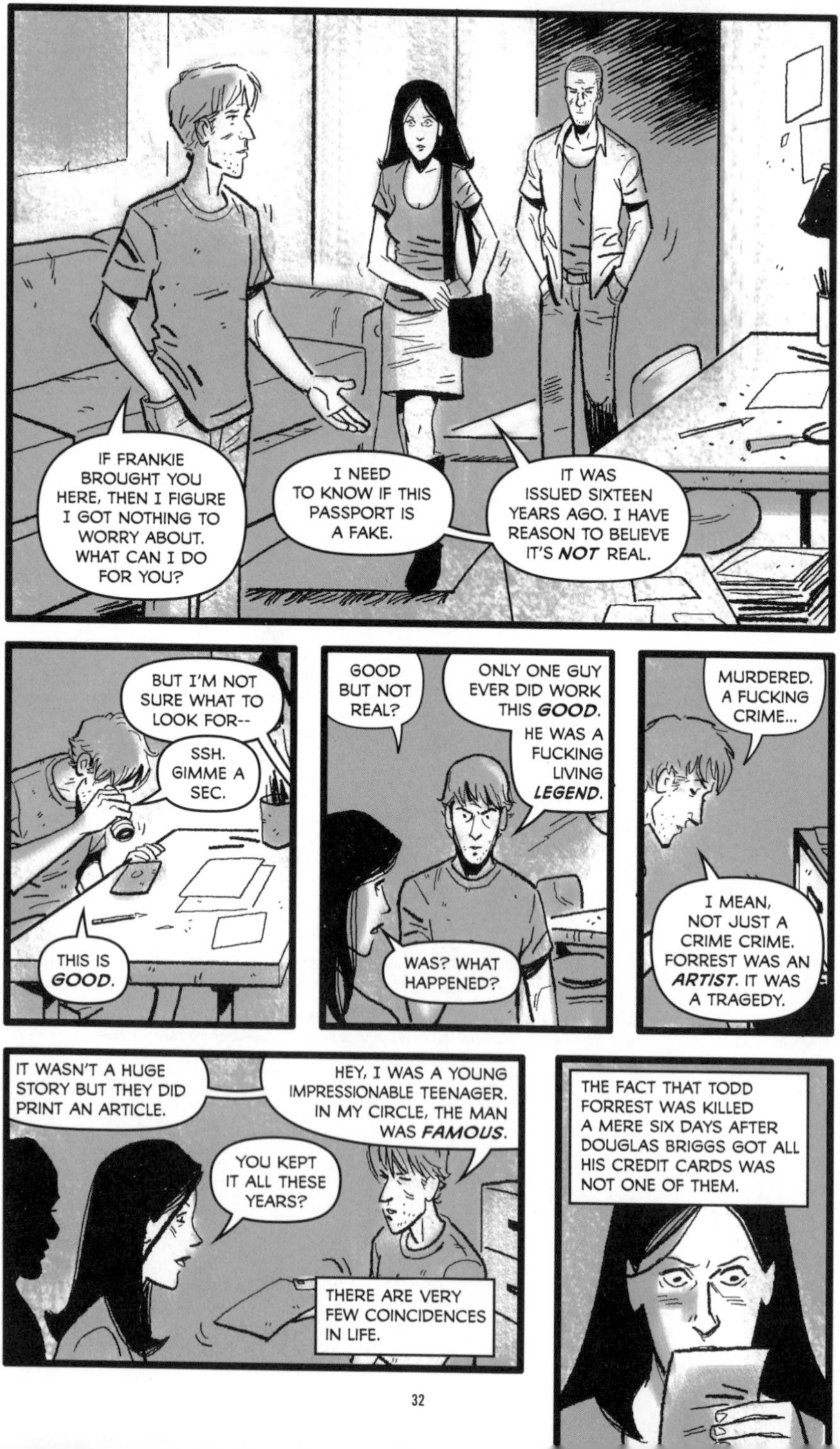
IF FRANKIE BROUGHT YOU HERE, THEN I FIGURE I GOT NOTHING TO WORRY ABOUT. WHAT CAN I DO FOR YOU?
I NEED TO KNOW IF THIS PASSPORT IS A FAKE.
IT WAS ISSUED SIXTEEN YEARS AGO. I HAVE REASON TO BELIEVE IT'S ***NOT*** REAL.
BUT I'M NOT SURE WHAT TO LOOK FOR--
SSH. GIMME A SEC.
THIS IS ***GOOD***.
GOOD BUT NOT REAL?
ONLY ONE GUY EVER DID WORK THIS ***GOOD***.
HE WAS A FUCKING LIVING ***LEGEND***.
WAS? WHAT HAPPENED?
MURDERED. A FUCKING CRIME...
I MEAN, NOT JUST A CRIME CRIME. FORREST WAS AN ***ARTIST***. IT WAS A TRAGEDY.
IT WASN'T A HUGE STORY BUT THEY DID PRINT AN ARTICLE.
HEY, I WAS A YOUNG IMPRESSIONABLE TEENAGER. IN MY CIRCLE, THE MAN WAS ***FAMOUS***.
YOU KEPT IT ALL THESE YEARS?
THERE ARE VERY FEW COINCIDENCES IN LIFE.
THE FACT THAT TODD FORREST WAS KILLED A MERE SIX DAYS AFTER DOUGLAS BRIGGS GOT ALL HIS CREDIT CARDS WAS NOT ONE OF THEM.

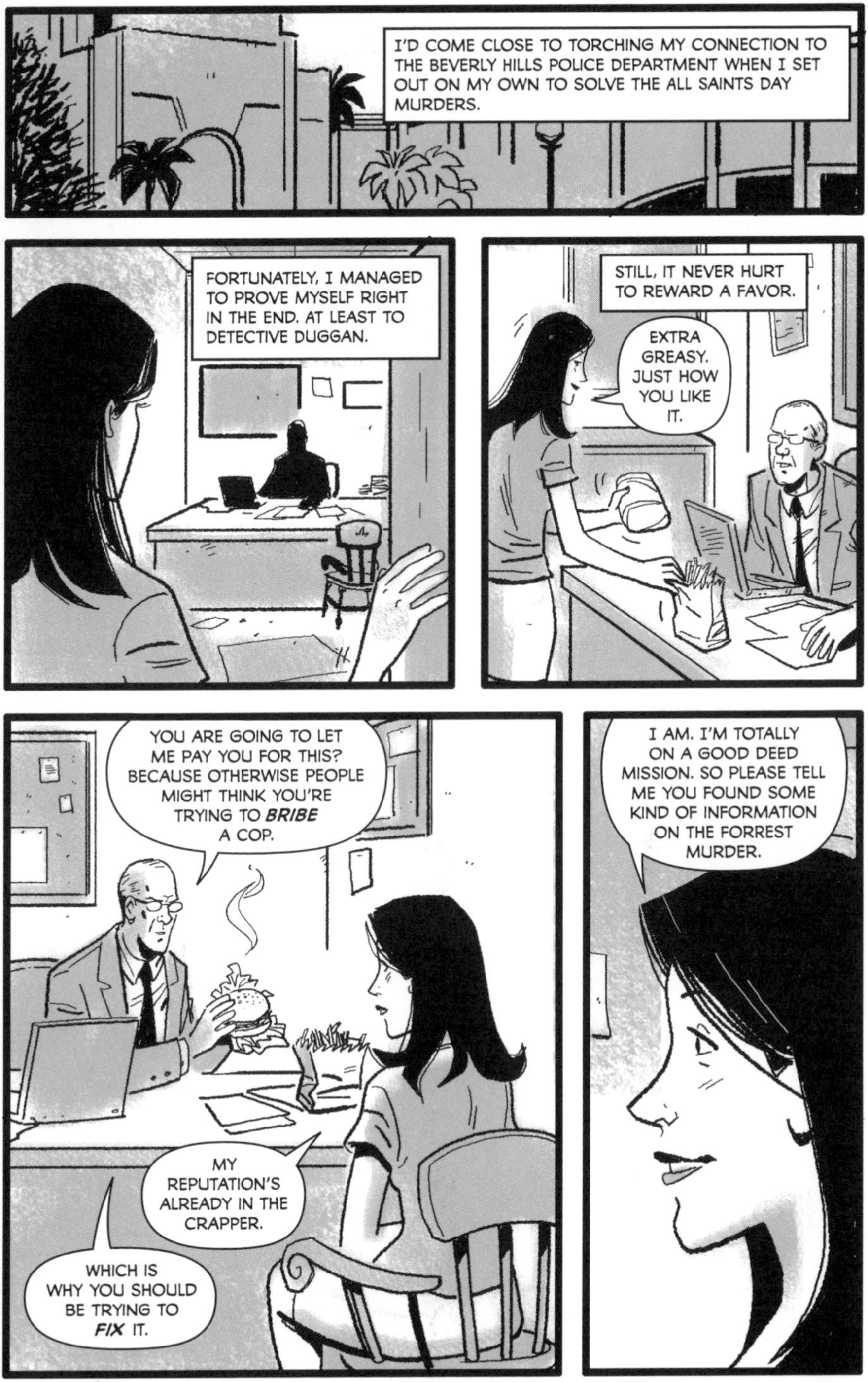
I'D COME CLOSE TO TORCHING MY CONNECTION TO THE BEVERLY HILLS POLICE DEPARTMENT WHEN I SET OUT ON MY OWN TO SOLVE THE ALL SAINTS DAY MURDERS.
FORTUNATELY, I MANAGED TO PROVE MYSELF RIGHT IN THE END. AT LEAST TO DETECTIVE DUGGAN.
STILL, IT NEVER HURT TO REWARD A FAVOR.
EXTRA GREASY. JUST HOW YOU LIKE IT.
YOU ARE GOING TO LET ME PAY YOU FOR THIS? BECAUSE OTHERWISE PEOPLE MIGHT THINK YOU'RE TRYING TO *BRIBE* A COP.
MY REPUTATION'S ALREADY IN THE CRAPPER.
WHICH IS WHY YOU SHOULD BE TRYING TO *FIX* IT.
I AM. I'M TOTALLY ON A GOOD DEED MISSION. SO PLEASE TELL ME YOU FOUND SOME KIND OF INFORMATION ON THE FORREST MURDER.

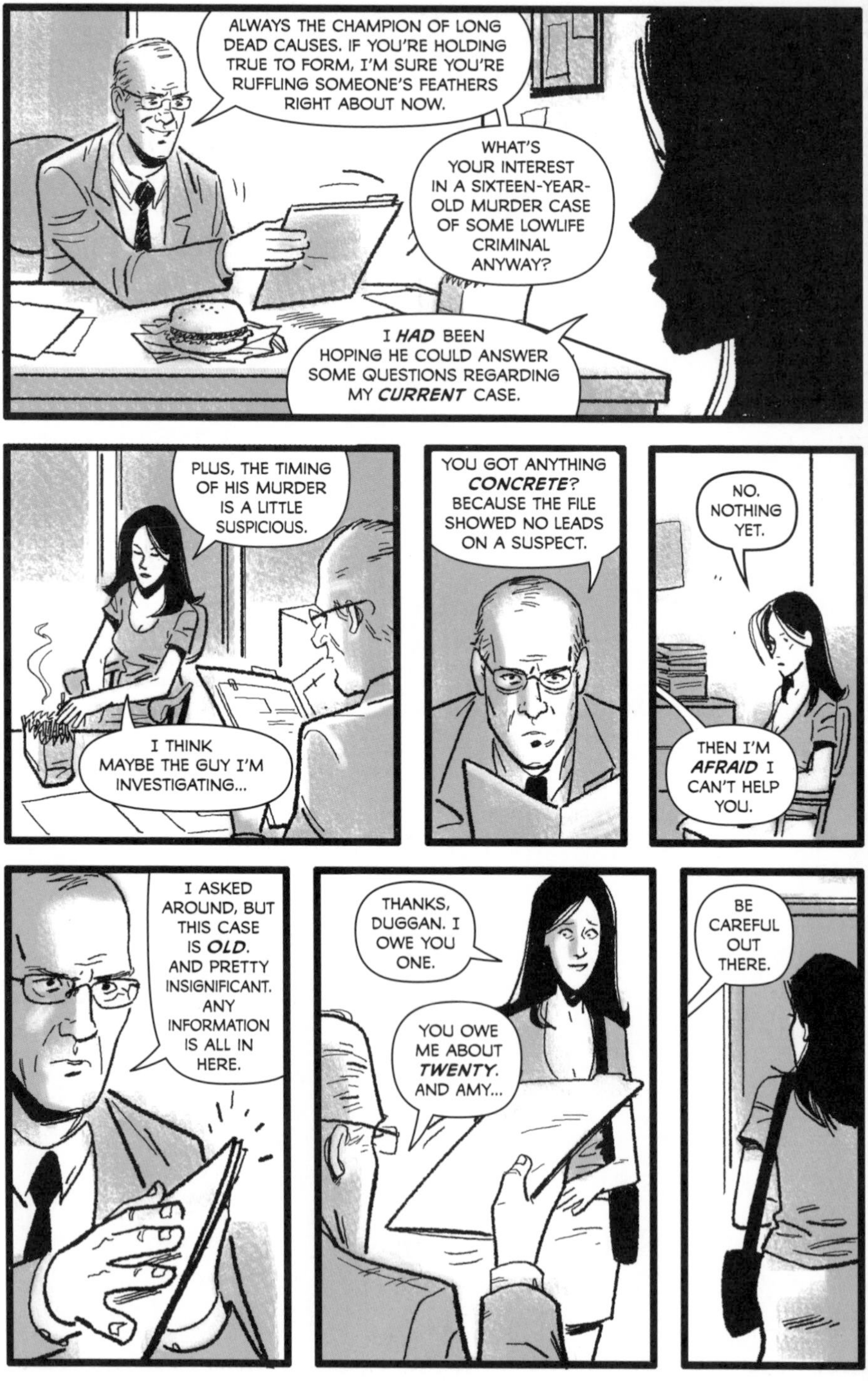
ALWAYS THE CHAMPION OF LONG DEAD CAUSES. IF YOU'RE HOLDING TRUE TO FORM, I'M SURE YOU'RE RUFFLING SOMEONE'S FEATHERS RIGHT ABOUT NOW.
WHAT'S YOUR INTEREST IN A SIXTEEN-YEAR-OLD MURDER CASE OF SOME LOWLIFE CRIMINAL ANYWAY?
I *HAD* BEEN HOPING HE COULD ANSWER SOME QUESTIONS REGARDING MY *CURRENT* CASE.
PLUS, THE TIMING OF HIS MURDER IS A LITTLE SUSPICIOUS.
I THINK MAYBE THE GUY I'M INVESTIGATING...
YOU GOT ANYTHING *CONCRETE*? BECAUSE THE FILE SHOWED NO LEADS ON A SUSPECT.
NO. NOTHING YET.
THEN I'M *AFRAID* I CAN'T HELP YOU.
I ASKED AROUND, BUT THIS CASE IS *OLD*. AND PRETTY INSIGNIFICANT. ANY INFORMATION IS ALL IN HERE.
THANKS, DUGGAN. I OWE YOU ONE.
YOU OWE ME ABOUT *TWENTY*. AND AMY...
BE CAREFUL OUT THERE.

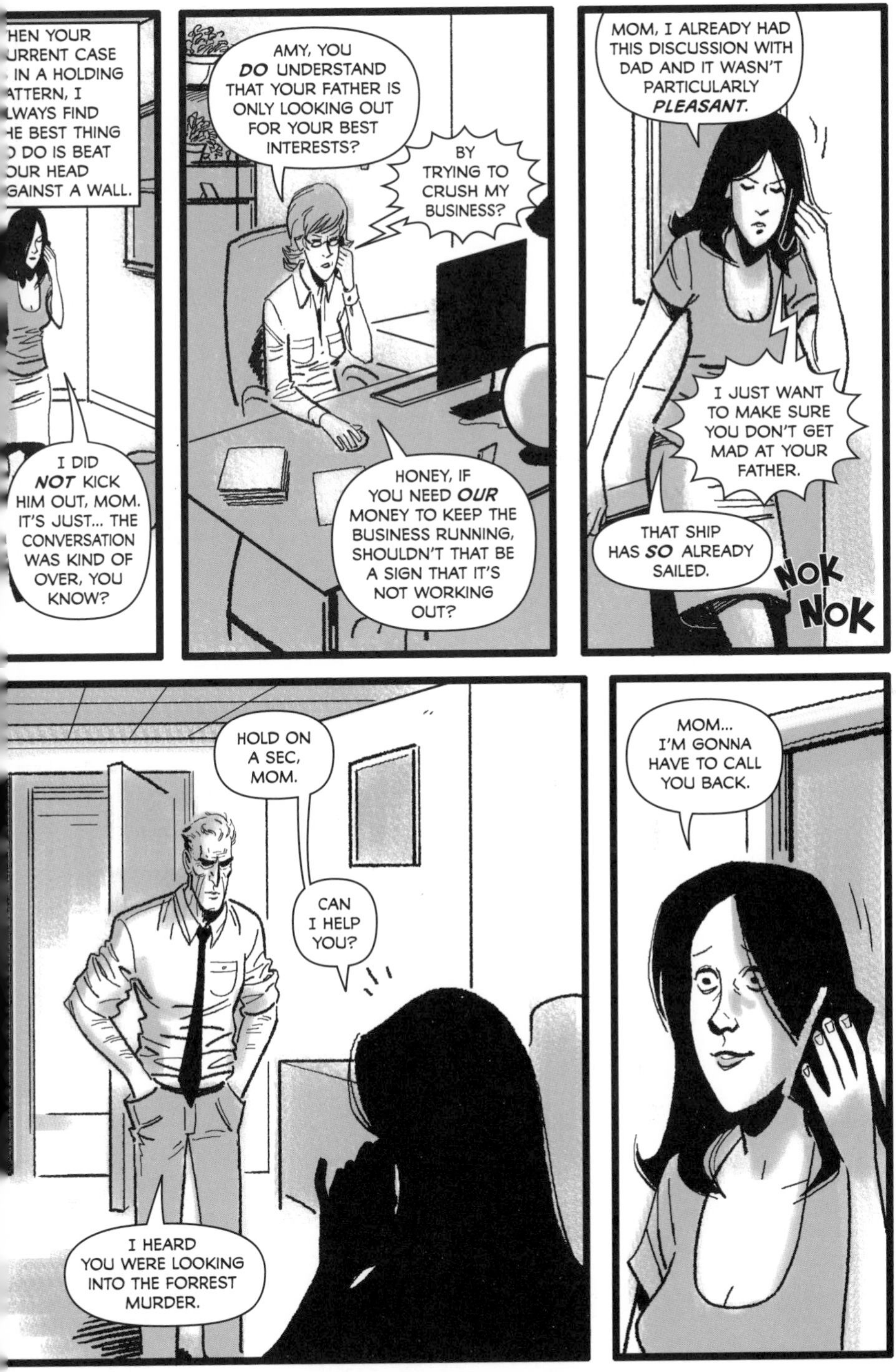

HEN YOUR
URRENT CASE
IN A HOLDING
ATTERN, I
LWAYS FIND
HE BEST THING
O DO IS BEAT
OUR HEAD
GAINST A WALL.
I DID NOT KICK HIM OUT, MOM. IT'S JUST... THE CONVERSATION WAS KIND OF OVER, YOU KNOW?
AMY, YOU DO UNDERSTAND THAT YOUR FATHER IS ONLY LOOKING OUT FOR YOUR BEST INTERESTS?
BY TRYING TO CRUSH MY BUSINESS?
HONEY, IF YOU NEED OUR MONEY TO KEEP THE BUSINESS RUNNING, SHOULDN'T THAT BE A SIGN THAT IT'S NOT WORKING OUT?
MOM, I ALREADY HAD THIS DISCUSSION WITH DAD AND IT WASN'T PARTICULARLY PLEASANT.
I JUST WANT TO MAKE SURE YOU DON'T GET MAD AT YOUR FATHER.
THAT SHIP HAS SO ALREADY SAILED.
NOK NOK
HOLD ON A SEC, MOM.
CAN I HELP YOU?
I HEARD YOU WERE LOOKING INTO THE FORREST MURDER.
MOM... I'M GONNA HAVE TO CALL YOU BACK.

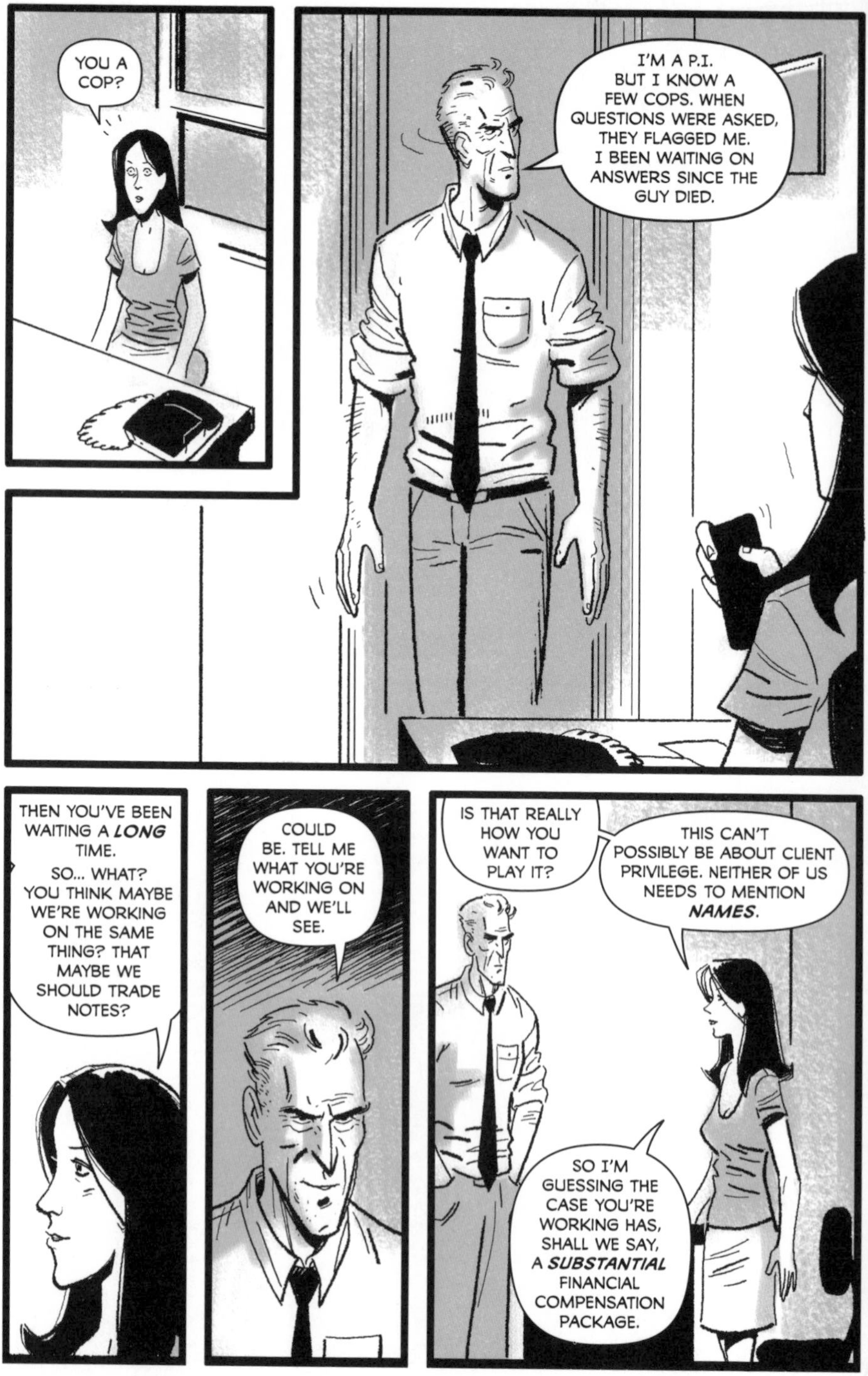
YOU A COP?
I'M A P.I. BUT I KNOW A FEW COPS. WHEN QUESTIONS WERE ASKED, THEY FLAGGED ME. I BEEN WAITING ON ANSWERS SINCE THE GUY DIED.
THEN YOU'VE BEEN WAITING A *LONG* TIME.
SO... WHAT? YOU THINK MAYBE WE'RE WORKING ON THE SAME THING? THAT MAYBE WE SHOULD TRADE NOTES?
COULD BE. TELL ME WHAT YOU'RE WORKING ON AND WE'LL SEE.
IS THAT REALLY HOW YOU WANT TO PLAY IT?
THIS CAN'T POSSIBLY BE ABOUT CLIENT PRIVILEGE. NEITHER OF US NEEDS TO MENTION ***NAMES***.
SO I'M GUESSING THE CASE YOU'RE WORKING HAS, SHALL WE SAY, A ***SUBSTANTIAL*** FINANCIAL COMPENSATION PACKAGE.

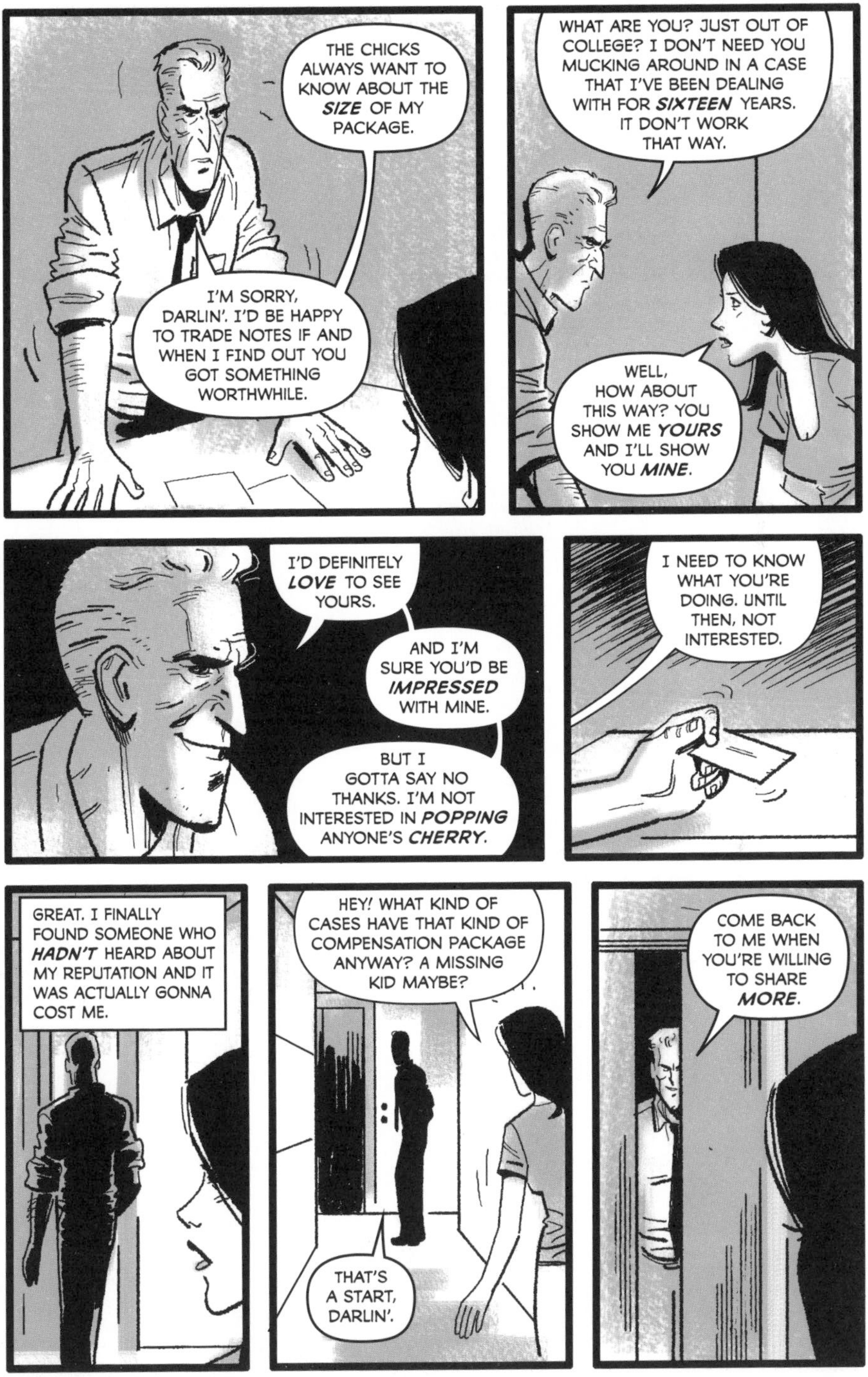
THE CHICKS ALWAYS WANT TO KNOW ABOUT THE *SIZE* OF MY PACKAGE.
I'M SORRY, DARLIN'. I'D BE HAPPY TO TRADE NOTES IF AND WHEN I FIND OUT YOU GOT SOMETHING WORTHWHILE.
WHAT ARE YOU? JUST OUT OF COLLEGE? I DON'T NEED YOU MUCKING AROUND IN A CASE THAT I'VE BEEN DEALING WITH FOR *SIXTEEN* YEARS. IT DON'T WORK THAT WAY.
WELL, HOW ABOUT THIS WAY? YOU SHOW ME *YOURS* AND I'LL SHOW YOU *MINE*.
I'D DEFINITELY *LOVE* TO SEE YOURS.
AND I'M SURE YOU'D BE *IMPRESSED* WITH MINE.
BUT I GOTTA SAY NO THANKS. I'M NOT INTERESTED IN *POPPING* ANYONE'S *CHERRY*.
I NEED TO KNOW WHAT YOU'RE DOING. UNTIL THEN, NOT INTERESTED.
GREAT. I FINALLY FOUND SOMEONE WHO *HADN'T* HEARD ABOUT MY REPUTATION AND IT WAS ACTUALLY GONNA COST ME.
HEY! WHAT KIND OF CASES HAVE THAT KIND OF COMPENSATION PACKAGE ANYWAY? A MISSING KID MAYBE?
THAT'S A START, DARLIN'.
COME BACK TO ME WHEN YOU'RE WILLING TO SHARE *MORE*.

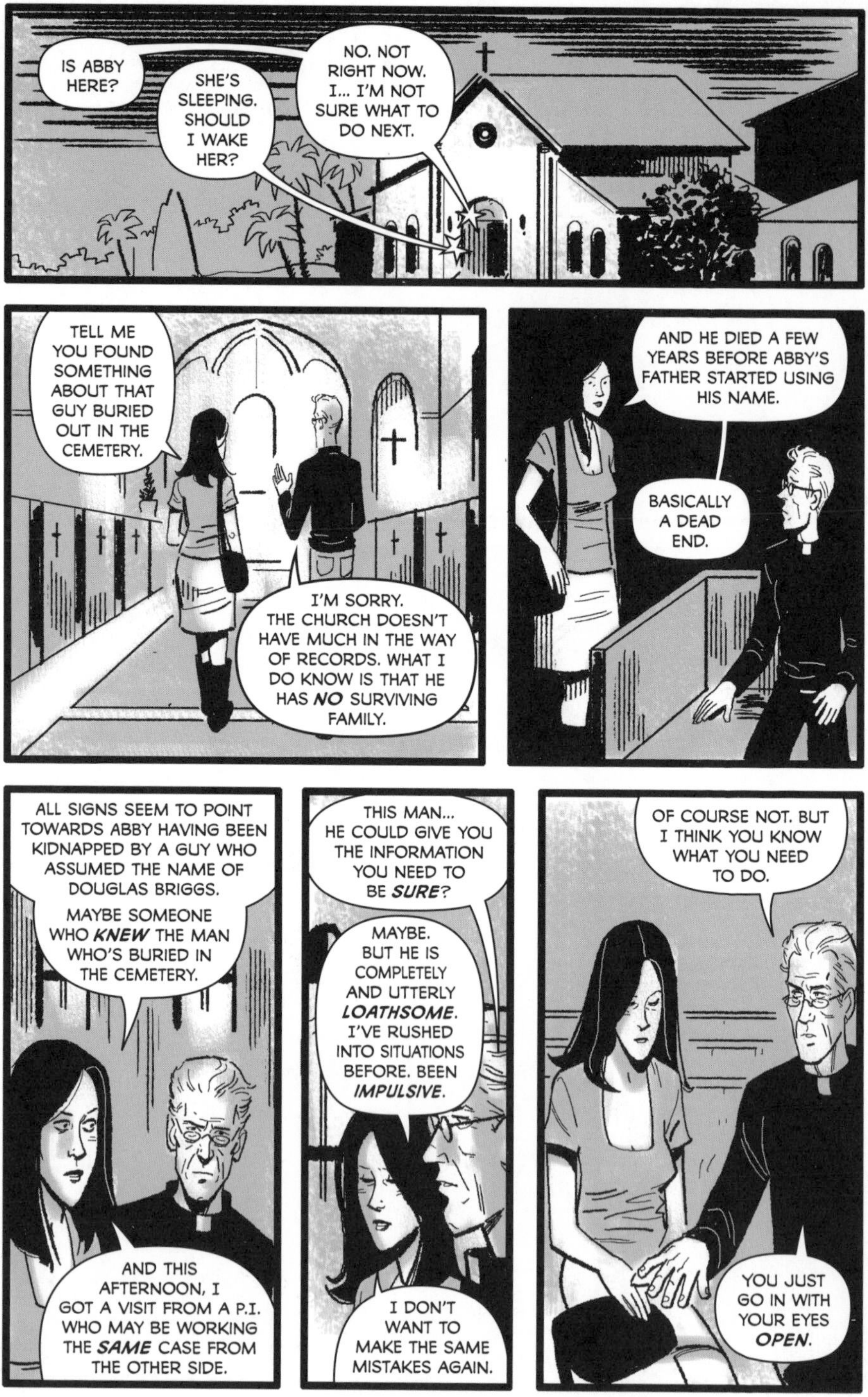
IS ABBY HERE?
SHE'S SLEEPING. SHOULD I WAKE HER?
NO. NOT RIGHT NOW. I... I'M NOT SURE WHAT TO DO NEXT.
TELL ME YOU FOUND SOMETHING ABOUT THAT GUY BURIED OUT IN THE CEMETERY.
I'M SORRY. THE CHURCH DOESN'T HAVE MUCH IN THE WAY OF RECORDS. WHAT I DO KNOW IS THAT HE HAS *NO* SURVIVING FAMILY.
AND HE DIED A FEW YEARS BEFORE ABBY'S FATHER STARTED USING HIS NAME.
BASICALLY A DEAD END.
ALL SIGNS SEEM TO POINT TOWARDS ABBY HAVING BEEN KIDNAPPED BY A GUY WHO ASSUMED THE NAME OF DOUGLAS BRIGGS.
MAYBE SOMEONE WHO *KNEW* THE MAN WHO'S BURIED IN THE CEMETERY.
AND THIS AFTERNOON, I GOT A VISIT FROM A P.I. WHO MAY BE WORKING THE *SAME* CASE FROM THE OTHER SIDE.
THIS MAN... HE COULD GIVE YOU THE INFORMATION YOU NEED TO BE *SURE*?
MAYBE. BUT HE IS COMPLETELY AND UTTERLY *LOATHSOME*. I'VE RUSHED INTO SITUATIONS BEFORE. BEEN *IMPULSIVE*.
I DON'T WANT TO MAKE THE SAME MISTAKES AGAIN.
OF COURSE NOT. BUT I THINK YOU KNOW WHAT YOU NEED TO DO.
YOU JUST GO IN WITH YOUR EYES *OPEN*.

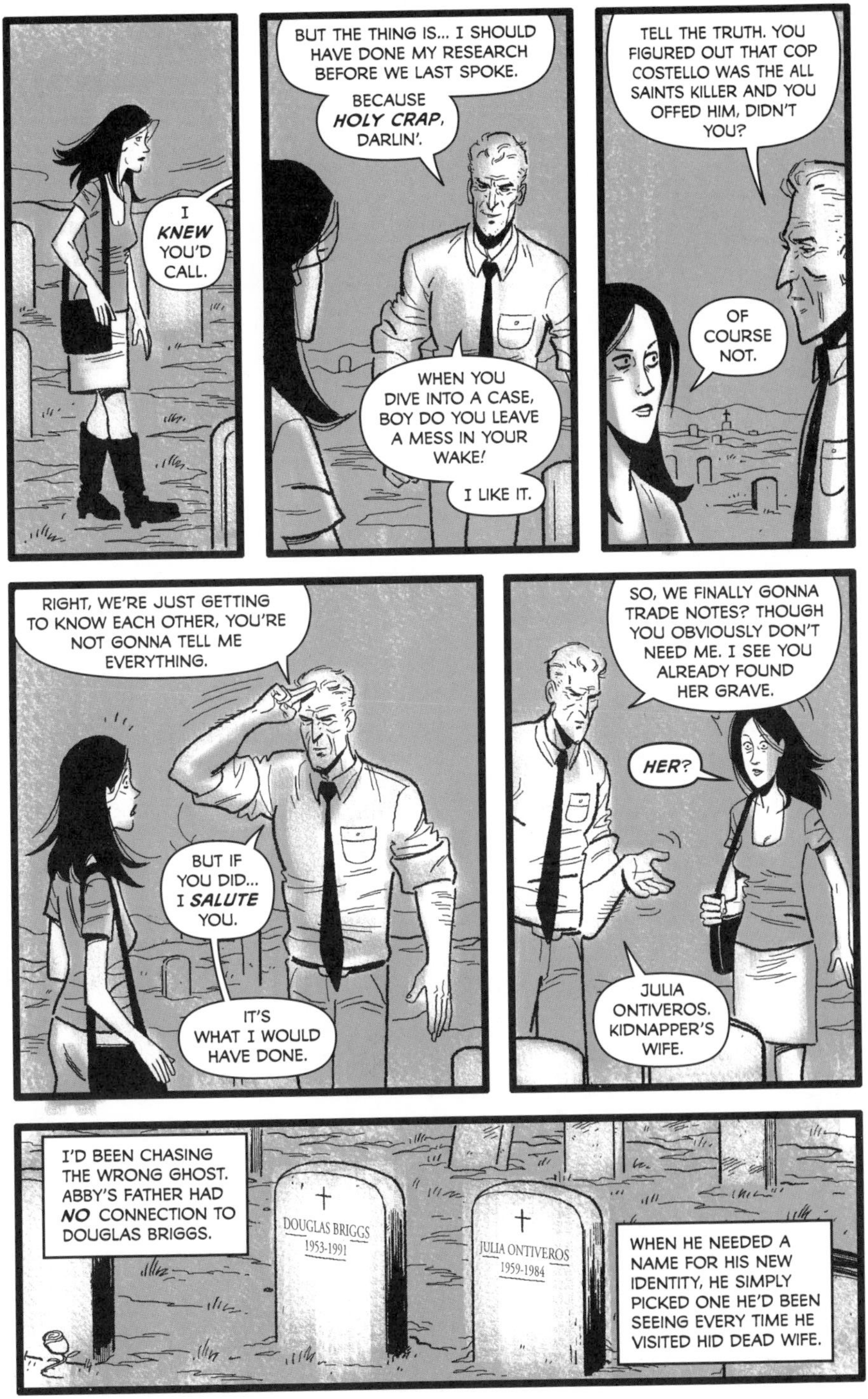

I KNEW YOU'D CALL.
BUT THE THING IS... I SHOULD HAVE DONE MY RESEARCH BEFORE WE LAST SPOKE.
BECAUSE HOLY CRAP, DARLIN'.
WHEN YOU DIVE INTO A CASE, BOY DO YOU LEAVE A MESS IN YOUR WAKE!
I LIKE IT.
TELL THE TRUTH. YOU FIGURED OUT THAT COP COSTELLO WAS THE ALL SAINTS KILLER AND YOU OFFED HIM, DIDN'T YOU?
OF COURSE NOT.
RIGHT, WE'RE JUST GETTING TO KNOW EACH OTHER, YOU'RE NOT GONNA TELL ME EVERYTHING.
BUT IF YOU DID... I SALUTE YOU.
IT'S WHAT I WOULD HAVE DONE.
SO, WE FINALLY GONNA TRADE NOTES? THOUGH YOU OBVIOUSLY DON'T NEED ME. I SEE YOU ALREADY FOUND HER GRAVE.
HER?
JULIA ONTIVEROS. KIDNAPPER'S WIFE.
I'D BEEN CHASING THE WRONG GHOST. ABBY'S FATHER HAD NO CONNECTION TO DOUGLAS BRIGGS.
DOUGLAS BRIGGS 1953-1991
JULIA ONTIVEROS 1959-1984
WHEN HE NEEDED A NAME FOR HIS NEW IDENTITY, HE SIMPLY PICKED ONE HE'D BEEN SEEING EVERY TIME HE VISITED HID DEAD WIFE.

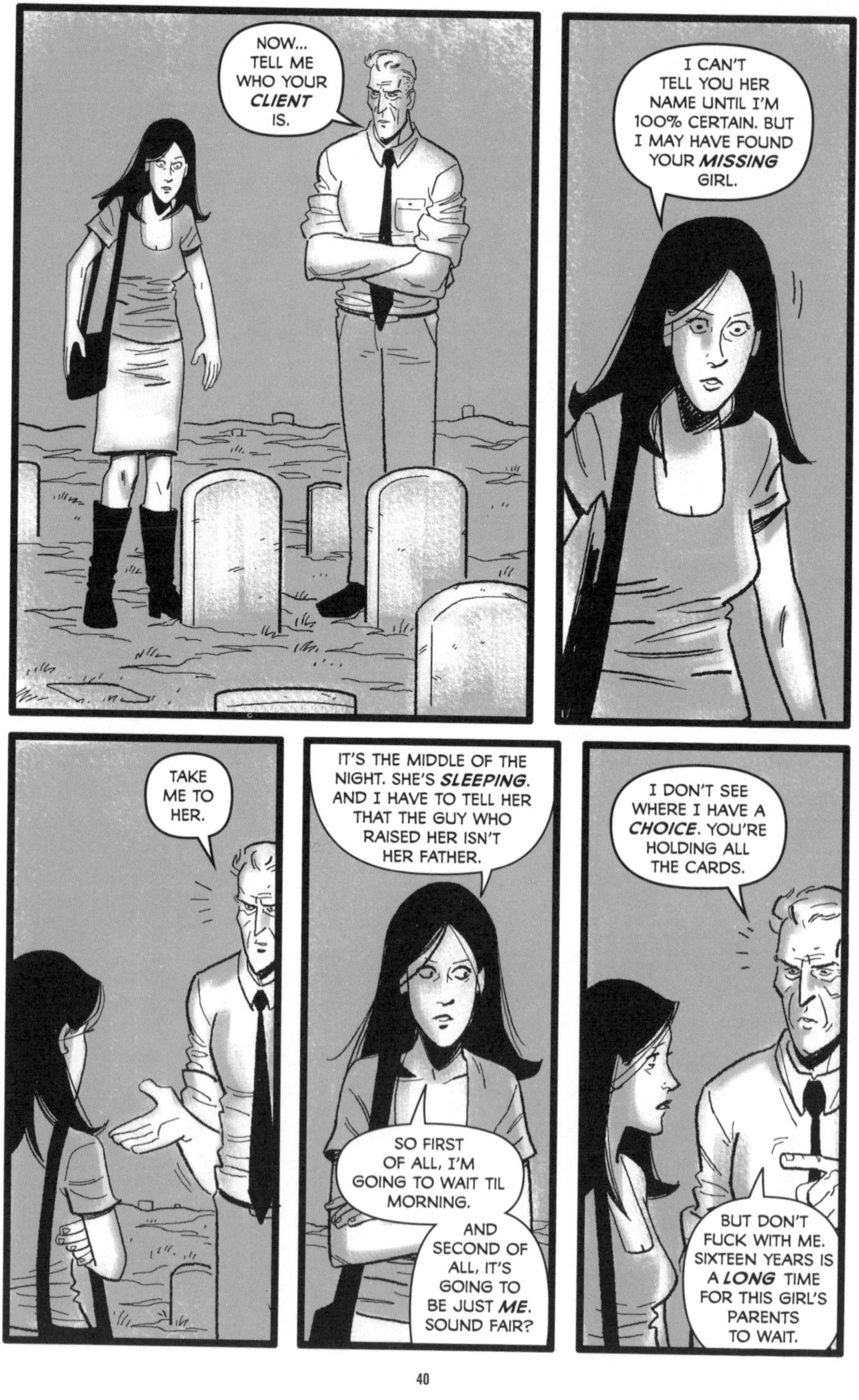
NOW... TELL ME WHO YOUR *CLIENT* IS.
I CAN'T TELL YOU HER NAME UNTIL I'M 100% CERTAIN. BUT I MAY HAVE FOUND YOUR *MISSING* GIRL.
TAKE ME TO HER.
IT'S THE MIDDLE OF THE NIGHT. SHE'S *SLEEPING*. AND I HAVE TO TELL HER THAT THE GUY WHO RAISED HER ISN'T HER FATHER.
SO FIRST OF ALL, I'M GOING TO WAIT TIL MORNING.
AND SECOND OF ALL, IT'S GOING TO BE JUST *ME*. SOUND FAIR?
I DON'T SEE WHERE I HAVE A *CHOICE*. YOU'RE HOLDING ALL THE CARDS.
BUT DON'T FUCK WITH ME. SIXTEEN YEARS IS A *LONG* TIME FOR THIS GIRL'S PARENTS TO WAIT.

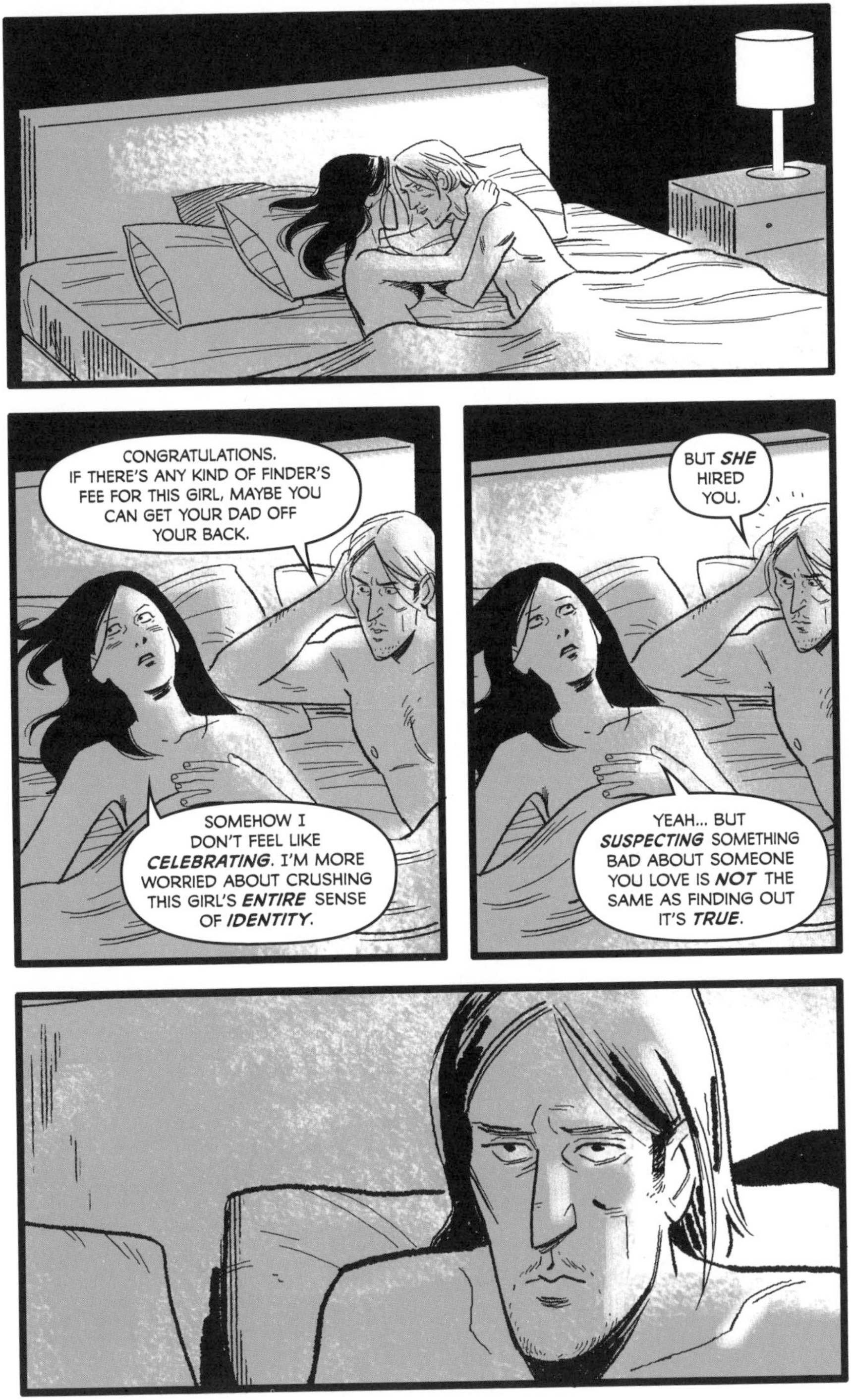
CONGRATULATIONS. IF THERE'S ANY KIND OF FINDER'S FEE FOR THIS GIRL, MAYBE YOU CAN GET YOUR DAD OFF YOUR BACK.
SOMEHOW I DON'T FEEL LIKE *CELEBRATING*. I'M MORE WORRIED ABOUT CRUSHING THIS GIRL'S *ENTIRE* SENSE OF *IDENTITY*.
BUT *SHE* HIRED YOU.
YEAH... BUT *SUSPECTING* SOMETHING BAD ABOUT SOMEONE YOU LOVE IS *NOT* THE SAME AS FINDING OUT IT'S *TRUE*.

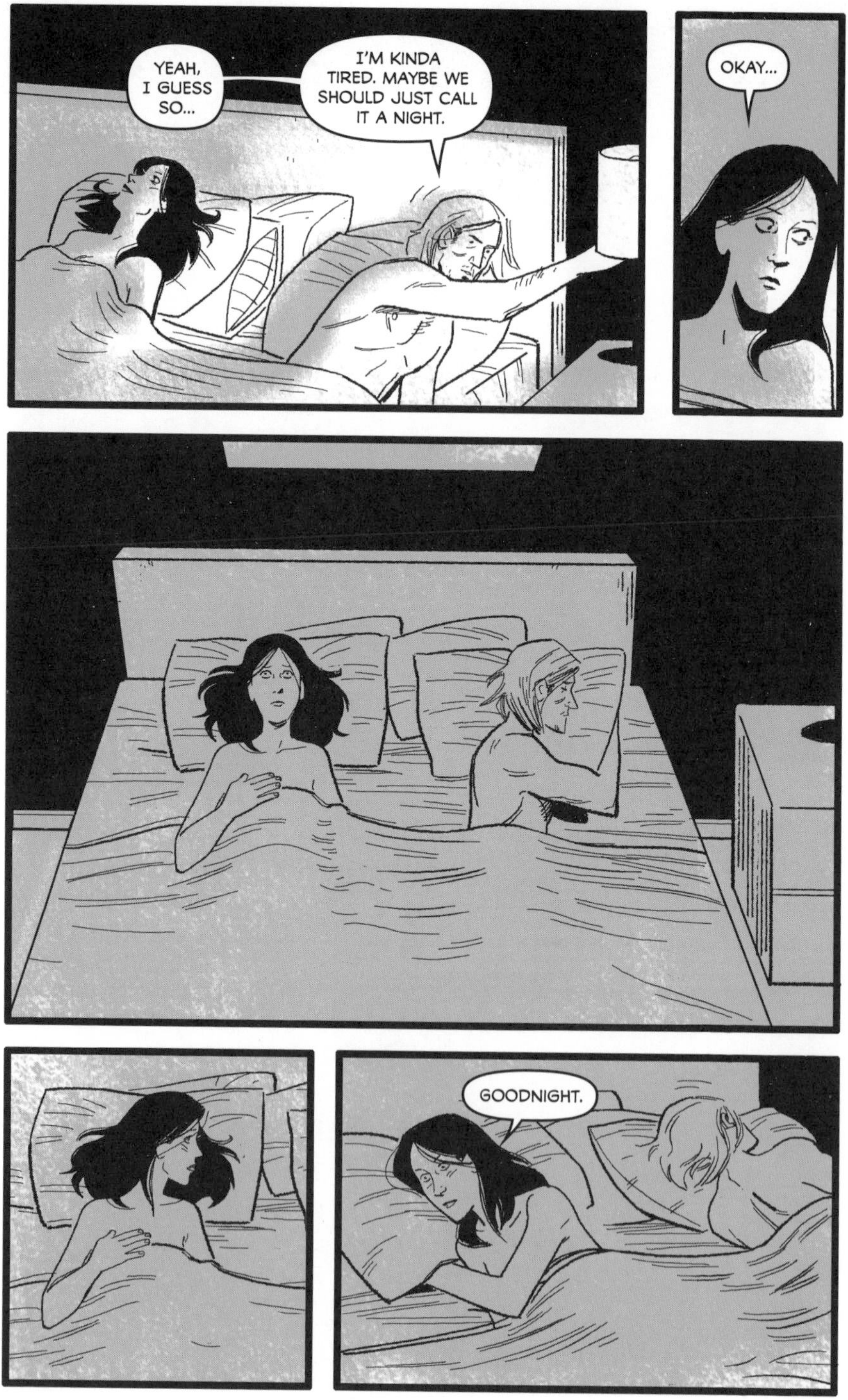
I'M KINDA TIRED. MAYBE WE SHOULD JUST CALL IT A NIGHT.
YEAH, I GUESS SO...
OKAY...
GOODNIGHT.

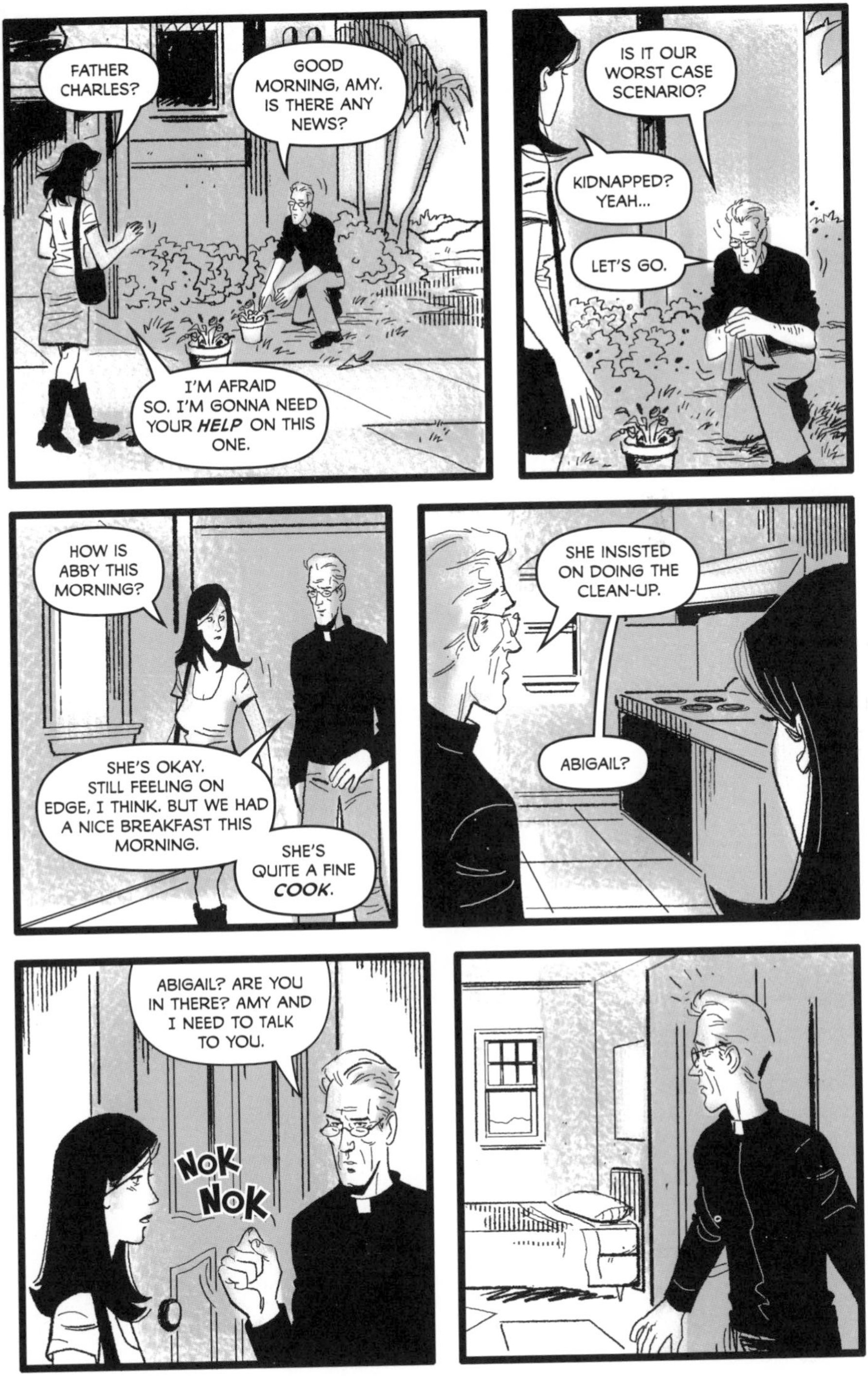
FATHER CHARLES?
GOOD MORNING, AMY. IS THERE ANY NEWS?
I'M AFRAID SO. I'M GONNA NEED YOUR **HELP** ON THIS ONE.
IS IT OUR WORST CASE SCENARIO?
KIDNAPPED? YEAH...
LET'S GO.
HOW IS ABBY THIS MORNING?
SHE'S OKAY. STILL FEELING ON EDGE, I THINK. BUT WE HAD A NICE BREAKFAST THIS MORNING.
SHE'S QUITE A FINE **COOK**.
SHE INSISTED ON DOING THE CLEAN-UP.
ABIGAIL?
ABIGAIL? ARE YOU IN THERE? AMY AND I NEED TO TALK TO YOU.
NOK NOK

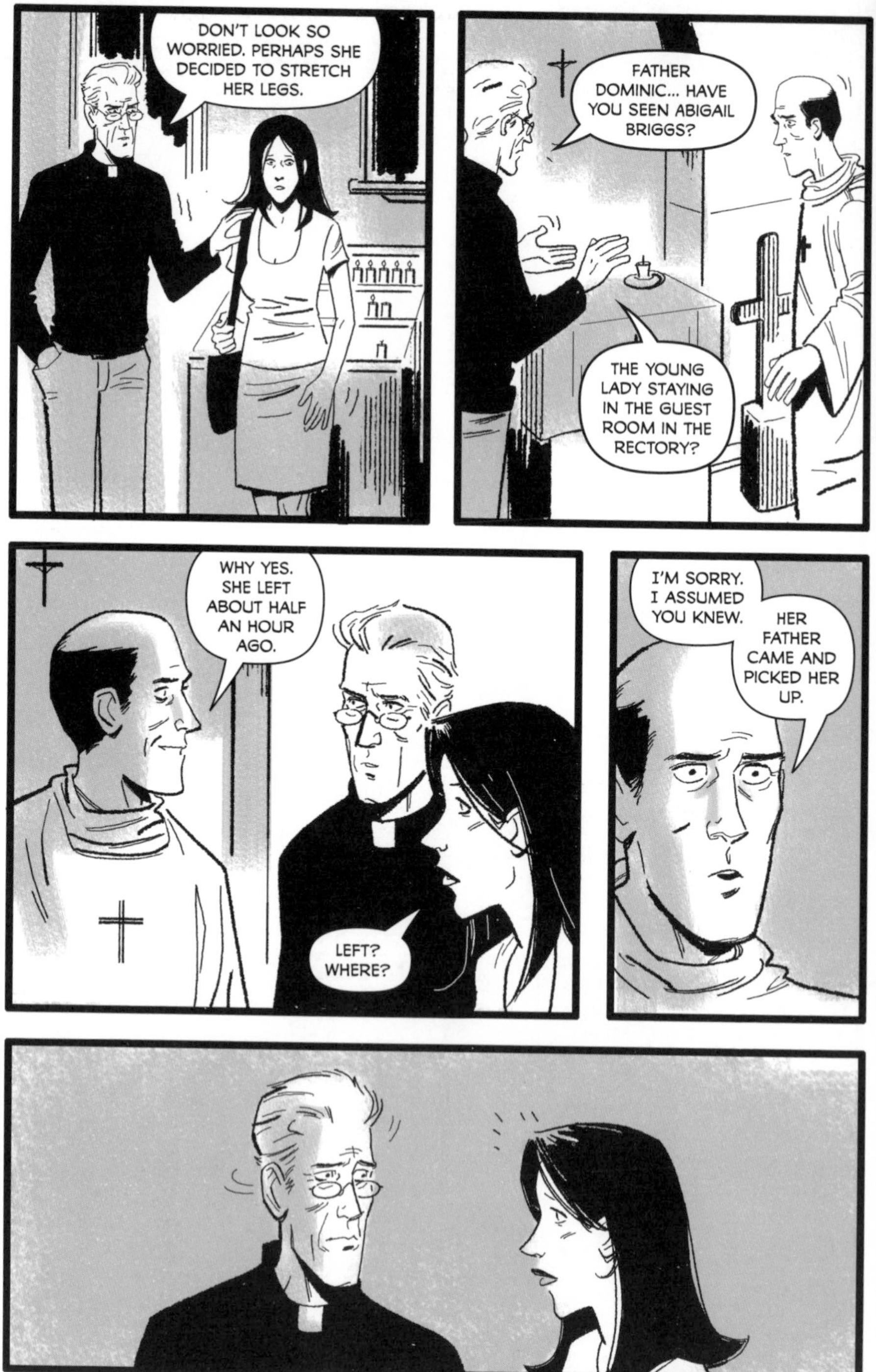
DON'T LOOK SO WORRIED. PERHAPS SHE DECIDED TO STRETCH HER LEGS.
FATHER DOMINIC... HAVE YOU SEEN ABIGAIL BRIGGS?
THE YOUNG LADY STAYING IN THE GUEST ROOM IN THE RECTORY?
WHY YES. SHE LEFT ABOUT HALF AN HOUR AGO.
LEFT? WHERE?
I'M SORRY. I ASSUMED YOU KNEW.
HER FATHER CAME AND PICKED HER UP.

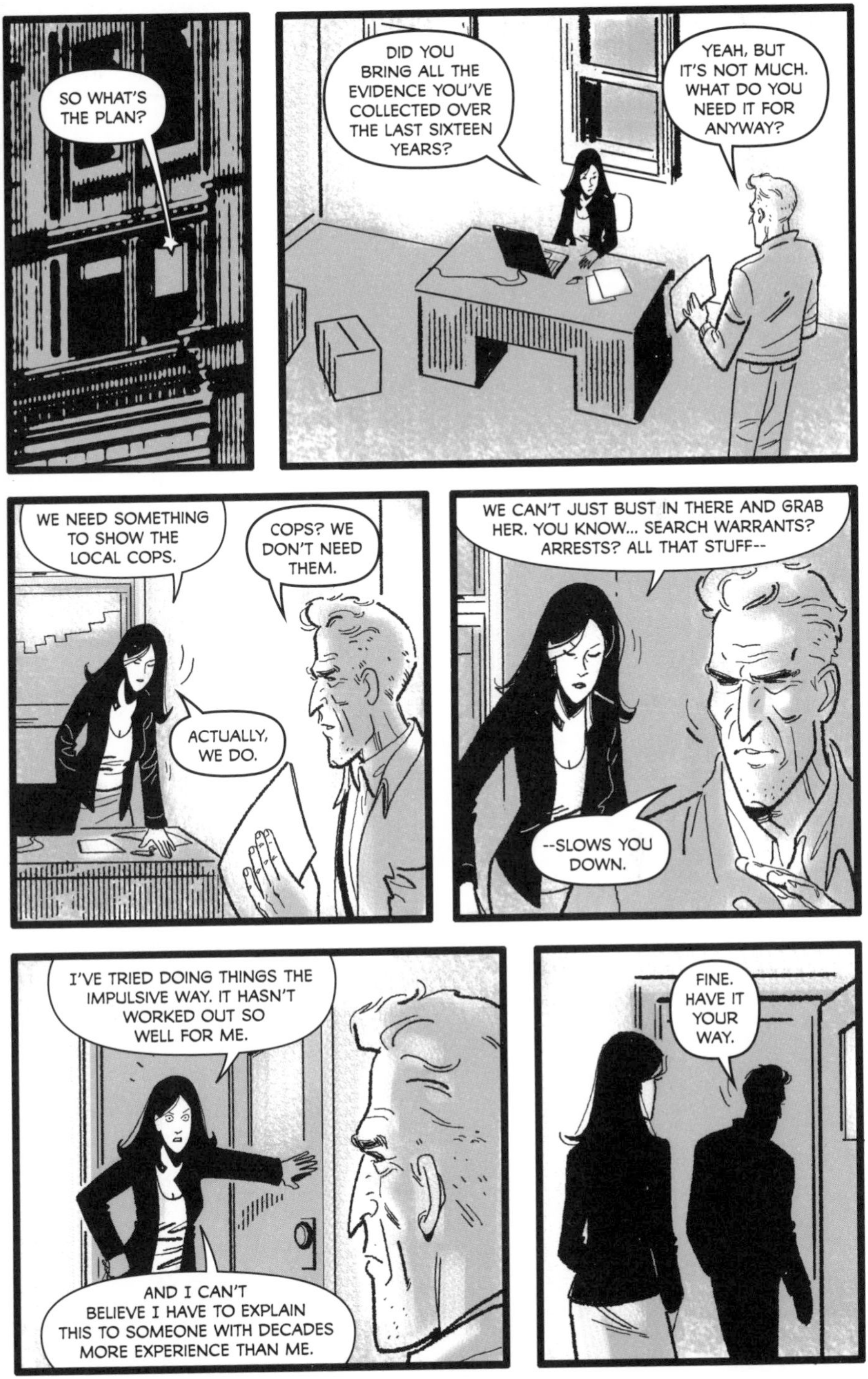
SO WHAT'S THE PLAN?
DID YOU BRING ALL THE EVIDENCE YOU'VE COLLECTED OVER THE LAST SIXTEEN YEARS?
YEAH, BUT IT'S NOT MUCH. WHAT DO YOU NEED IT FOR ANYWAY?
WE NEED SOMETHING TO SHOW THE LOCAL COPS.
COPS? WE DON'T NEED THEM.
ACTUALLY, WE DO.
WE CAN'T JUST BUST IN THERE AND GRAB HER. YOU KNOW... SEARCH WARRANTS? ARRESTS? ALL THAT STUFF--
--SLOWS YOU DOWN.
I'VE TRIED DOING THINGS THE IMPULSIVE WAY. IT HASN'T WORKED OUT SO WELL FOR ME.
AND I CAN'T BELIEVE I HAVE TO EXPLAIN THIS TO SOMEONE WITH DECADES MORE EXPERIENCE THAN ME.
FINE. HAVE IT YOUR WAY.

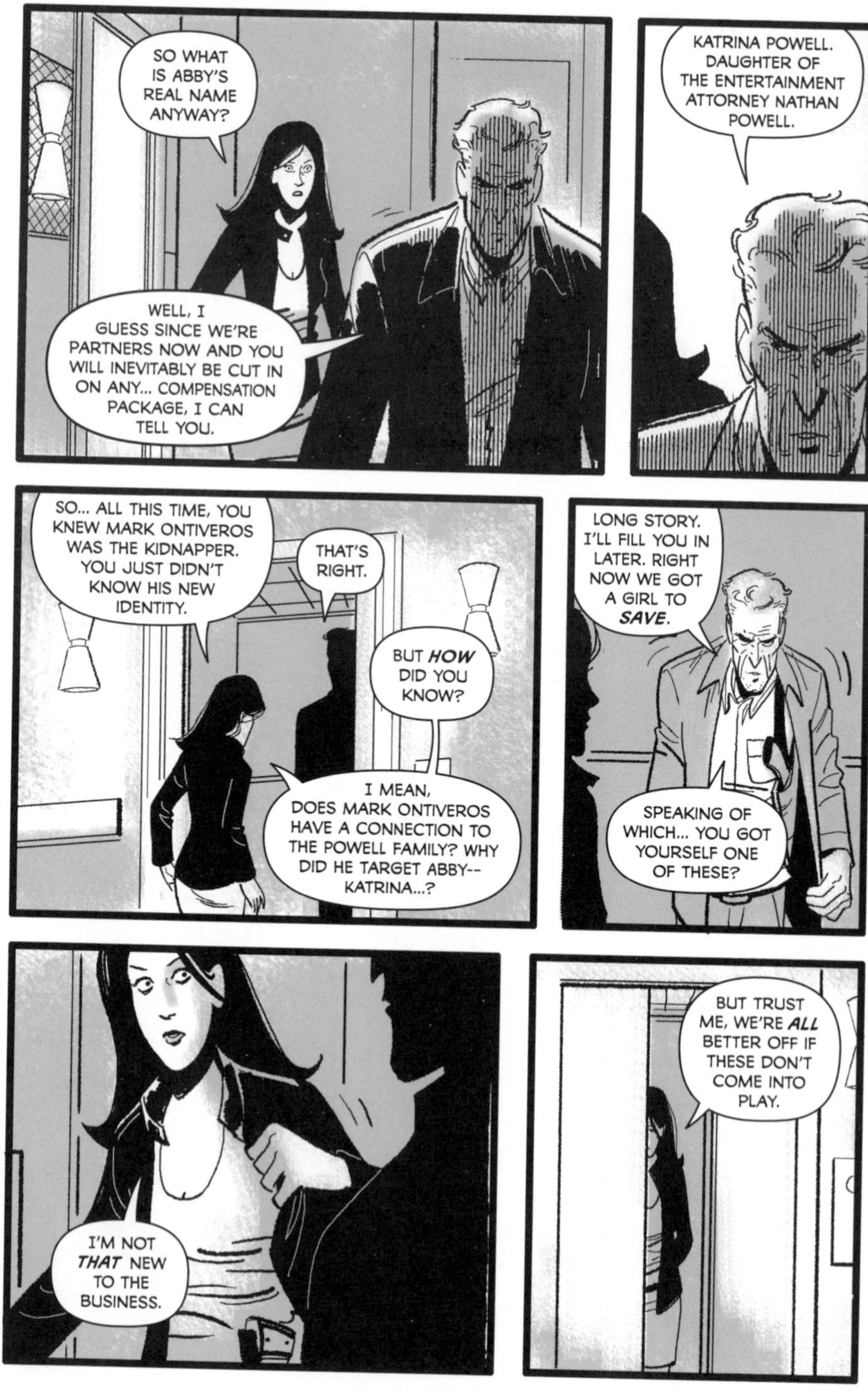
SO WHAT IS ABBY'S REAL NAME ANYWAY?
WELL, I GUESS SINCE WE'RE PARTNERS NOW AND YOU WILL INEVITABLY BE CUT IN ON ANY... COMPENSATION PACKAGE, I CAN TELL YOU.
KATRINA POWELL. DAUGHTER OF THE ENTERTAINMENT ATTORNEY NATHAN POWELL.
SO... ALL THIS TIME, YOU KNEW MARK ONTIVEROS WAS THE KIDNAPPER. YOU JUST DIDN'T KNOW HIS NEW IDENTITY.
THAT'S RIGHT.
BUT *HOW* DID YOU KNOW?
I MEAN, DOES MARK ONTIVEROS HAVE A CONNECTION TO THE POWELL FAMILY? WHY DID HE TARGET ABBY-- KATRINA...?
LONG STORY. I'LL FILL YOU IN LATER. RIGHT NOW WE GOT A GIRL TO ***SAVE***.
SPEAKING OF WHICH... YOU GOT YOURSELF ONE OF THESE?
I'M NOT ***THAT*** NEW TO THE BUSINESS.
BUT TRUST ME, WE'RE ***ALL*** BETTER OFF IF THESE DON'T COME INTO PLAY.

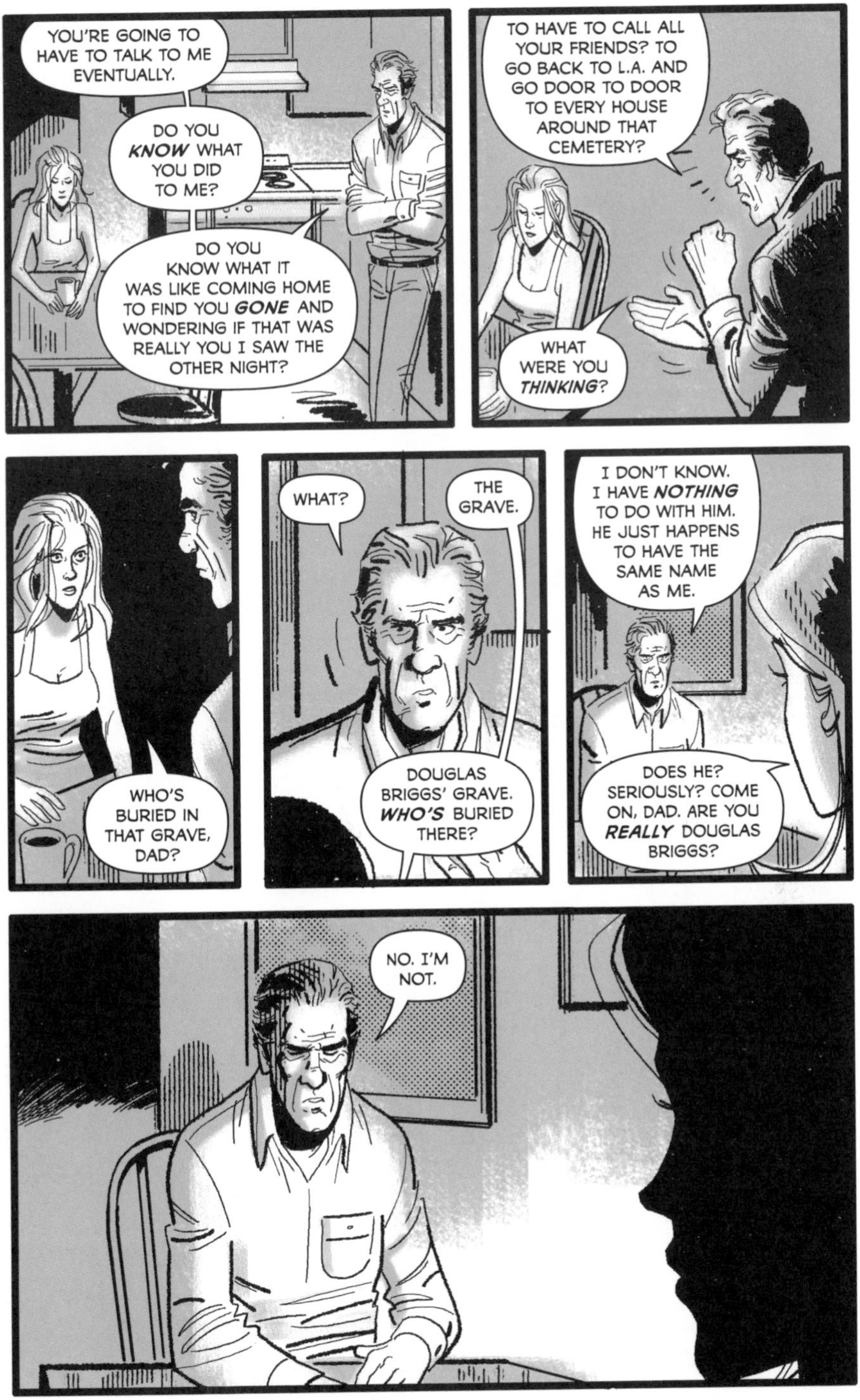
YOU'RE GOING TO HAVE TO TALK TO ME EVENTUALLY.
DO YOU KNOW WHAT YOU DID TO ME?
DO YOU KNOW WHAT IT WAS LIKE COMING HOME TO FIND YOU GONE AND WONDERING IF THAT WAS REALLY YOU I SAW THE OTHER NIGHT?
TO HAVE TO CALL ALL YOUR FRIENDS? TO GO BACK TO L.A. AND GO DOOR TO DOOR TO EVERY HOUSE AROUND THAT CEMETERY?
WHAT WERE YOU THINKING?
WHO'S BURIED IN THAT GRAVE, DAD?
WHAT?
THE GRAVE.
DOUGLAS BRIGGS' GRAVE. WHO'S BURIED THERE?
I DON'T KNOW. I HAVE NOTHING TO DO WITH HIM. HE JUST HAPPENS TO HAVE THE SAME NAME AS ME.
DOES HE? SERIOUSLY? COME ON, DAD. ARE YOU REALLY DOUGLAS BRIGGS?
NO. I'M NOT.

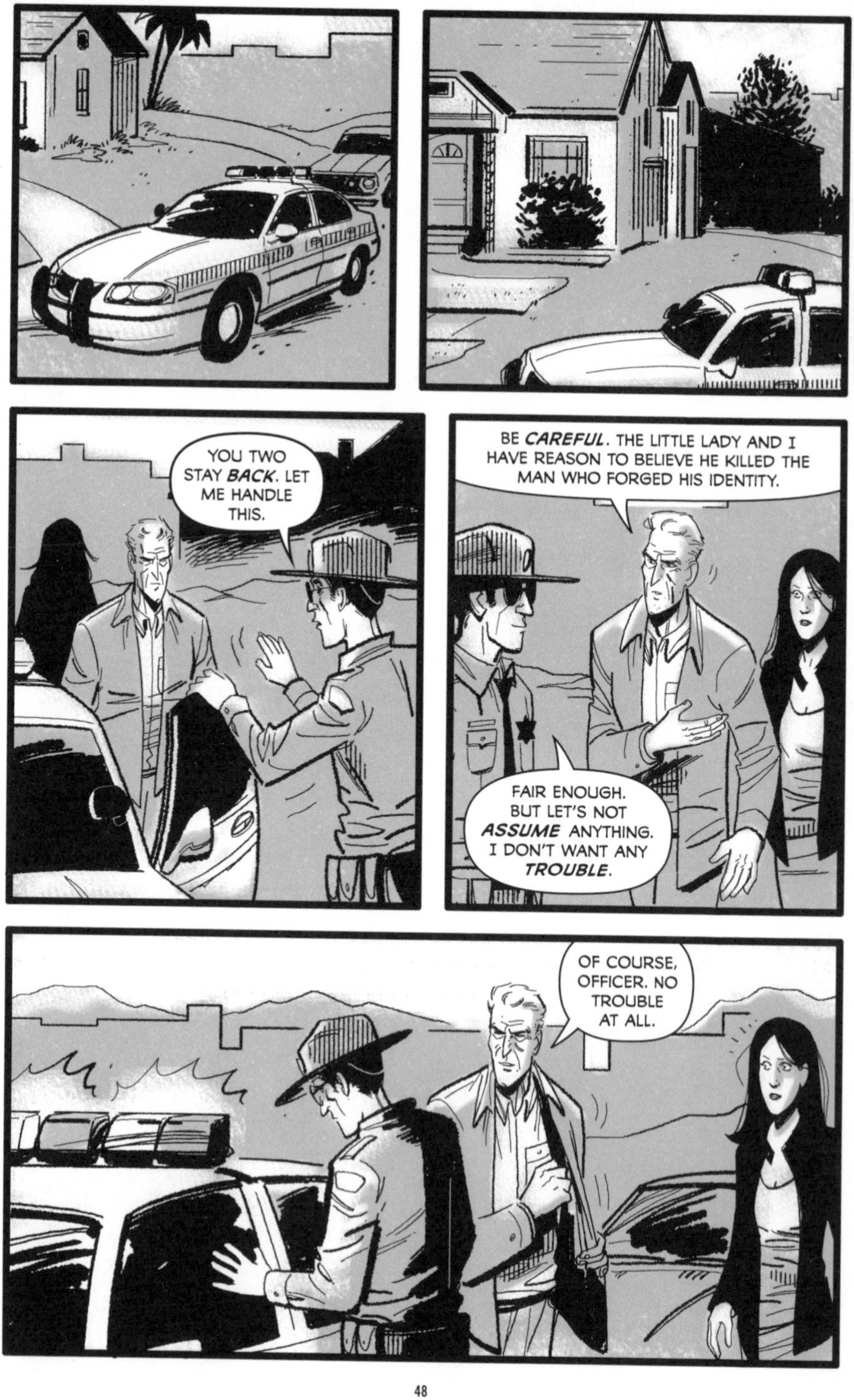
YOU TWO STAY BACK. LET ME HANDLE THIS.
BE CAREFUL. THE LITTLE LADY AND I HAVE REASON TO BELIEVE HE KILLED THE MAN WHO FORGED HIS IDENTITY.
FAIR ENOUGH. BUT LET'S NOT ASSUME ANYTHING. I DON'T WANT ANY TROUBLE.
OF COURSE, OFFICER. NO TROUBLE AT ALL.

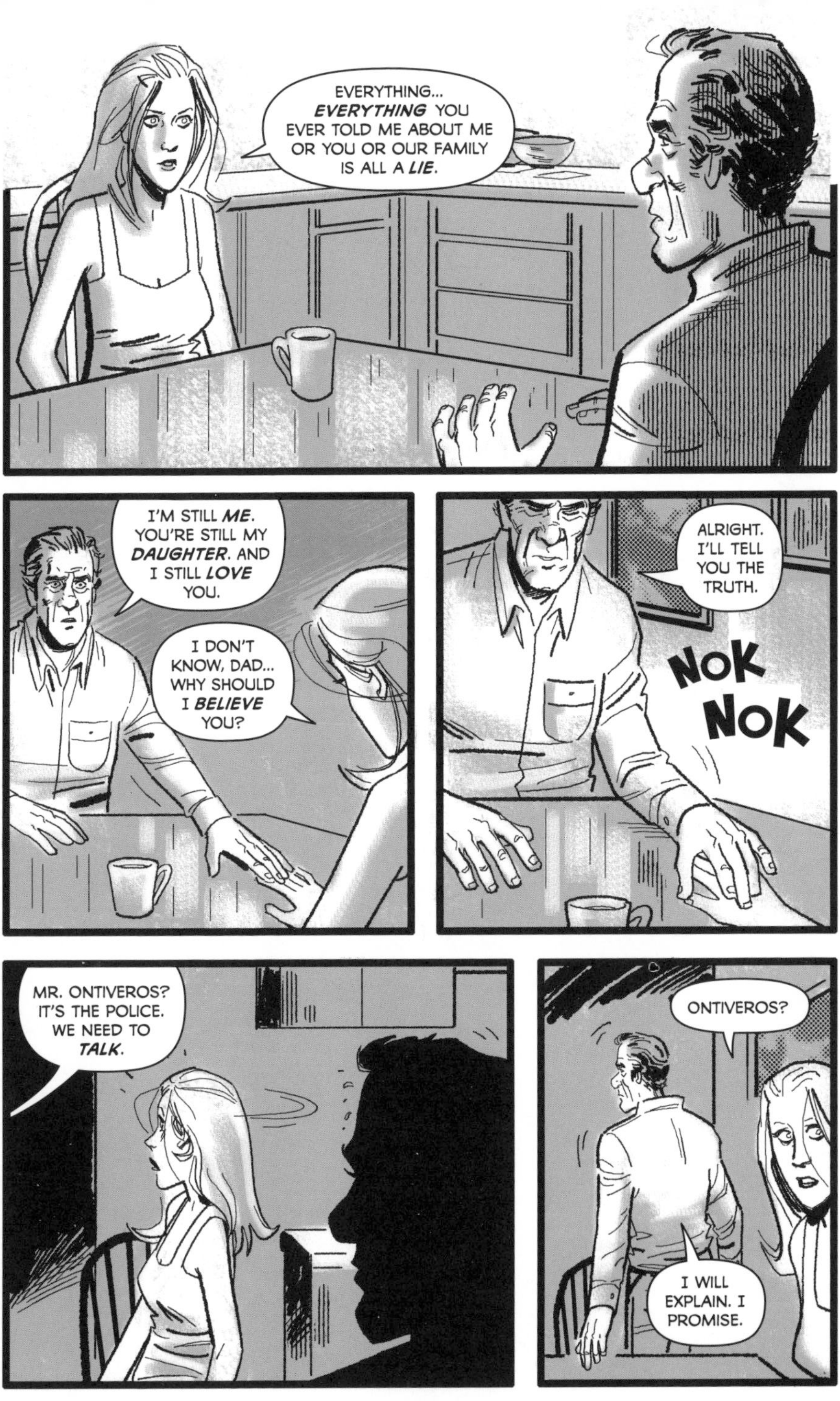
EVERYTHING... *EVERYTHING* YOU EVER TOLD ME ABOUT ME OR YOU OR OUR FAMILY IS ALL A *LIE*.
I'M STILL *ME*. YOU'RE STILL MY *DAUGHTER*. AND I STILL *LOVE* YOU.
I DON'T KNOW, DAD... WHY SHOULD I *BELIEVE* YOU?
ALRIGHT. I'LL TELL YOU THE TRUTH.
NOK NOK
MR. ONTIVEROS? IT'S THE POLICE. WE NEED TO *TALK*.
ONTIVEROS?
I WILL EXPLAIN. I PROMISE.

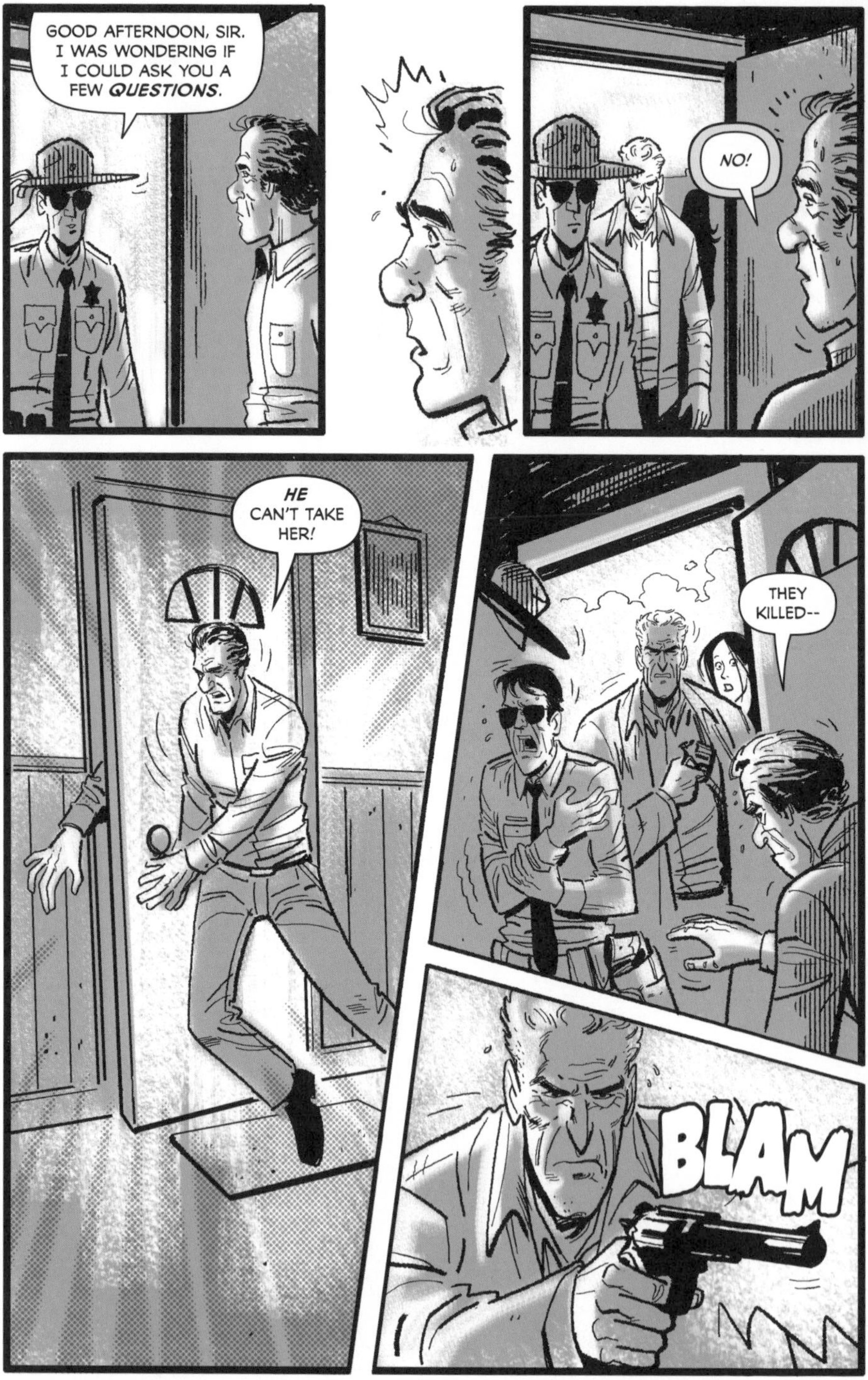

GOOD AFTERNOON, SIR. I WAS WONDERING IF I COULD ASK YOU A FEW *QUESTIONS*.
NO!
HE CAN'T TAKE *HER!*
THEY KILLED--
BLAM

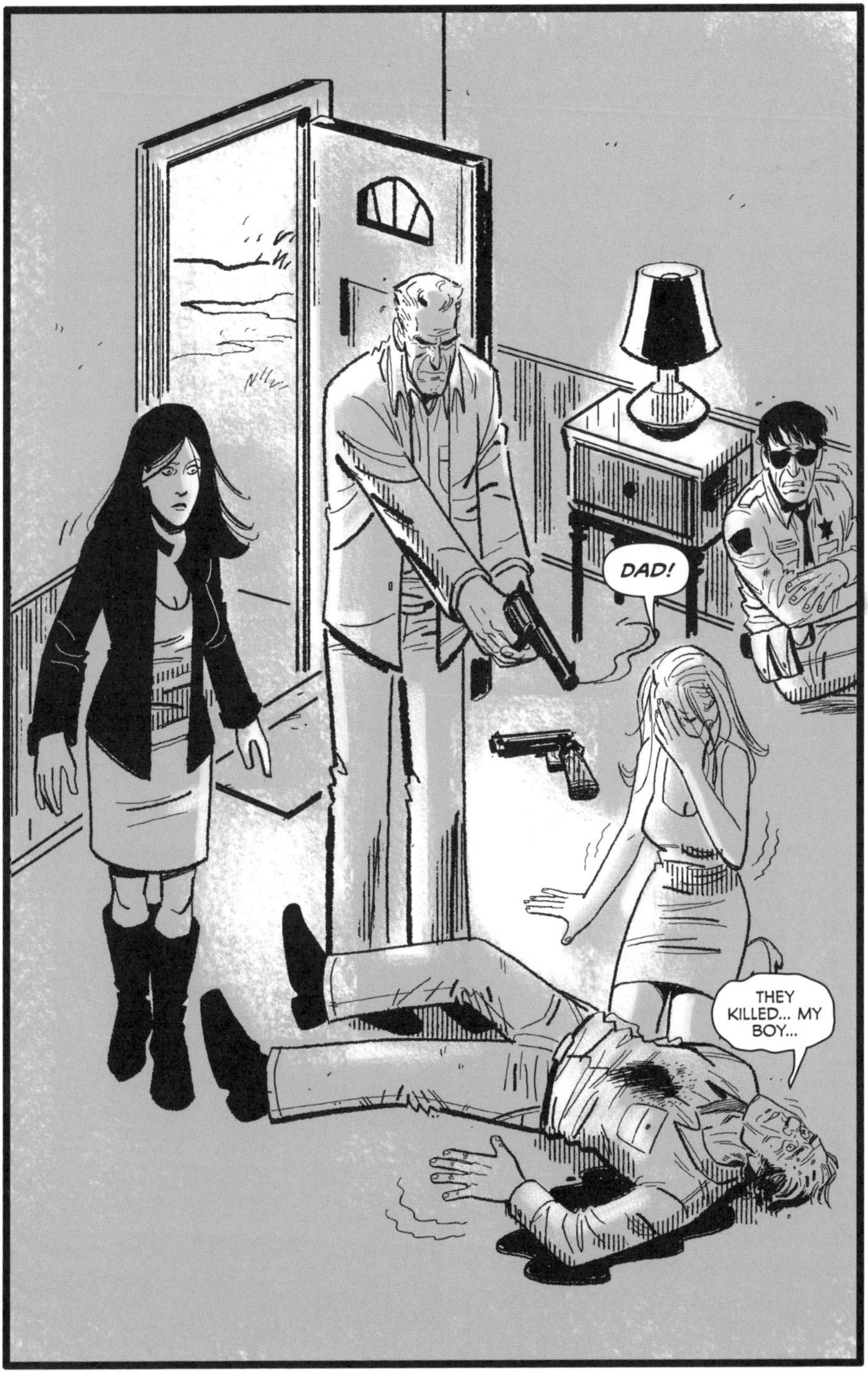
DAD!
THEY KILLED... MY BOY...

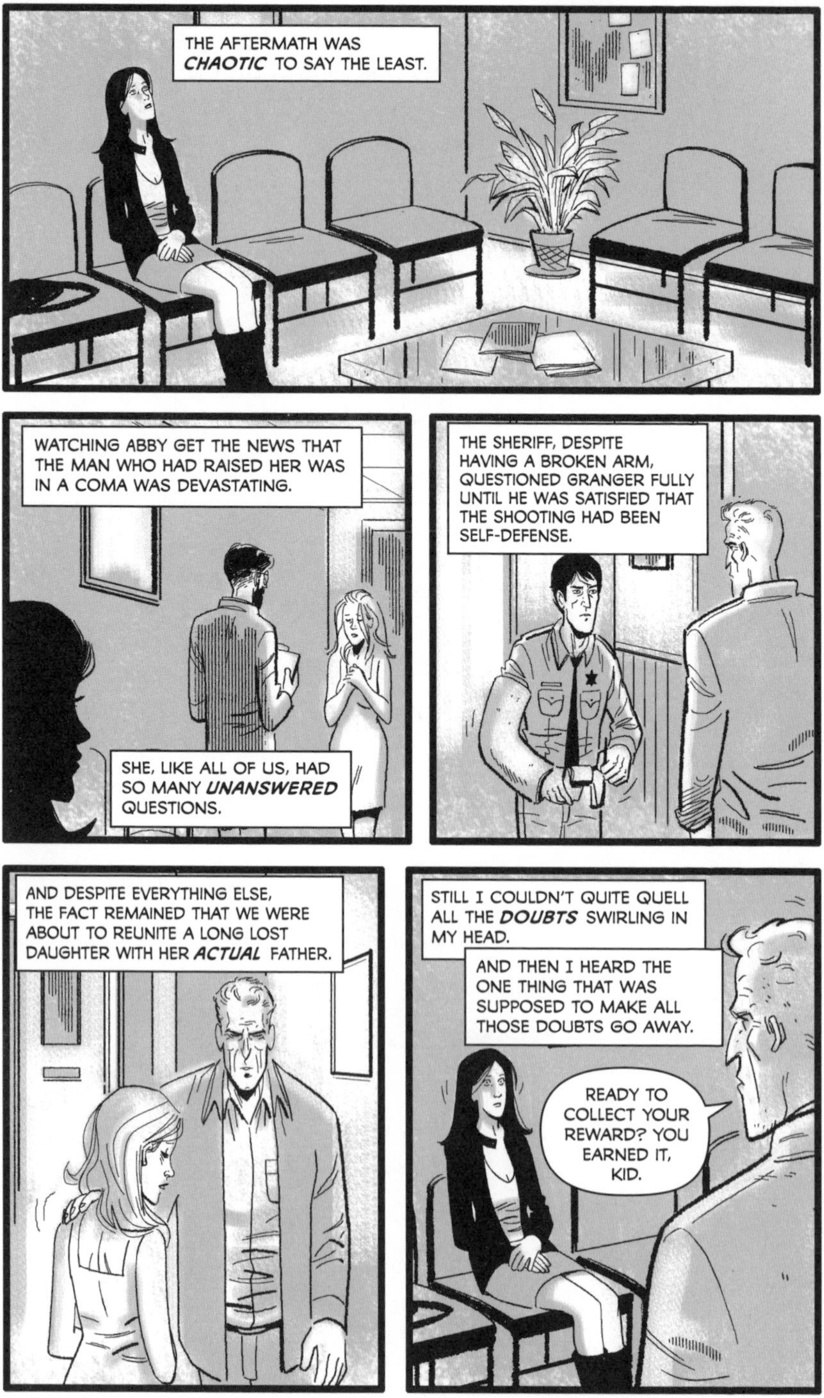
THE AFTERMATH WAS CHAOTIC TO SAY THE LEAST.
WATCHING ABBY GET THE NEWS THAT THE MAN WHO HAD RAISED HER WAS IN A COMA WAS DEVASTATING.
SHE, LIKE ALL OF US, HAD SO MANY UNANSWERED QUESTIONS.
THE SHERIFF, DESPITE HAVING A BROKEN ARM, QUESTIONED GRANGER FULLY UNTIL HE WAS SATISFIED THAT THE SHOOTING HAD BEEN SELF-DEFENSE.
AND DESPITE EVERYTHING ELSE, THE FACT REMAINED THAT WE WERE ABOUT TO REUNITE A LONG LOST DAUGHTER WITH HER ACTUAL FATHER.
STILL I COULDN'T QUITE QUELL ALL THE DOUBTS SWIRLING IN MY HEAD.
AND THEN I HEARD THE ONE THING THAT WAS SUPPOSED TO MAKE ALL THOSE DOUBTS GO AWAY.
READY TO COLLECT YOUR REWARD? YOU EARNED IT, KID.

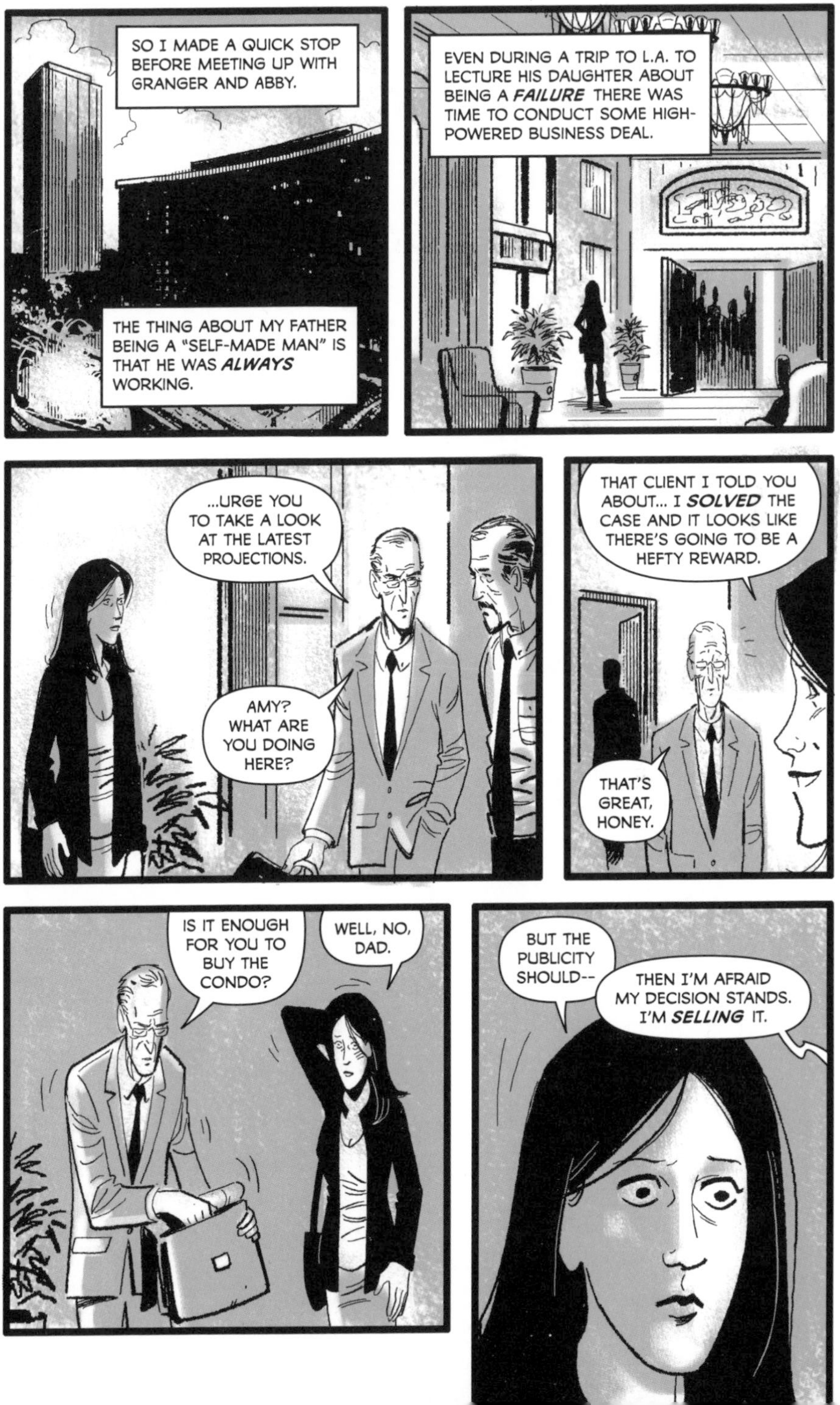
SO I MADE A QUICK STOP BEFORE MEETING UP WITH GRANGER AND ABBY.
THE THING ABOUT MY FATHER BEING A "SELF-MADE MAN" IS THAT HE WAS ALWAYS WORKING.
EVEN DURING A TRIP TO L.A. TO LECTURE HIS DAUGHTER ABOUT BEING A FAILURE THERE WAS TIME TO CONDUCT SOME HIGH-POWERED BUSINESS DEAL.
...URGE YOU TO TAKE A LOOK AT THE LATEST PROJECTIONS.
AMY? WHAT ARE YOU DOING HERE?
THAT CLIENT I TOLD YOU ABOUT... I SOLVED THE CASE AND IT LOOKS LIKE THERE'S GOING TO BE A HEFTY REWARD.
THAT'S GREAT, HONEY.
IS IT ENOUGH FOR YOU TO BUY THE CONDO?
WELL, NO, DAD.
BUT THE PUBLICITY SHOULD--
THEN I'M AFRAID MY DECISION STANDS. I'M SELLING IT.

READY TO MEET YOUR *FATHER*?

WE ARRIVED AT THE HOUSE OF NATHAN POWELL. BIG TIME ENTERTAINMENT ATTORNEY, AND FATHER OF KATRINA POWELL.

COME ON... YOU'LL BE OKAY.

THE WOMAN NOW KNOWN AS ABIGAIL BRIGGS.

...KATRINA?

SWEETHEART...?

ABBY SEEMED WARY, BUT I FOUND MYSELF HOPING IT WOULD WORK OUT FOR HER.

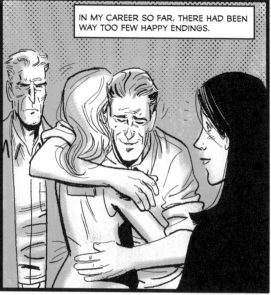

IN MY CAREER SO FAR, THERE HAD BEEN WAY TOO FEW HAPPY ENDINGS.

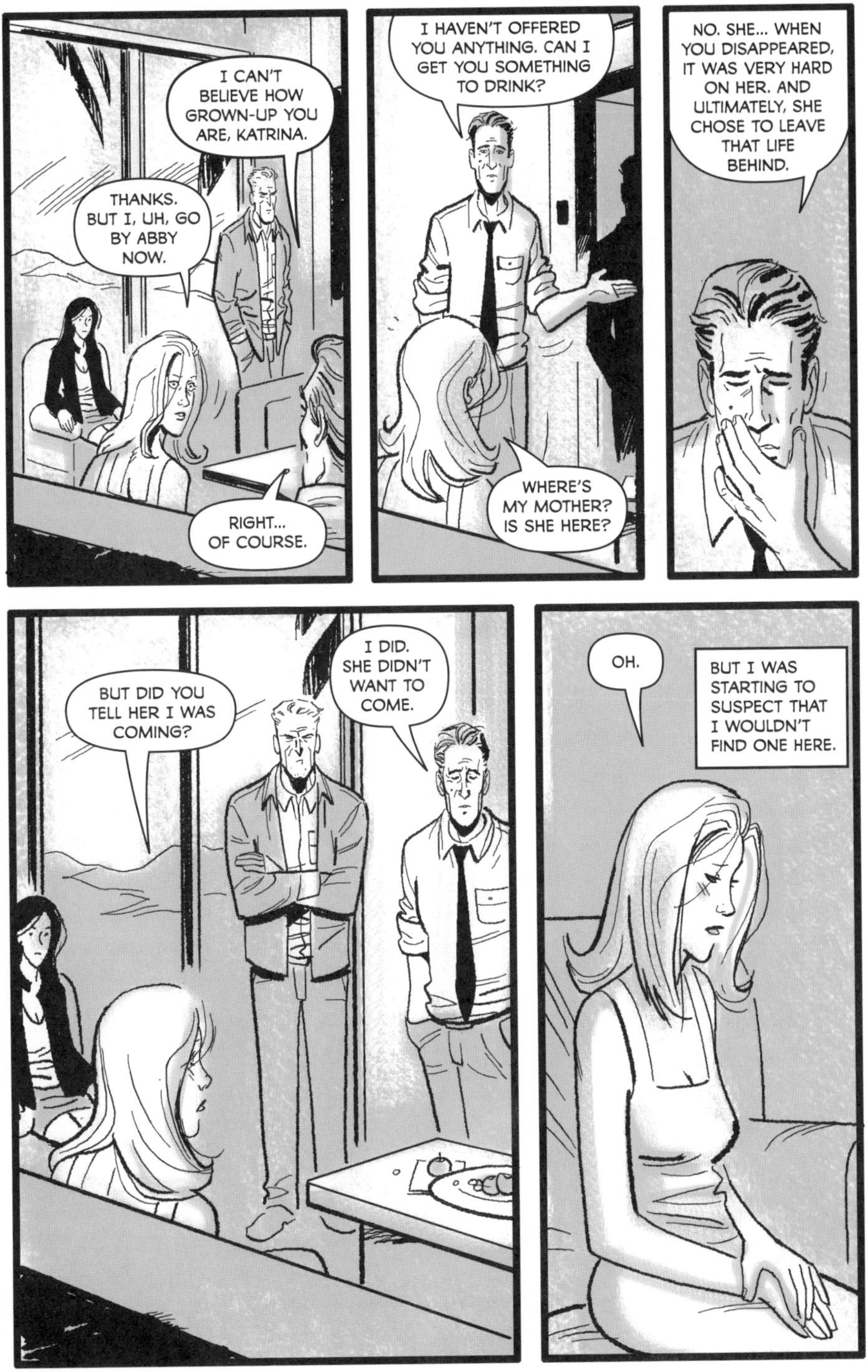
I CAN'T BELIEVE HOW GROWN-UP YOU ARE, KATRINA.
THANKS. BUT I, UH, GO BY ABBY NOW.
RIGHT... OF COURSE.
I HAVEN'T OFFERED YOU ANYTHING. CAN I GET YOU SOMETHING TO DRINK?
WHERE'S MY MOTHER? IS SHE HERE?
NO. SHE... WHEN YOU DISAPPEARED, IT WAS VERY HARD ON HER. AND ULTIMATELY, SHE CHOSE TO LEAVE THAT LIFE BEHIND.
BUT DID YOU TELL HER I WAS COMING?
I DID. SHE DIDN'T WANT TO COME.
OH.
BUT I WAS STARTING TO SUSPECT THAT I WOULDN'T FIND ONE HERE.

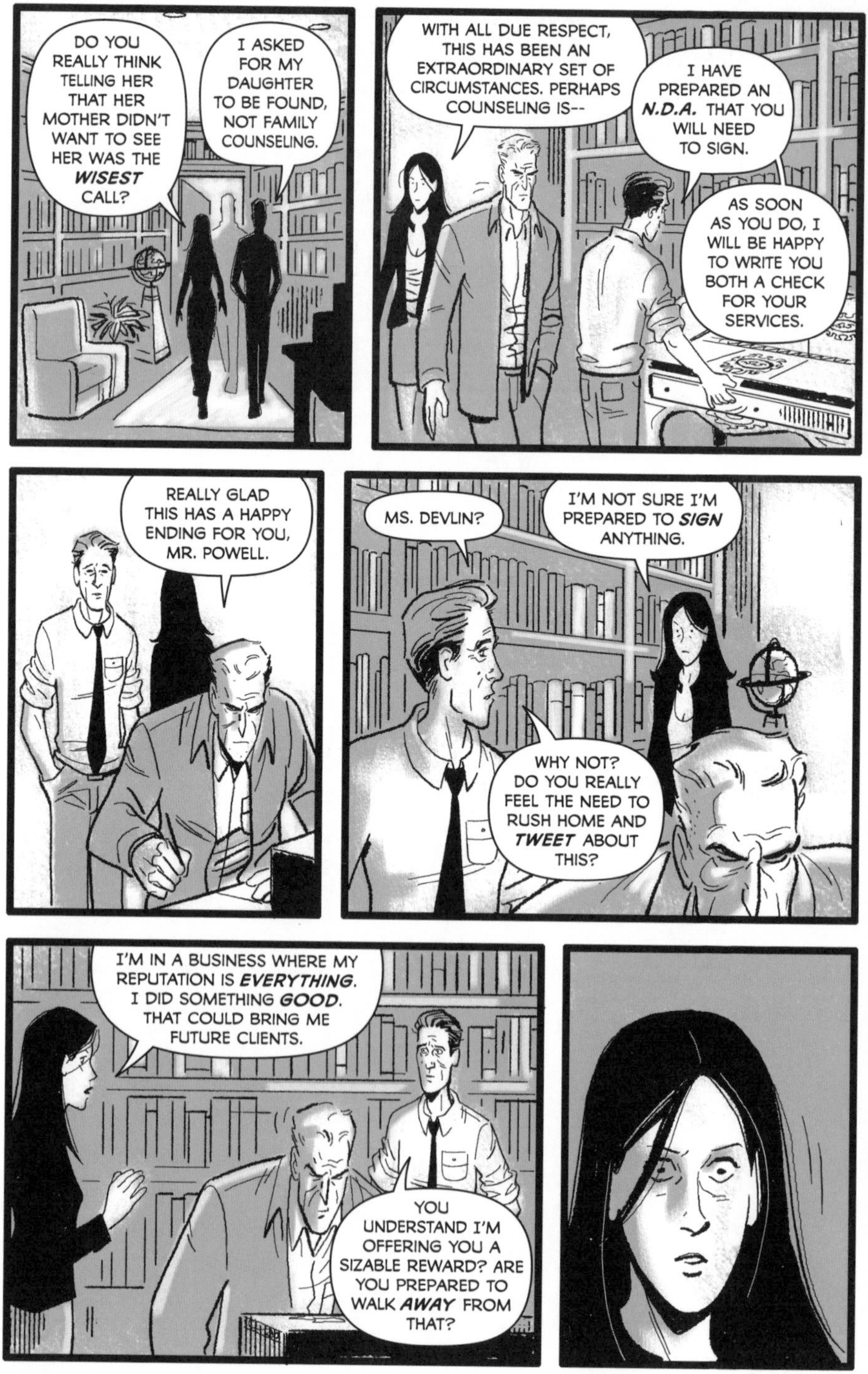
DO YOU REALLY THINK TELLING HER THAT HER MOTHER DIDN'T WANT TO SEE HER WAS THE *WISEST* CALL?
I ASKED FOR MY DAUGHTER TO BE FOUND, NOT FAMILY COUNSELING.
WITH ALL DUE RESPECT, THIS HAS BEEN AN EXTRAORDINARY SET OF CIRCUMSTANCES. PERHAPS COUNSELING IS--
I HAVE PREPARED AN *N.D.A.* THAT YOU WILL NEED TO SIGN.
AS SOON AS YOU DO, I WILL BE HAPPY TO WRITE YOU BOTH A CHECK FOR YOUR SERVICES.
REALLY GLAD THIS HAS A HAPPY ENDING FOR YOU, MR. POWELL.
MS. DEVLIN?
I'M NOT SURE I'M PREPARED TO *SIGN* ANYTHING.
WHY NOT? DO YOU REALLY FEEL THE NEED TO RUSH HOME AND *TWEET* ABOUT THIS?
I'M IN A BUSINESS WHERE MY REPUTATION IS *EVERYTHING*. I DID SOMETHING *GOOD*. THAT COULD BRING ME FUTURE CLIENTS.
YOU UNDERSTAND I'M OFFERING YOU A SIZABLE REWARD? ARE YOU PREPARED TO WALK *AWAY* FROM THAT?

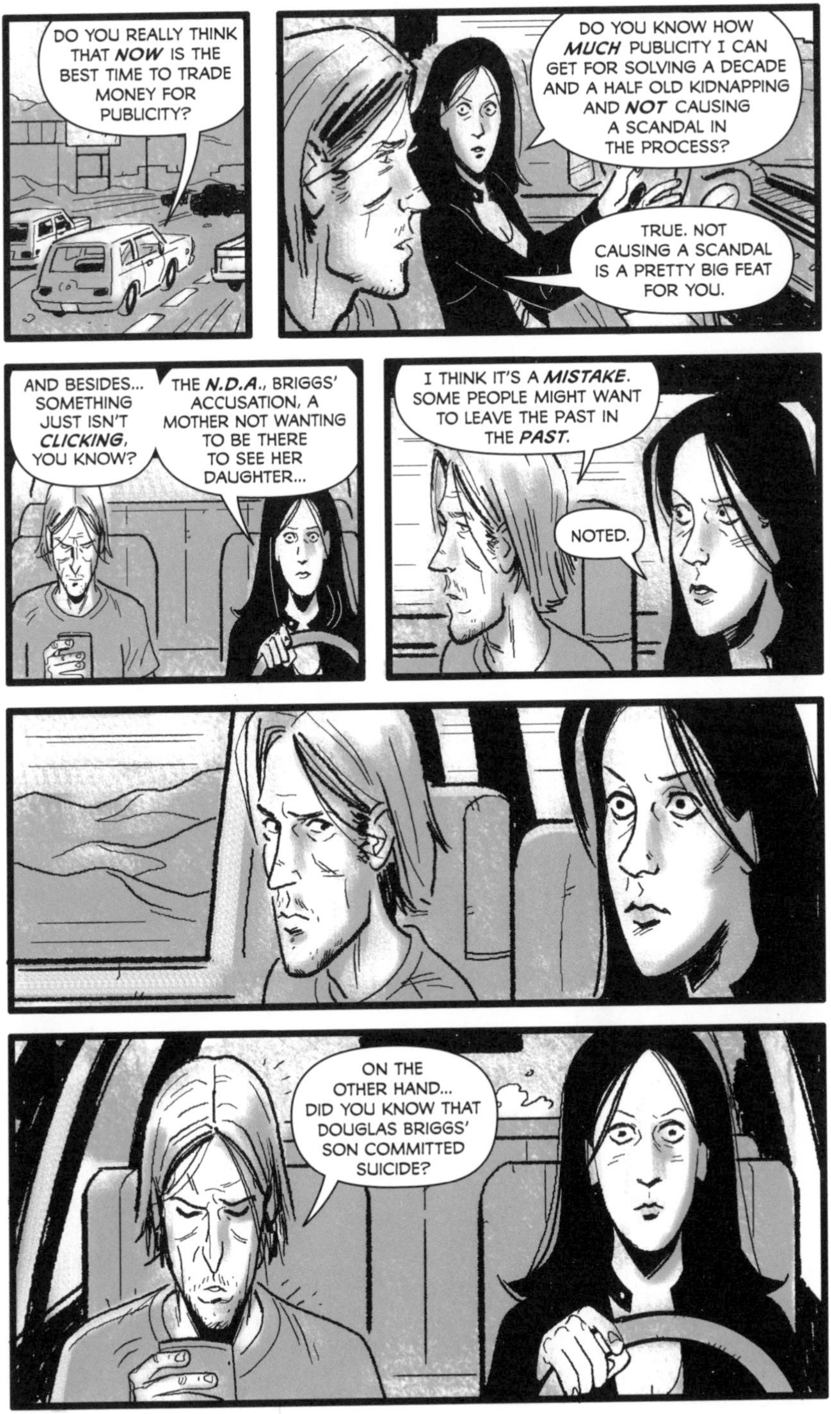
DO YOU REALLY THINK THAT NOW IS THE BEST TIME TO TRADE MONEY FOR PUBLICITY?
DO YOU KNOW HOW MUCH PUBLICITY I CAN GET FOR SOLVING A DECADE AND A HALF OLD KIDNAPPING AND NOT CAUSING A SCANDAL IN THE PROCESS?
TRUE. NOT CAUSING A SCANDAL IS A PRETTY BIG FEAT FOR YOU.
AND BESIDES... SOMETHING JUST ISN'T CLICKING, YOU KNOW?
THE N.D.A., BRIGGS' ACCUSATION, A MOTHER NOT WANTING TO BE THERE TO SEE HER DAUGHTER...
I THINK IT'S A MISTAKE. SOME PEOPLE MIGHT WANT TO LEAVE THE PAST IN THE PAST.
NOTED.
ON THE OTHER HAND... DID YOU KNOW THAT DOUGLAS BRIGGS' SON COMMITTED SUICIDE?

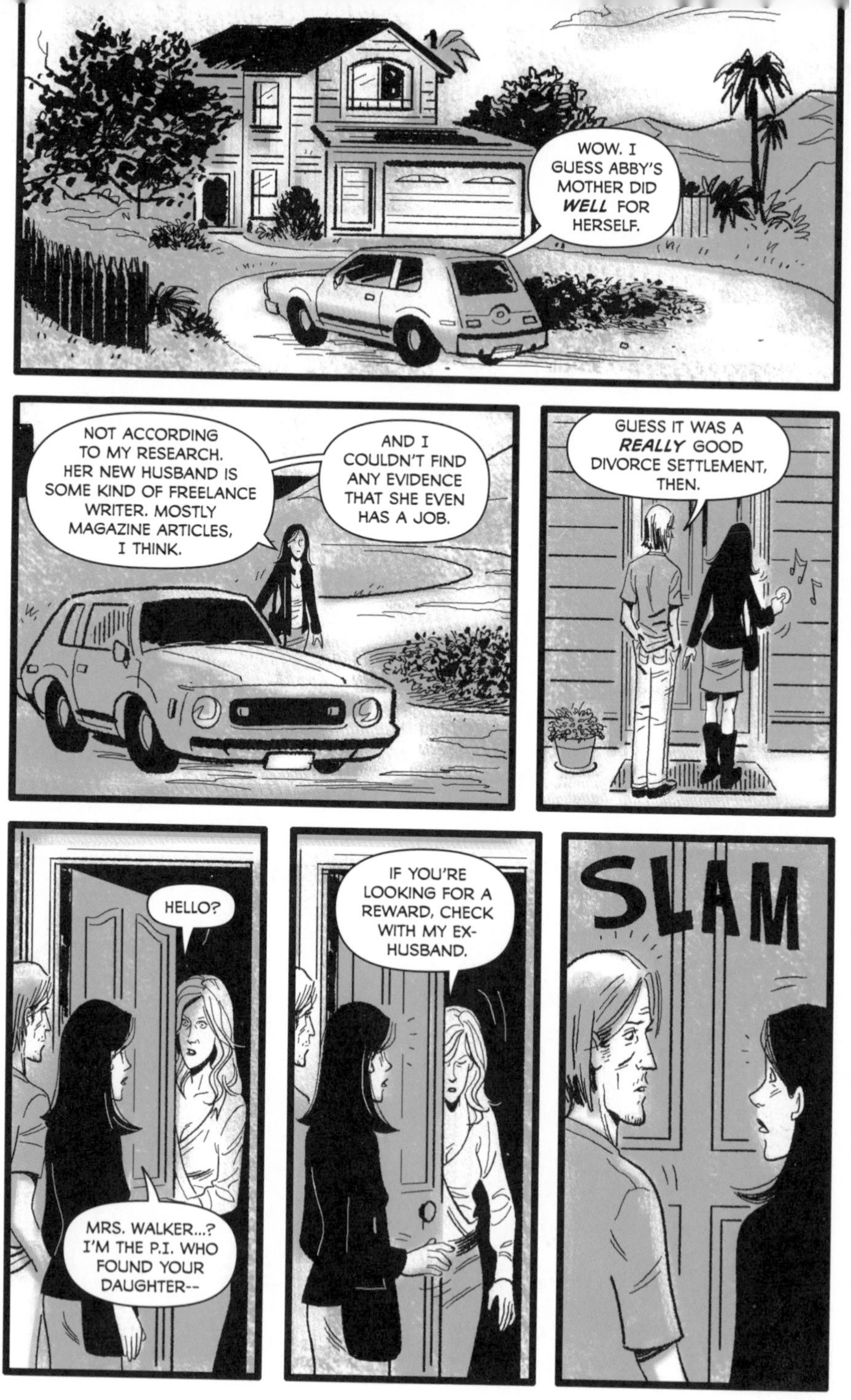
WOW. I GUESS ABBY'S MOTHER DID *WELL* FOR HERSELF.
NOT ACCORDING TO MY RESEARCH. HER NEW HUSBAND IS SOME KIND OF FREELANCE WRITER. MOSTLY MAGAZINE ARTICLES, I THINK.
AND I COULDN'T FIND ANY EVIDENCE THAT SHE EVEN HAS A JOB.
GUESS IT WAS A *REALLY* GOOD DIVORCE SETTLEMENT, THEN.
HELLO?
MRS. WALKER...? I'M THE P.I. WHO FOUND YOUR DAUGHTER--
IF YOU'RE LOOKING FOR A REWARD, CHECK WITH MY EX-HUSBAND.
SLAM

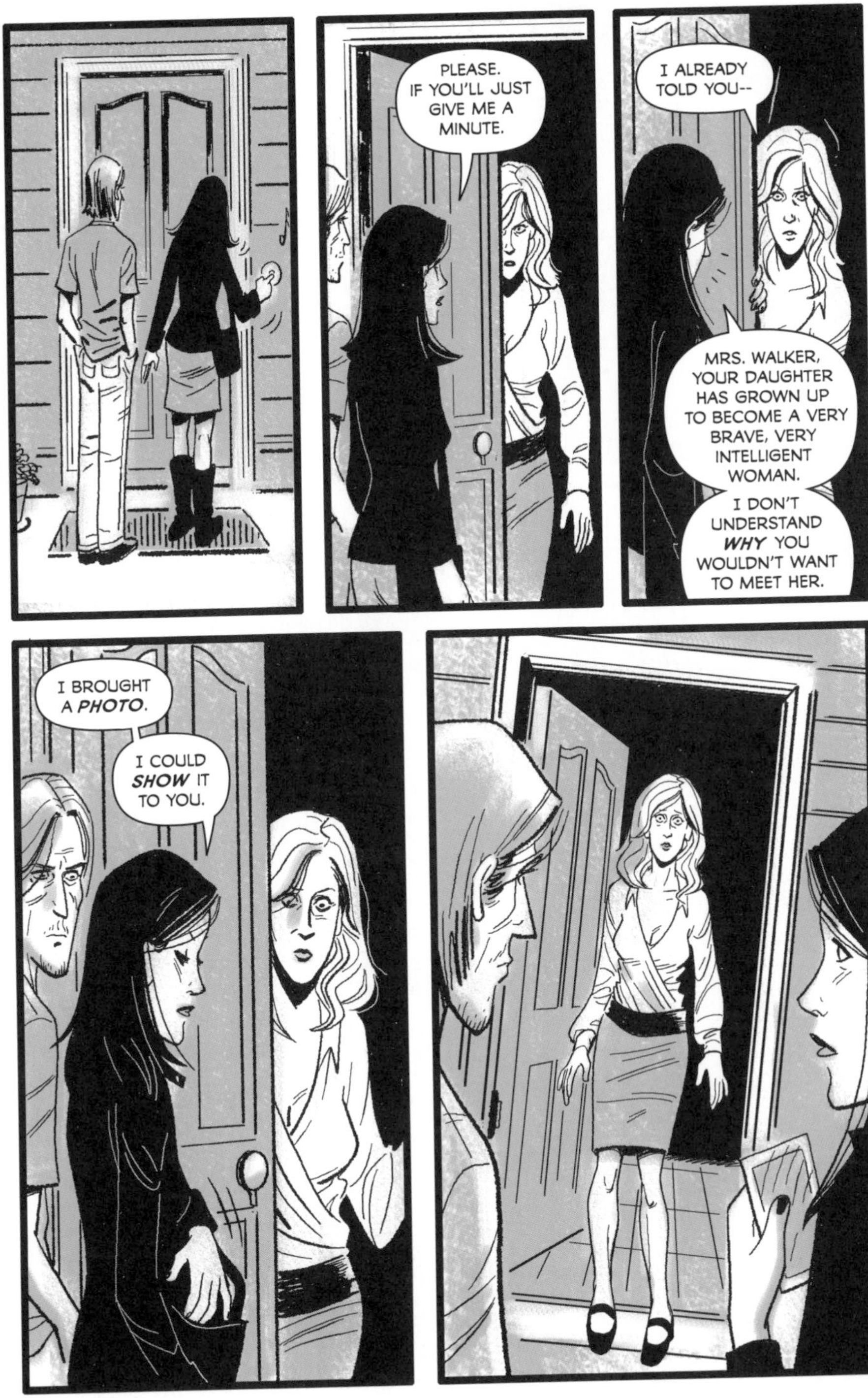
PLEASE. IF YOU'LL JUST GIVE ME A MINUTE.
I ALREADY TOLD YOU--
MRS. WALKER, YOUR DAUGHTER HAS GROWN UP TO BECOME A VERY BRAVE, VERY INTELLIGENT WOMAN.
I DON'T UNDERSTAND *WHY* YOU WOULDN'T WANT TO MEET HER.
I BROUGHT A *PHOTO*.
I COULD *SHOW* IT TO YOU.

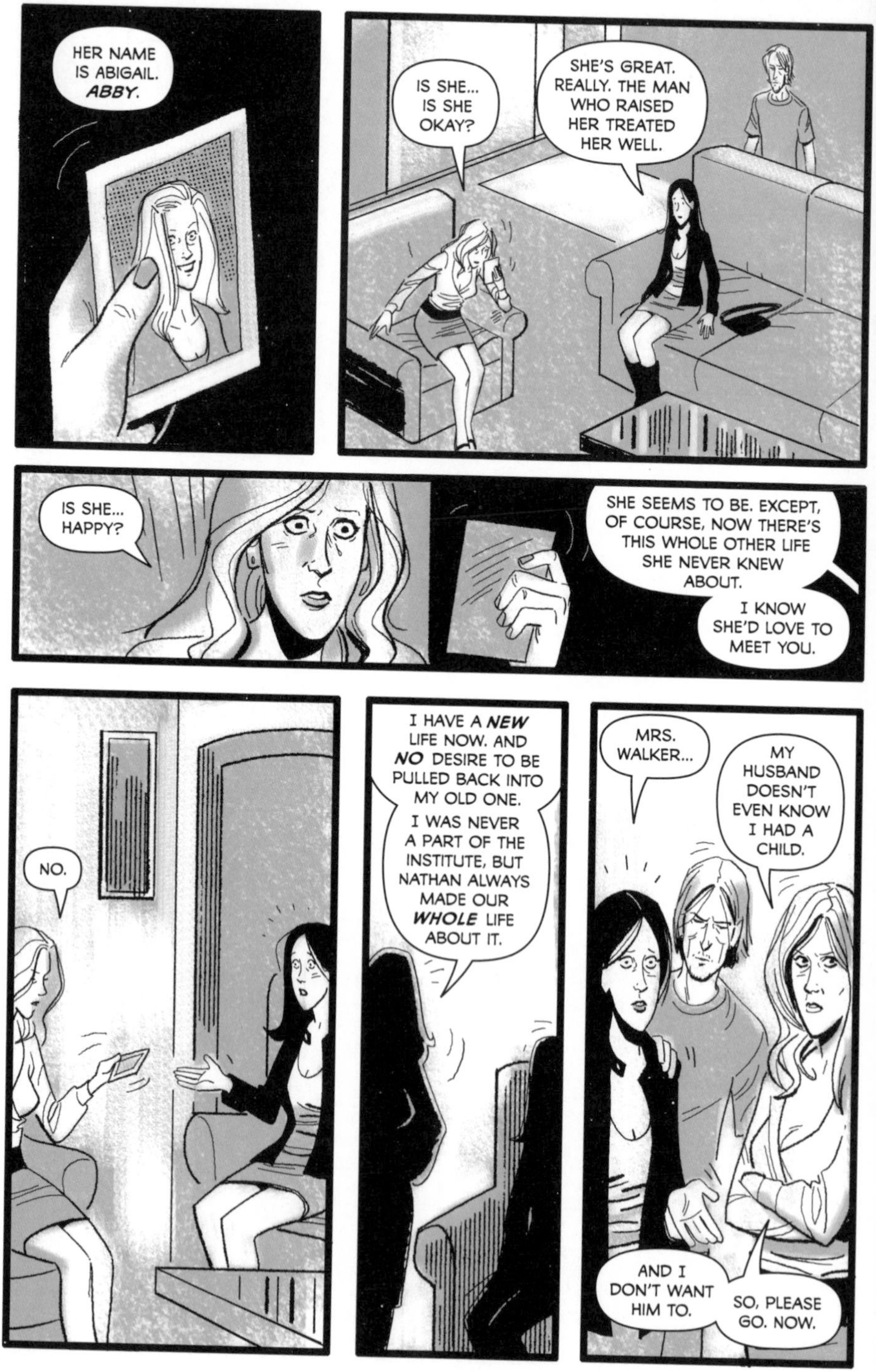
HER NAME IS ABIGAIL. *ABBY*.
IS SHE... IS SHE OKAY?
SHE'S GREAT. REALLY. THE MAN WHO RAISED HER TREATED HER WELL.
IS SHE... HAPPY?
SHE SEEMS TO BE. EXCEPT, OF COURSE, NOW THERE'S THIS WHOLE OTHER LIFE SHE NEVER KNEW ABOUT.
I KNOW SHE'D LOVE TO MEET YOU.
NO.
I HAVE A ***NEW*** LIFE NOW. AND ***NO*** DESIRE TO BE PULLED BACK INTO MY OLD ONE.
I WAS NEVER A PART OF THE INSTITUTE, BUT NATHAN ALWAYS MADE OUR ***WHOLE*** LIFE ABOUT IT.
MRS. WALKER...
MY HUSBAND DOESN'T EVEN KNOW I HAD A CHILD.
AND I DON'T WANT HIM TO.
SO, PLEASE GO. NOW.

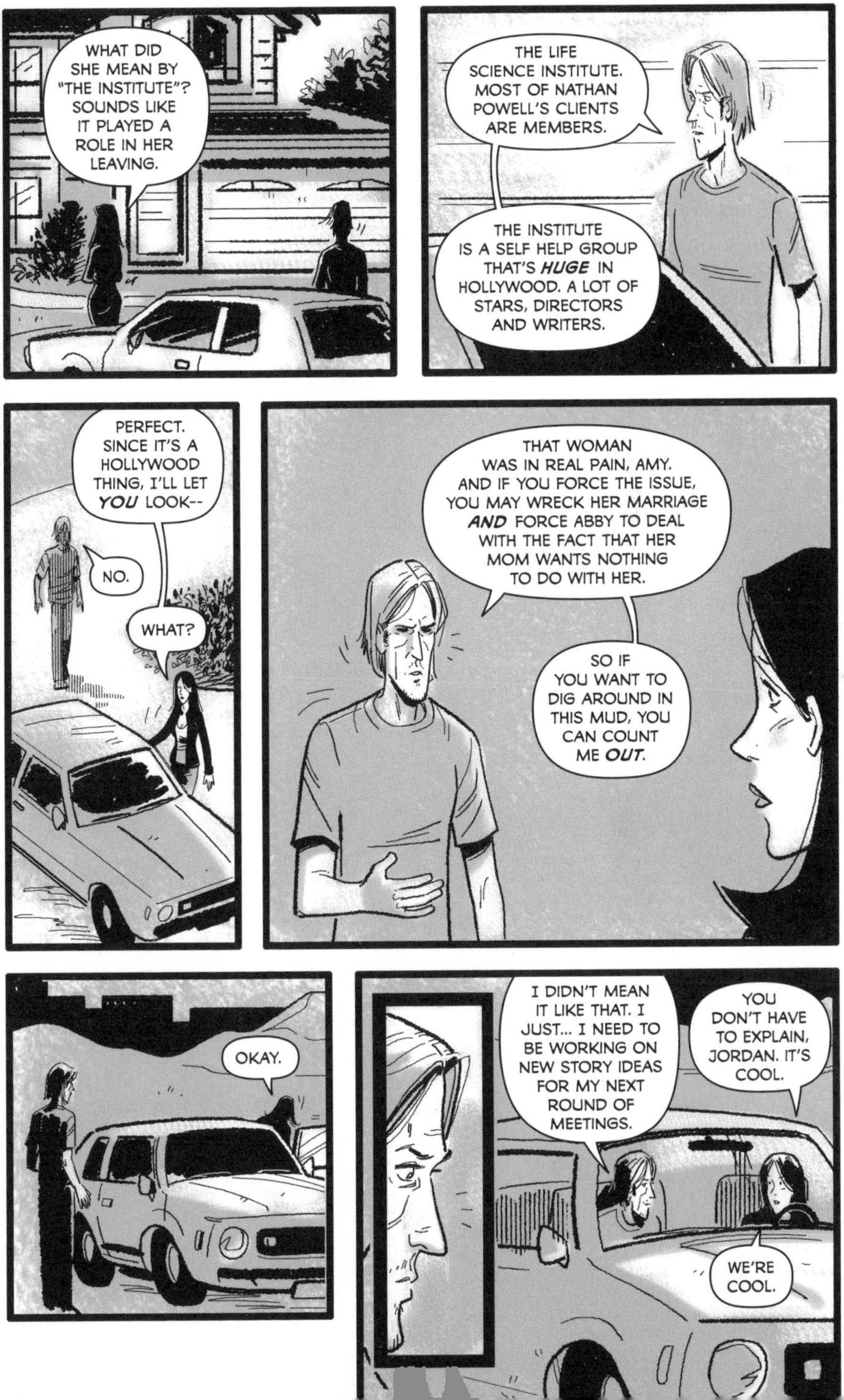
WHAT DID SHE MEAN BY "THE INSTITUTE"? SOUNDS LIKE IT PLAYED A ROLE IN HER LEAVING.
THE LIFE SCIENCE INSTITUTE. MOST OF NATHAN POWELL'S CLIENTS ARE MEMBERS.
THE INSTITUTE IS A SELF HELP GROUP THAT'S *HUGE* IN HOLLYWOOD. A LOT OF STARS, DIRECTORS AND WRITERS.
PERFECT. SINCE IT'S A HOLLYWOOD THING, I'LL LET *YOU* LOOK--
NO.
WHAT?
THAT WOMAN WAS IN REAL PAIN, AMY. AND IF YOU FORCE THE ISSUE, YOU MAY WRECK HER MARRIAGE *AND* FORCE ABBY TO DEAL WITH THE FACT THAT HER MOM WANTS NOTHING TO DO WITH HER.
SO IF YOU WANT TO DIG AROUND IN THIS MUD, YOU CAN COUNT ME *OUT*.
OKAY.
I DIDN'T MEAN IT LIKE THAT. I JUST... I NEED TO BE WORKING ON NEW STORY IDEAS FOR MY NEXT ROUND OF MEETINGS.
YOU DON'T HAVE TO EXPLAIN, JORDAN. IT'S COOL.
WE'RE COOL.

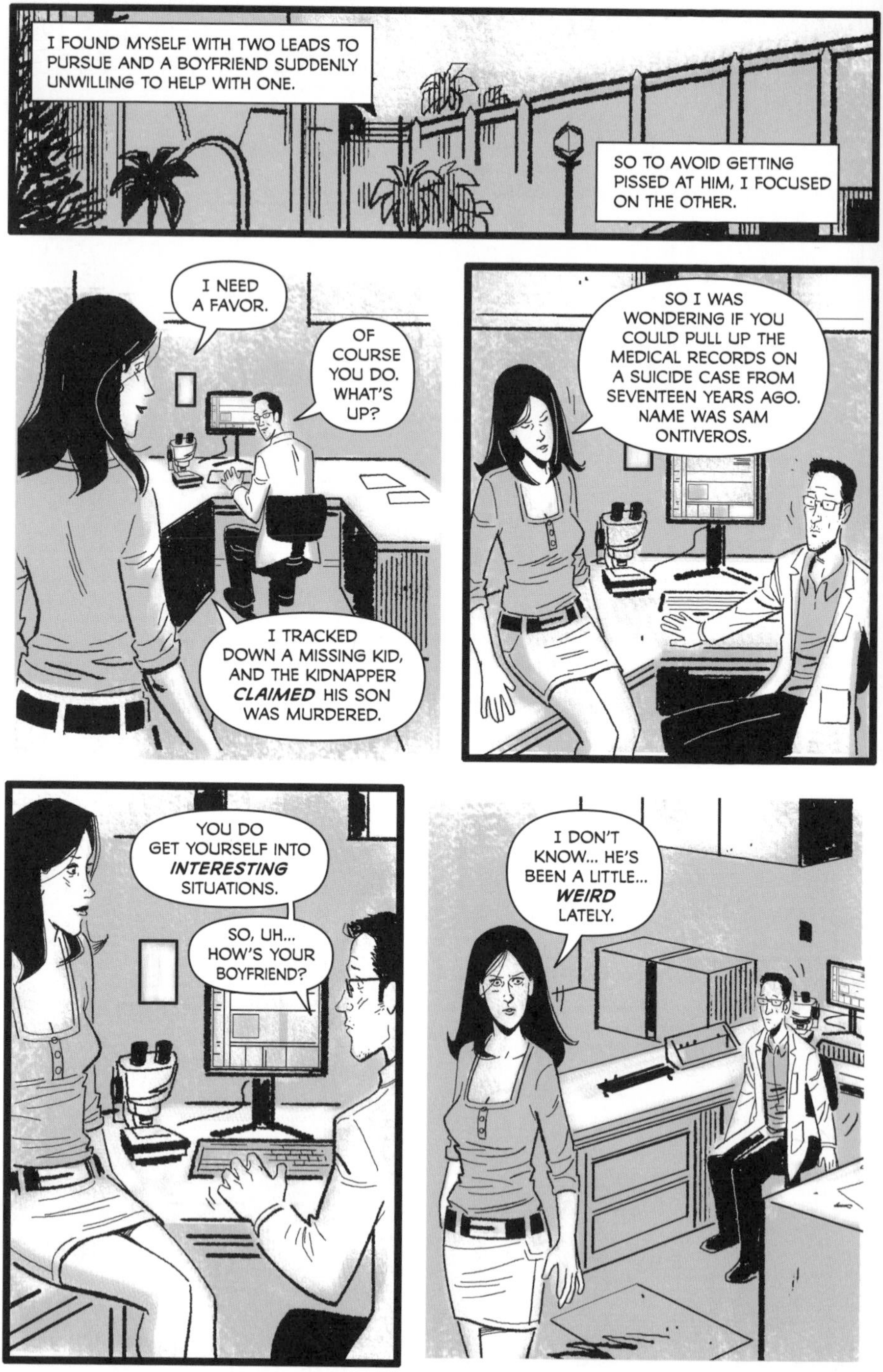
I FOUND MYSELF WITH TWO LEADS TO PURSUE AND A BOYFRIEND SUDDENLY UNWILLING TO HELP WITH ONE.
SO TO AVOID GETTING PISSED AT HIM, I FOCUSED ON THE OTHER.
I NEED A FAVOR.
OF COURSE YOU DO. WHAT'S UP?
I TRACKED DOWN A MISSING KID, AND THE KIDNAPPER *CLAIMED* HIS SON WAS MURDERED.
SO I WAS WONDERING IF YOU COULD PULL UP THE MEDICAL RECORDS ON A SUICIDE CASE FROM SEVENTEEN YEARS AGO. NAME WAS SAM ONTIVEROS.
YOU DO GET YOURSELF INTO *INTERESTING* SITUATIONS.
SO, UH... HOW'S YOUR BOYFRIEND?
I DON'T KNOW... HE'S BEEN A LITTLE... *WEIRD* LATELY.

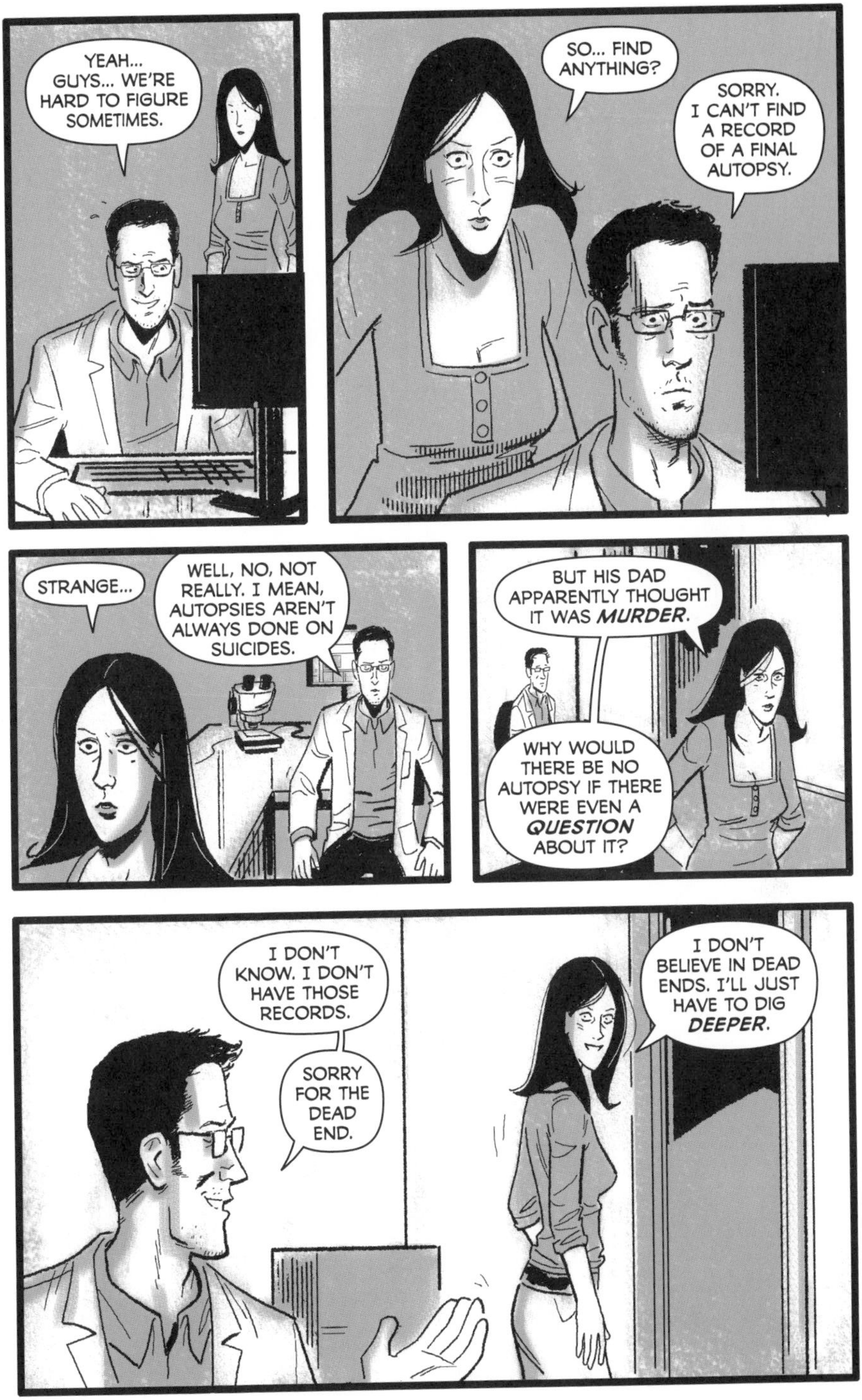
YEAH... GUYS... WE'RE HARD TO FIGURE SOMETIMES.
SO... FIND ANYTHING?
SORRY. I CAN'T FIND A RECORD OF A FINAL AUTOPSY.
STRANGE...
WELL, NO, NOT REALLY. I MEAN, AUTOPSIES AREN'T ALWAYS DONE ON SUICIDES.
BUT HIS DAD APPARENTLY THOUGHT IT WAS MURDER.
WHY WOULD THERE BE NO AUTOPSY IF THERE WERE EVEN A QUESTION ABOUT IT?
I DON'T KNOW. I DON'T HAVE THOSE RECORDS.
SORRY FOR THE DEAD END.
I DON'T BELIEVE IN DEAD ENDS. I'LL JUST HAVE TO DIG DEEPER.

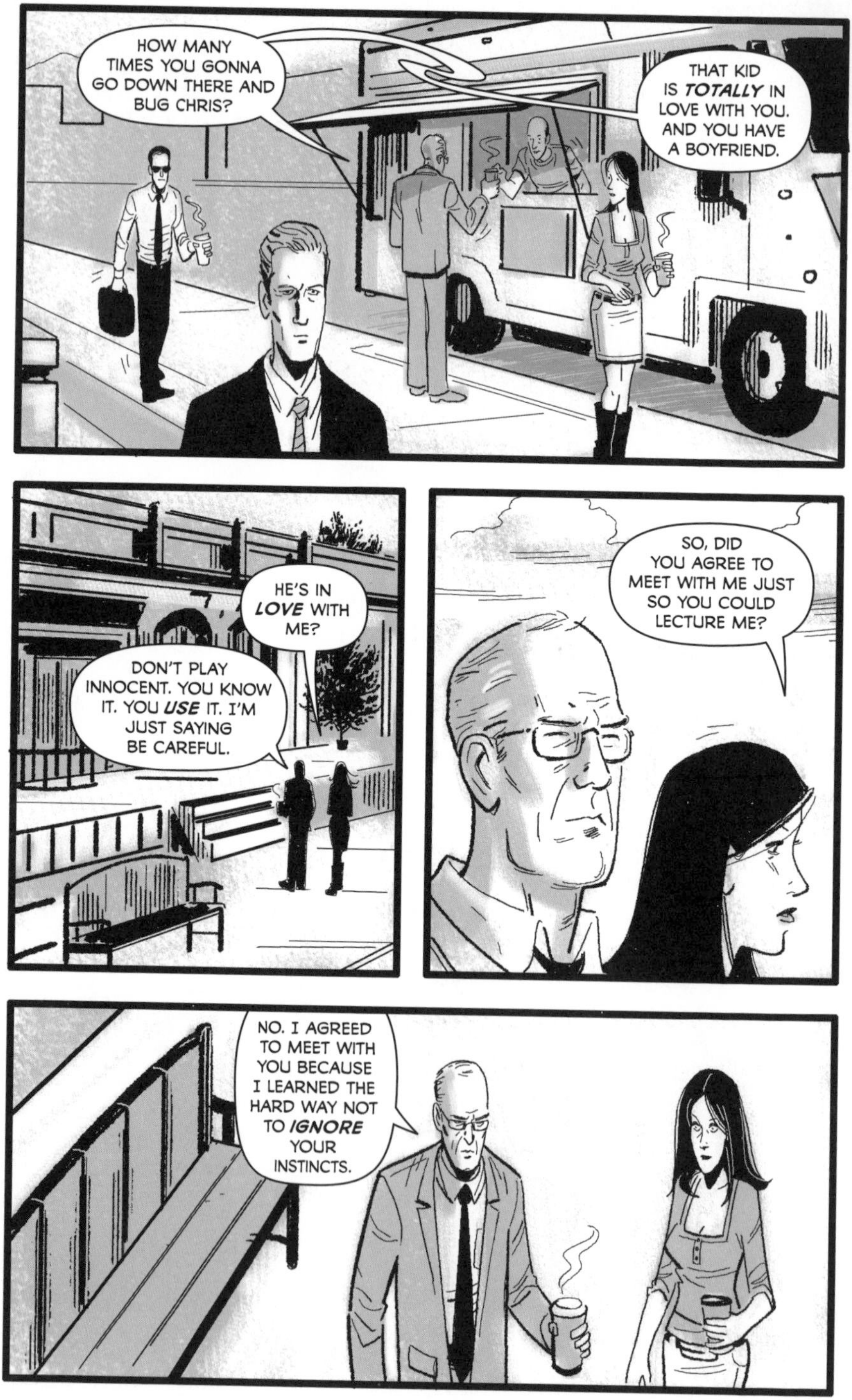
HOW MANY TIMES YOU GONNA GO DOWN THERE AND BUG CHRIS?
THAT KID IS TOTALLY IN LOVE WITH YOU. AND YOU HAVE A BOYFRIEND.
HE'S IN LOVE WITH ME?
DON'T PLAY INNOCENT. YOU KNOW IT. YOU USE IT. I'M JUST SAYING BE CAREFUL.
SO, DID YOU AGREE TO MEET WITH ME JUST SO YOU COULD LECTURE ME?
NO. I AGREED TO MEET WITH YOU BECAUSE I LEARNED THE HARD WAY NOT TO IGNORE YOUR INSTINCTS.

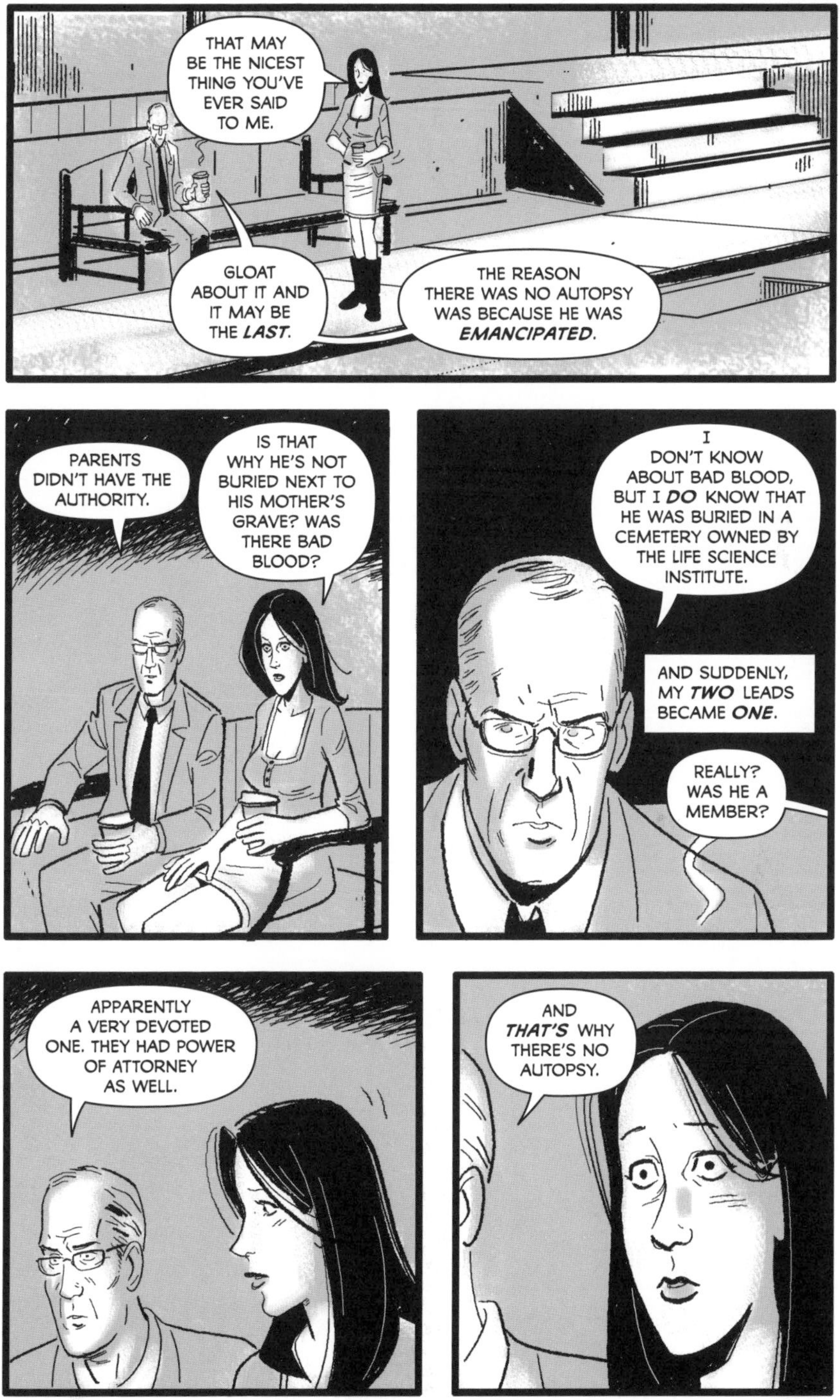
THAT MAY BE THE NICEST THING YOU'VE EVER SAID TO ME.
GLOAT ABOUT IT AND IT MAY BE THE *LAST*.
THE REASON THERE WAS NO AUTOPSY WAS BECAUSE HE WAS *EMANCIPATED*.
PARENTS DIDN'T HAVE THE AUTHORITY.
IS THAT WHY HE'S NOT BURIED NEXT TO HIS MOTHER'S GRAVE? WAS THERE BAD BLOOD?
I DON'T KNOW ABOUT BAD BLOOD, BUT I *DO* KNOW THAT HE WAS BURIED IN A CEMETERY OWNED BY THE LIFE SCIENCE INSTITUTE.
AND SUDDENLY, MY *TWO* LEADS BECAME *ONE*.
REALLY? WAS HE A MEMBER?
APPARENTLY A VERY DEVOTED ONE. THEY HAD POWER OF ATTORNEY AS WELL.
AND *THAT'S* WHY THERE'S NO AUTOPSY.

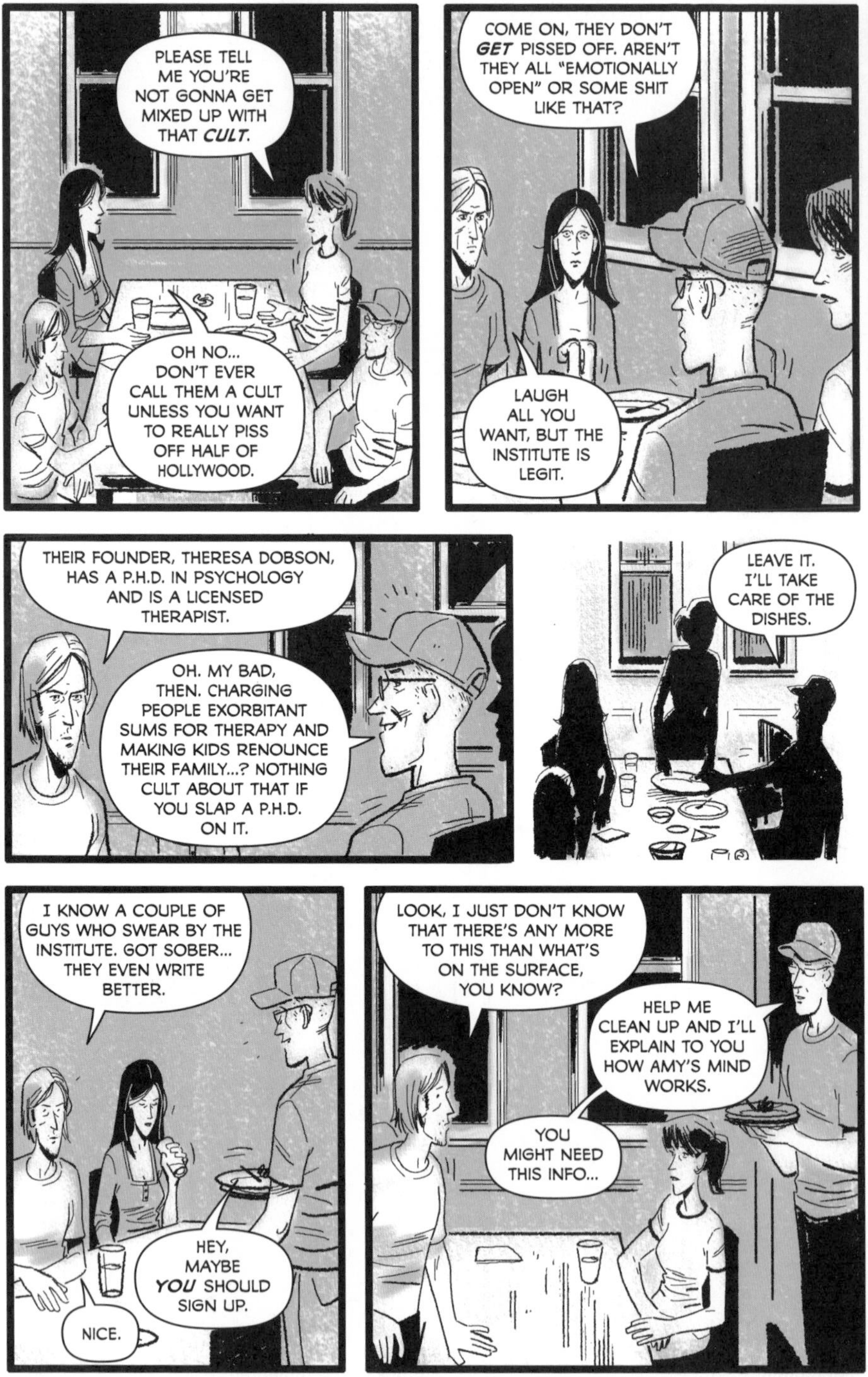
PLEASE TELL ME YOU'RE NOT GONNA GET MIXED UP WITH THAT *CULT*.
OH NO... DON'T EVER CALL THEM A CULT UNLESS YOU WANT TO REALLY PISS OFF HALF OF HOLLYWOOD.
COME ON, THEY DON'T *GET* PISSED OFF. AREN'T THEY ALL "EMOTIONALLY OPEN" OR SOME SHIT LIKE THAT?
LAUGH ALL YOU WANT, BUT THE INSTITUTE IS LEGIT.
THEIR FOUNDER, THERESA DOBSON, HAS A P.H.D. IN PSYCHOLOGY AND IS A LICENSED THERAPIST.
OH. MY BAD, THEN. CHARGING PEOPLE EXORBITANT SUMS FOR THERAPY AND MAKING KIDS RENOUNCE THEIR FAMILY...? NOTHING CULT ABOUT THAT IF YOU SLAP A P.H.D. ON IT.
LEAVE IT. I'LL TAKE CARE OF THE DISHES.
I KNOW A COUPLE OF GUYS WHO SWEAR BY THE INSTITUTE. GOT SOBER... THEY EVEN WRITE BETTER.
HEY, MAYBE *YOU* SHOULD SIGN UP.
NICE.
LOOK, I JUST DON'T KNOW THAT THERE'S ANY MORE TO THIS THAN WHAT'S ON THE SURFACE, YOU KNOW?
HELP ME CLEAN UP AND I'LL EXPLAIN TO YOU HOW AMY'S MIND WORKS.
YOU MIGHT NEED THIS INFO...

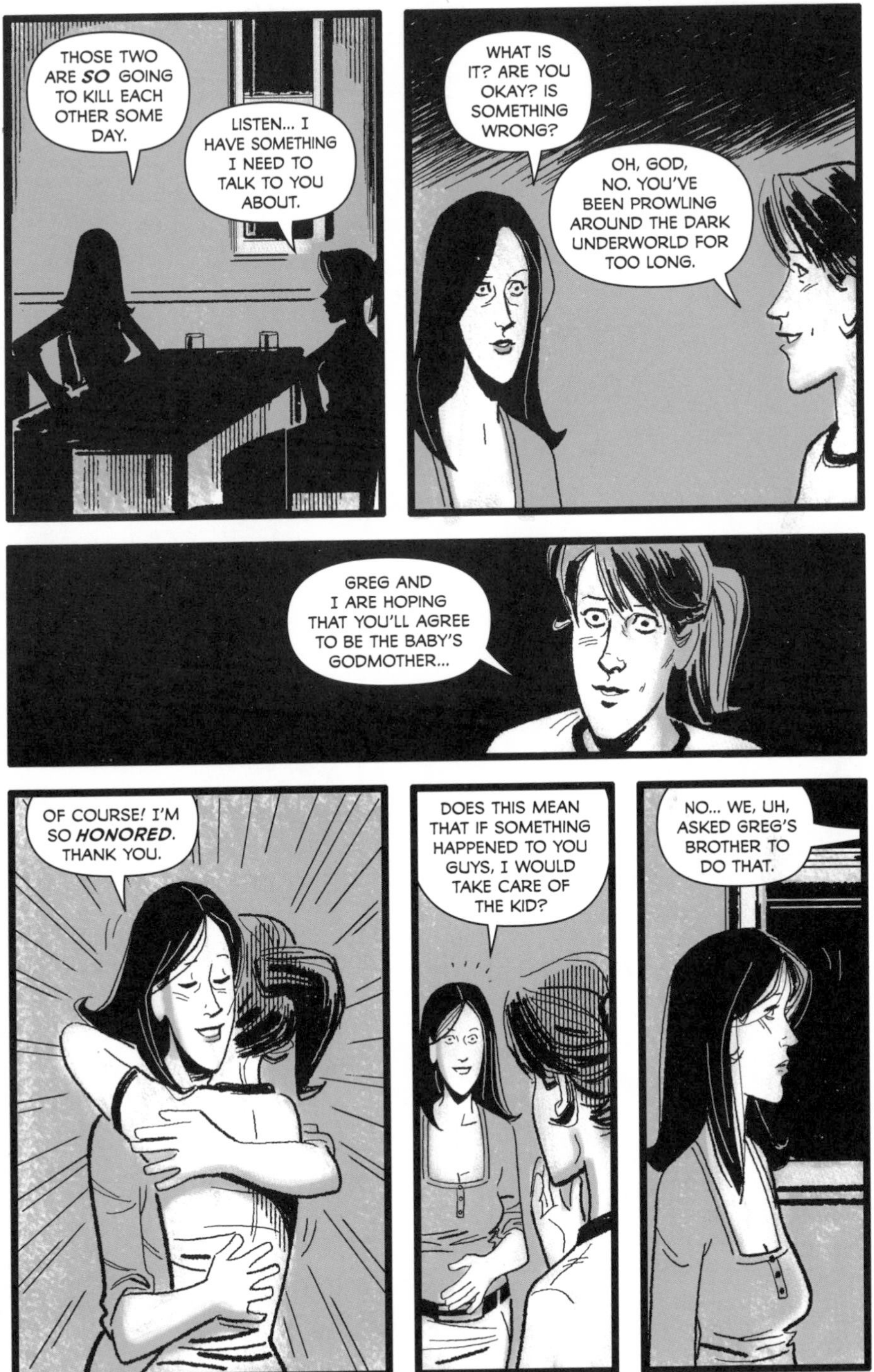
THOSE TWO ARE **SO** GOING TO KILL EACH OTHER SOME DAY.
LISTEN... I HAVE SOMETHING I NEED TO TALK TO YOU ABOUT.
WHAT IS IT? ARE YOU OKAY? IS SOMETHING WRONG?
OH, GOD, NO. YOU'VE BEEN PROWLING AROUND THE DARK UNDERWORLD FOR TOO LONG.
GREG AND I ARE HOPING THAT YOU'LL AGREE TO BE THE BABY'S GODMOTHER...
OF COURSE! I'M SO ***HONORED***. THANK YOU.
DOES THIS MEAN THAT IF SOMETHING HAPPENED TO YOU GUYS, I WOULD TAKE CARE OF THE KID?
NO... WE, UH, ASKED GREG'S BROTHER TO DO THAT.

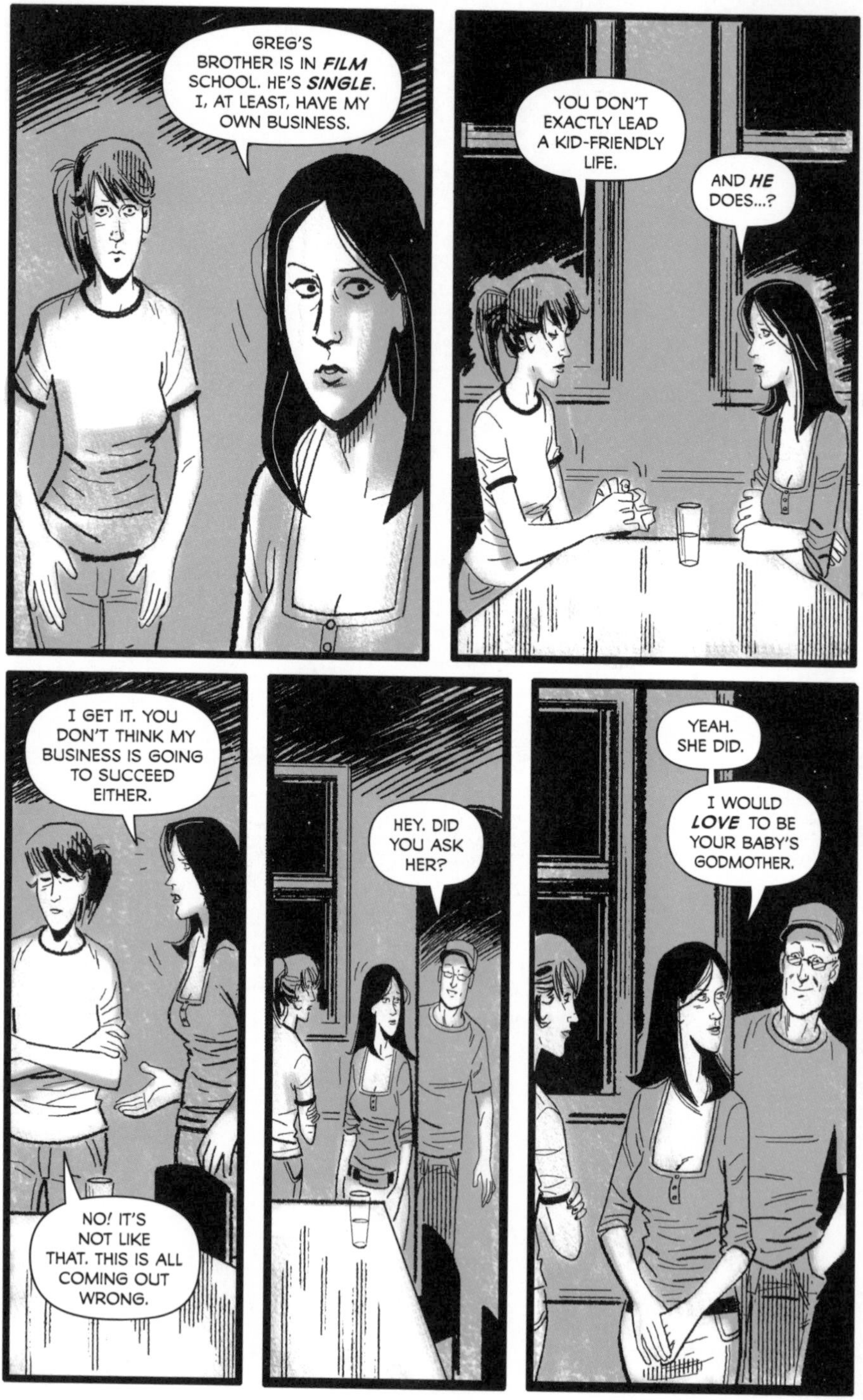
GREG'S BROTHER IS IN *FILM* SCHOOL. HE'S *SINGLE*. I, AT LEAST, HAVE MY OWN BUSINESS.
YOU DON'T EXACTLY LEAD A KID-FRIENDLY LIFE.
AND *HE* DOES...?
I GET IT. YOU DON'T THINK MY BUSINESS IS GOING TO SUCCEED EITHER.
NO! IT'S NOT LIKE THAT. THIS IS ALL COMING OUT WRONG.
HEY. DID YOU ASK HER?
YEAH. SHE DID.
I WOULD *LOVE* TO BE YOUR BABY'S GODMOTHER.

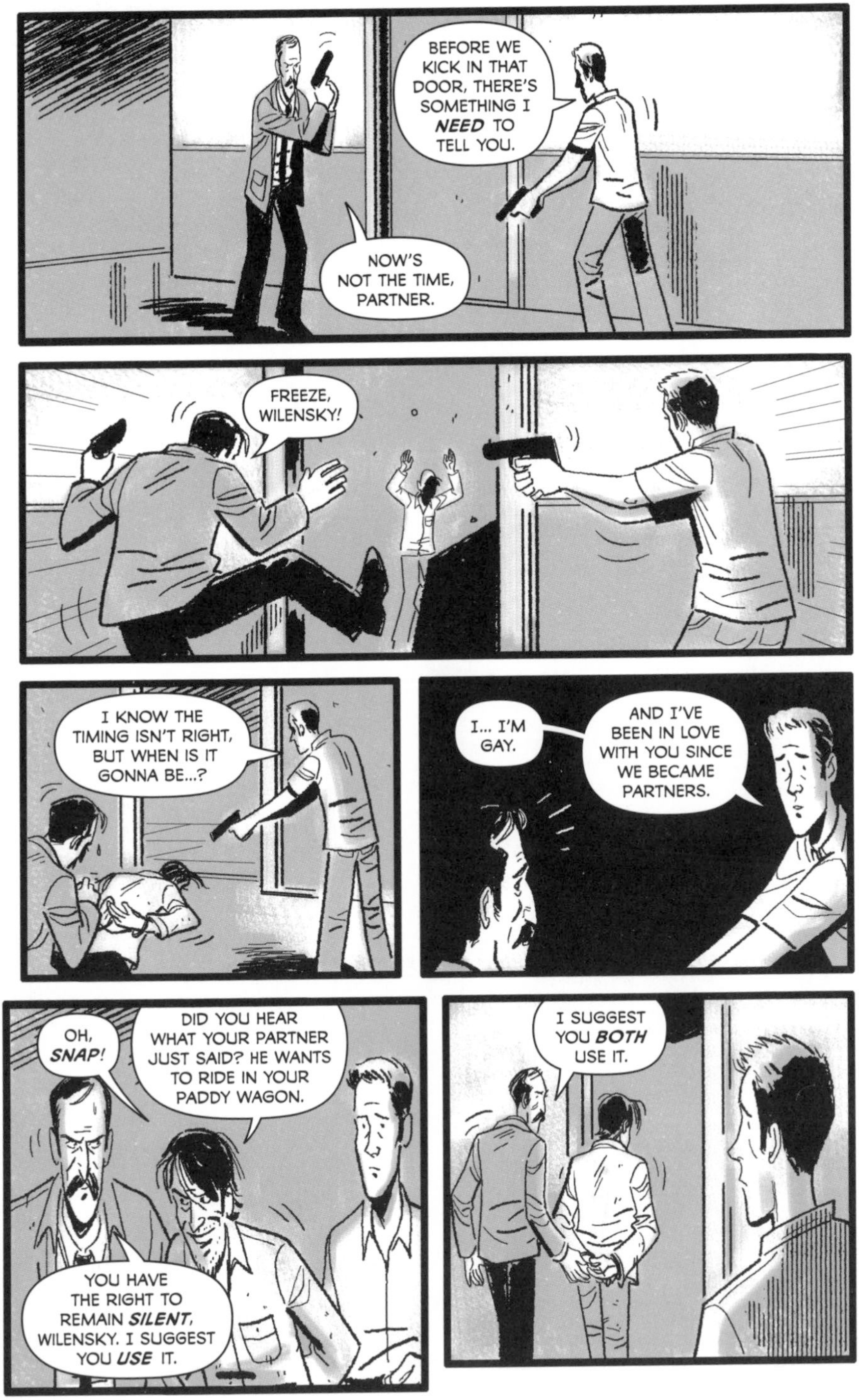
BEFORE WE KICK IN THAT DOOR, THERE'S SOMETHING I *NEED* TO TELL YOU.
NOW'S NOT THE TIME, PARTNER.
FREEZE, WILENSKY!
I KNOW THE TIMING ISN'T RIGHT, BUT WHEN IS IT GONNA BE...?
I... I'M GAY.
AND I'VE BEEN IN LOVE WITH YOU SINCE WE BECAME PARTNERS.
OH, *SNAP!*
DID YOU HEAR WHAT YOUR PARTNER JUST SAID? HE WANTS TO RIDE IN YOUR PADDY WAGON.
YOU HAVE THE RIGHT TO REMAIN *SILENT*, WILENSKY. I SUGGEST YOU *USE* IT.
I SUGGEST YOU *BOTH* USE IT.

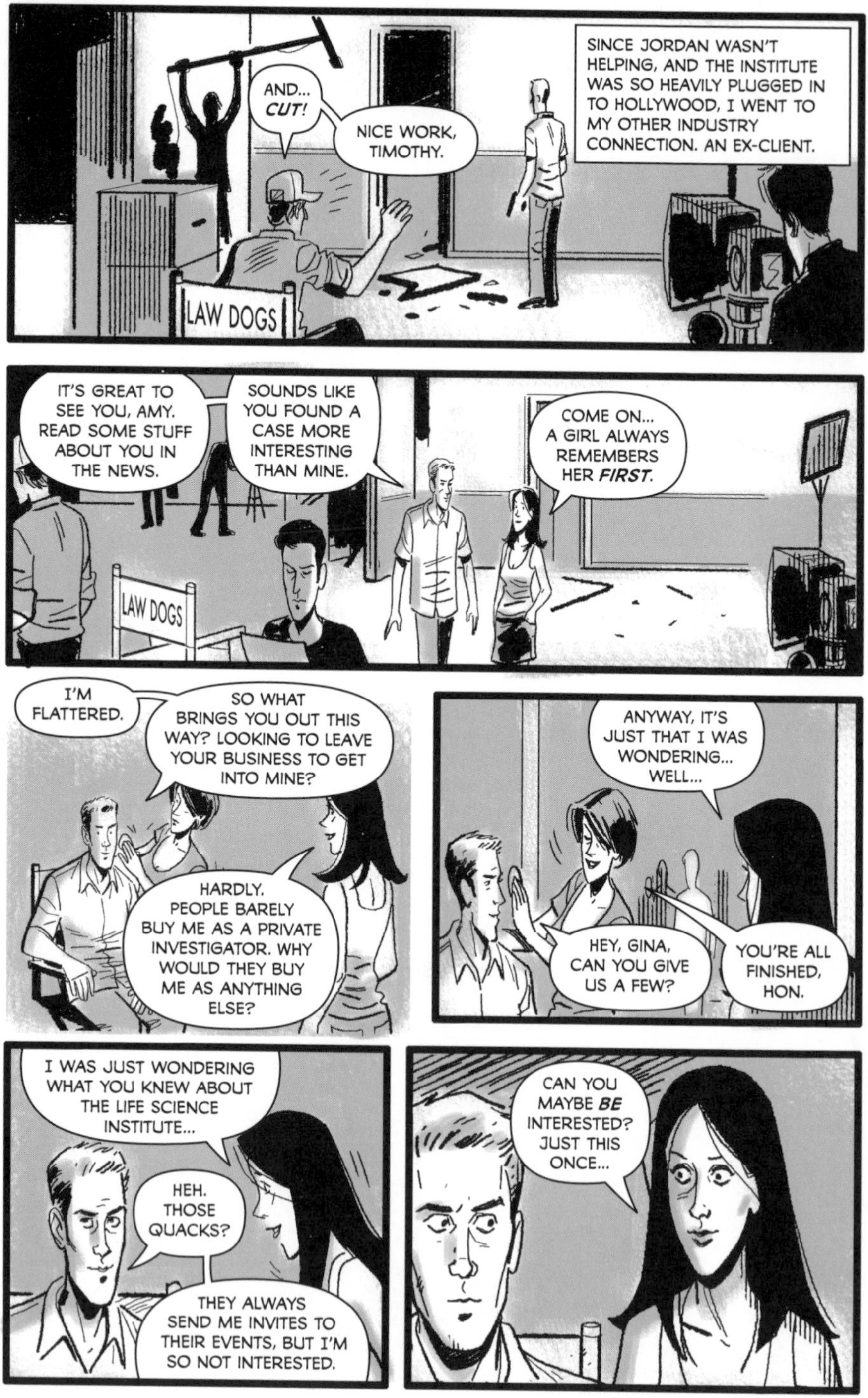
SINCE JORDAN WASN'T HELPING, AND THE INSTITUTE WAS SO HEAVILY PLUGGED IN TO HOLLYWOOD, I WENT TO MY OTHER INDUSTRY CONNECTION. AN EX-CLIENT.
AND... *CUT!*
NICE WORK, TIMOTHY.
LAW DOGS
IT'S GREAT TO SEE YOU, AMY. READ SOME STUFF ABOUT YOU IN THE NEWS.
SOUNDS LIKE YOU FOUND A CASE MORE INTERESTING THAN MINE.
COME ON... A GIRL ALWAYS REMEMBERS HER *FIRST*.
LAW DOGS
I'M FLATTERED.
SO WHAT BRINGS YOU OUT THIS WAY? LOOKING TO LEAVE YOUR BUSINESS TO GET INTO MINE?
HARDLY. PEOPLE BARELY BUY ME AS A PRIVATE INVESTIGATOR. WHY WOULD THEY BUY ME AS ANYTHING ELSE?
ANYWAY, IT'S JUST THAT I WAS WONDERING... WELL...
HEY, GINA, CAN YOU GIVE US A FEW?
YOU'RE ALL FINISHED, HON.
I WAS JUST WONDERING WHAT YOU KNEW ABOUT THE LIFE SCIENCE INSTITUTE...
HEH. THOSE QUACKS?
THEY ALWAYS SEND ME INVITES TO THEIR EVENTS, BUT I'M SO NOT INTERESTED.
CAN YOU MAYBE *BE* INTERESTED? JUST THIS ONCE...

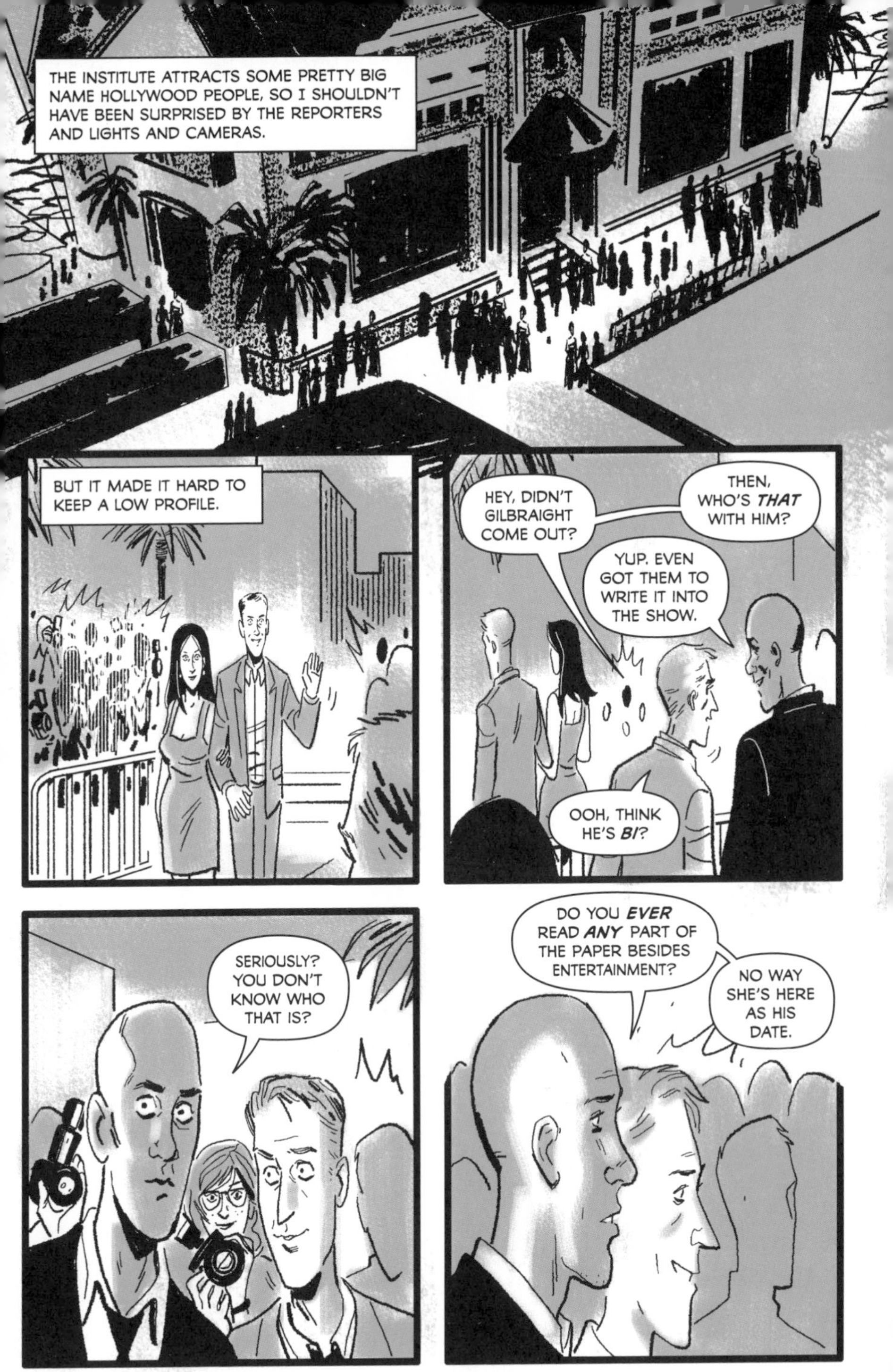
THE INSTITUTE ATTRACTS SOME PRETTY BIG NAME HOLLYWOOD PEOPLE, SO I SHOULDN'T HAVE BEEN SURPRISED BY THE REPORTERS AND LIGHTS AND CAMERAS.
BUT IT MADE IT HARD TO KEEP A LOW PROFILE.
HEY, DIDN'T GILBRAIGHT COME OUT?
THEN, WHO'S *THAT* WITH HIM?
YUP. EVEN GOT THEM TO WRITE IT INTO THE SHOW.
OOH, THINK HE'S *BI*?
SERIOUSLY? YOU DON'T KNOW WHO THAT IS?
DO YOU *EVER* READ *ANY* PART OF THE PAPER BESIDES ENTERTAINMENT?
NO WAY SHE'S HERE AS HIS DATE.

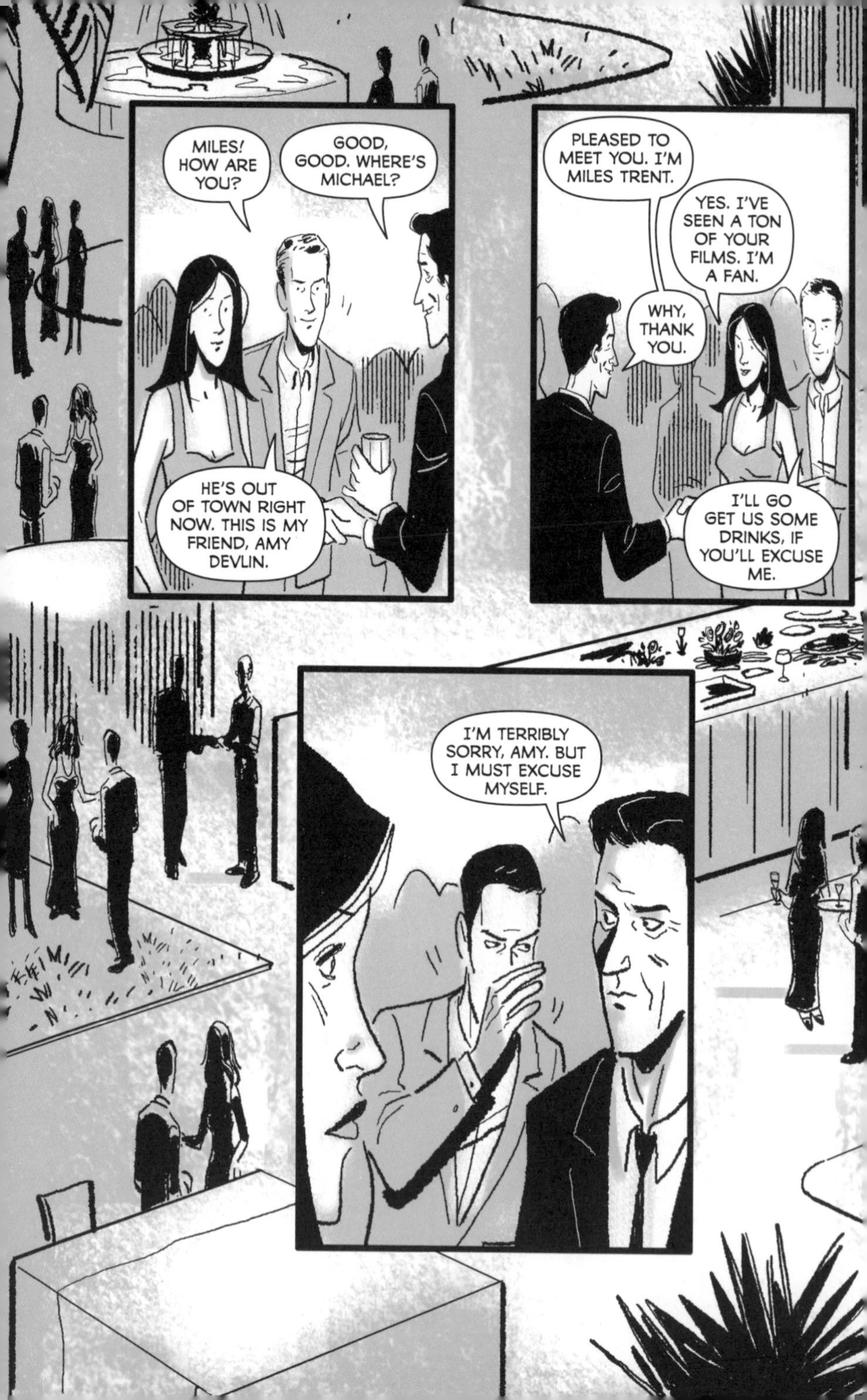
MILES! HOW ARE YOU?
GOOD, GOOD. WHERE'S MICHAEL?
HE'S OUT OF TOWN RIGHT NOW. THIS IS MY FRIEND, AMY DEVLIN.
PLEASED TO MEET YOU. I'M MILES TRENT.
YES. I'VE SEEN A TON OF YOUR FILMS. I'M A FAN.
WHY, THANK YOU.
I'LL GO GET US SOME DRINKS, IF YOU'LL EXCUSE ME.
I'M TERRIBLY SORRY, AMY. BUT I MUST EXCUSE MYSELF.

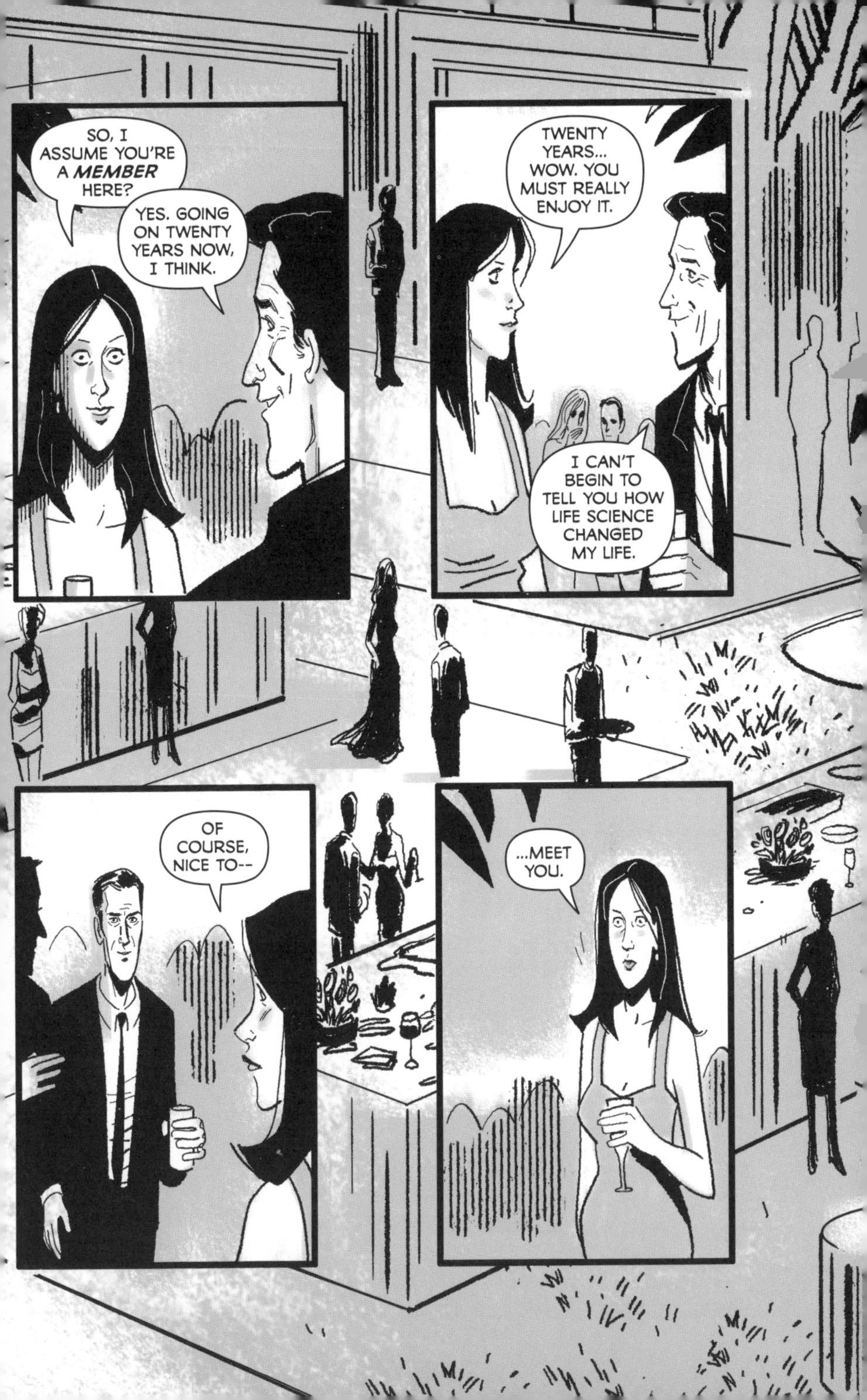
SO, I ASSUME YOU'RE A *MEMBER* HERE?
YES. GOING ON TWENTY YEARS NOW, I THINK.
TWENTY YEARS... WOW. YOU MUST REALLY ENJOY IT.
I CAN'T BEGIN TO TELL YOU HOW LIFE SCIENCE CHANGED MY LIFE.
OF COURSE, NICE TO--
...MEET YOU.

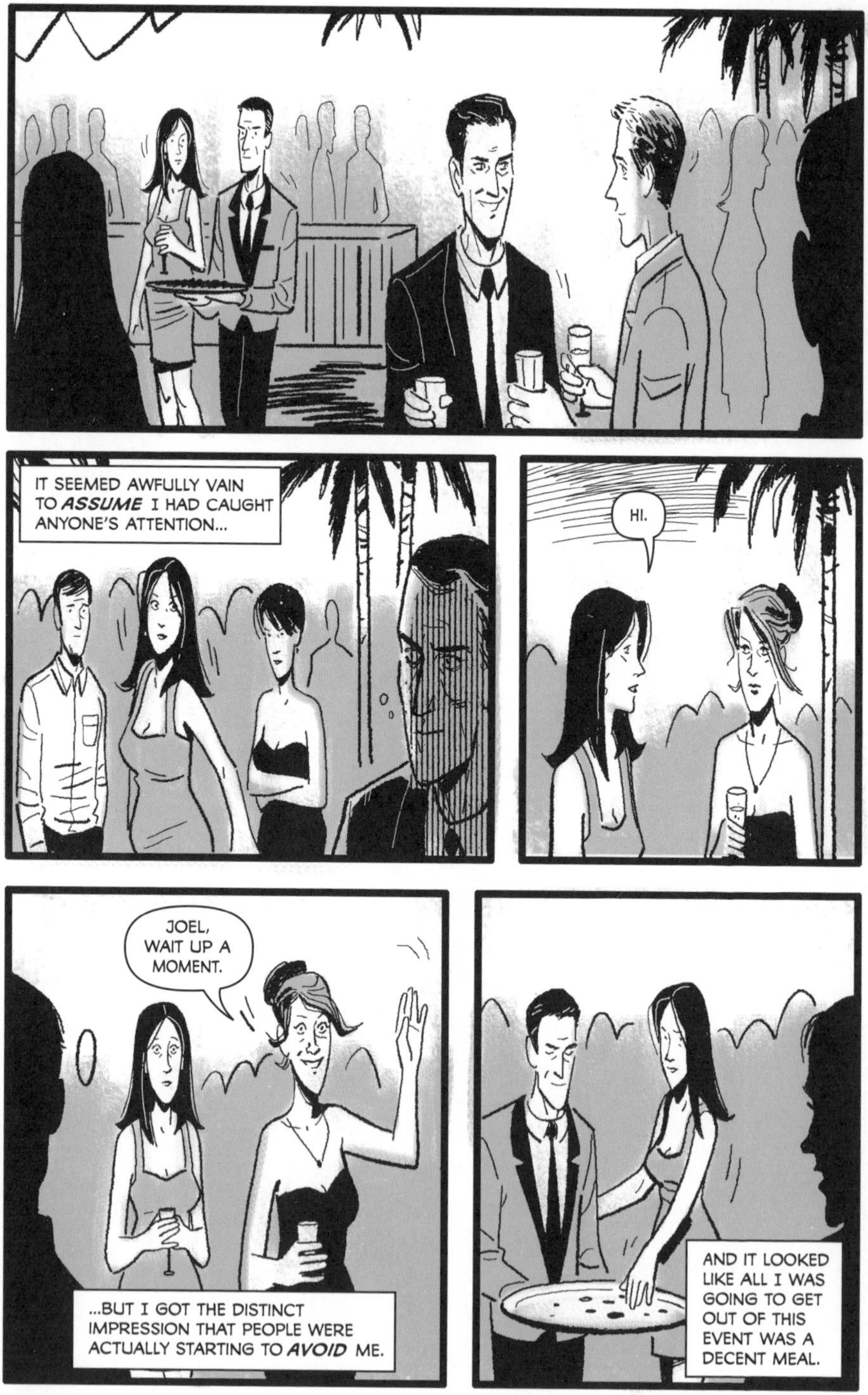
IT SEEMED AWFULLY VAIN TO ASSUME I HAD CAUGHT ANYONE'S ATTENTION...
HI.
JOEL, WAIT UP A MOMENT.
...BUT I GOT THE DISTINCT IMPRESSION THAT PEOPLE WERE ACTUALLY STARTING TO AVOID ME.
AND IT LOOKED LIKE ALL I WAS GOING TO GET OUT OF THIS EVENT WAS A DECENT MEAL.

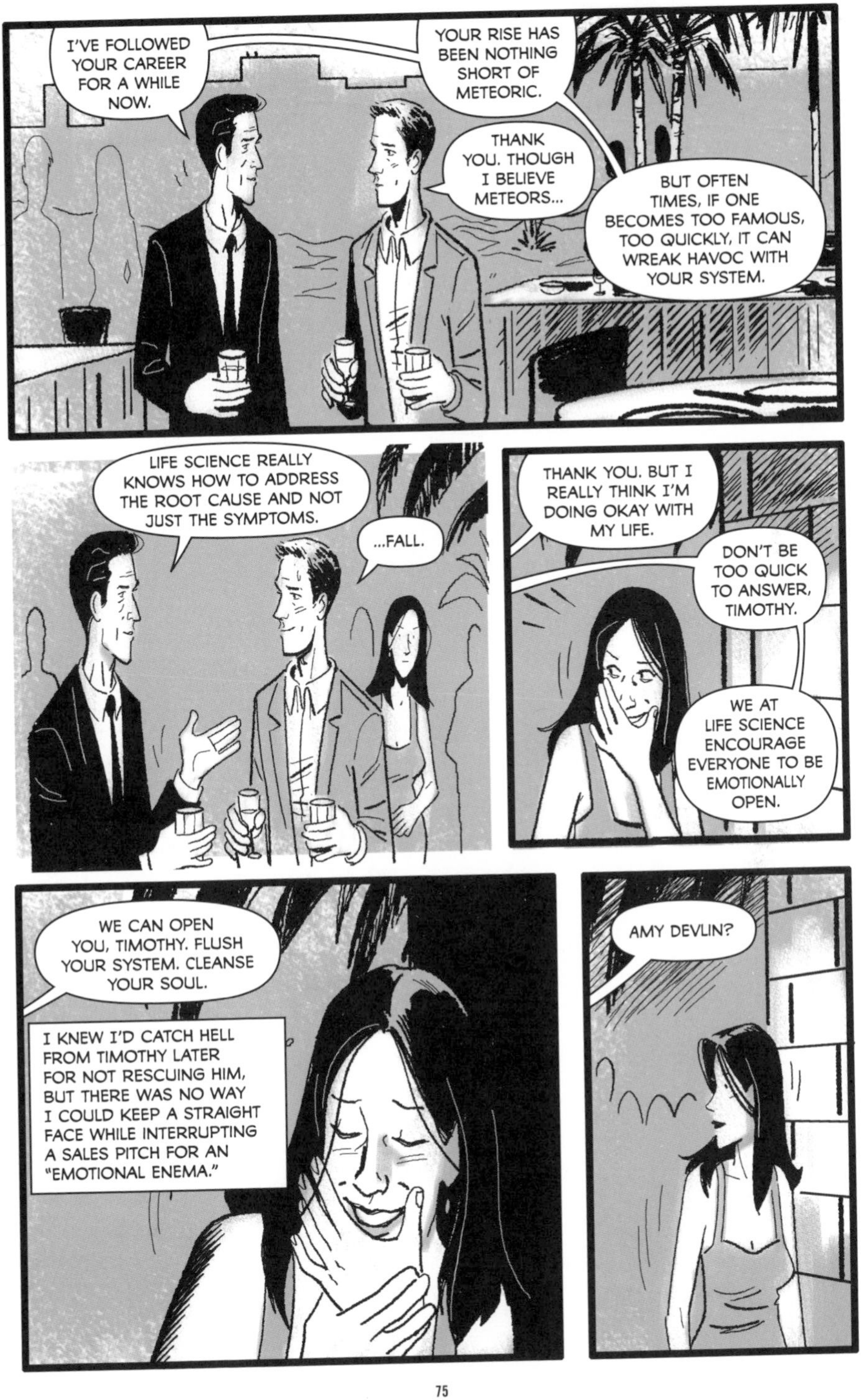
I'VE FOLLOWED YOUR CAREER FOR A WHILE NOW.
YOUR RISE HAS BEEN NOTHING SHORT OF METEORIC.
THANK YOU. THOUGH I BELIEVE METEORS...
BUT OFTEN TIMES, IF ONE BECOMES TOO FAMOUS, TOO QUICKLY, IT CAN WREAK HAVOC WITH YOUR SYSTEM.
LIFE SCIENCE REALLY KNOWS HOW TO ADDRESS THE ROOT CAUSE AND NOT JUST THE SYMPTOMS.
...FALL.
THANK YOU. BUT I REALLY THINK I'M DOING OKAY WITH MY LIFE.
DON'T BE TOO QUICK TO ANSWER, TIMOTHY.
WE AT LIFE SCIENCE ENCOURAGE EVERYONE TO BE EMOTIONALLY OPEN.
WE CAN OPEN YOU, TIMOTHY. FLUSH YOUR SYSTEM. CLEANSE YOUR SOUL.
I KNEW I'D CATCH HELL FROM TIMOTHY LATER FOR NOT RESCUING HIM, BUT THERE WAS NO WAY I COULD KEEP A STRAIGHT FACE WHILE INTERRUPTING A SALES PITCH FOR AN "EMOTIONAL ENEMA."
AMY DEVLIN?

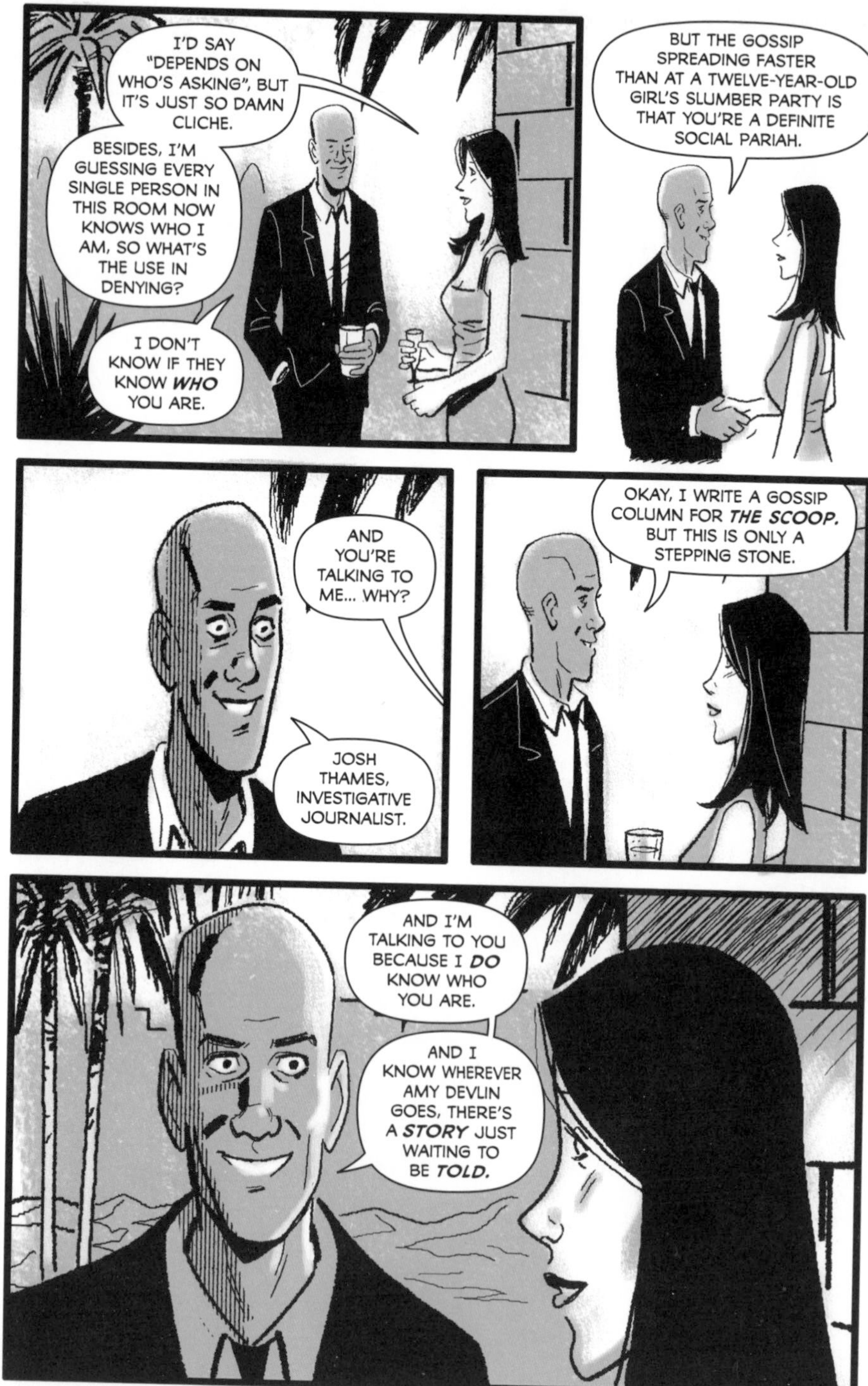
I'D SAY "DEPENDS ON WHO'S ASKING", BUT IT'S JUST SO DAMN CLICHE.
BESIDES, I'M GUESSING EVERY SINGLE PERSON IN THIS ROOM NOW KNOWS WHO I AM, SO WHAT'S THE USE IN DENYING?
I DON'T KNOW IF THEY KNOW ***WHO*** YOU ARE.
BUT THE GOSSIP SPREADING FASTER THAN AT A TWELVE-YEAR-OLD GIRL'S SLUMBER PARTY IS THAT YOU'RE A DEFINITE SOCIAL PARIAH.
AND YOU'RE TALKING TO ME... WHY?
JOSH THAMES, INVESTIGATIVE JOURNALIST.
OKAY, I WRITE A GOSSIP COLUMN FOR ***THE SCOOP.*** BUT THIS IS ONLY A STEPPING STONE.
AND I'M TALKING TO YOU BECAUSE I ***DO*** KNOW WHO YOU ARE.
AND I KNOW WHEREVER AMY DEVLIN GOES, THERE'S A ***STORY*** JUST WAITING TO BE ***TOLD.***

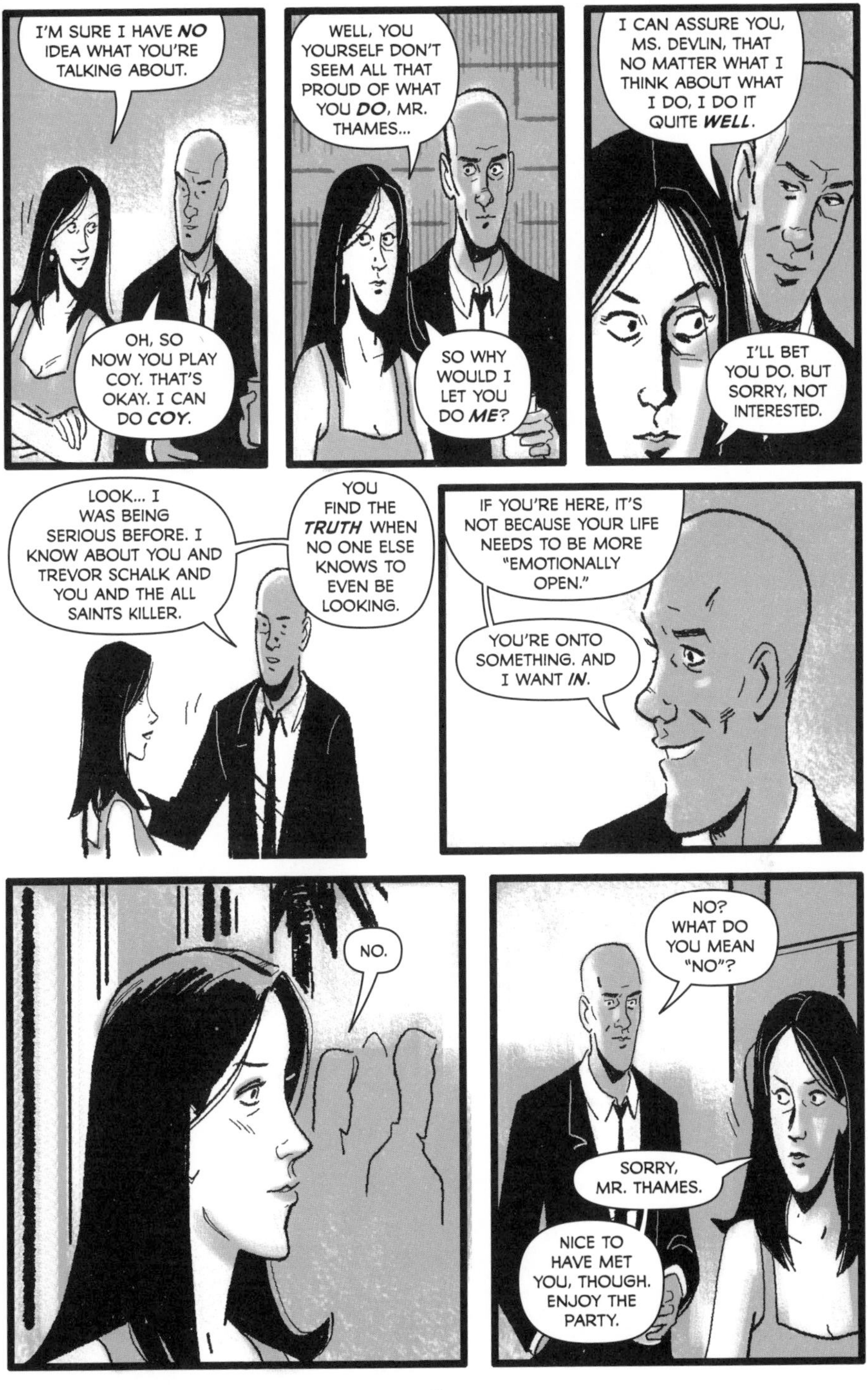
I'M SURE I HAVE NO IDEA WHAT YOU'RE TALKING ABOUT.
OH, SO NOW YOU PLAY COY. THAT'S OKAY. I CAN DO COY.
WELL, YOU YOURSELF DON'T SEEM ALL THAT PROUD OF WHAT YOU DO, MR. THAMES...
SO WHY WOULD I LET YOU DO ME?
I CAN ASSURE YOU, MS. DEVLIN, THAT NO MATTER WHAT I THINK ABOUT WHAT I DO, I DO IT QUITE WELL.
I'LL BET YOU DO. BUT SORRY, NOT INTERESTED.
LOOK... I WAS BEING SERIOUS BEFORE. I KNOW ABOUT YOU AND TREVOR SCHALK AND YOU AND THE ALL SAINTS KILLER.
YOU FIND THE TRUTH WHEN NO ONE ELSE KNOWS TO EVEN BE LOOKING.
IF YOU'RE HERE, IT'S NOT BECAUSE YOUR LIFE NEEDS TO BE MORE "EMOTIONALLY OPEN."
YOU'RE ONTO SOMETHING. AND I WANT IN.
NO.
NO? WHAT DO YOU MEAN "NO"?
SORRY, MR. THAMES.
NICE TO HAVE MET YOU, THOUGH. ENJOY THE PARTY.

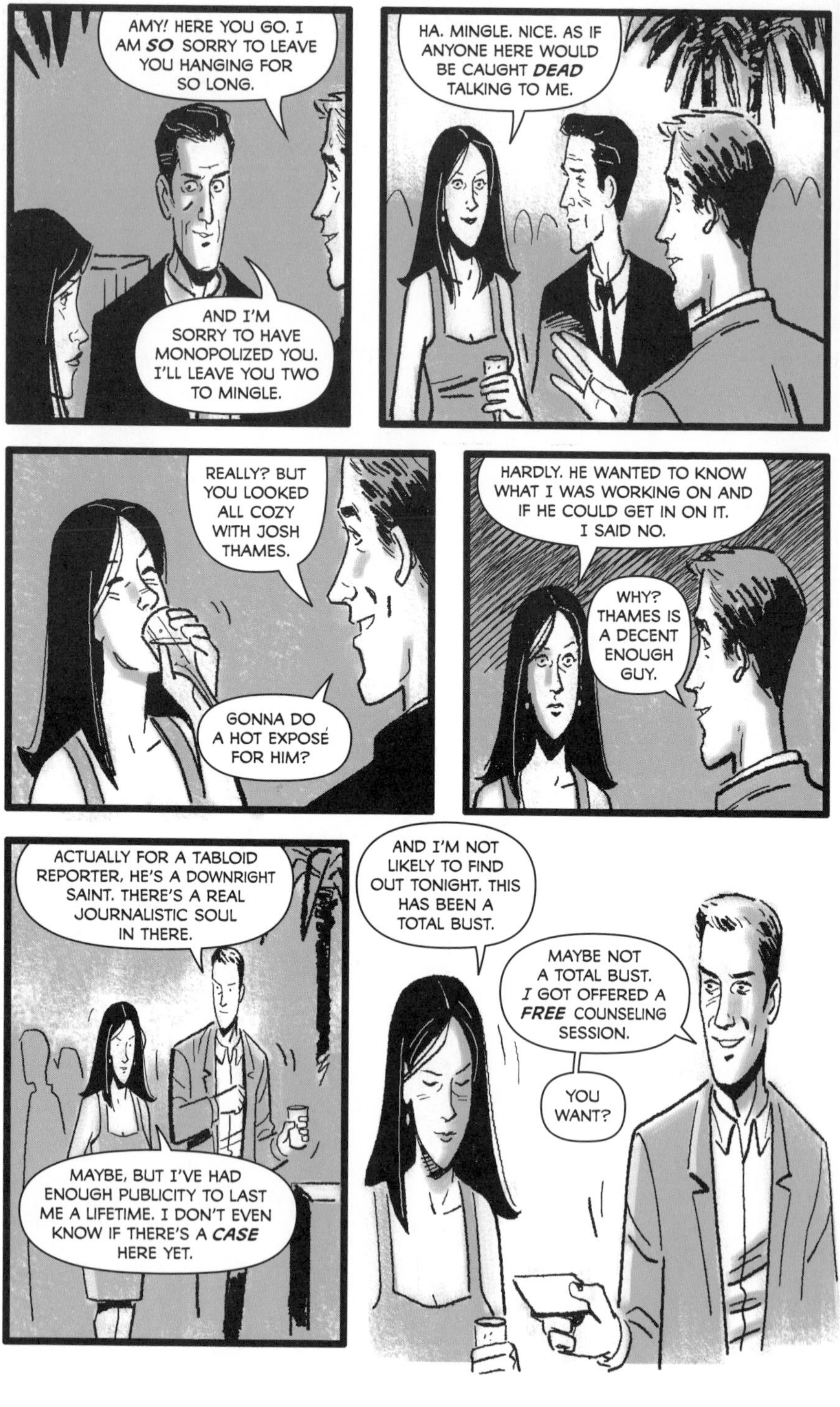
AMY! HERE YOU GO. I AM *SO* SORRY TO LEAVE YOU HANGING FOR SO LONG.
AND I'M SORRY TO HAVE MONOPOLIZED YOU. I'LL LEAVE YOU TWO TO MINGLE.
HA. MINGLE. NICE. AS IF ANYONE HERE WOULD BE CAUGHT *DEAD* TALKING TO ME.
REALLY? BUT YOU LOOKED ALL COZY WITH JOSH THAMES.
GONNA DO A HOT EXPOSÉ FOR HIM?
HARDLY. HE WANTED TO KNOW WHAT I WAS WORKING ON AND IF HE COULD GET IN ON IT. I SAID NO.
WHY? THAMES IS A DECENT ENOUGH GUY.
ACTUALLY FOR A TABLOID REPORTER, HE'S A DOWNRIGHT SAINT. THERE'S A REAL JOURNALISTIC SOUL IN THERE.
MAYBE, BUT I'VE HAD ENOUGH PUBLICITY TO LAST ME A LIFETIME. I DON'T EVEN KNOW IF THERE'S A *CASE* HERE YET.
AND I'M NOT LIKELY TO FIND OUT TONIGHT. THIS HAS BEEN A TOTAL BUST.
MAYBE NOT A TOTAL BUST. *I* GOT OFFERED A *FREE* COUNSELING SESSION.
YOU WANT?

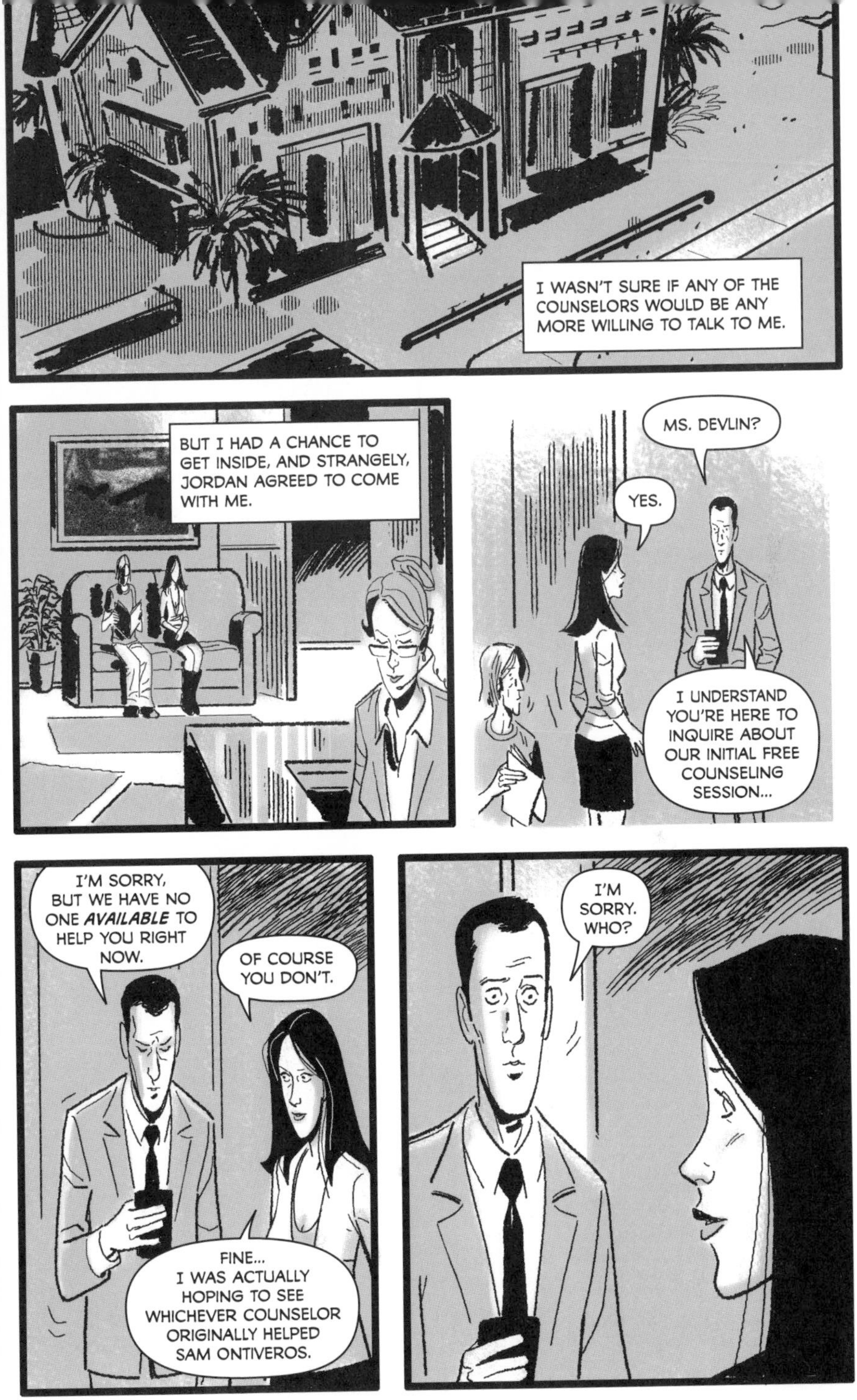
I WASN'T SURE IF ANY OF THE COUNSELORS WOULD BE ANY MORE WILLING TO TALK TO ME.
BUT I HAD A CHANCE TO GET INSIDE, AND STRANGELY, JORDAN AGREED TO COME WITH ME.
MS. DEVLIN?
YES.
I UNDERSTAND YOU'RE HERE TO INQUIRE ABOUT OUR INITIAL FREE COUNSELING SESSION...
I'M SORRY, BUT WE HAVE NO ONE *AVAILABLE* TO HELP YOU RIGHT NOW.
OF COURSE YOU DON'T.
FINE... I WAS ACTUALLY HOPING TO SEE WHICHEVER COUNSELOR ORIGINALLY HELPED SAM ONTIVEROS.
I'M SORRY. WHO?

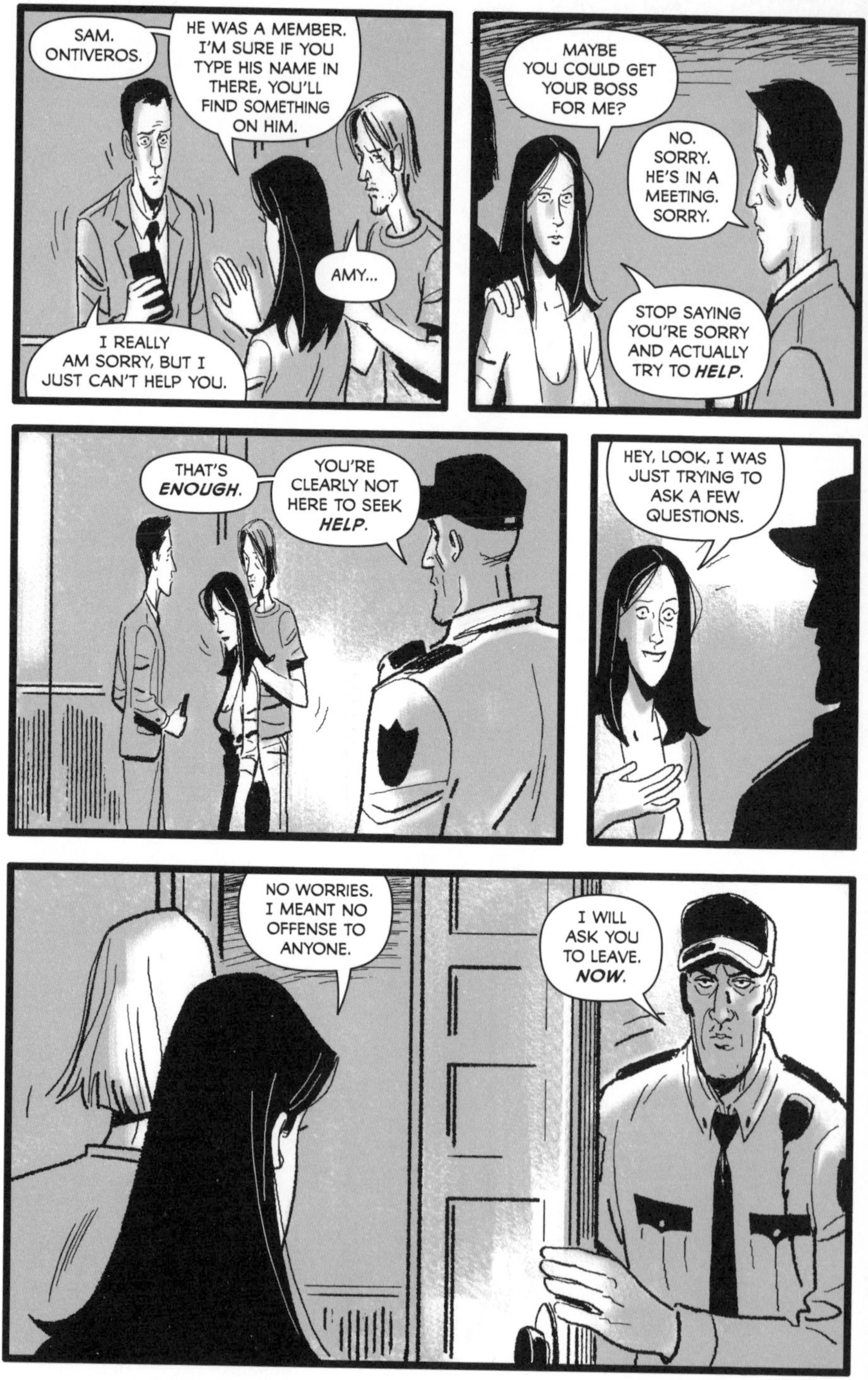
SAM. ONTIVEROS.
HE WAS A MEMBER. I'M SURE IF YOU TYPE HIS NAME IN THERE, YOU'LL FIND SOMETHING ON HIM.
AMY...
I REALLY AM SORRY, BUT I JUST CAN'T HELP YOU.
MAYBE YOU COULD GET YOUR BOSS FOR ME?
NO. SORRY. HE'S IN A MEETING. SORRY.
STOP SAYING YOU'RE SORRY AND ACTUALLY TRY TO ***HELP***.
THAT'S ***ENOUGH***.
YOU'RE CLEARLY NOT HERE TO SEEK ***HELP***.
HEY, LOOK, I WAS JUST TRYING TO ASK A FEW QUESTIONS.
NO WORRIES. I MEANT NO OFFENSE TO ANYONE.
I WILL ASK YOU TO LEAVE. ***NOW***.

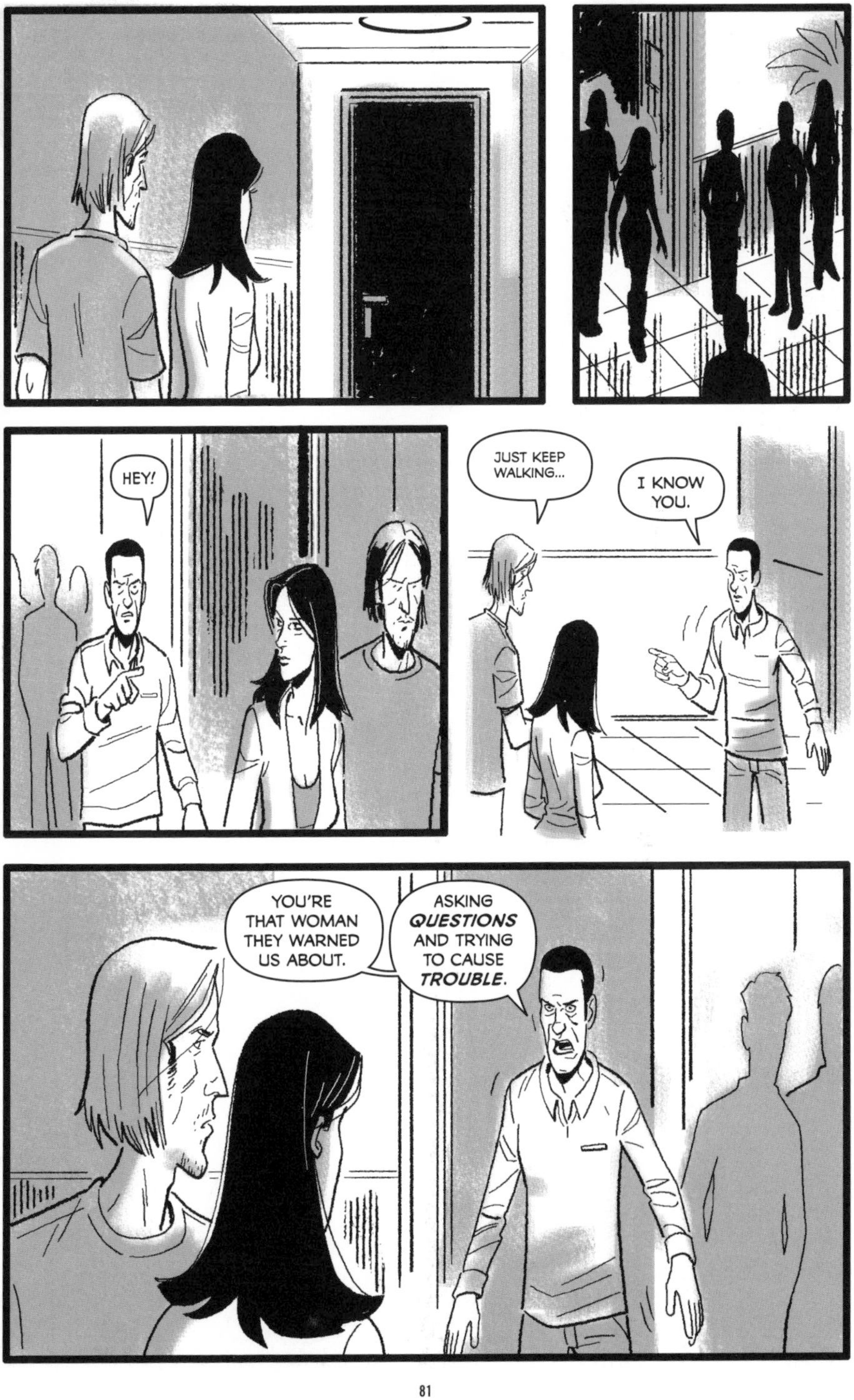
HEY!
JUST KEEP WALKING...
I KNOW YOU.
YOU'RE THAT WOMAN THEY WARNED US ABOUT.
ASKING *QUESTIONS* AND TRYING TO CAUSE *TROUBLE*.

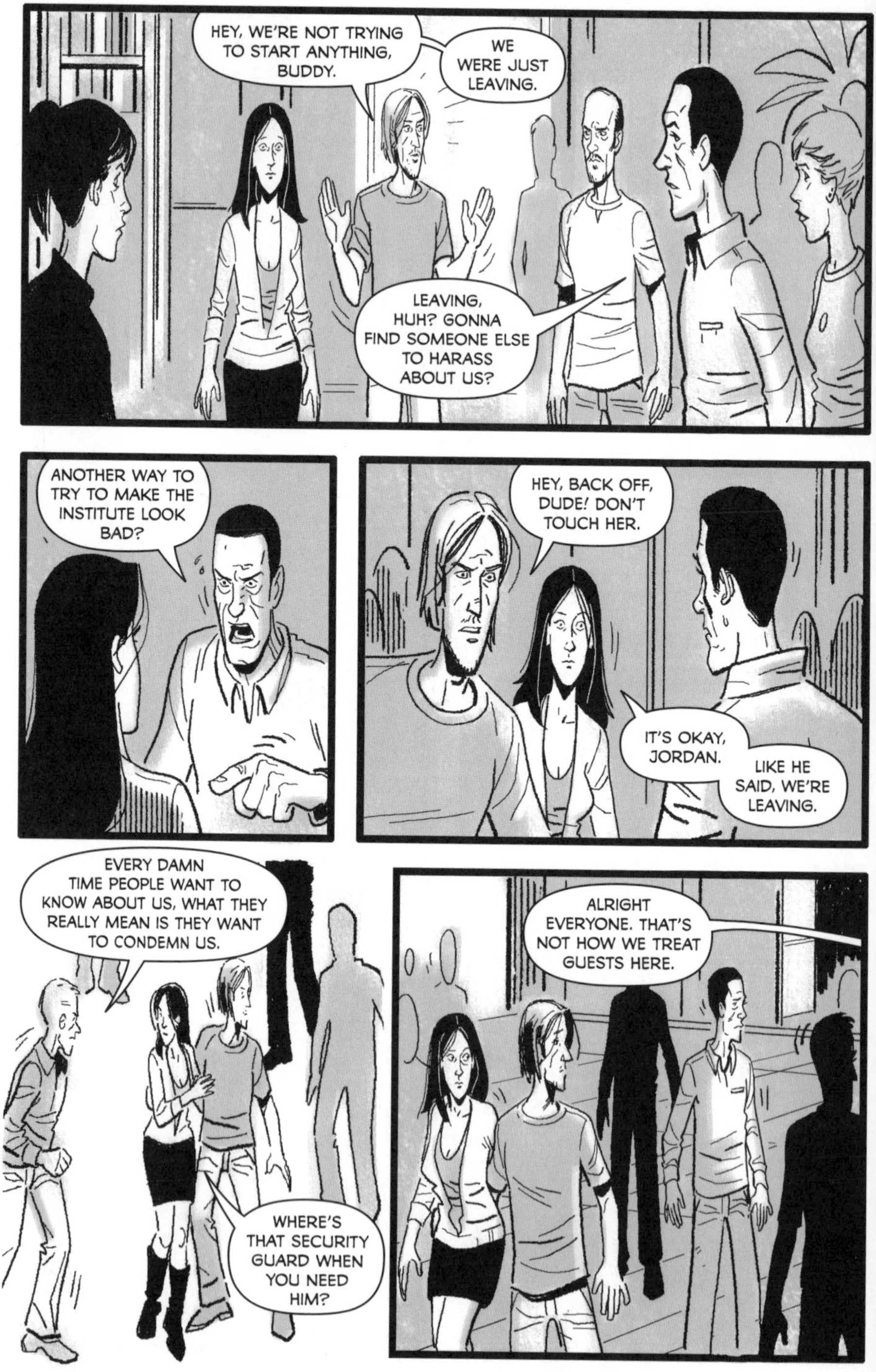
HEY, WE'RE NOT TRYING TO START ANYTHING, BUDDY.
WE WERE JUST LEAVING.
LEAVING, HUH? GONNA FIND SOMEONE ELSE TO HARASS ABOUT US?
ANOTHER WAY TO TRY TO MAKE THE INSTITUTE LOOK BAD?
HEY, BACK OFF, DUDE! DON'T TOUCH HER.
IT'S OKAY, JORDAN.
LIKE HE SAID, WE'RE LEAVING.
EVERY DAMN TIME PEOPLE WANT TO KNOW ABOUT US, WHAT THEY REALLY MEAN IS THEY WANT TO CONDEMN US.
WHERE'S THAT SECURITY GUARD WHEN YOU NEED HIM?
ALRIGHT EVERYONE. THAT'S NOT HOW WE TREAT GUESTS HERE.

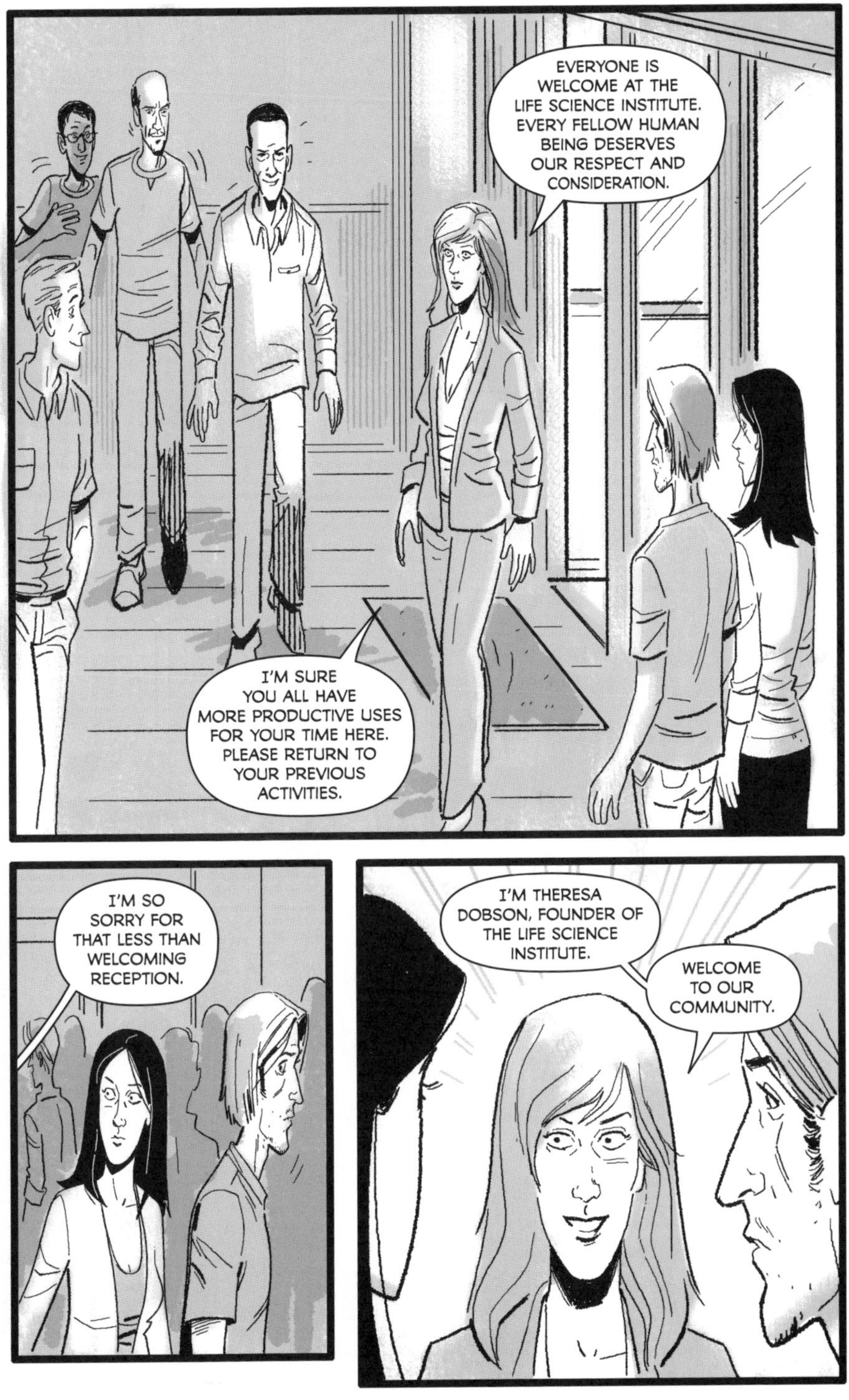
EVERYONE IS WELCOME AT THE LIFE SCIENCE INSTITUTE. EVERY FELLOW HUMAN BEING DESERVES OUR RESPECT AND CONSIDERATION.
I'M SURE YOU ALL HAVE MORE PRODUCTIVE USES FOR YOUR TIME HERE. PLEASE RETURN TO YOUR PREVIOUS ACTIVITIES.
I'M SO SORRY FOR THAT LESS THAN WELCOMING RECEPTION.
I'M THERESA DOBSON, FOUNDER OF THE LIFE SCIENCE INSTITUTE.
WELCOME TO OUR COMMUNITY.

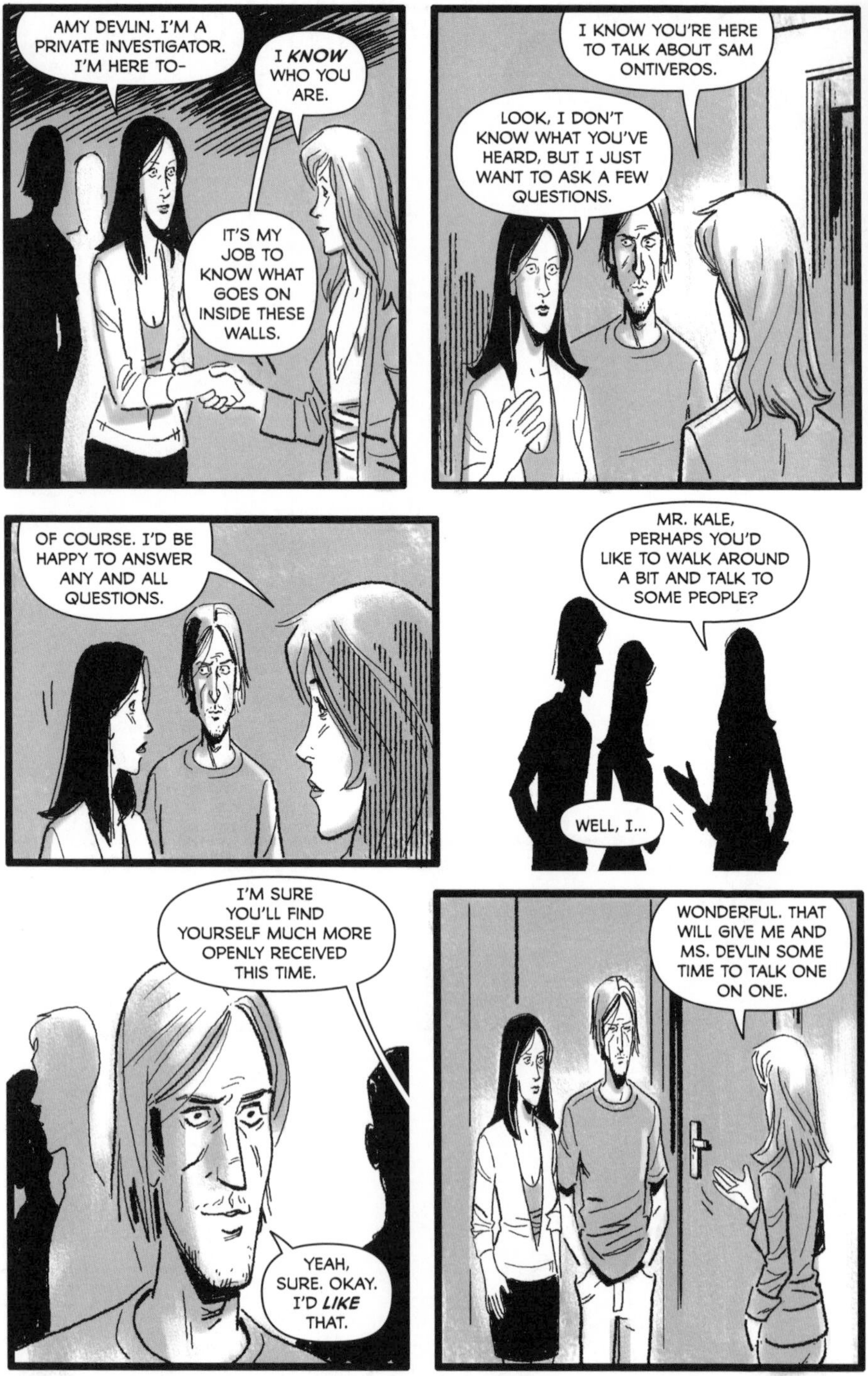
AMY DEVLIN. I'M A PRIVATE INVESTIGATOR. I'M HERE TO-
I ***KNOW*** WHO YOU ARE.
IT'S MY JOB TO KNOW WHAT GOES ON INSIDE THESE WALLS.
I KNOW YOU'RE HERE TO TALK ABOUT SAM ONTIVEROS.
LOOK, I DON'T KNOW WHAT YOU'VE HEARD, BUT I JUST WANT TO ASK A FEW QUESTIONS.
OF COURSE. I'D BE HAPPY TO ANSWER ANY AND ALL QUESTIONS.
MR. KALE, PERHAPS YOU'D LIKE TO WALK AROUND A BIT AND TALK TO SOME PEOPLE?
WELL, I...
I'M SURE YOU'LL FIND YOURSELF MUCH MORE OPENLY RECEIVED THIS TIME.
YEAH, SURE. OKAY. I'D ***LIKE*** THAT.
WONDERFUL. THAT WILL GIVE ME AND MS. DEVLIN SOME TIME TO TALK ONE ON ONE.

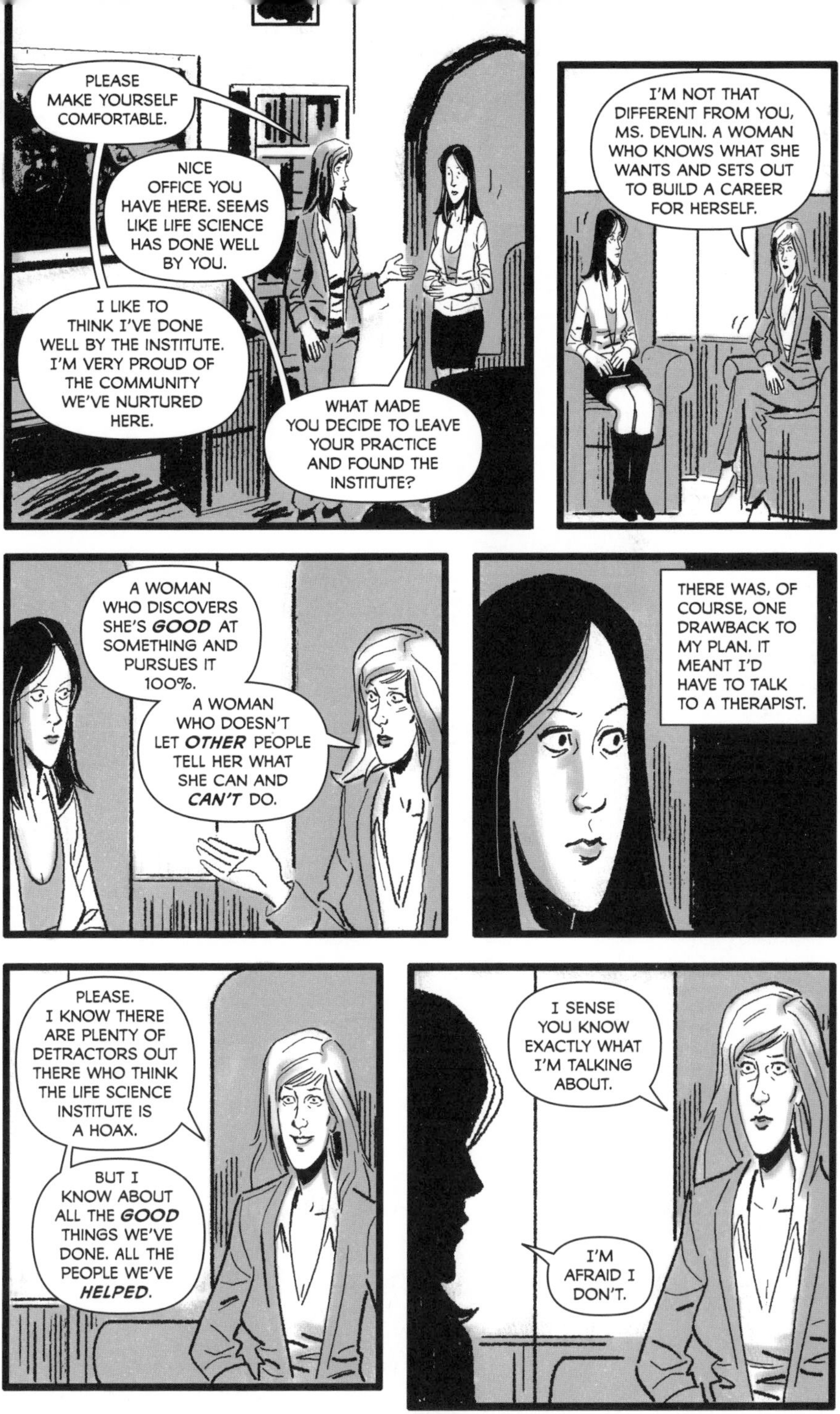
PLEASE MAKE YOURSELF COMFORTABLE.
NICE OFFICE YOU HAVE HERE. SEEMS LIKE LIFE SCIENCE HAS DONE WELL BY YOU.
I LIKE TO THINK I'VE DONE WELL BY THE INSTITUTE. I'M VERY PROUD OF THE COMMUNITY WE'VE NURTURED HERE.
WHAT MADE YOU DECIDE TO LEAVE YOUR PRACTICE AND FOUND THE INSTITUTE?
I'M NOT THAT DIFFERENT FROM YOU, MS. DEVLIN. A WOMAN WHO KNOWS WHAT SHE WANTS AND SETS OUT TO BUILD A CAREER FOR HERSELF.
A WOMAN WHO DISCOVERS SHE'S ***GOOD*** AT SOMETHING AND PURSUES IT 100%.
A WOMAN WHO DOESN'T LET ***OTHER*** PEOPLE TELL HER WHAT SHE CAN AND ***CAN'T*** DO.
THERE WAS, OF COURSE, ONE DRAWBACK TO MY PLAN. IT MEANT I'D HAVE TO TALK TO A THERAPIST.
PLEASE. I KNOW THERE ARE PLENTY OF DETRACTORS OUT THERE WHO THINK THE LIFE SCIENCE INSTITUTE IS A HOAX.
BUT I KNOW ABOUT ALL THE ***GOOD*** THINGS WE'VE DONE. ALL THE PEOPLE WE'VE ***HELPED***.
I SENSE YOU KNOW EXACTLY WHAT I'M TALKING ABOUT.
I'M AFRAID I DON'T.

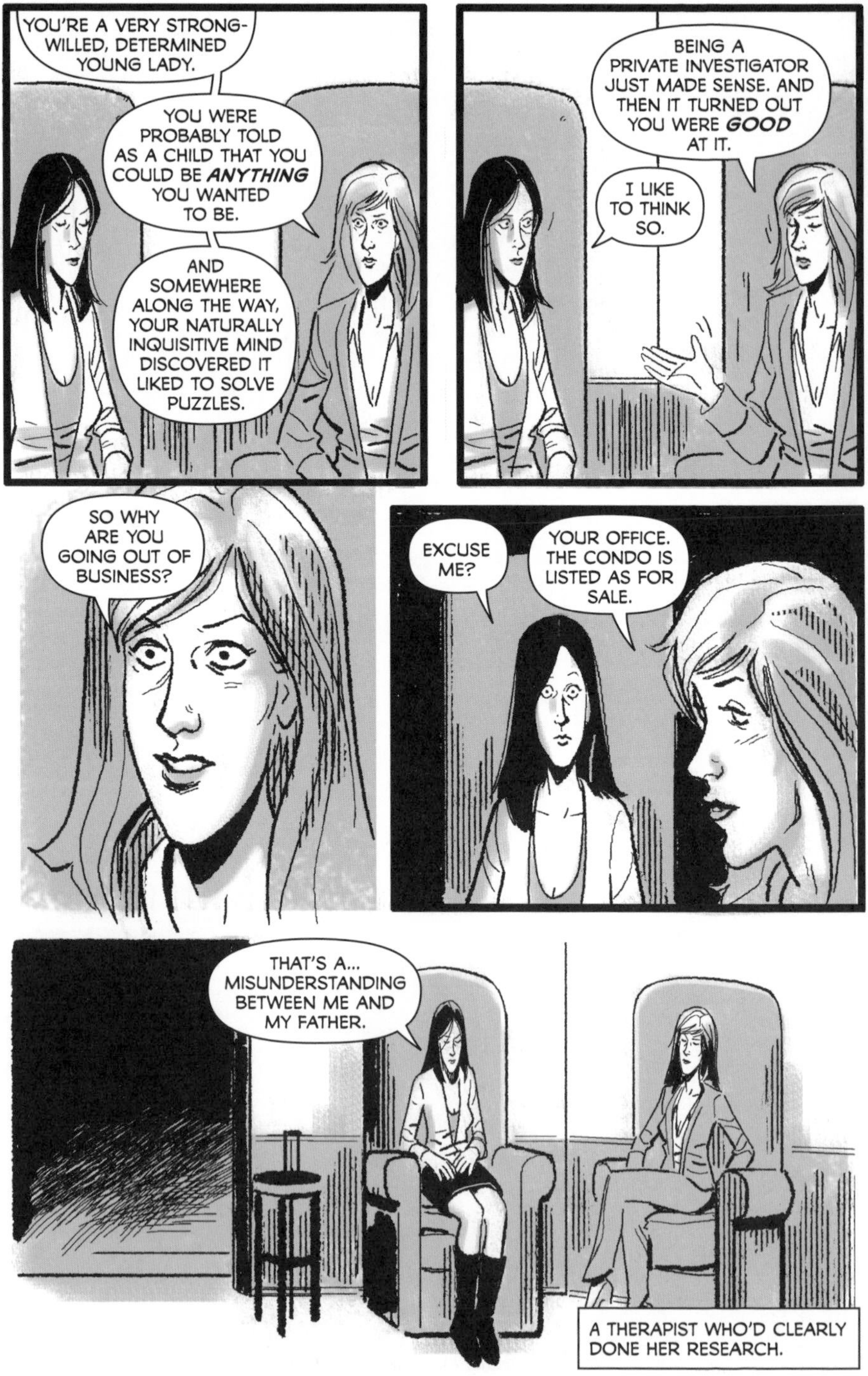
YOU'RE A VERY STRONG-WILLED, DETERMINED YOUNG LADY.
YOU WERE PROBABLY TOLD AS A CHILD THAT YOU COULD BE *ANYTHING* YOU WANTED TO BE.
AND SOMEWHERE ALONG THE WAY, YOUR NATURALLY INQUISITIVE MIND DISCOVERED IT LIKED TO SOLVE PUZZLES.
BEING A PRIVATE INVESTIGATOR JUST MADE SENSE. AND THEN IT TURNED OUT YOU WERE *GOOD* AT IT.
I LIKE TO THINK SO.
SO WHY ARE YOU GOING OUT OF BUSINESS?
EXCUSE ME?
YOUR OFFICE. THE CONDO IS LISTED AS FOR SALE.
THAT'S A... MISUNDERSTANDING BETWEEN ME AND MY FATHER.
A THERAPIST WHO'D CLEARLY DONE HER RESEARCH.

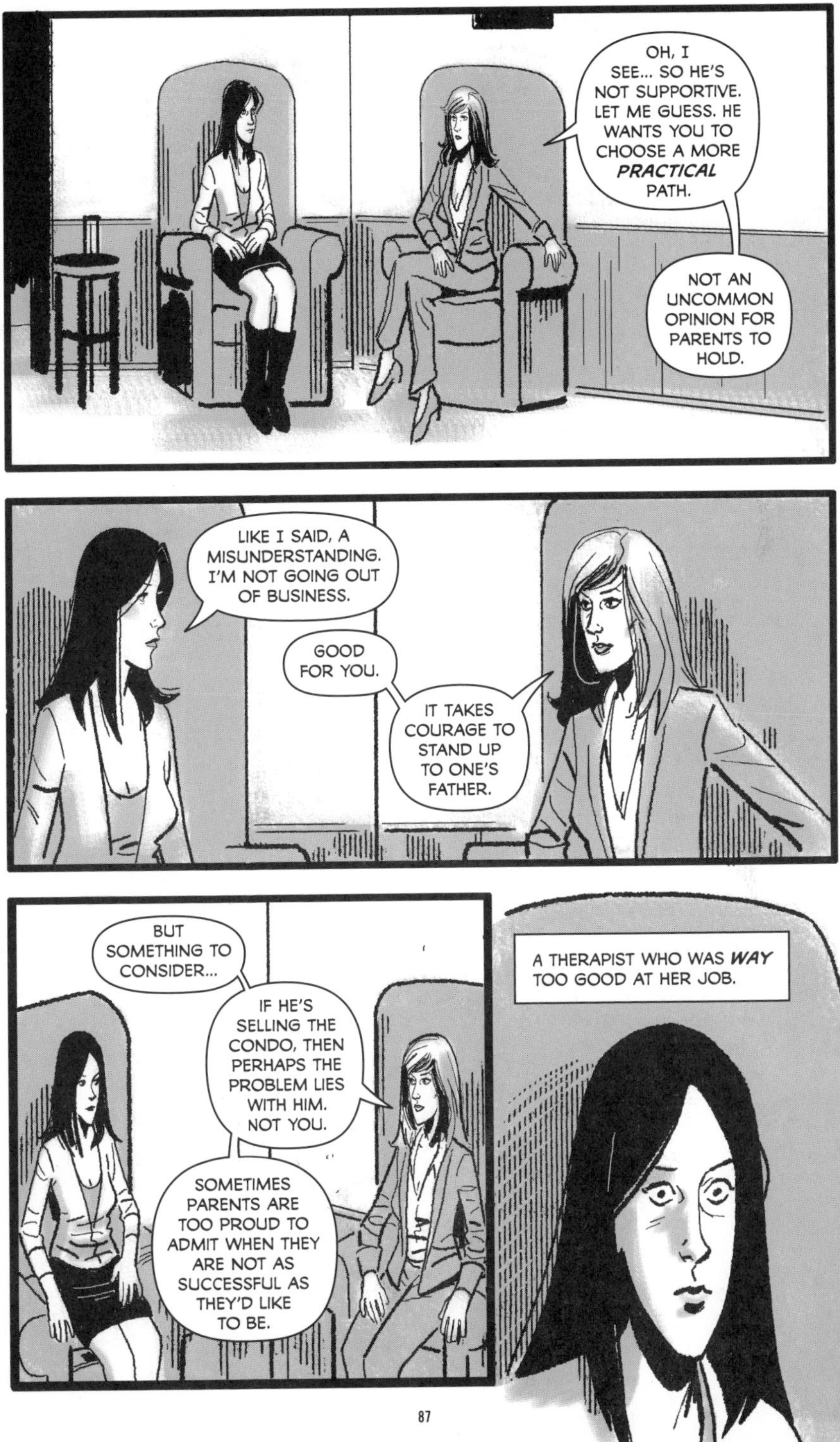
OH, I SEE... SO HE'S NOT SUPPORTIVE. LET ME GUESS. HE WANTS YOU TO CHOOSE A MORE ***PRACTICAL*** PATH.
NOT AN UNCOMMON OPINION FOR PARENTS TO HOLD.
LIKE I SAID, A MISUNDERSTANDING. I'M NOT GOING OUT OF BUSINESS.
GOOD FOR YOU.
IT TAKES COURAGE TO STAND UP TO ONE'S FATHER.
BUT SOMETHING TO CONSIDER...
IF HE'S SELLING THE CONDO, THEN PERHAPS THE PROBLEM LIES WITH HIM. NOT YOU.
SOMETIMES PARENTS ARE TOO PROUD TO ADMIT WHEN THEY ARE NOT AS SUCCESSFUL AS THEY'D LIKE TO BE.
A THERAPIST WHO WAS ***WAY*** TOO GOOD AT HER JOB.

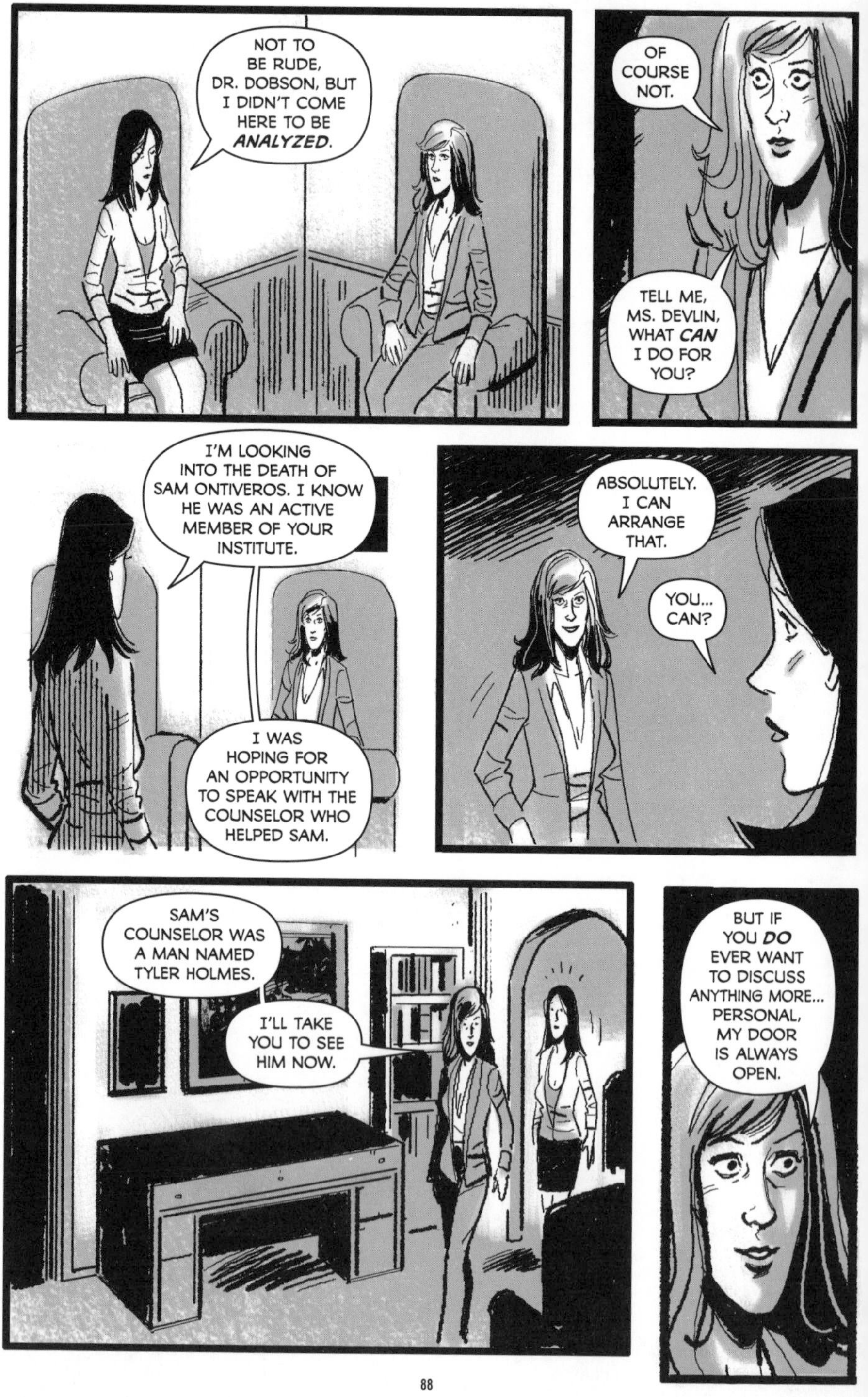

NOT TO BE RUDE, DR. DOBSON, BUT I DIDN'T COME HERE TO BE *ANALYZED*.
OF COURSE NOT.
TELL ME, MS. DEVLIN, WHAT *CAN* I DO FOR YOU?
I'M LOOKING INTO THE DEATH OF SAM ONTIVEROS. I KNOW HE WAS AN ACTIVE MEMBER OF YOUR INSTITUTE.
I WAS HOPING FOR AN OPPORTUNITY TO SPEAK WITH THE COUNSELOR WHO HELPED SAM.
ABSOLUTELY. I CAN ARRANGE THAT.
YOU... CAN?
SAM'S COUNSELOR WAS A MAN NAMED TYLER HOLMES.
I'LL TAKE YOU TO SEE HIM NOW.
BUT IF YOU *DO* EVER WANT TO DISCUSS ANYTHING MORE... PERSONAL, MY DOOR IS ALWAYS OPEN.

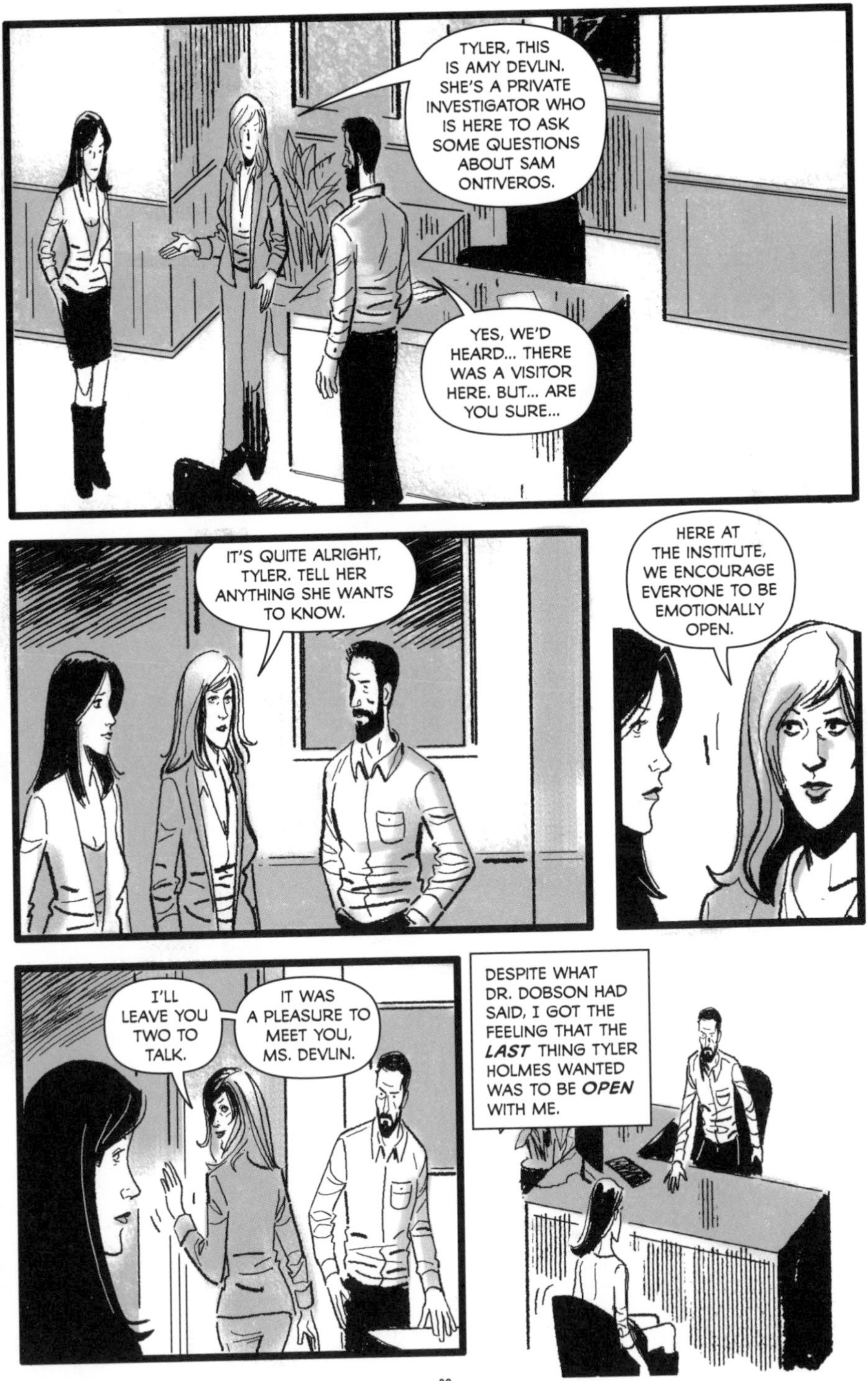

TYLER, THIS IS AMY DEVLIN. SHE'S A PRIVATE INVESTIGATOR WHO IS HERE TO ASK SOME QUESTIONS ABOUT SAM ONTIVEROS.
YES, WE'D HEARD... THERE WAS A VISITOR HERE. BUT... ARE YOU SURE...
IT'S QUITE ALRIGHT, TYLER. TELL HER ANYTHING SHE WANTS TO KNOW.
HERE AT THE INSTITUTE, WE ENCOURAGE EVERYONE TO BE EMOTIONALLY OPEN.
I'LL LEAVE YOU TWO TO TALK.
IT WAS A PLEASURE TO MEET YOU, MS. DEVLIN.
DESPITE WHAT DR. DOBSON HAD SAID, I GOT THE FEELING THAT THE ***LAST*** THING TYLER HOLMES WANTED WAS TO BE ***OPEN*** WITH ME.

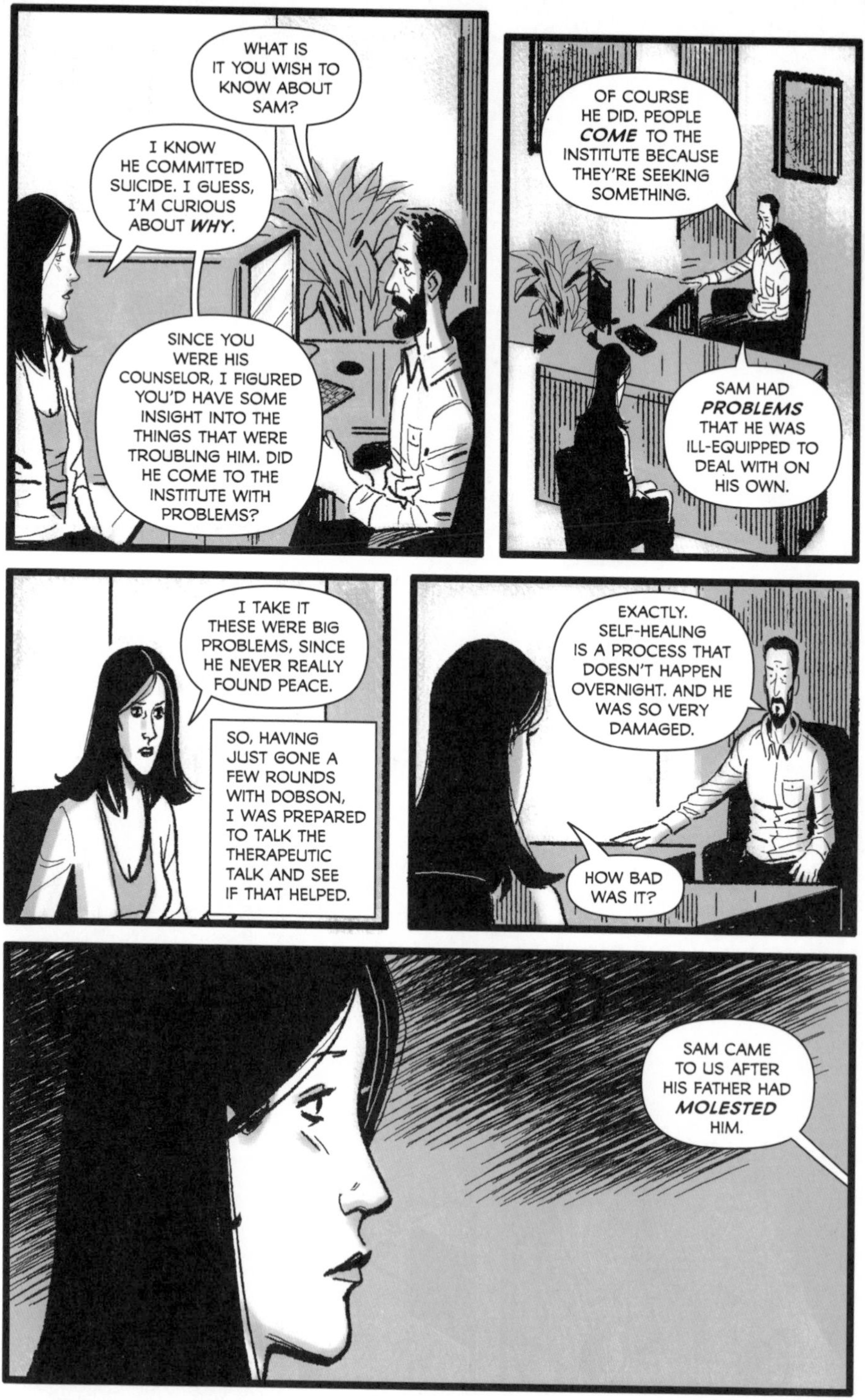
WHAT IS IT YOU WISH TO KNOW ABOUT SAM?
I KNOW HE COMMITTED SUICIDE. I GUESS, I'M CURIOUS ABOUT *WHY*.
SINCE YOU WERE HIS COUNSELOR, I FIGURED YOU'D HAVE SOME INSIGHT INTO THE THINGS THAT WERE TROUBLING HIM. DID HE COME TO THE INSTITUTE WITH PROBLEMS?
OF COURSE HE DID. PEOPLE *COME* TO THE INSTITUTE BECAUSE THEY'RE SEEKING SOMETHING.
SAM HAD *PROBLEMS* THAT HE WAS ILL-EQUIPPED TO DEAL WITH ON HIS OWN.
I TAKE IT THESE WERE BIG PROBLEMS, SINCE HE NEVER REALLY FOUND PEACE.
SO, HAVING JUST GONE A FEW ROUNDS WITH DOBSON, I WAS PREPARED TO TALK THE THERAPEUTIC TALK AND SEE IF THAT HELPED.
EXACTLY. SELF-HEALING IS A PROCESS THAT DOESN'T HAPPEN OVERNIGHT. AND HE WAS SO VERY DAMAGED.
HOW BAD WAS IT?
SAM CAME TO US AFTER HIS FATHER HAD *MOLESTED* HIM.

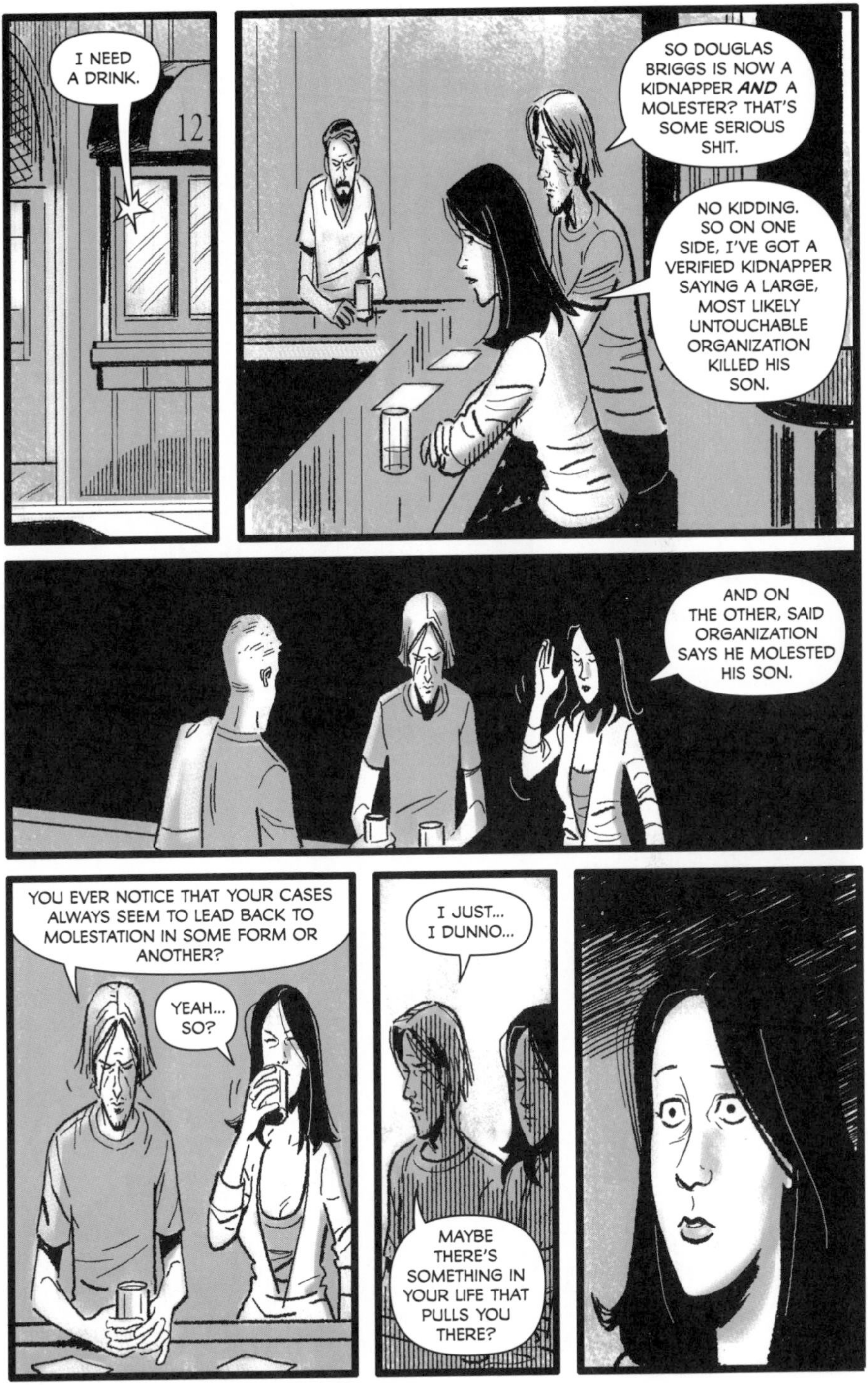

I NEED A DRINK.
121
SO DOUGLAS BRIGGS IS NOW A KIDNAPPER *AND* A MOLESTER? THAT'S SOME SERIOUS SHIT.
NO KIDDING. SO ON ONE SIDE, I'VE GOT A VERIFIED KIDNAPPER SAYING A LARGE, MOST LIKELY UNTOUCHABLE ORGANIZATION KILLED HIS SON.
AND ON THE OTHER, SAID ORGANIZATION SAYS HE MOLESTED HIS SON.
YOU EVER NOTICE THAT YOUR CASES ALWAYS SEEM TO LEAD BACK TO MOLESTATION IN SOME FORM OR ANOTHER?
YEAH... SO?
I JUST... I DUNNO...
MAYBE THERE'S SOMETHING IN YOUR LIFE THAT PULLS YOU THERE?

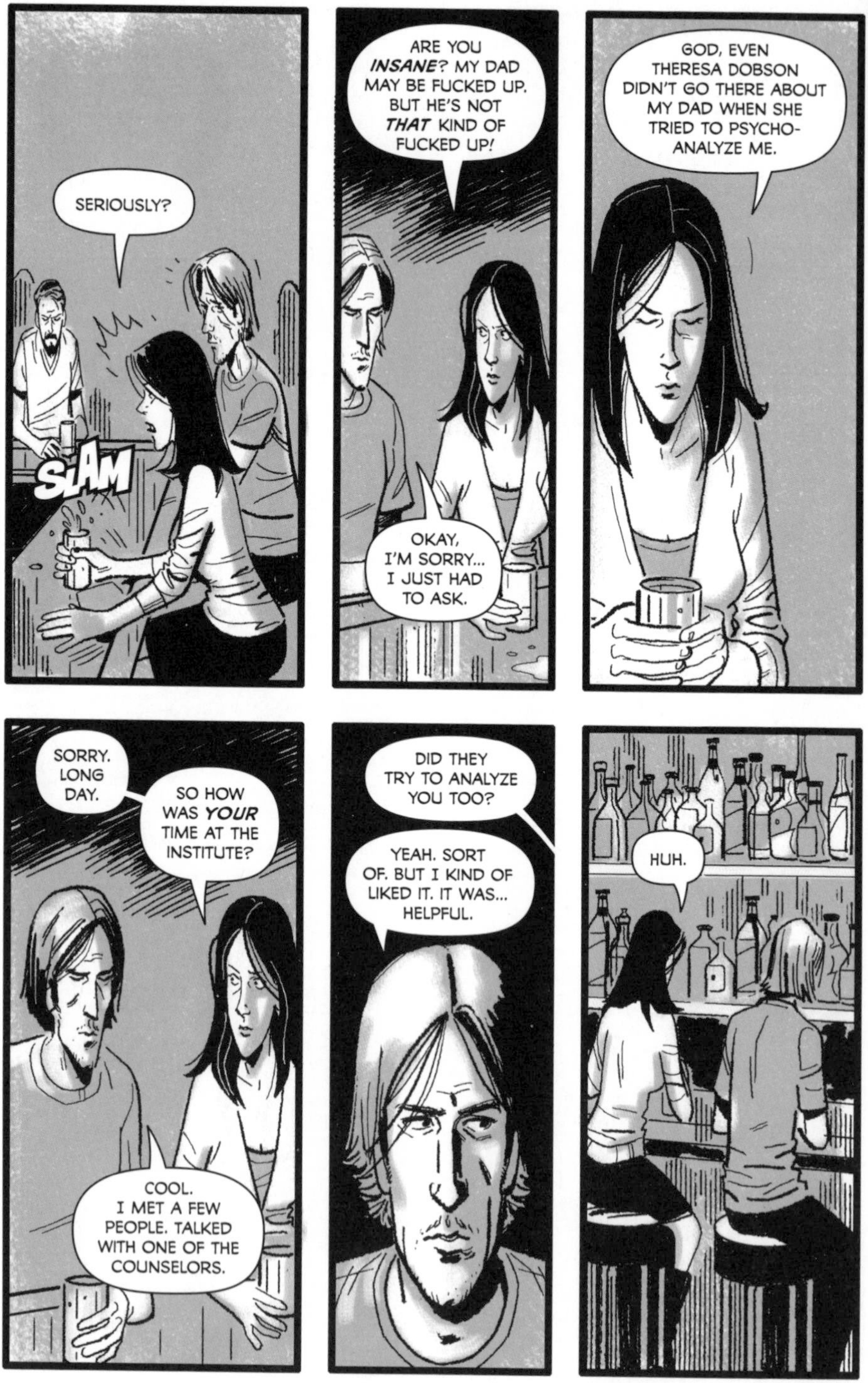
SERIOUSLY?
SLAM
ARE YOU INSANE? MY DAD MAY BE FUCKED UP. BUT HE'S NOT THAT KIND OF FUCKED UP!
OKAY, I'M SORRY... I JUST HAD TO ASK.
GOD, EVEN THERESA DOBSON DIDN'T GO THERE ABOUT MY DAD WHEN SHE TRIED TO PSYCHO-ANALYZE ME.
SORRY. LONG DAY.
SO HOW WAS YOUR TIME AT THE INSTITUTE?
COOL. I MET A FEW PEOPLE. TALKED WITH ONE OF THE COUNSELORS.
DID THEY TRY TO ANALYZE YOU TOO?
YEAH. SORT OF. BUT I KIND OF LIKED IT. IT WAS... HELPFUL.
HUH.

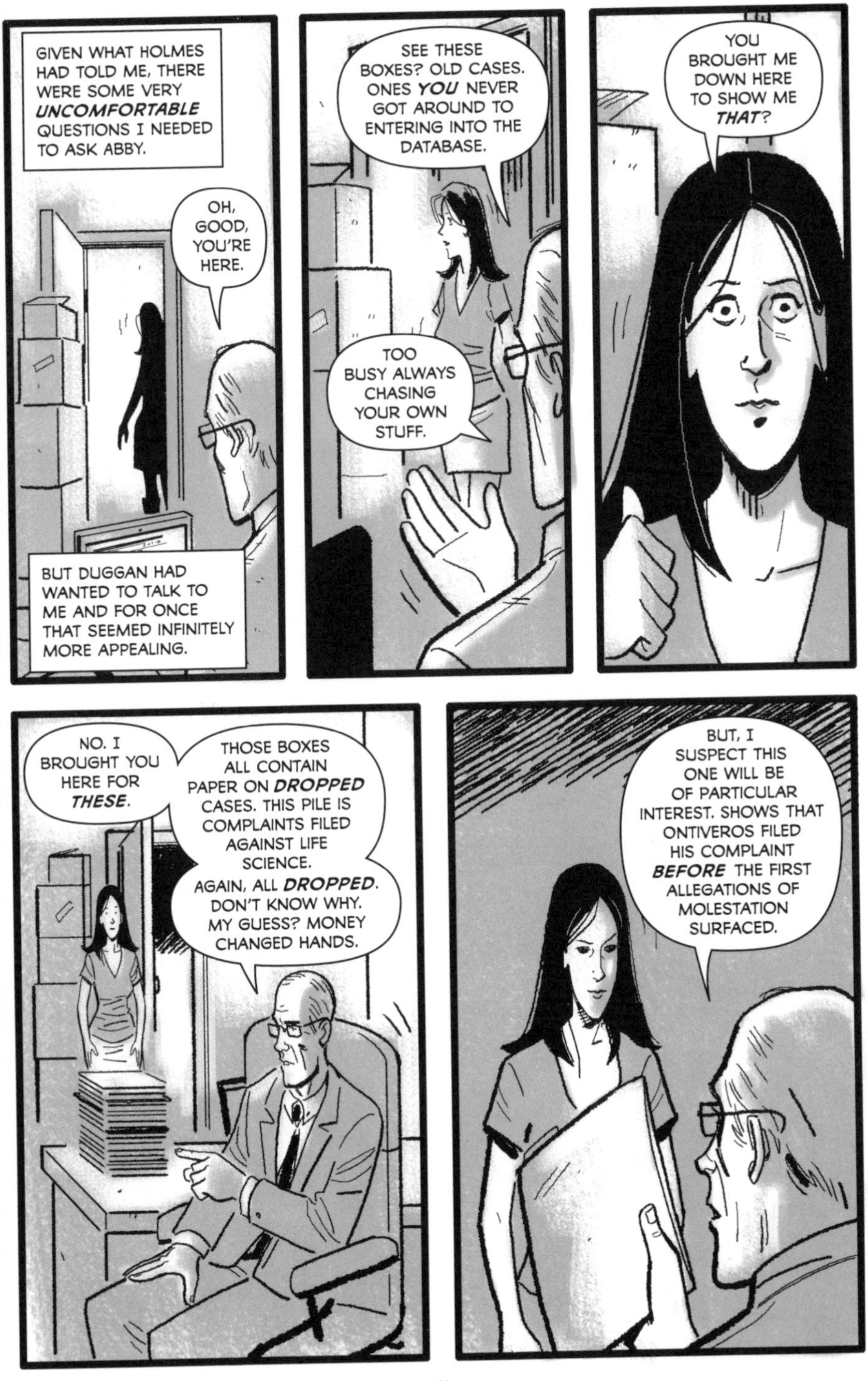
GIVEN WHAT HOLMES HAD TOLD ME, THERE WERE SOME VERY UNCOMFORTABLE QUESTIONS I NEEDED TO ASK ABBY.
OH, GOOD, YOU'RE HERE.
BUT DUGGAN HAD WANTED TO TALK TO ME AND FOR ONCE THAT SEEMED INFINITELY MORE APPEALING.
SEE THESE BOXES? OLD CASES. ONES YOU NEVER GOT AROUND TO ENTERING INTO THE DATABASE.
TOO BUSY ALWAYS CHASING YOUR OWN STUFF.
YOU BROUGHT ME DOWN HERE TO SHOW ME THAT?
NO. I BROUGHT YOU HERE FOR THESE.
THOSE BOXES ALL CONTAIN PAPER ON DROPPED CASES. THIS PILE IS COMPLAINTS FILED AGAINST LIFE SCIENCE.
AGAIN, ALL DROPPED. DON'T KNOW WHY. MY GUESS? MONEY CHANGED HANDS.
BUT, I SUSPECT THIS ONE WILL BE OF PARTICULAR INTEREST. SHOWS THAT ONTIVEROS FILED HIS COMPLAINT BEFORE THE FIRST ALLEGATIONS OF MOLESTATION SURFACED.

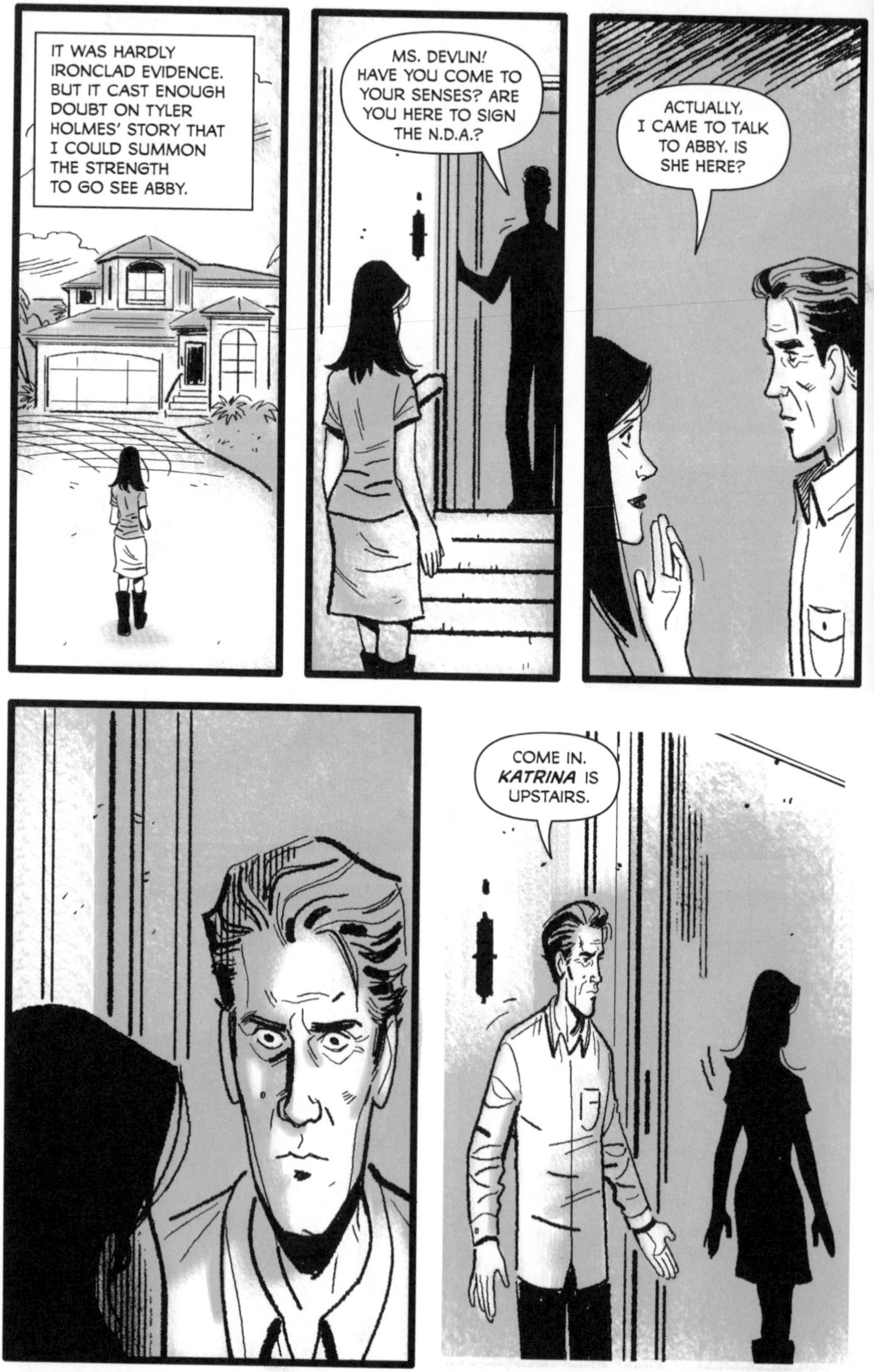
IT WAS HARDLY IRONCLAD EVIDENCE. BUT IT CAST ENOUGH DOUBT ON TYLER HOLMES' STORY THAT I COULD SUMMON THE STRENGTH TO GO SEE ABBY.
MS. DEVLIN! HAVE YOU COME TO YOUR SENSES? ARE YOU HERE TO SIGN THE N.D.A.?
ACTUALLY, I CAME TO TALK TO ABBY. IS SHE HERE?
COME IN. *KATRINA* IS UPSTAIRS.

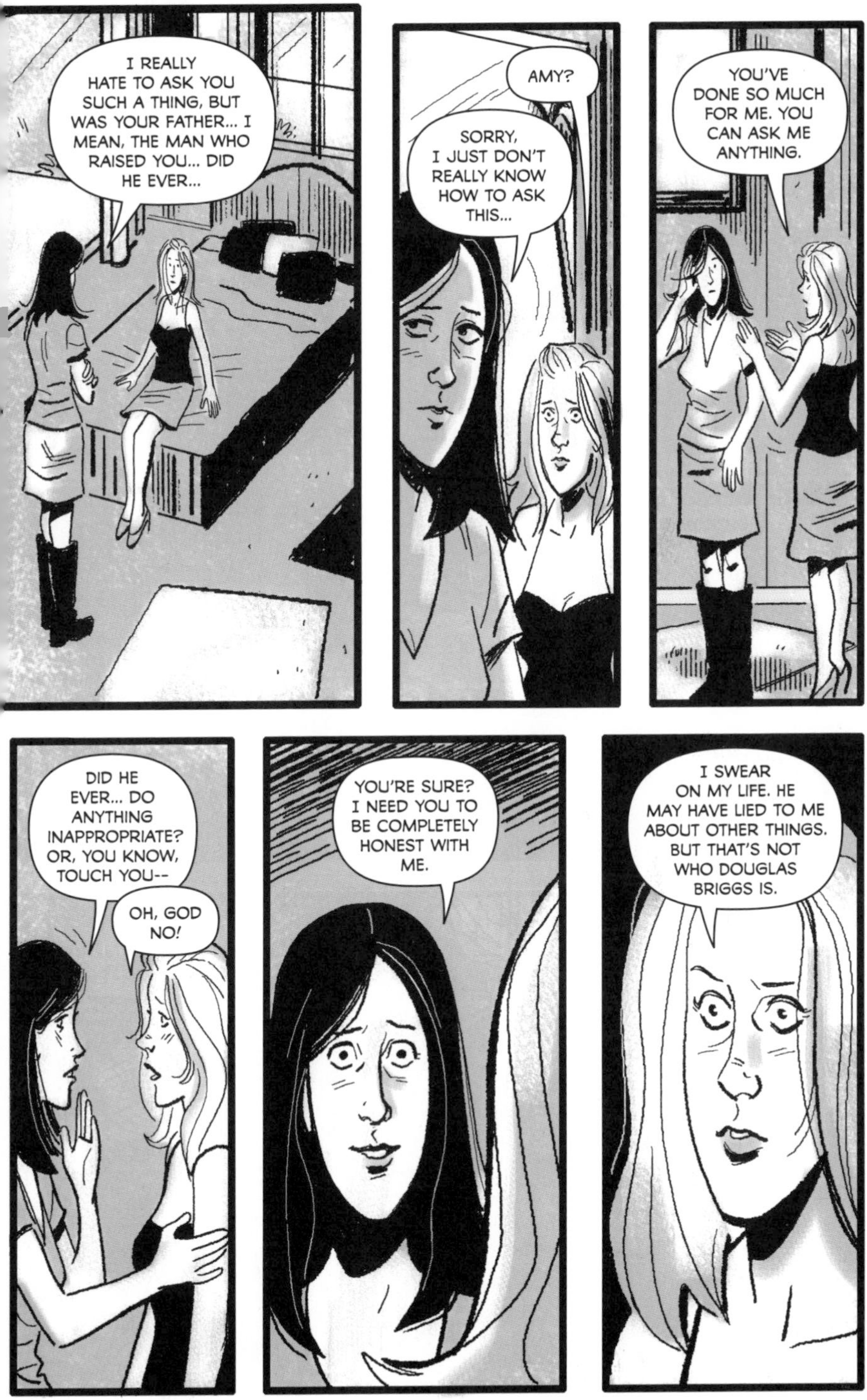
I REALLY HATE TO ASK YOU SUCH A THING, BUT WAS YOUR FATHER... I MEAN, THE MAN WHO RAISED YOU... DID HE EVER...
AMY?
SORRY, I JUST DON'T REALLY KNOW HOW TO ASK THIS...
YOU'VE DONE SO MUCH FOR ME. YOU CAN ASK ME ANYTHING.
DID HE EVER... DO ANYTHING INAPPROPRIATE? OR, YOU KNOW, TOUCH YOU--
OH, GOD NO!
YOU'RE SURE? I NEED YOU TO BE COMPLETELY HONEST WITH ME.
I SWEAR ON MY LIFE. HE MAY HAVE LIED TO ME ABOUT OTHER THINGS. BUT THAT'S NOT WHO DOUGLAS BRIGGS IS.

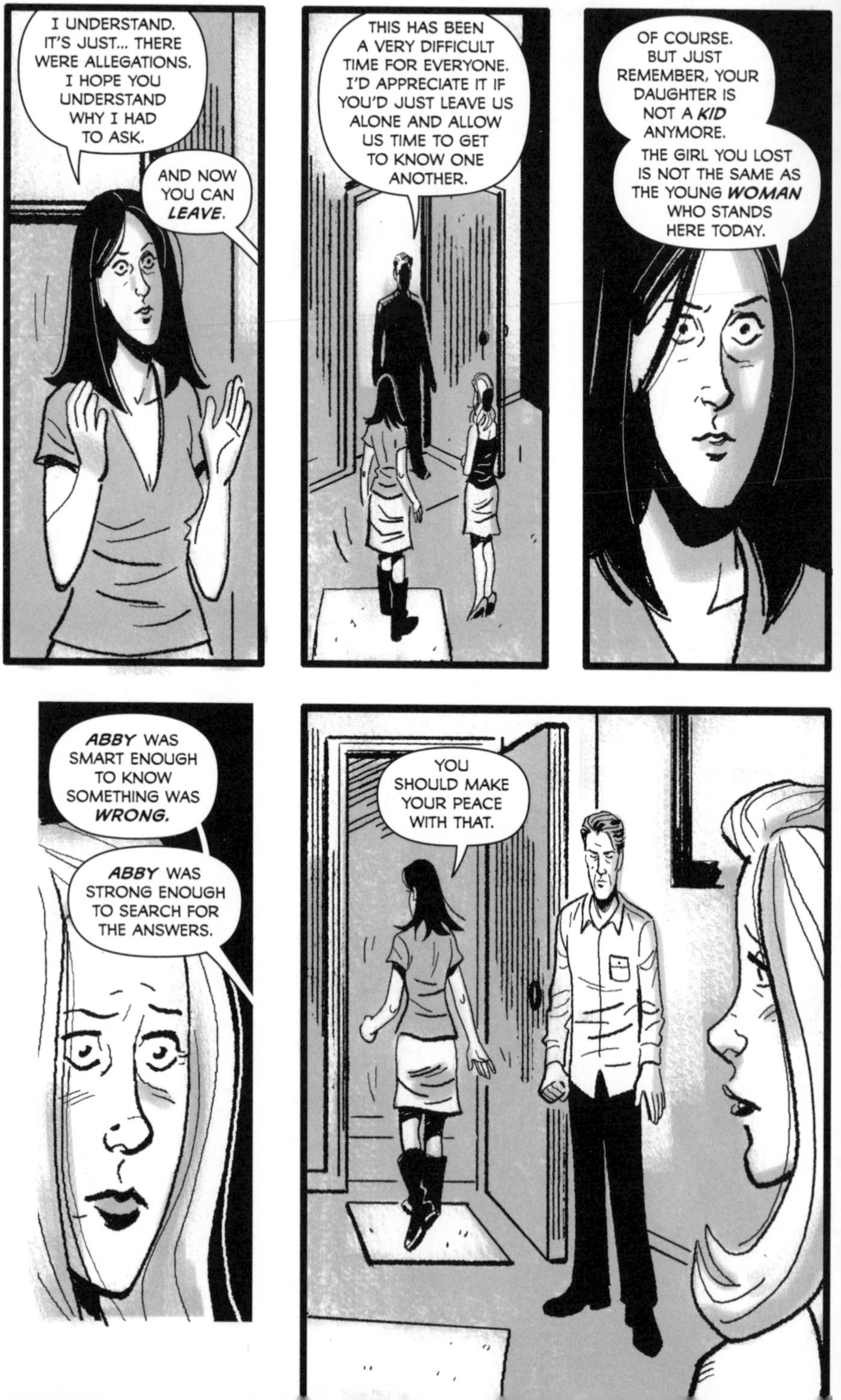
I UNDERSTAND. IT'S JUST... THERE WERE ALLEGATIONS. I HOPE YOU UNDERSTAND WHY I HAD TO ASK.
AND NOW YOU CAN *LEAVE*.
THIS HAS BEEN A VERY DIFFICULT TIME FOR EVERYONE. I'D APPRECIATE IT IF YOU'D JUST LEAVE US ALONE AND ALLOW US TIME TO GET TO KNOW ONE ANOTHER.
OF COURSE. BUT JUST REMEMBER, YOUR DAUGHTER IS NOT A *KID* ANYMORE.
THE GIRL YOU LOST IS NOT THE SAME AS THE YOUNG *WOMAN* WHO STANDS HERE TODAY.
ABBY WAS SMART ENOUGH TO KNOW SOMETHING WAS *WRONG.*
ABBY WAS STRONG ENOUGH TO SEARCH FOR THE ANSWERS.
YOU SHOULD MAKE YOUR PEACE WITH THAT.

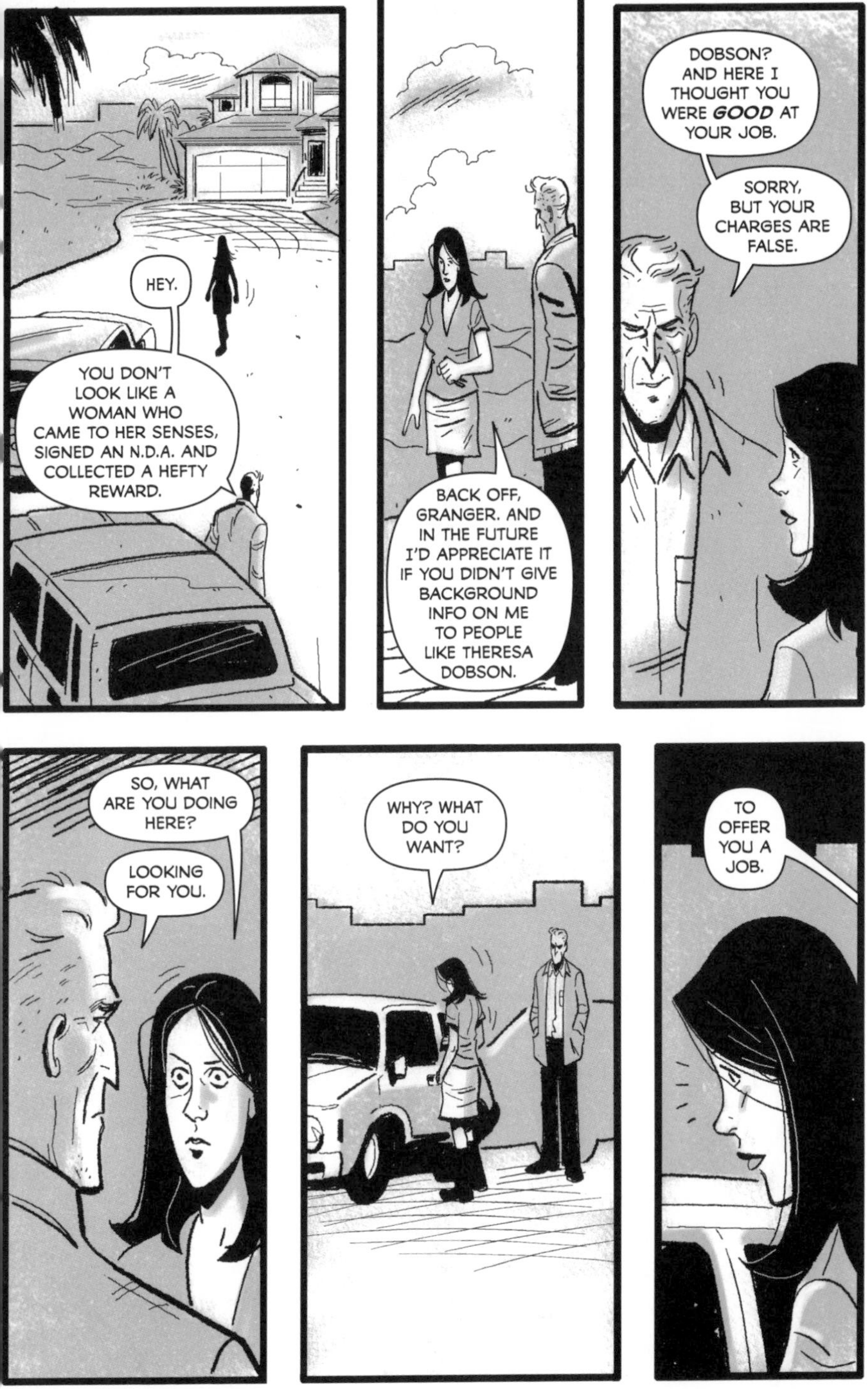
HEY.
YOU DON'T LOOK LIKE A WOMAN WHO CAME TO HER SENSES, SIGNED AN N.D.A. AND COLLECTED A HEFTY REWARD.
BACK OFF, GRANGER. AND IN THE FUTURE I'D APPRECIATE IT IF YOU DIDN'T GIVE BACKGROUND INFO ON ME TO PEOPLE LIKE THERESA DOBSON.
DOBSON? AND HERE I THOUGHT YOU WERE *GOOD* AT YOUR JOB.
SORRY, BUT YOUR CHARGES ARE FALSE.
SO, WHAT ARE YOU DOING HERE?
LOOKING FOR YOU.
WHY? WHAT DO YOU WANT?
TO OFFER YOU A JOB.

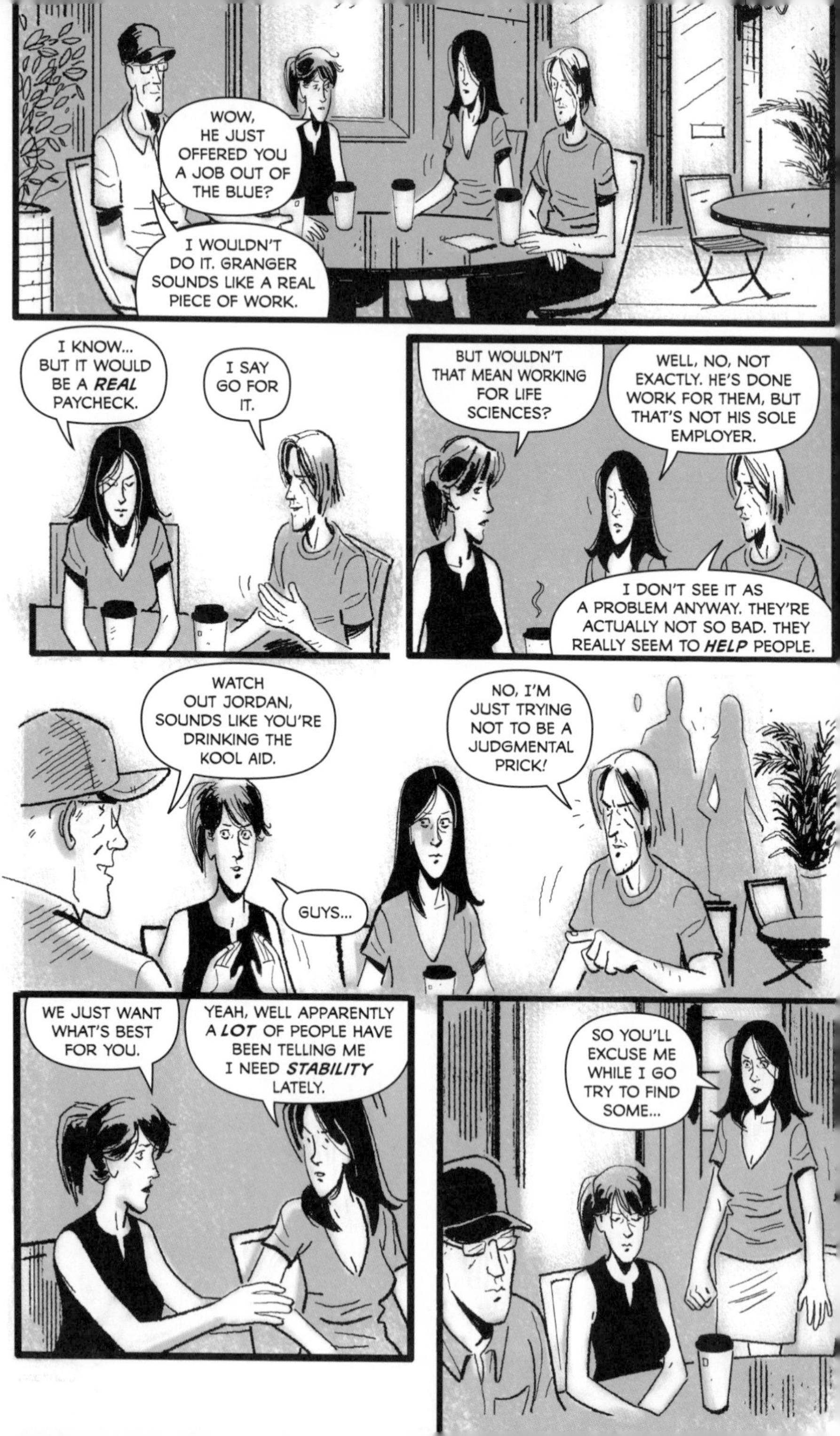
WOW, HE JUST OFFERED YOU A JOB OUT OF THE BLUE?
I WOULDN'T DO IT. GRANGER SOUNDS LIKE A REAL PIECE OF WORK.
I KNOW... BUT IT WOULD BE A *REAL* PAYCHECK.
I SAY GO FOR IT.
BUT WOULDN'T THAT MEAN WORKING FOR LIFE SCIENCES?
WELL, NO, NOT EXACTLY. HE'S DONE WORK FOR THEM, BUT THAT'S NOT HIS SOLE EMPLOYER.
I DON'T SEE IT AS A PROBLEM ANYWAY. THEY'RE ACTUALLY NOT SO BAD. THEY REALLY SEEM TO *HELP* PEOPLE.
WATCH OUT JORDAN, SOUNDS LIKE YOU'RE DRINKING THE KOOL AID.
NO, I'M JUST TRYING NOT TO BE A JUDGMENTAL PRICK!
GUYS...
WE JUST WANT WHAT'S BEST FOR YOU.
YEAH, WELL APPARENTLY A *LOT* OF PEOPLE HAVE BEEN TELLING ME I NEED *STABILITY* LATELY.
SO YOU'LL EXCUSE ME WHILE I GO TRY TO FIND SOME...

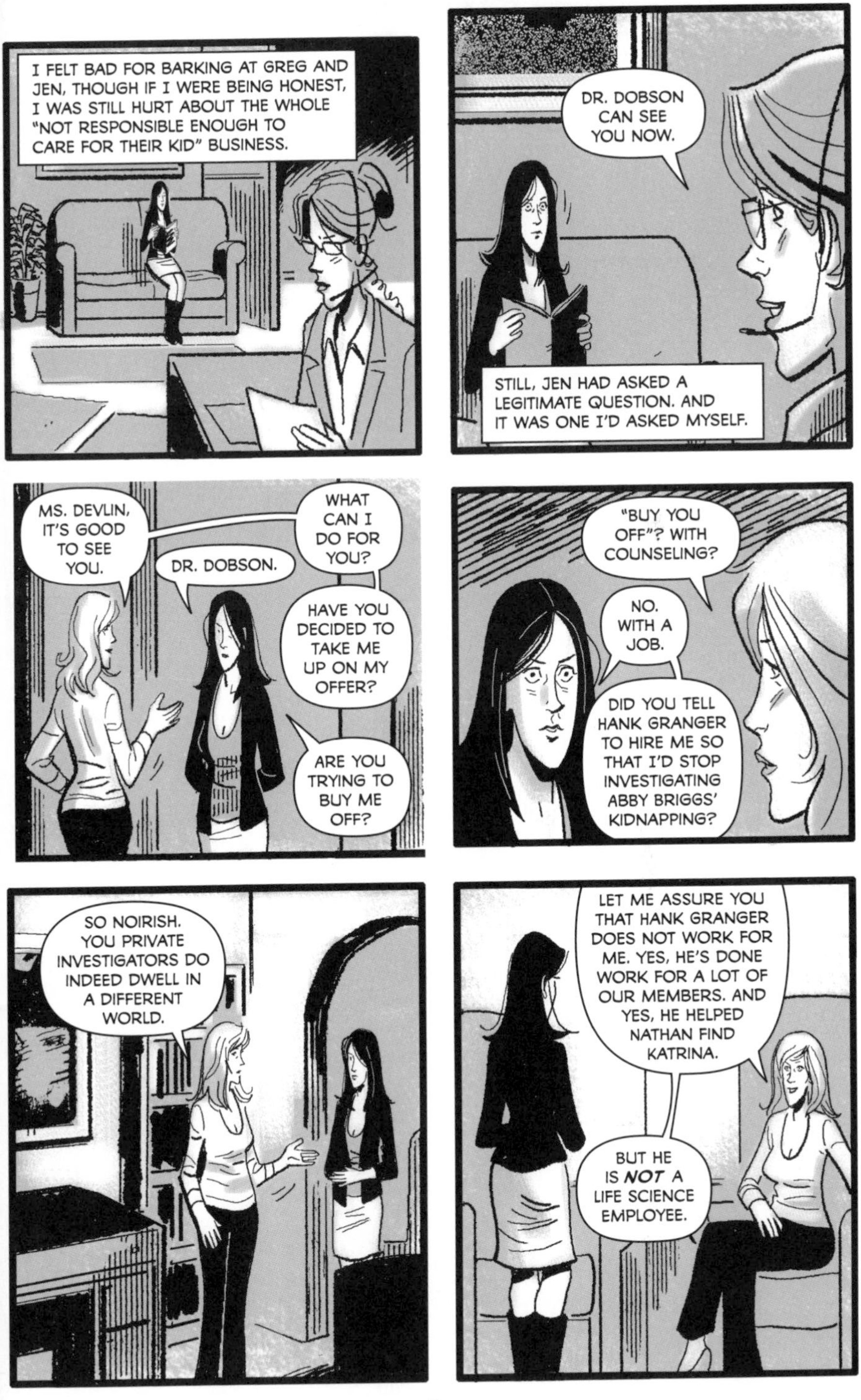
I FELT BAD FOR BARKING AT GREG AND JEN, THOUGH IF I WERE BEING HONEST, I WAS STILL HURT ABOUT THE WHOLE "NOT RESPONSIBLE ENOUGH TO CARE FOR THEIR KID" BUSINESS.
DR. DOBSON CAN SEE YOU NOW.
STILL, JEN HAD ASKED A LEGITIMATE QUESTION. AND IT WAS ONE I'D ASKED MYSELF.
MS. DEVLIN, IT'S GOOD TO SEE YOU.
DR. DOBSON.
WHAT CAN I DO FOR YOU?
HAVE YOU DECIDED TO TAKE ME UP ON MY OFFER?
ARE YOU TRYING TO BUY ME OFF?
"BUY YOU OFF"? WITH COUNSELING?
NO. WITH A JOB.
DID YOU TELL HANK GRANGER TO HIRE ME SO THAT I'D STOP INVESTIGATING ABBY BRIGGS' KIDNAPPING?
SO NOIRISH. YOU PRIVATE INVESTIGATORS DO INDEED DWELL IN A DIFFERENT WORLD.
LET ME ASSURE YOU THAT HANK GRANGER DOES NOT WORK FOR ME. YES, HE'S DONE WORK FOR A LOT OF OUR MEMBERS. AND YES, HE HELPED NATHAN FIND KATRINA.
BUT HE IS ***NOT*** A LIFE SCIENCE EMPLOYEE.

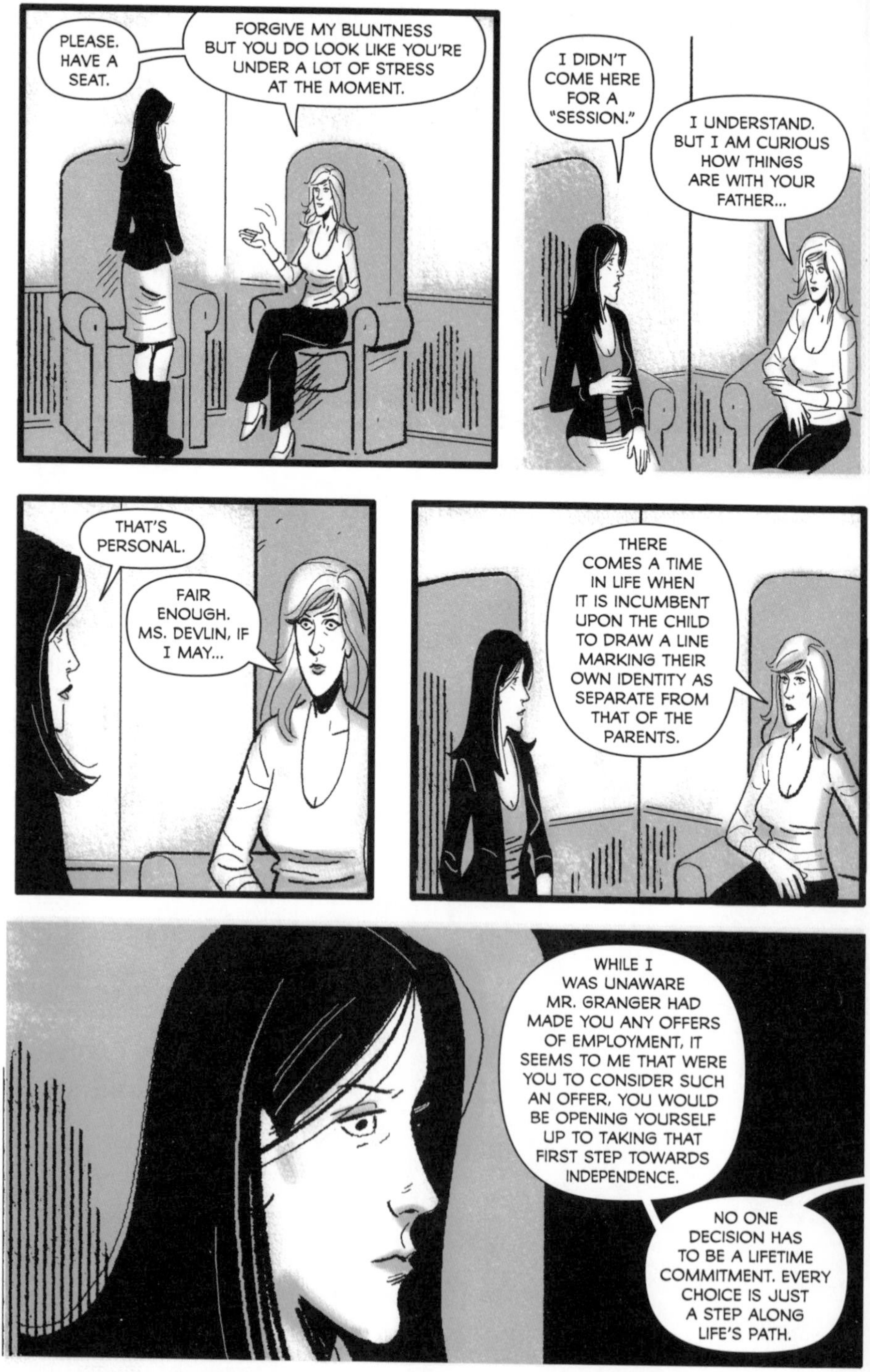
PLEASE. HAVE A SEAT.
FORGIVE MY BLUNTNESS BUT YOU DO LOOK LIKE YOU'RE UNDER A LOT OF STRESS AT THE MOMENT.
I DIDN'T COME HERE FOR A "SESSION."
I UNDERSTAND. BUT I AM CURIOUS HOW THINGS ARE WITH YOUR FATHER...
THAT'S PERSONAL.
FAIR ENOUGH. MS. DEVLIN, IF I MAY...
THERE COMES A TIME IN LIFE WHEN IT IS INCUMBENT UPON THE CHILD TO DRAW A LINE MARKING THEIR OWN IDENTITY AS SEPARATE FROM THAT OF THE PARENTS.
WHILE I WAS UNAWARE MR. GRANGER HAD MADE YOU ANY OFFERS OF EMPLOYMENT, IT SEEMS TO ME THAT WERE YOU TO CONSIDER SUCH AN OFFER, YOU WOULD BE OPENING YOURSELF UP TO TAKING THAT FIRST STEP TOWARDS INDEPENDENCE.
NO ONE DECISION HAS TO BE A LIFETIME COMMITMENT. EVERY CHOICE IS JUST A STEP ALONG LIFE'S PATH.

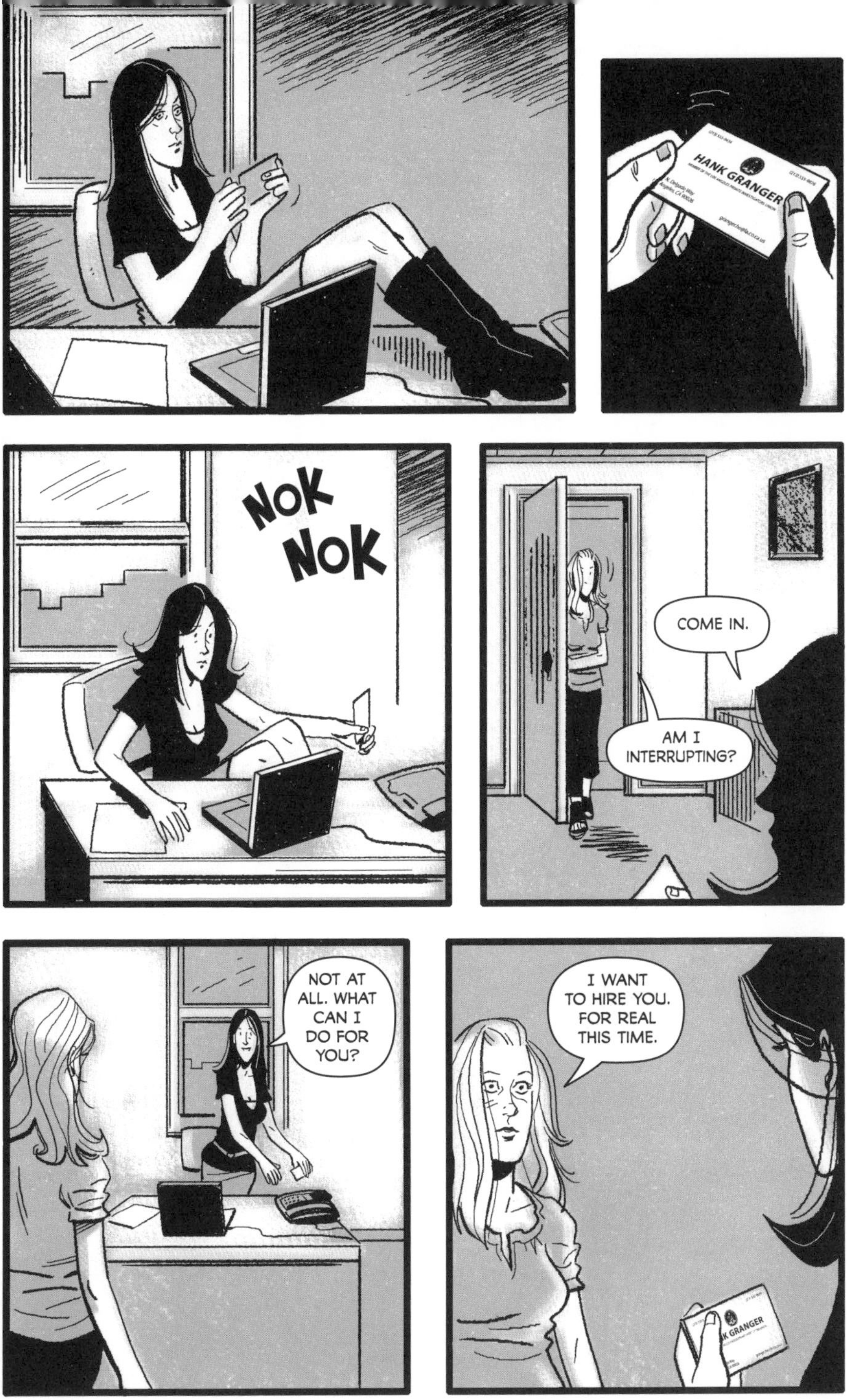
HANK GRANGER
NOK NOK
COME IN.
AM I INTERRUPTING?
NOT AT ALL. WHAT CAN I DO FOR YOU?
I WANT TO HIRE YOU. FOR REAL THIS TIME.

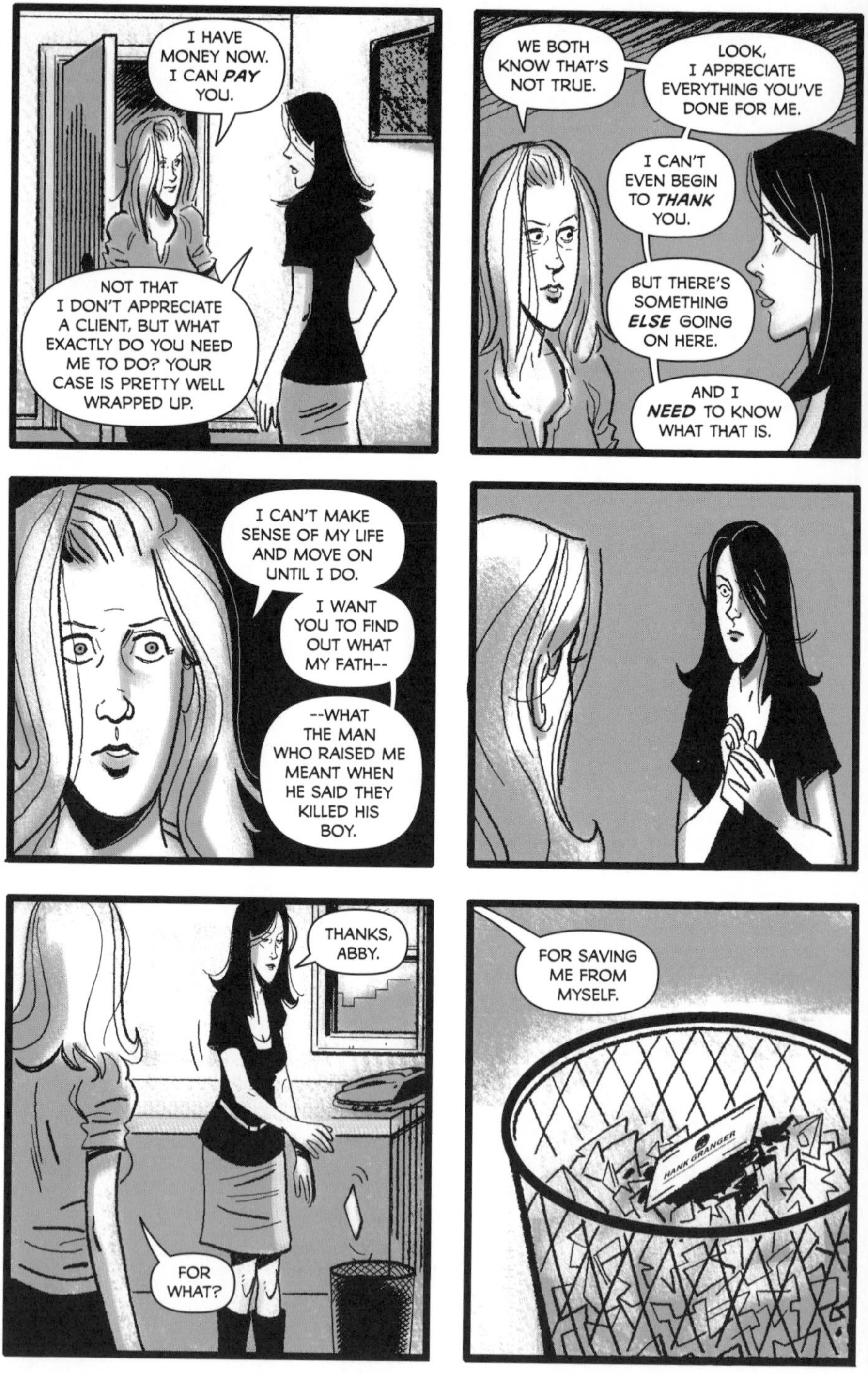
I HAVE MONEY NOW. I CAN *PAY* YOU.
NOT THAT I DON'T APPRECIATE A CLIENT, BUT WHAT EXACTLY DO YOU NEED ME TO DO? YOUR CASE IS PRETTY WELL WRAPPED UP.
WE BOTH KNOW THAT'S NOT TRUE.
LOOK, I APPRECIATE EVERYTHING YOU'VE DONE FOR ME.
I CAN'T EVEN BEGIN TO *THANK* YOU.
BUT THERE'S SOMETHING *ELSE* GOING ON HERE.
AND I *NEED* TO KNOW WHAT THAT IS.
I CAN'T MAKE SENSE OF MY LIFE AND MOVE ON UNTIL I DO.
I WANT YOU TO FIND OUT WHAT MY FATH--
--WHAT THE MAN WHO RAISED ME MEANT WHEN HE SAID THEY KILLED HIS BOY.
THANKS, ABBY.
FOR WHAT?
FOR SAVING ME FROM MYSELF.
HANK GRANGER

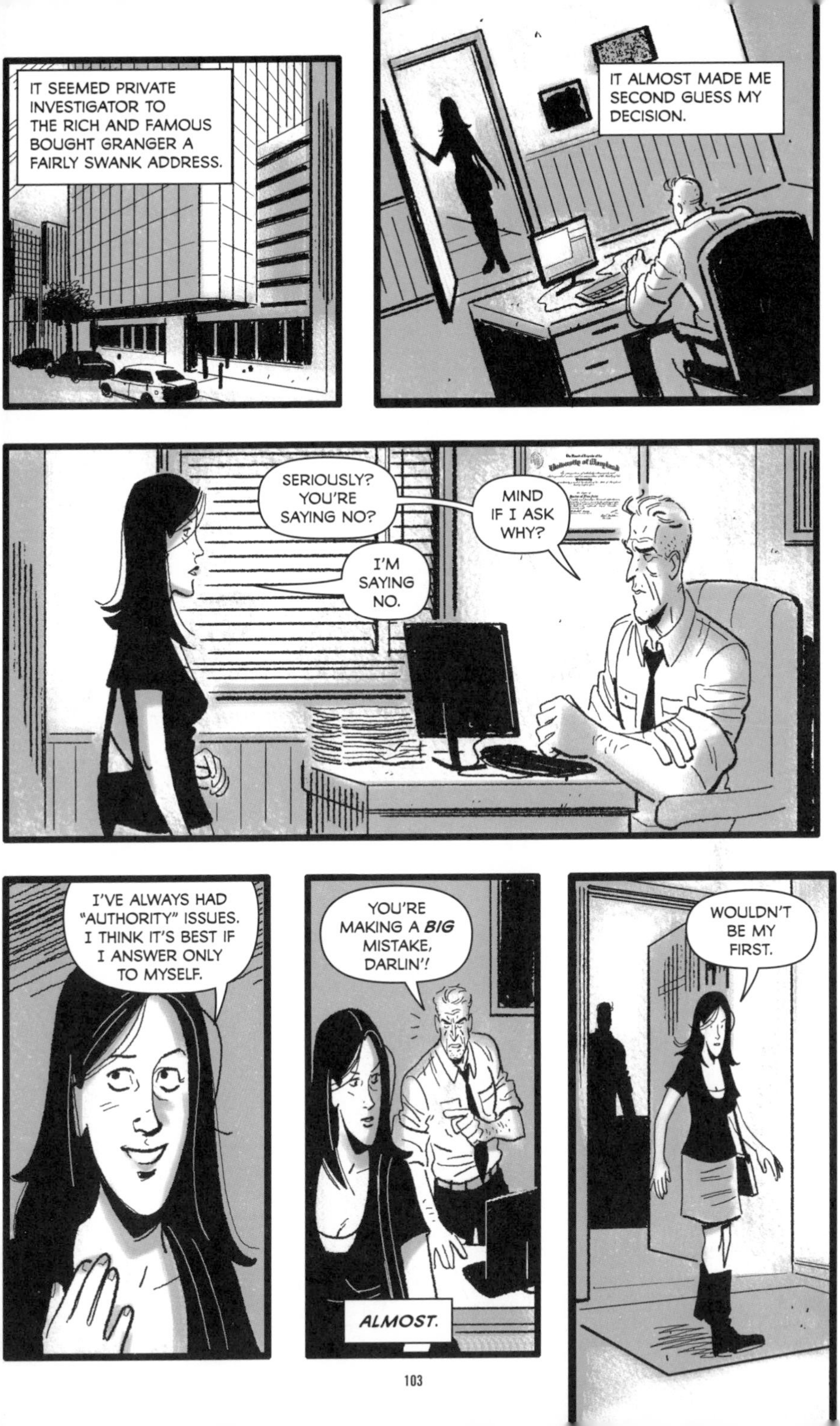
IT SEEMED PRIVATE INVESTIGATOR TO THE RICH AND FAMOUS BOUGHT GRANGER A FAIRLY SWANK ADDRESS.
IT ALMOST MADE ME SECOND GUESS MY DECISION.
SERIOUSLY? YOU'RE SAYING NO?
MIND IF I ASK WHY?
I'M SAYING NO.
I'VE ALWAYS HAD "AUTHORITY" ISSUES. I THINK IT'S BEST IF I ANSWER ONLY TO MYSELF.
YOU'RE MAKING A *BIG* MISTAKE, DARLIN'!
ALMOST.
WOULDN'T BE MY FIRST.

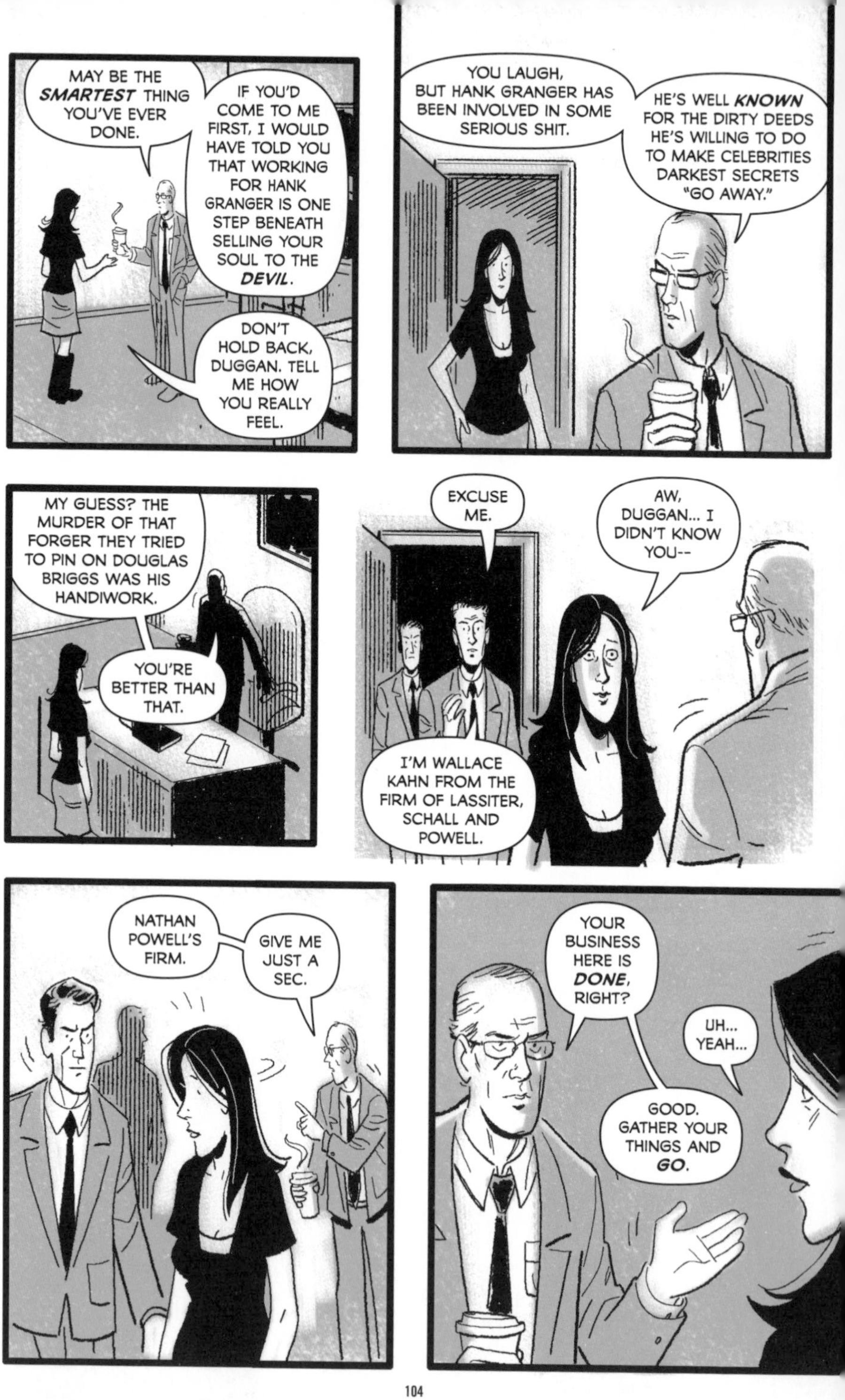
MAY BE THE SMARTEST THING YOU'VE EVER DONE.
IF YOU'D COME TO ME FIRST, I WOULD HAVE TOLD YOU THAT WORKING FOR HANK GRANGER IS ONE STEP BENEATH SELLING YOUR SOUL TO THE DEVIL.
DON'T HOLD BACK, DUGGAN. TELL ME HOW YOU REALLY FEEL.
YOU LAUGH, BUT HANK GRANGER HAS BEEN INVOLVED IN SOME SERIOUS SHIT.
HE'S WELL KNOWN FOR THE DIRTY DEEDS HE'S WILLING TO DO TO MAKE CELEBRITIES DARKEST SECRETS "GO AWAY."
MY GUESS? THE MURDER OF THAT FORGER THEY TRIED TO PIN ON DOUGLAS BRIGGS WAS HIS HANDIWORK.
YOU'RE BETTER THAN THAT.
EXCUSE ME.
AW, DUGGAN... I DIDN'T KNOW YOU--
I'M WALLACE KAHN FROM THE FIRM OF LASSITER, SCHALL AND POWELL.
NATHAN POWELL'S FIRM.
GIVE ME JUST A SEC.
YOUR BUSINESS HERE IS DONE, RIGHT?
UH... YEAH...
GOOD. GATHER YOUR THINGS AND GO.

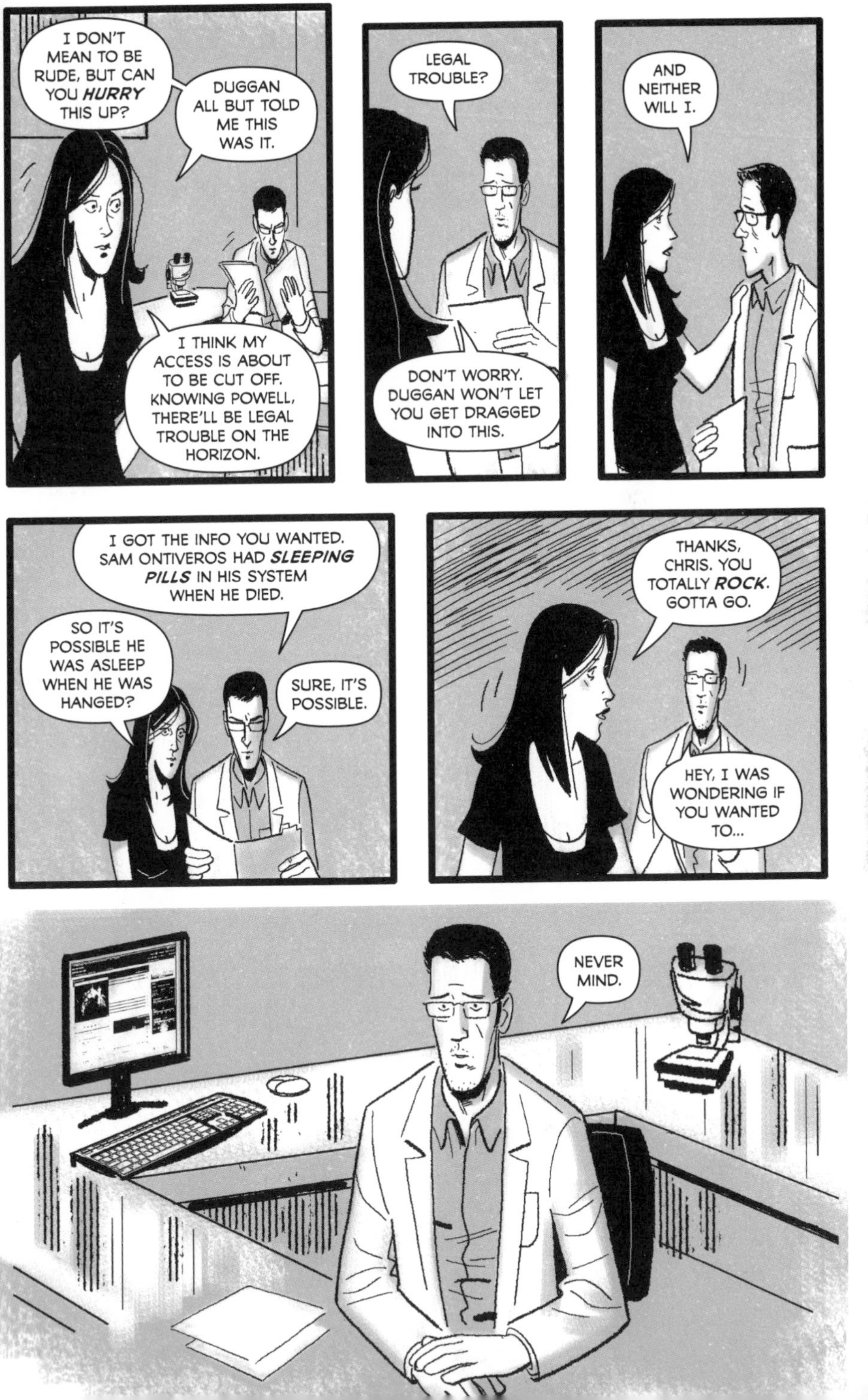
I DON'T MEAN TO BE RUDE, BUT CAN YOU *HURRY* THIS UP?
DUGGAN ALL BUT TOLD ME THIS WAS IT.
I THINK MY ACCESS IS ABOUT TO BE CUT OFF. KNOWING POWELL, THERE'LL BE LEGAL TROUBLE ON THE HORIZON.
LEGAL TROUBLE?
DON'T WORRY. DUGGAN WON'T LET YOU GET DRAGGED INTO THIS.
AND NEITHER WILL I.
I GOT THE INFO YOU WANTED. SAM ONTIVEROS HAD *SLEEPING PILLS* IN HIS SYSTEM WHEN HE DIED.
SO IT'S POSSIBLE HE WAS ASLEEP WHEN HE WAS HANGED?
SURE, IT'S POSSIBLE.
THANKS, CHRIS. YOU TOTALLY *ROCK*. GOTTA GO.
HEY, I WAS WONDERING IF YOU WANTED TO...
NEVER MIND.

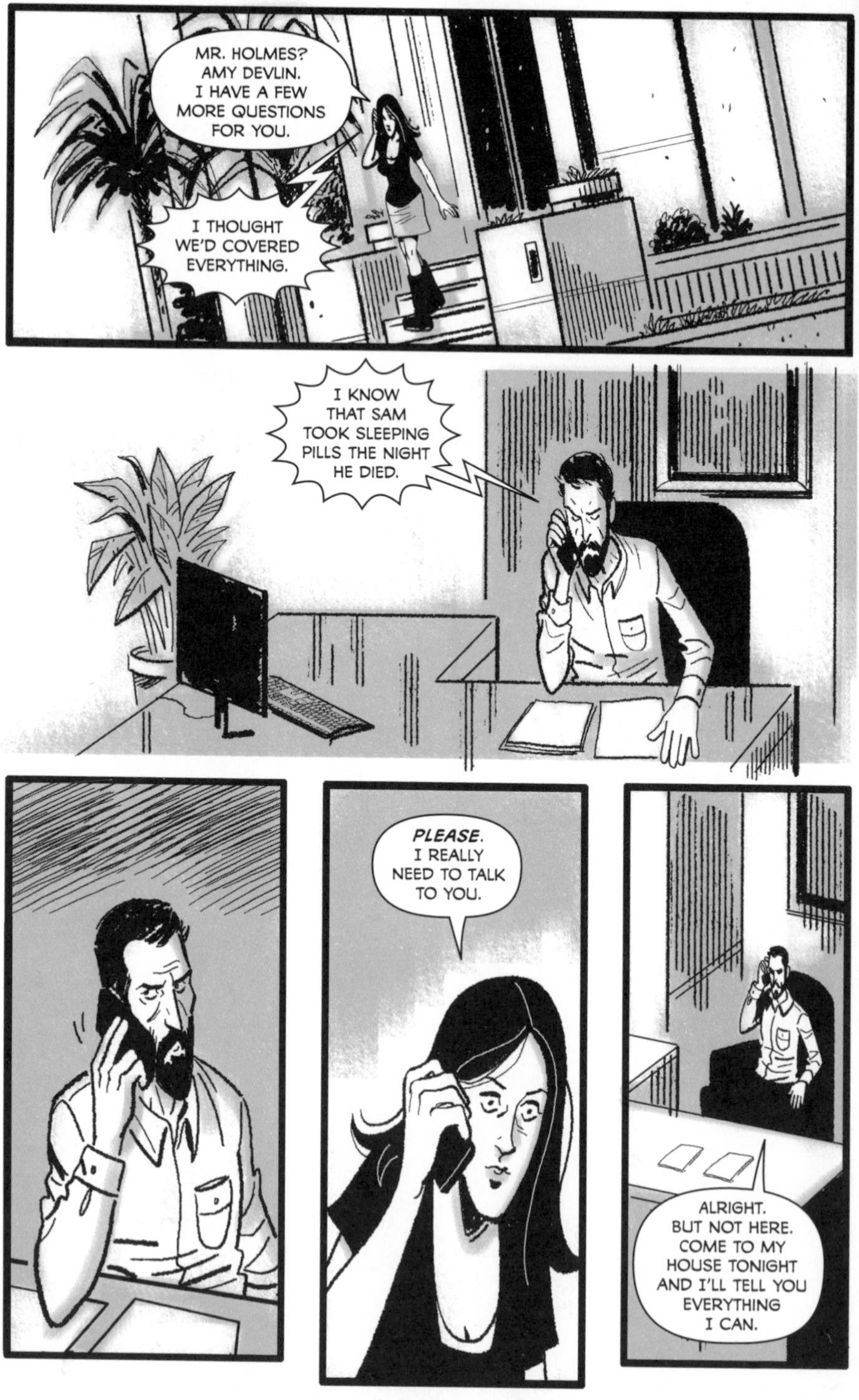
MR. HOLMES? AMY DEVLIN. I HAVE A FEW MORE QUESTIONS FOR YOU.
I THOUGHT WE'D COVERED EVERYTHING.
I KNOW THAT SAM TOOK SLEEPING PILLS THE NIGHT HE DIED.
PLEASE. I REALLY NEED TO TALK TO YOU.
ALRIGHT. BUT NOT HERE. COME TO MY HOUSE TONIGHT AND I'LL TELL YOU EVERYTHING I CAN.

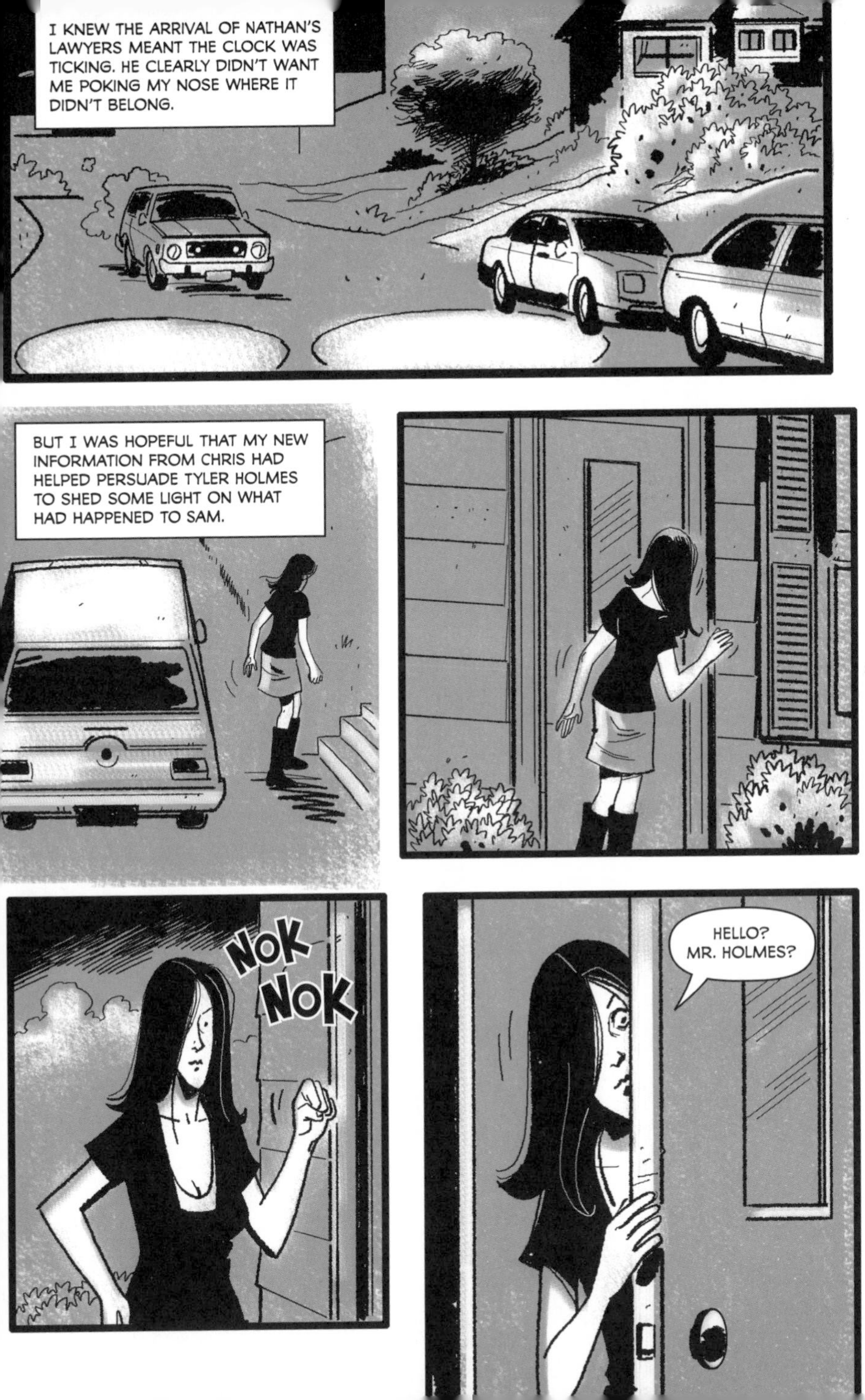
I KNEW THE ARRIVAL OF NATHAN'S LAWYERS MEANT THE CLOCK WAS TICKING. HE CLEARLY DIDN'T WANT ME POKING MY NOSE WHERE IT DIDN'T BELONG.
BUT I WAS HOPEFUL THAT MY NEW INFORMATION FROM CHRIS HAD HELPED PERSUADE TYLER HOLMES TO SHED SOME LIGHT ON WHAT HAD HAPPENED TO SAM.
NOK NOK
HELLO? MR. HOLMES?

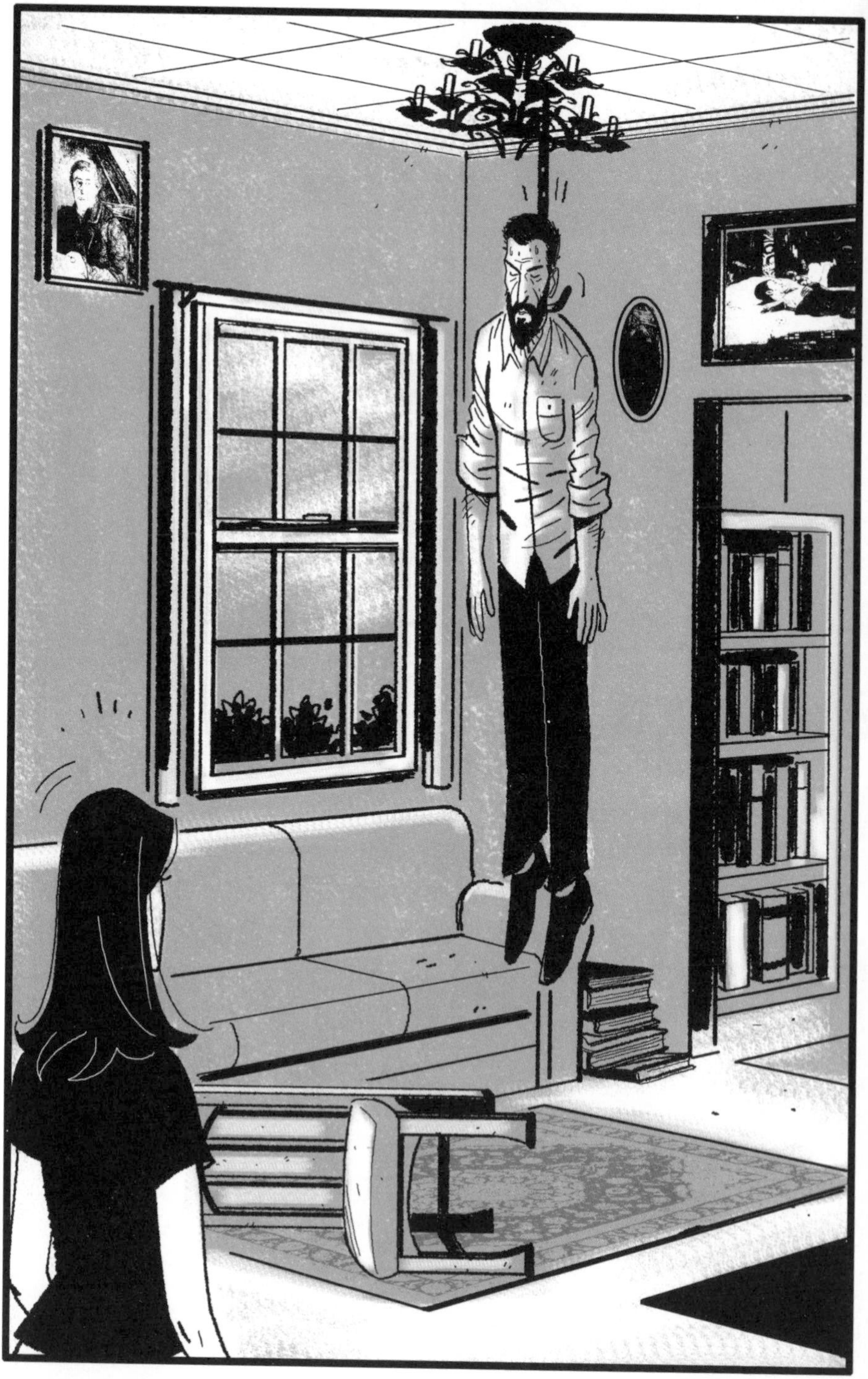

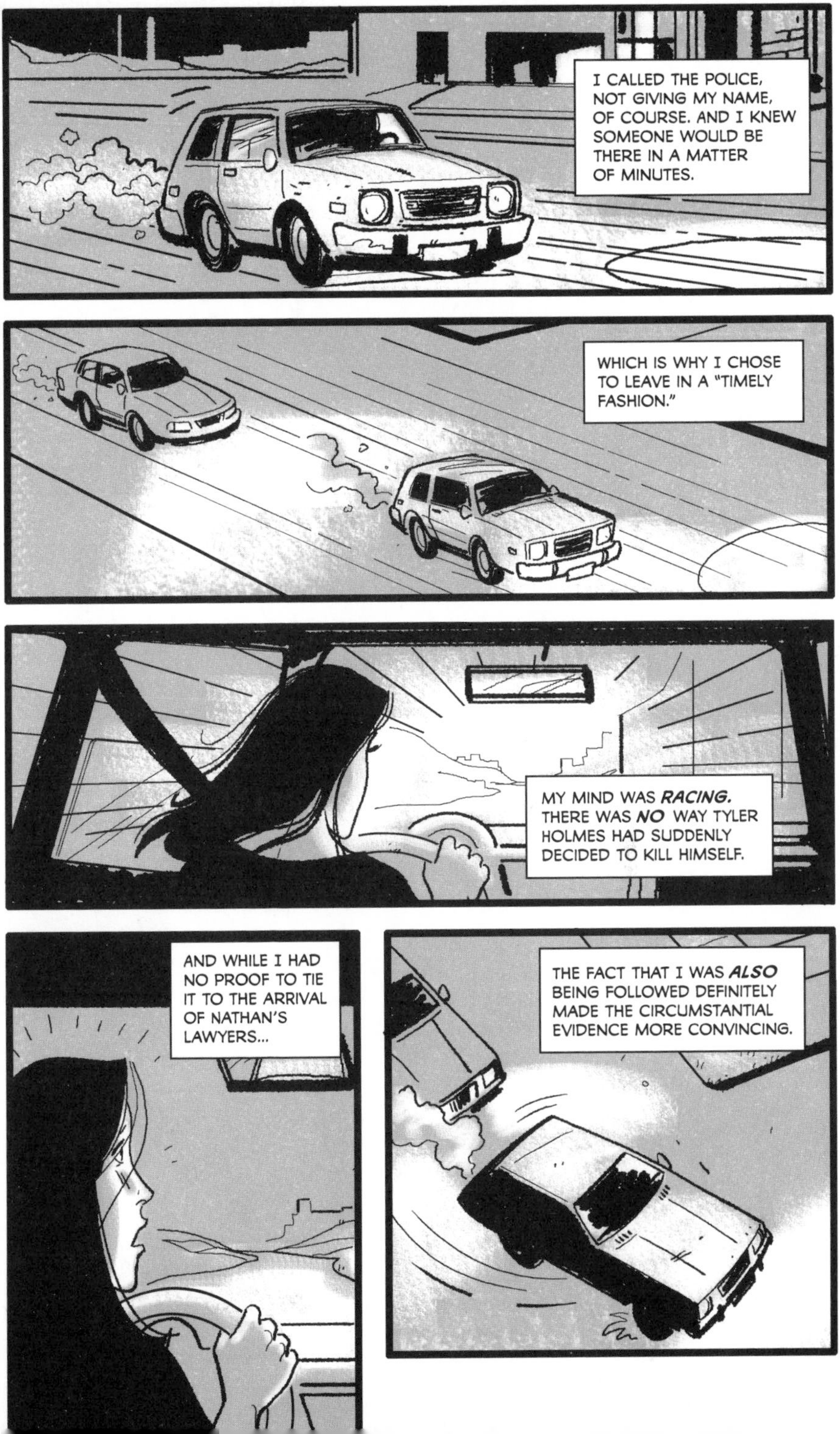
I CALLED THE POLICE, NOT GIVING MY NAME, OF COURSE. AND I KNEW SOMEONE WOULD BE THERE IN A MATTER OF MINUTES.
WHICH IS WHY I CHOSE TO LEAVE IN A "TIMELY FASHION."
MY MIND WAS *RACING.* THERE WAS *NO* WAY TYLER HOLMES HAD SUDDENLY DECIDED TO KILL HIMSELF.
AND WHILE I HAD NO PROOF TO TIE IT TO THE ARRIVAL OF NATHAN'S LAWYERS...
THE FACT THAT I WAS *ALSO* BEING FOLLOWED DEFINITELY MADE THE CIRCUMSTANTIAL EVIDENCE MORE CONVINCING.

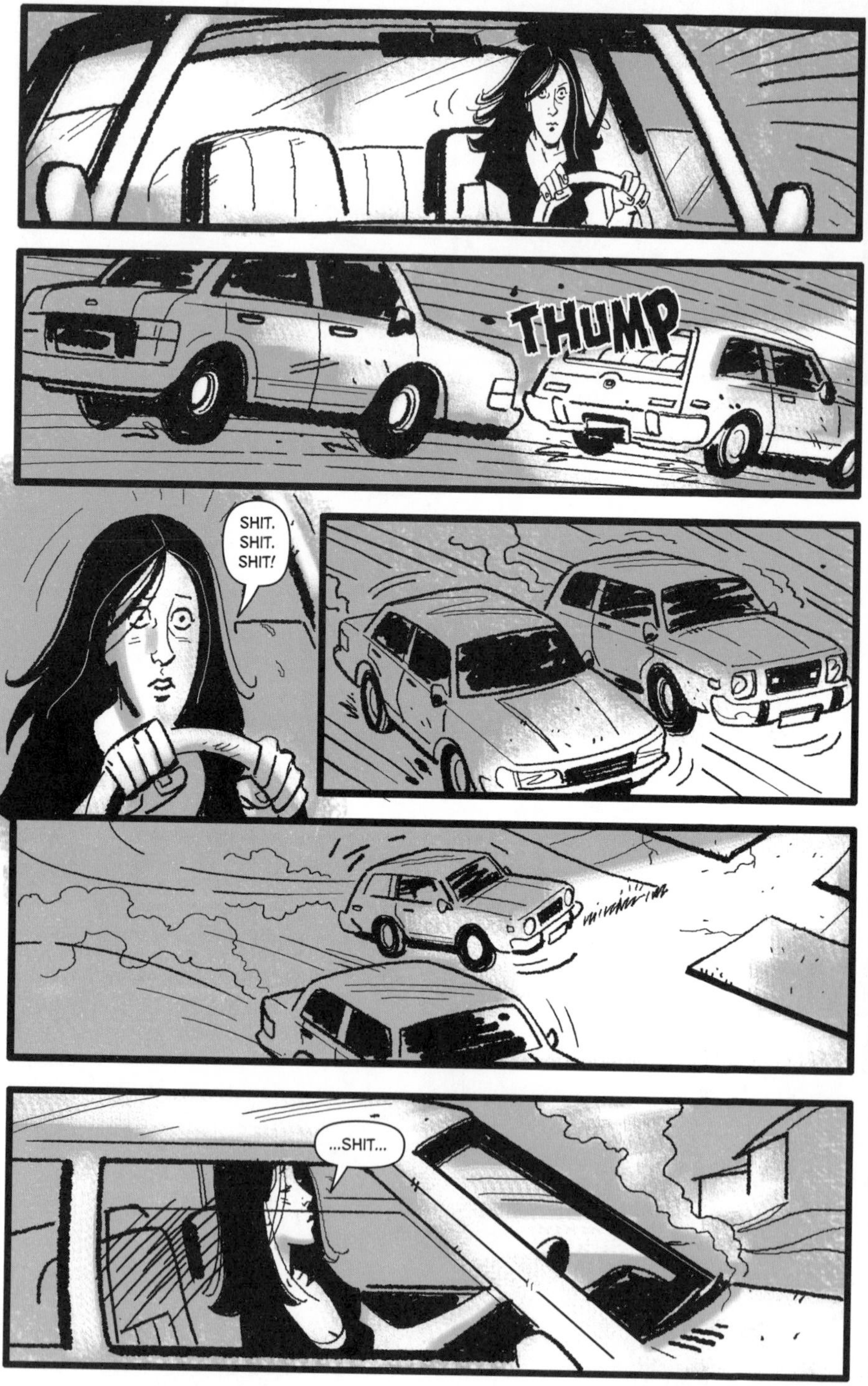
THUMP
SHIT. SHIT. SHIT!
...SHIT...

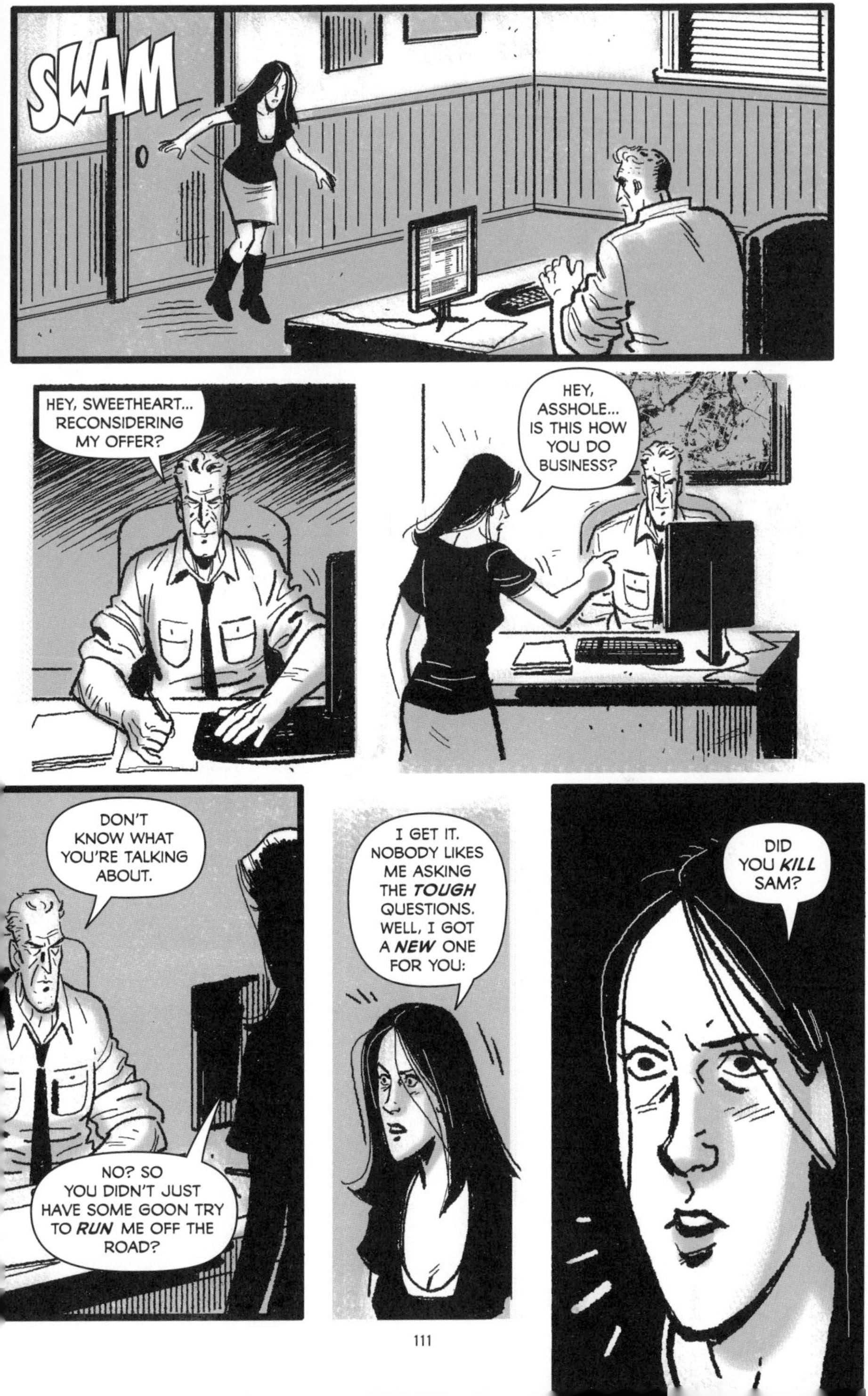
SLAM
HEY, SWEETHEART... RECONSIDERING MY OFFER?
HEY, ASSHOLE... IS THIS HOW YOU DO BUSINESS?
DON'T KNOW WHAT YOU'RE TALKING ABOUT.
NO? SO YOU DIDN'T JUST HAVE SOME GOON TRY TO RUN ME OFF THE ROAD?
I GET IT. NOBODY LIKES ME ASKING THE TOUGH QUESTIONS. WELL, I GOT A NEW ONE FOR YOU:
DID YOU KILL SAM?

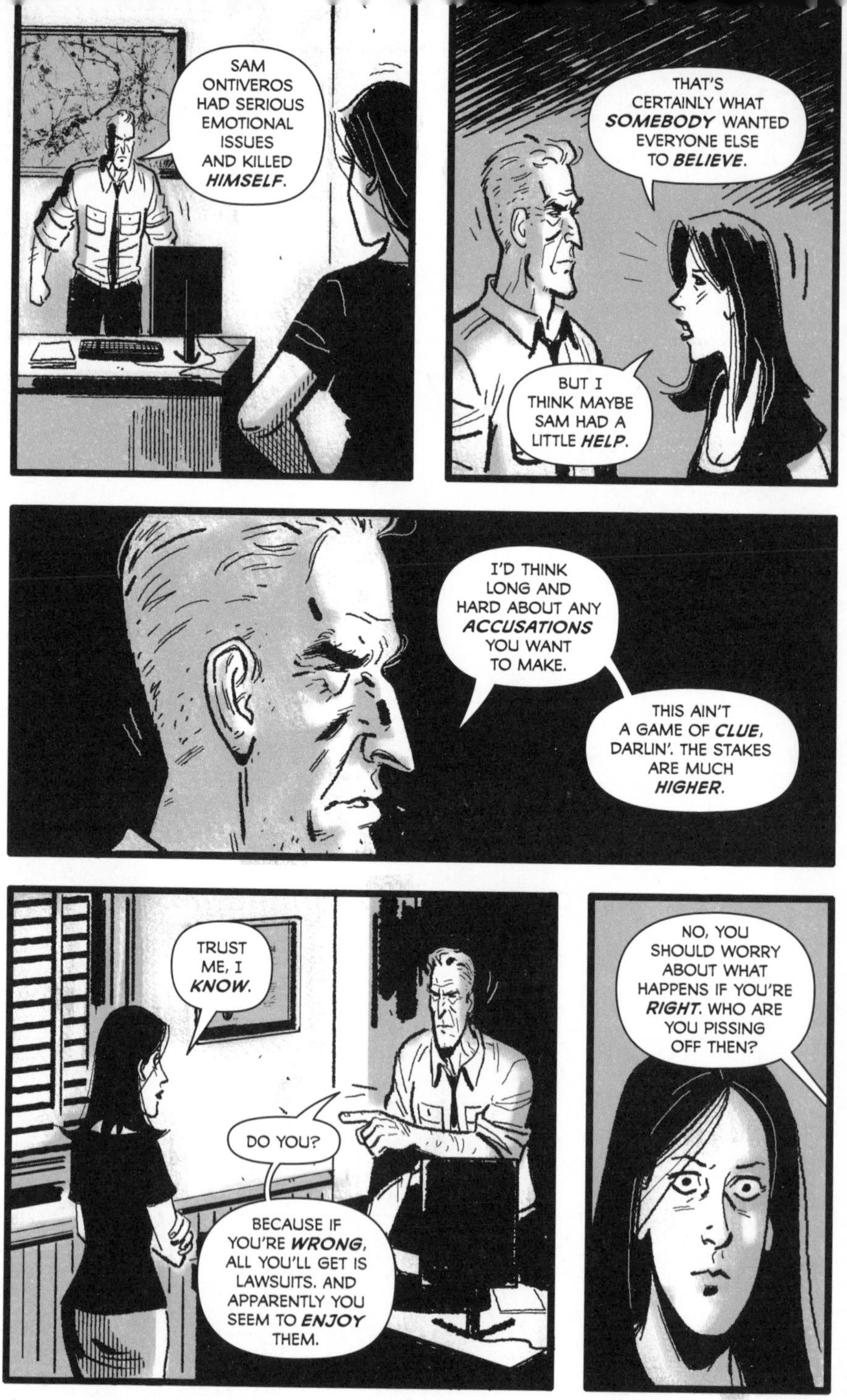
SAM ONTIVEROS HAD SERIOUS EMOTIONAL ISSUES AND KILLED HIMSELF.
THAT'S CERTAINLY WHAT SOMEBODY WANTED EVERYONE ELSE TO BELIEVE.
BUT I THINK MAYBE SAM HAD A LITTLE HELP.
I'D THINK LONG AND HARD ABOUT ANY ACCUSATIONS YOU WANT TO MAKE.
THIS AIN'T A GAME OF CLUE, DARLIN'. THE STAKES ARE MUCH HIGHER.
TRUST ME, I KNOW.
DO YOU?
BECAUSE IF YOU'RE WRONG, ALL YOU'LL GET IS LAWSUITS. AND APPARENTLY YOU SEEM TO ENJOY THEM.
NO, YOU SHOULD WORRY ABOUT WHAT HAPPENS IF YOU'RE RIGHT. WHO ARE YOU PISSING OFF THEN?

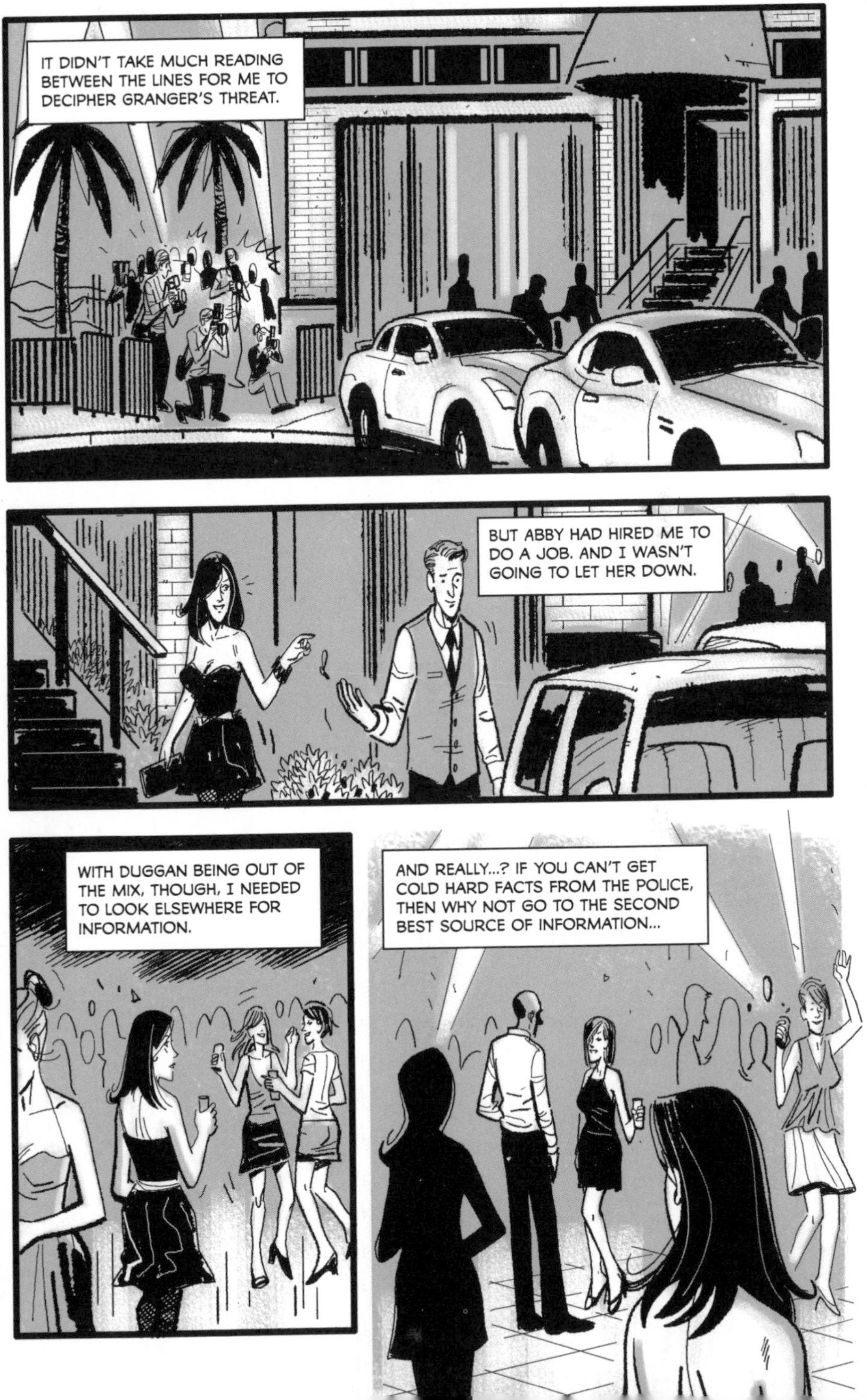
IT DIDN'T TAKE MUCH READING BETWEEN THE LINES FOR ME TO DECIPHER GRANGER'S THREAT.
BUT ABBY HAD HIRED ME TO DO A JOB. AND I WASN'T GOING TO LET HER DOWN.
WITH DUGGAN BEING OUT OF THE MIX, THOUGH, I NEEDED TO LOOK ELSEWHERE FOR INFORMATION.
AND REALLY...? IF YOU CAN'T GET COLD HARD FACTS FROM THE POLICE, THEN WHY NOT GO TO THE SECOND BEST SOURCE OF INFORMATION...

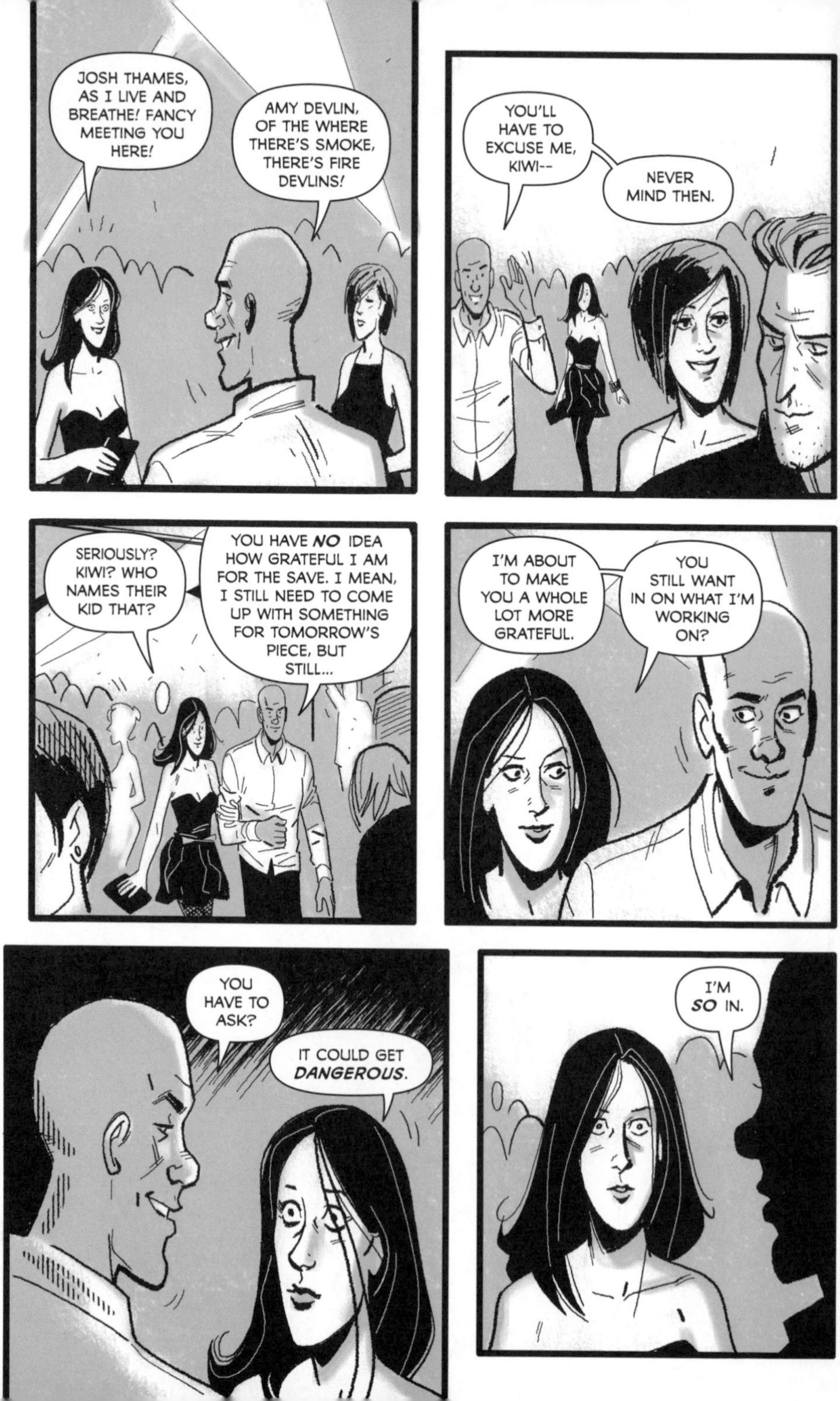
JOSH THAMES, AS I LIVE AND BREATHE! FANCY MEETING YOU HERE!
AMY DEVLIN, OF THE WHERE THERE'S SMOKE, THERE'S FIRE DEVLINS!
YOU'LL HAVE TO EXCUSE ME, KIWI--
NEVER MIND THEN.
SERIOUSLY? KIWI? WHO NAMES THEIR KID THAT?
YOU HAVE ***NO*** IDEA HOW GRATEFUL I AM FOR THE SAVE. I MEAN, I STILL NEED TO COME UP WITH SOMETHING FOR TOMORROW'S PIECE, BUT STILL...
I'M ABOUT TO MAKE YOU A WHOLE LOT MORE GRATEFUL.
YOU STILL WANT IN ON WHAT I'M WORKING ON?
YOU HAVE TO ASK?
IT COULD GET ***DANGEROUS***.
I'M ***SO*** IN.

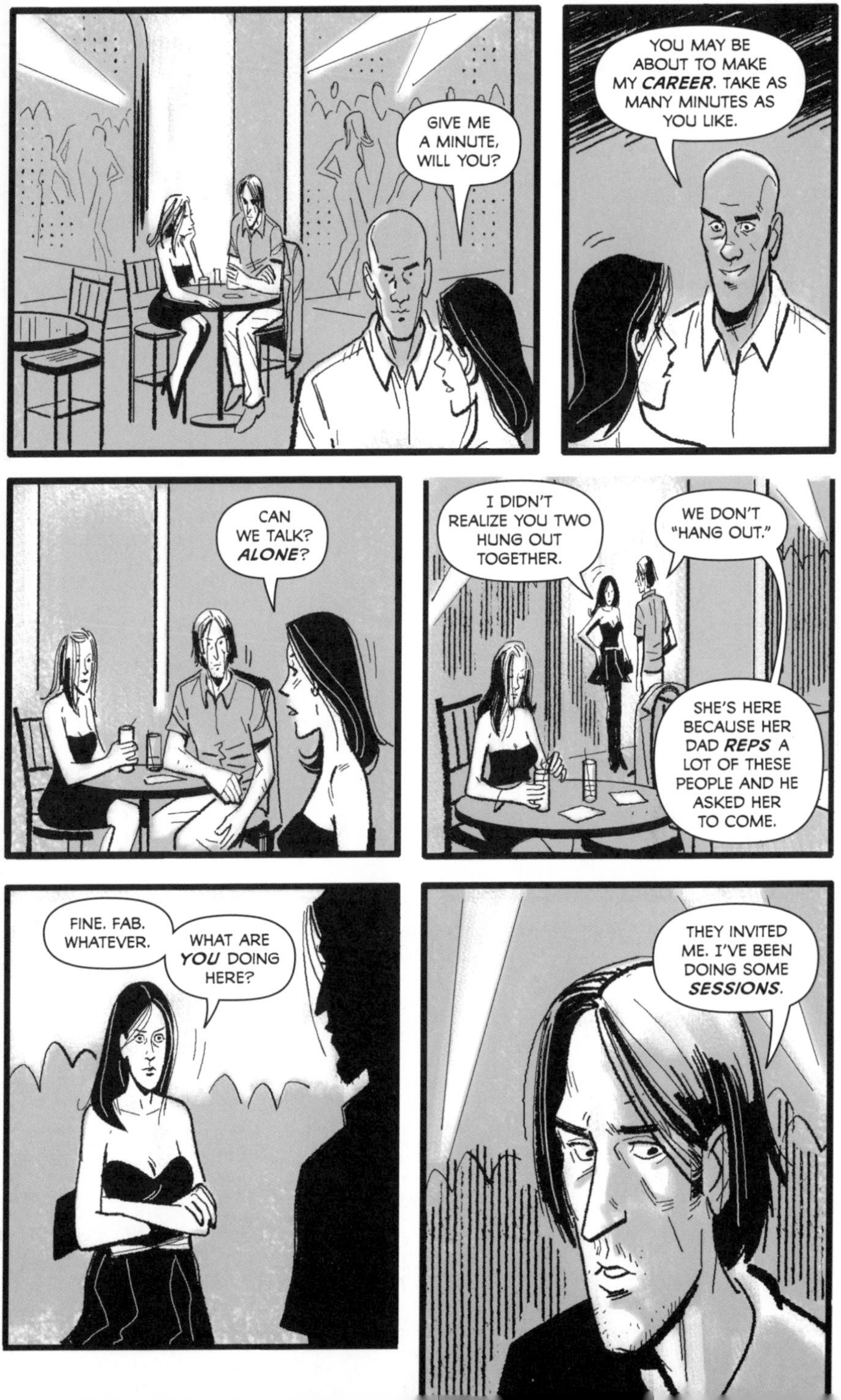
GIVE ME A MINUTE, WILL YOU?
YOU MAY BE ABOUT TO MAKE MY *CAREER*. TAKE AS MANY MINUTES AS YOU LIKE.
CAN WE TALK? *ALONE*?
I DIDN'T REALIZE YOU TWO HUNG OUT TOGETHER.
WE DON'T "HANG OUT."
SHE'S HERE BECAUSE HER DAD *REPS* A LOT OF THESE PEOPLE AND HE ASKED HER TO COME.
FINE. FAB. WHATEVER.
WHAT ARE *YOU* DOING HERE?
THEY INVITED ME. I'VE BEEN DOING SOME *SESSIONS*.

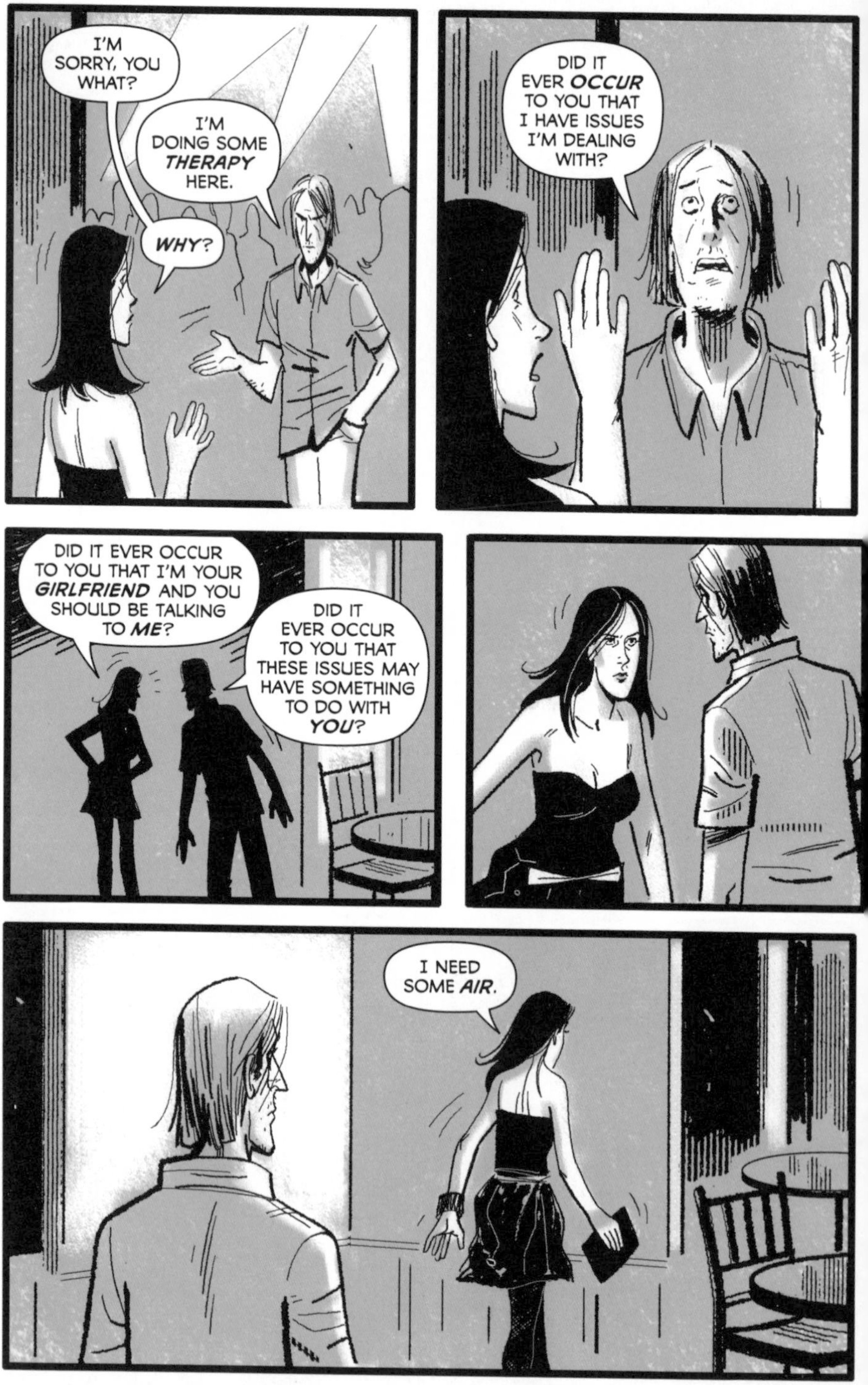
I'M SORRY, YOU WHAT?
I'M DOING SOME THERAPY HERE.
WHY?
DID IT EVER OCCUR TO YOU THAT I HAVE ISSUES I'M DEALING WITH?
DID IT EVER OCCUR TO YOU THAT I'M YOUR GIRLFRIEND AND YOU SHOULD BE TALKING TO ME?
DID IT EVER OCCUR TO YOU THAT THESE ISSUES MAY HAVE SOMETHING TO DO WITH YOU?
I NEED SOME AIR.

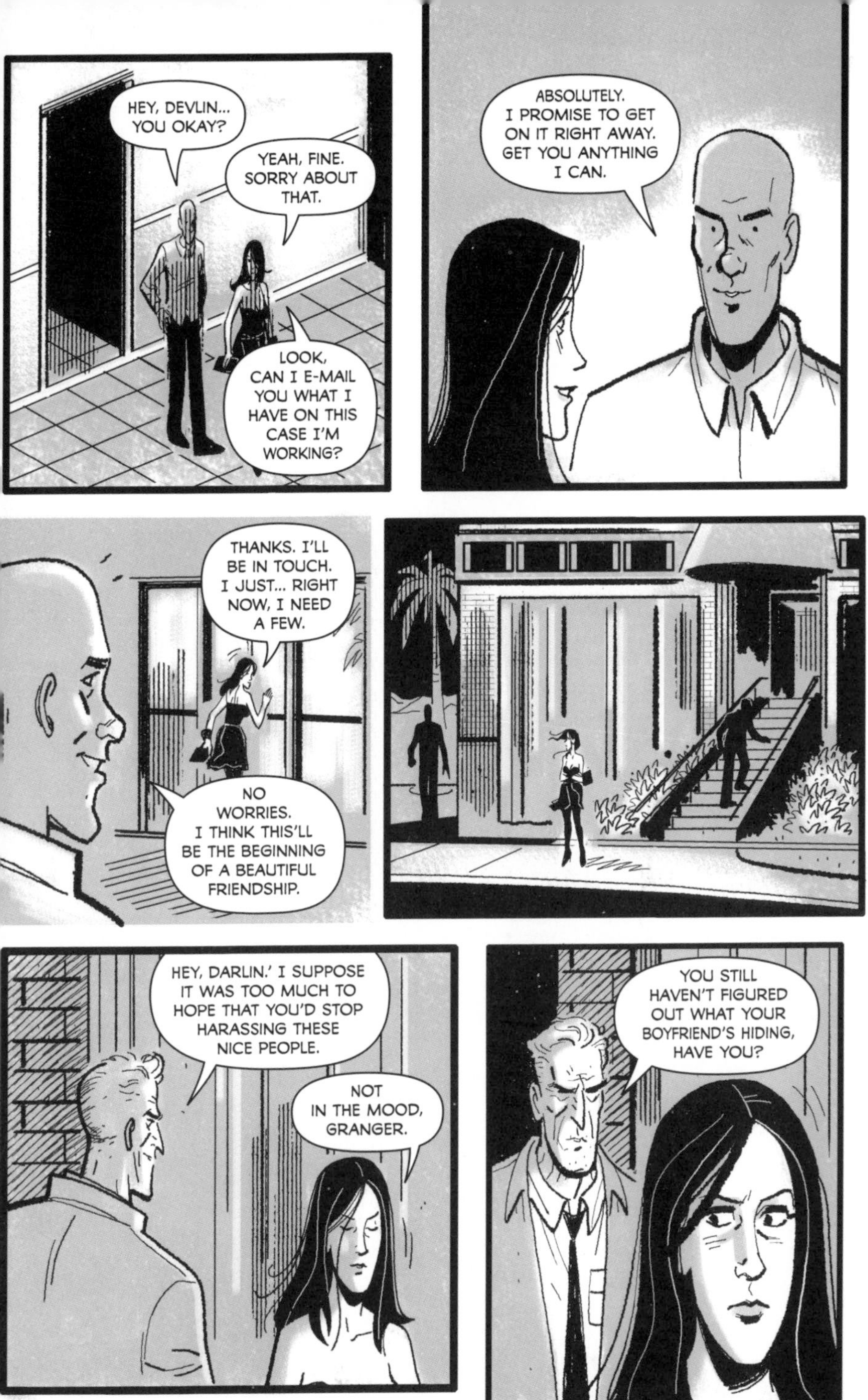
HEY, DEVLIN... YOU OKAY?
YEAH, FINE. SORRY ABOUT THAT.
LOOK, CAN I E-MAIL YOU WHAT I HAVE ON THIS CASE I'M WORKING?
ABSOLUTELY. I PROMISE TO GET ON IT RIGHT AWAY. GET YOU ANYTHING I CAN.
THANKS. I'LL BE IN TOUCH. I JUST... RIGHT NOW, I NEED A FEW.
NO WORRIES. I THINK THIS'LL BE THE BEGINNING OF A BEAUTIFUL FRIENDSHIP.
HEY, DARLIN.' I SUPPOSE IT WAS TOO MUCH TO HOPE THAT YOU'D STOP HARASSING THESE NICE PEOPLE.
NOT IN THE MOOD, GRANGER.
YOU STILL HAVEN'T FIGURED OUT WHAT YOUR BOYFRIEND'S HIDING, HAVE YOU?

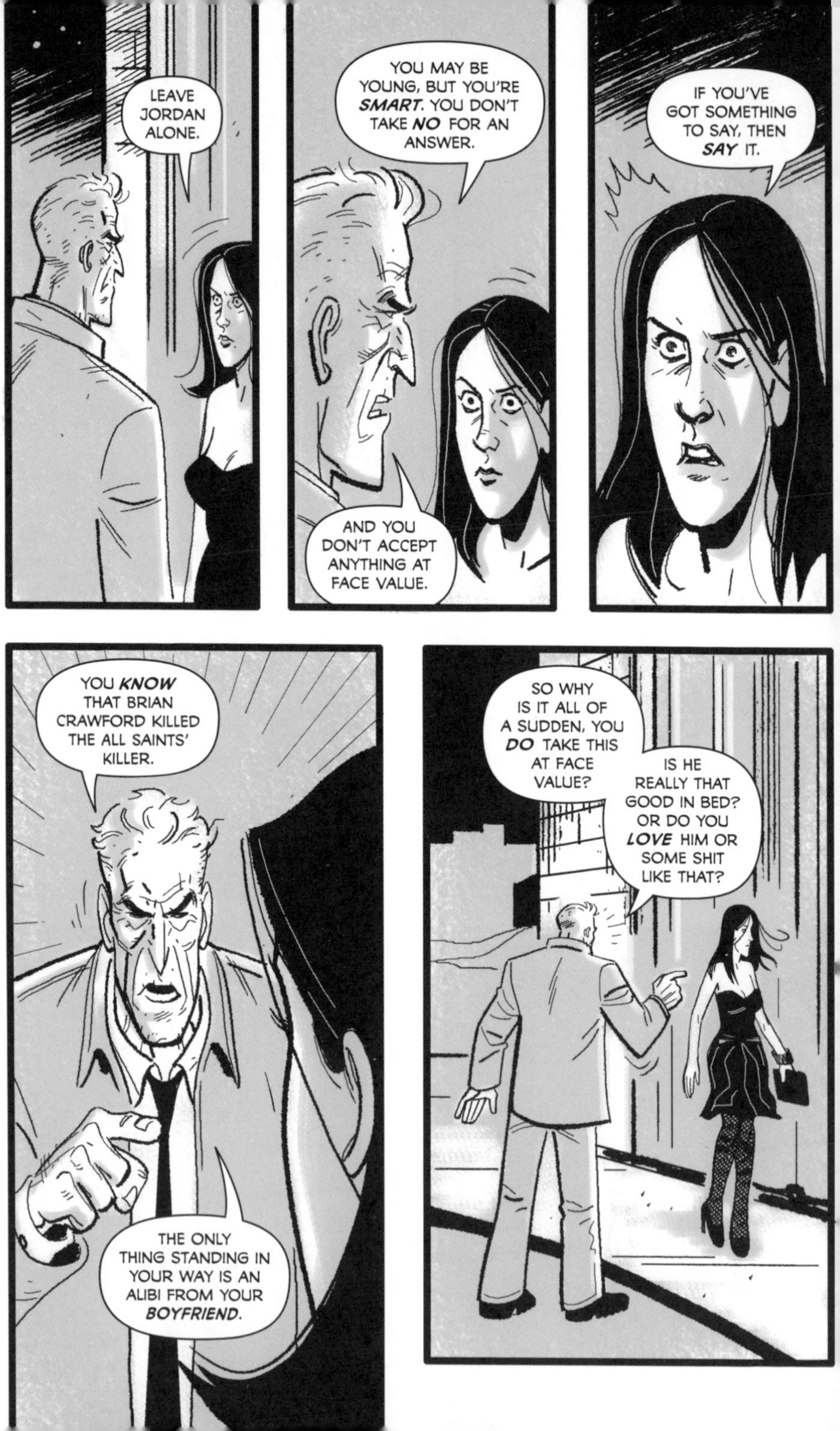
LEAVE JORDAN ALONE.
YOU MAY BE YOUNG, BUT YOU'RE SMART. YOU DON'T TAKE NO FOR AN ANSWER.
AND YOU DON'T ACCEPT ANYTHING AT FACE VALUE.
IF YOU'VE GOT SOMETHING TO SAY, THEN SAY IT.
YOU KNOW THAT BRIAN CRAWFORD KILLED THE ALL SAINTS' KILLER.
THE ONLY THING STANDING IN YOUR WAY IS AN ALIBI FROM YOUR BOYFRIEND.
SO WHY IS IT ALL OF A SUDDEN, YOU DO TAKE THIS AT FACE VALUE?
IS HE REALLY THAT GOOD IN BED? OR DO YOU LOVE HIM OR SOME SHIT LIKE THAT?

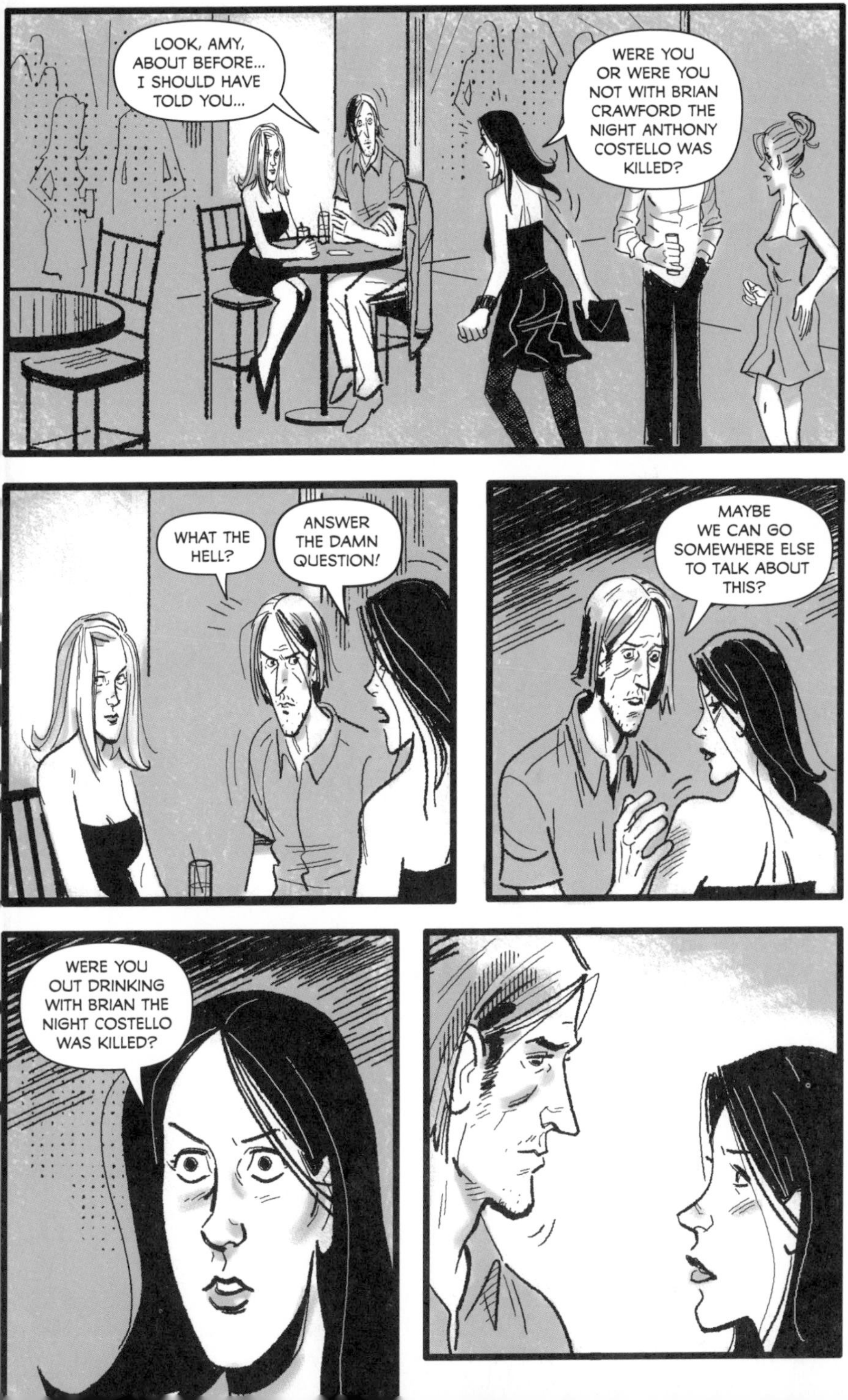
LOOK, AMY, ABOUT BEFORE... I SHOULD HAVE TOLD YOU...
WERE YOU OR WERE YOU NOT WITH BRIAN CRAWFORD THE NIGHT ANTHONY COSTELLO WAS KILLED?
WHAT THE HELL?
ANSWER THE DAMN QUESTION!
MAYBE WE CAN GO SOMEWHERE ELSE TO TALK ABOUT THIS?
WERE YOU OUT DRINKING WITH BRIAN THE NIGHT COSTELLO WAS KILLED?

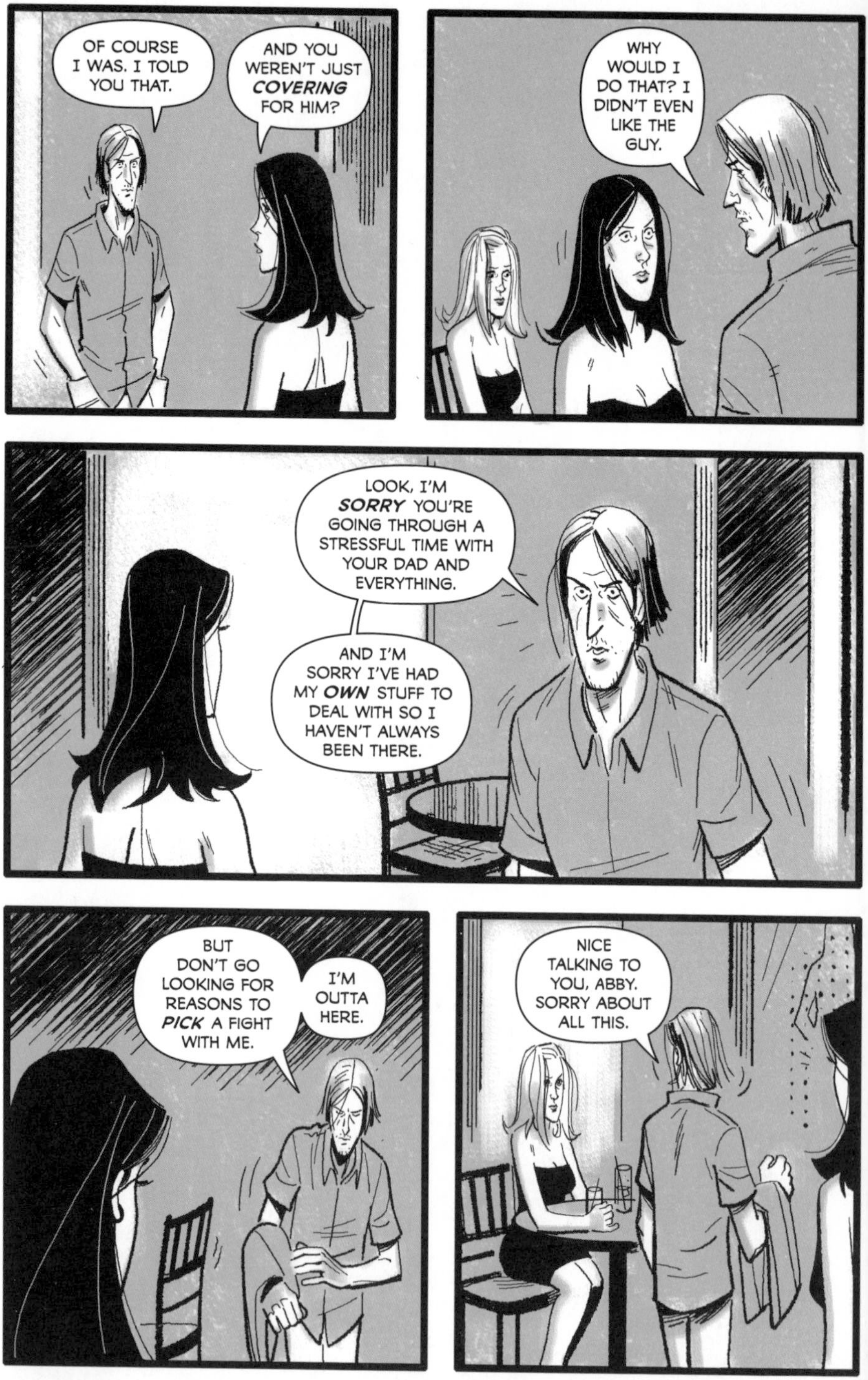
OF COURSE I WAS. I TOLD YOU THAT.
AND YOU WEREN'T JUST *COVERING* FOR HIM?
WHY WOULD I DO THAT? I DIDN'T EVEN LIKE THE GUY.
LOOK, I'M *SORRY* YOU'RE GOING THROUGH A STRESSFUL TIME WITH YOUR DAD AND EVERYTHING.
AND I'M SORRY I'VE HAD MY *OWN* STUFF TO DEAL WITH SO I HAVEN'T ALWAYS BEEN THERE.
BUT DON'T GO LOOKING FOR REASONS TO *PICK* A FIGHT WITH ME.
I'M OUTTA HERE.
NICE TALKING TO YOU, ABBY. SORRY ABOUT ALL THIS.

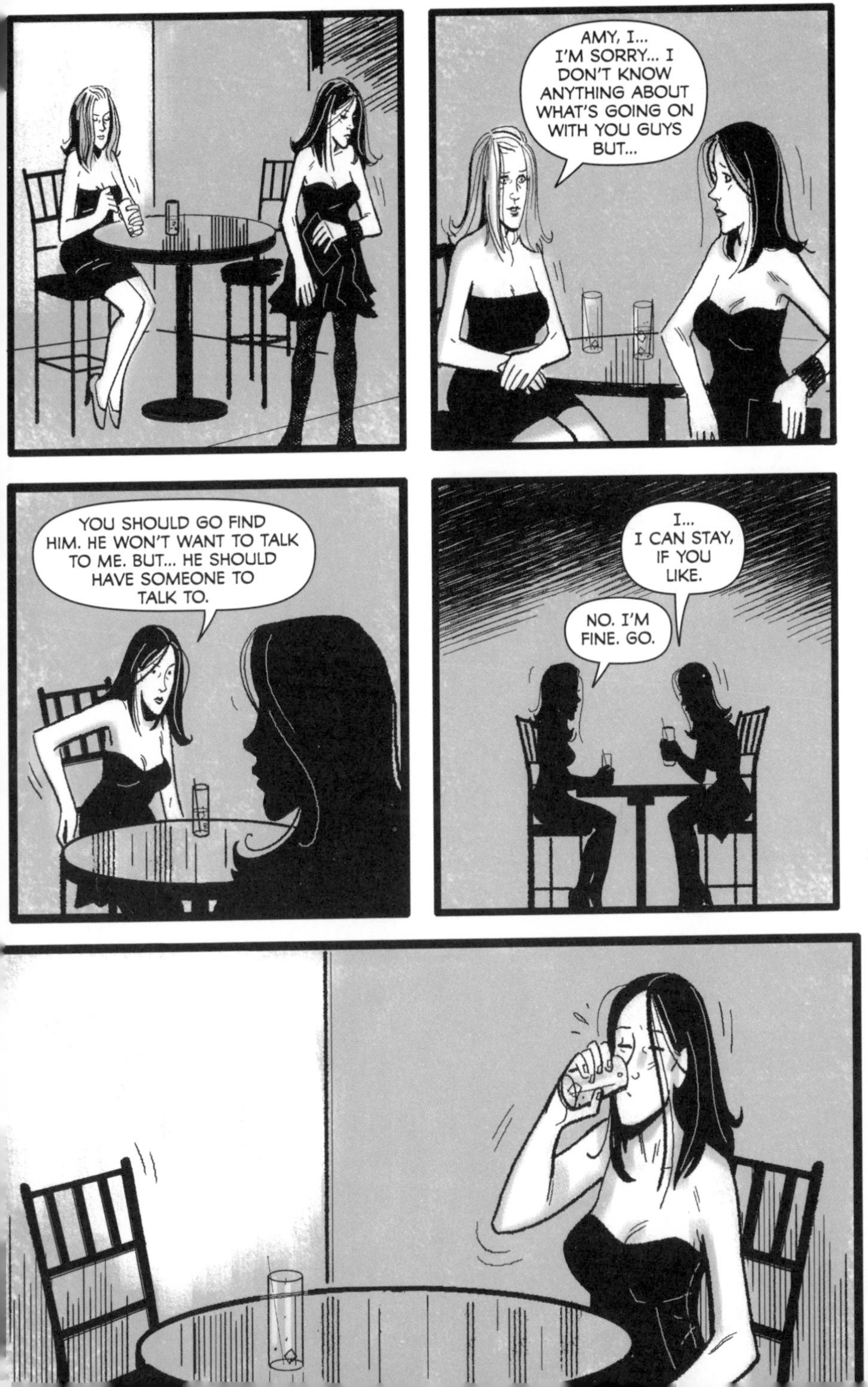
AMY, I... I'M SORRY... I DON'T KNOW ANYTHING ABOUT WHAT'S GOING ON WITH YOU GUYS BUT...
YOU SHOULD GO FIND HIM. HE WON'T WANT TO TALK TO ME. BUT... HE SHOULD HAVE SOMEONE TO TALK TO.
I... I CAN STAY, IF YOU LIKE.
NO. I'M FINE. GO.

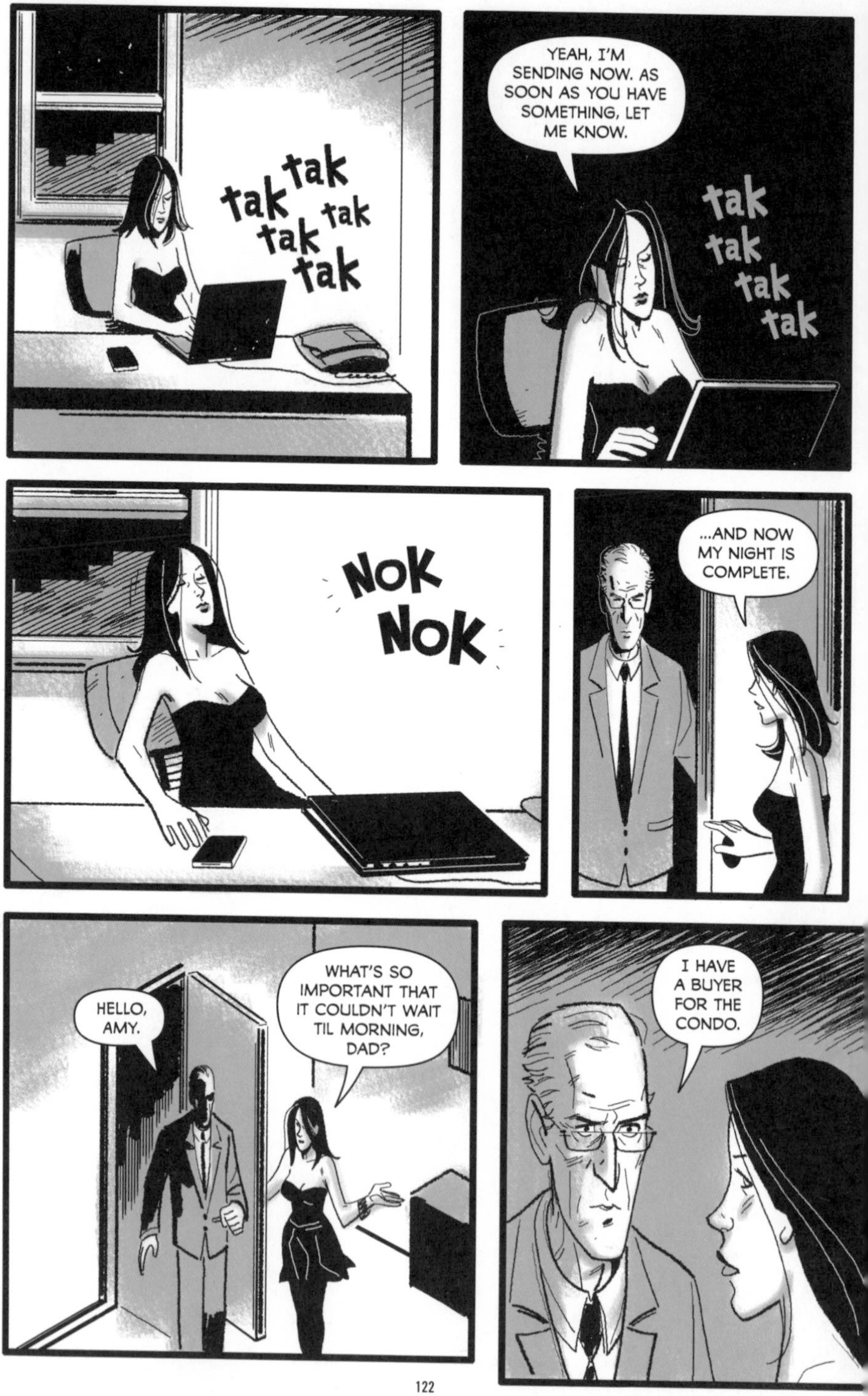
tak tak tak tak tak tak
YEAH, I'M SENDING NOW. AS SOON AS YOU HAVE SOMETHING, LET ME KNOW.
tak tak tak tak
NOK NOK
...AND NOW MY NIGHT IS COMPLETE.
HELLO, AMY.
WHAT'S SO IMPORTANT THAT IT COULDN'T WAIT TIL MORNING, DAD?
I HAVE A BUYER FOR THE CONDO.

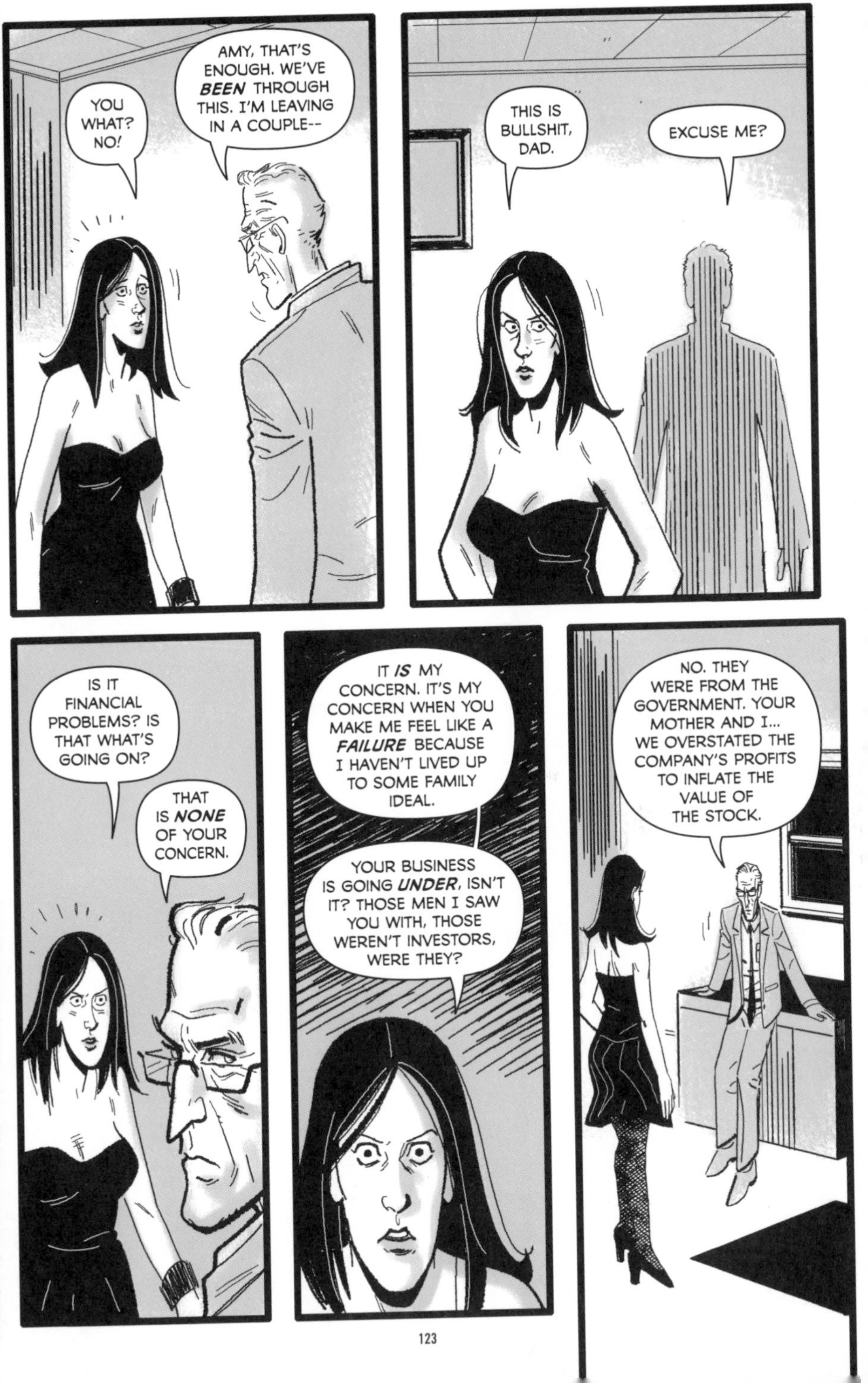
YOU WHAT? NO!
AMY, THAT'S ENOUGH. WE'VE BEEN THROUGH THIS. I'M LEAVING IN A COUPLE--
THIS IS BULLSHIT, DAD.
EXCUSE ME?
IS IT FINANCIAL PROBLEMS? IS THAT WHAT'S GOING ON?
THAT IS NONE OF YOUR CONCERN.
IT IS MY CONCERN. IT'S MY CONCERN WHEN YOU MAKE ME FEEL LIKE A FAILURE BECAUSE I HAVEN'T LIVED UP TO SOME FAMILY IDEAL.
YOUR BUSINESS IS GOING UNDER, ISN'T IT? THOSE MEN I SAW YOU WITH, THOSE WEREN'T INVESTORS, WERE THEY?
NO. THEY WERE FROM THE GOVERNMENT. YOUR MOTHER AND I... WE OVERSTATED THE COMPANY'S PROFITS TO INFLATE THE VALUE OF THE STOCK.

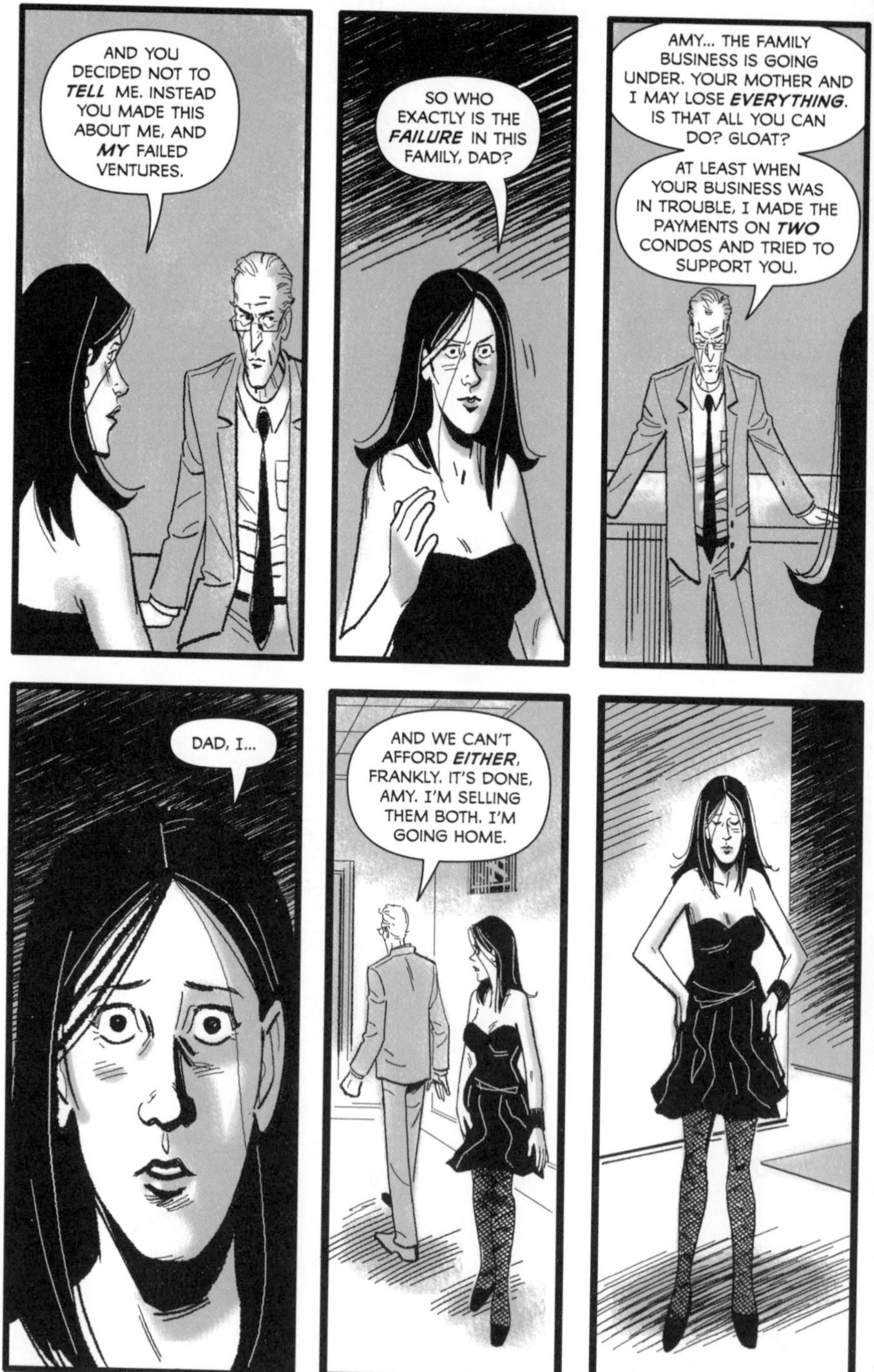
AND YOU DECIDED NOT TO TELL ME. INSTEAD YOU MADE THIS ABOUT ME, AND MY FAILED VENTURES.
SO WHO EXACTLY IS THE FAILURE IN THIS FAMILY, DAD?
AMY... THE FAMILY BUSINESS IS GOING UNDER. YOUR MOTHER AND I MAY LOSE EVERYTHING. IS THAT ALL YOU CAN DO? GLOAT?
AT LEAST WHEN YOUR BUSINESS WAS IN TROUBLE, I MADE THE PAYMENTS ON TWO CONDOS AND TRIED TO SUPPORT YOU.
DAD, I...
AND WE CAN'T AFFORD EITHER, FRANKLY. IT'S DONE, AMY. I'M SELLING THEM BOTH. I'M GOING HOME.

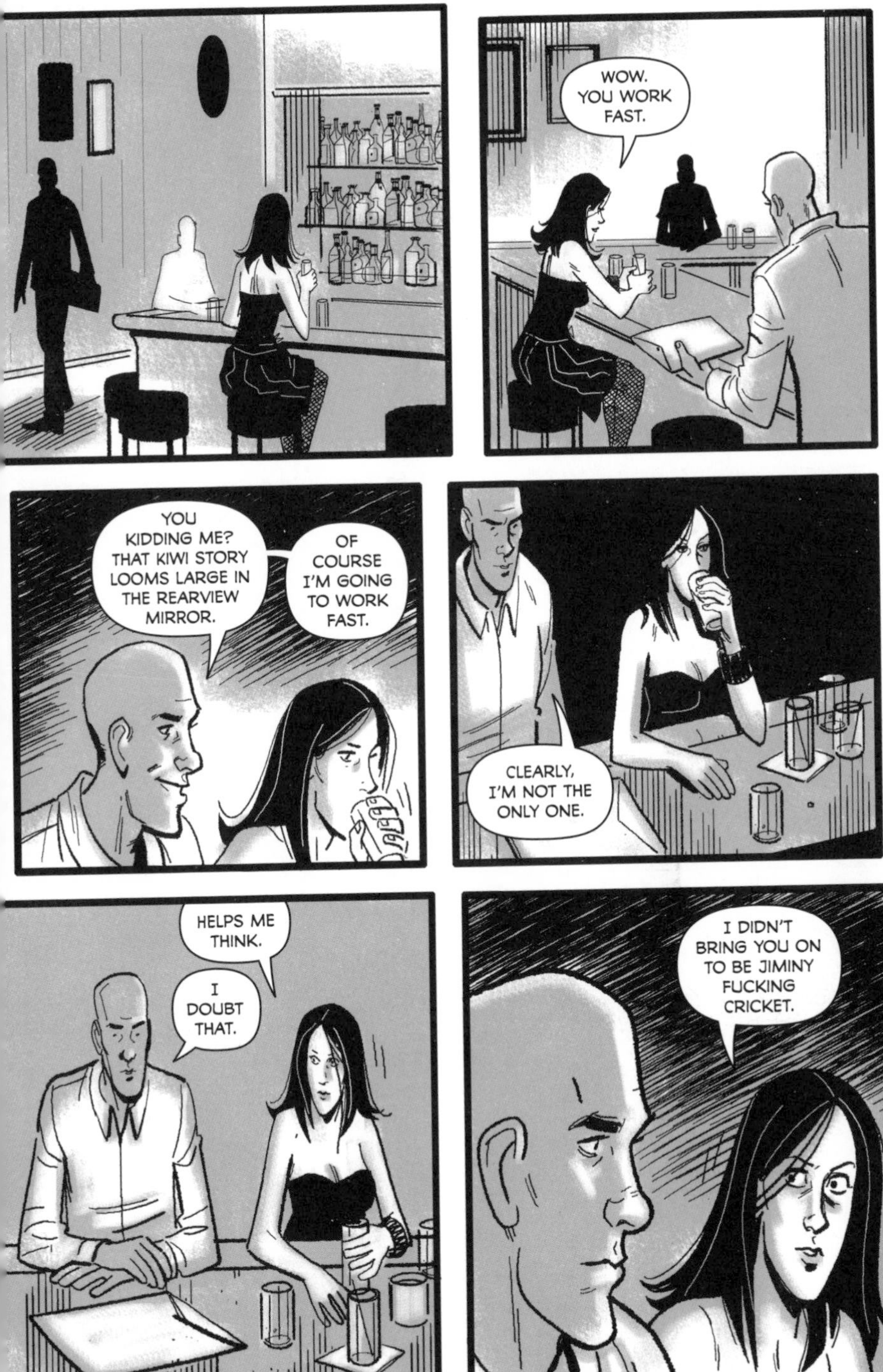
WOW. YOU WORK FAST.
YOU KIDDING ME? THAT KIWI STORY LOOMS LARGE IN THE REARVIEW MIRROR.
OF COURSE I'M GOING TO WORK FAST.
CLEARLY, I'M NOT THE ONLY ONE.
HELPS ME THINK.
I DOUBT THAT.
I DIDN'T BRING YOU ON TO BE JIMINY FUCKING CRICKET.

MESSAGE RECEIVED LOUD AND CLEAR. SO LET'S GET TO THE GOOD STUFF.

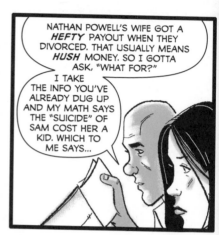

NATHAN POWELL'S WIFE GOT A *HEFTY* PAYOUT WHEN THEY DIVORCED. THAT USUALLY MEANS *HUSH* MONEY. SO I GOTTA ASK, "WHAT FOR?"

I TAKE THE INFO YOU'VE ALREADY DUG UP AND MY MATH SAYS THE "SUICIDE" OF SAM COST HER A KID. WHICH TO ME SAYS...

...AND YOU'RE NOT HEARING A THING I'M SAYING.

WHAT IF SOMEONE YOU KNEW TURNED OUT TO BE NOT WHO YOU THOUGHT THEY WERE?

I'M A PRIVATE INVESTIGATOR. I'M *PAID* TO KNOW WHEN PEOPLE ARE LYING. BUT... SUDDENLY I DON'T KNOW WHAT TO BELIEVE.

IN MY LINE OF WORK...? THE LOUDER SOMEONE PROTESTS, THE GUILTIER THEY ARE.

YEAH. MY LINE OF WORK, TOO...

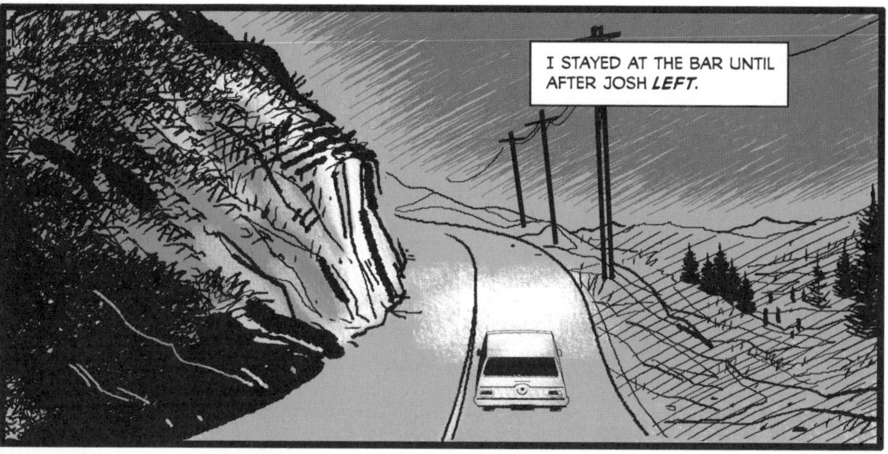
I STAYED AT THE BAR UNTIL AFTER JOSH *LEFT*.

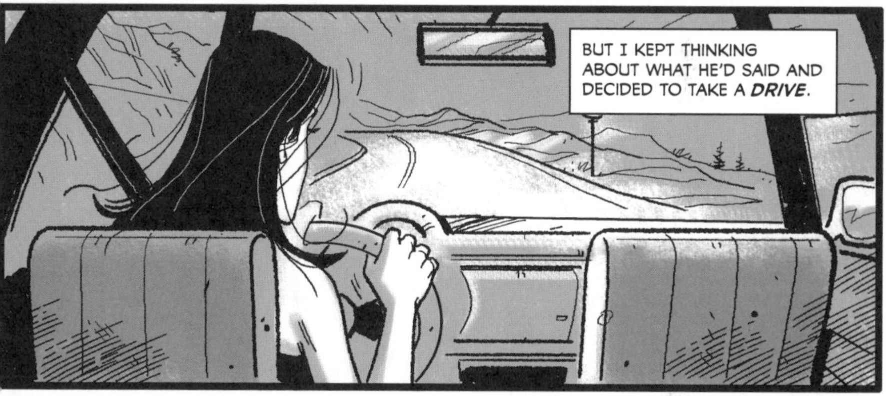
BUT I KEPT THINKING ABOUT WHAT HE'D SAID AND DECIDED TO TAKE A *DRIVE*.

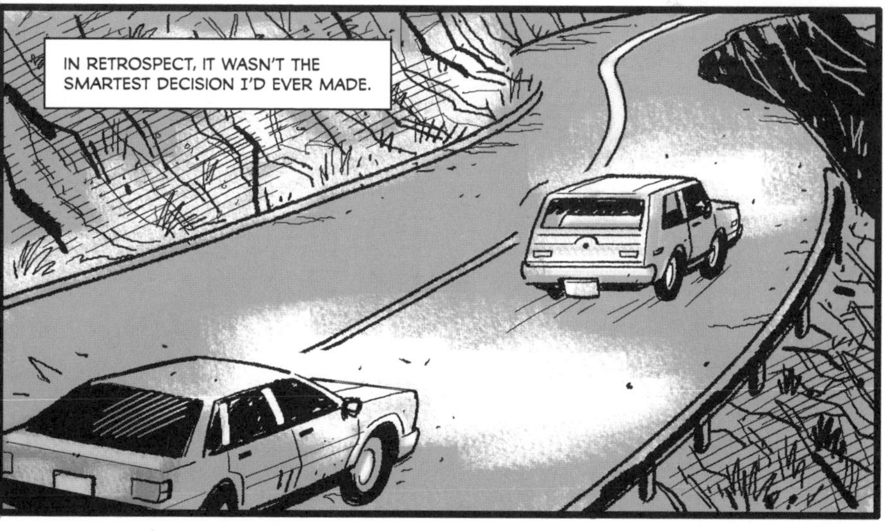
IN RETROSPECT, IT WASN'T THE SMARTEST DECISION I'D EVER MADE.

NOK
NOK
AMY?
HI... WE NEED TO--
JORDAN? WHO IS IT?

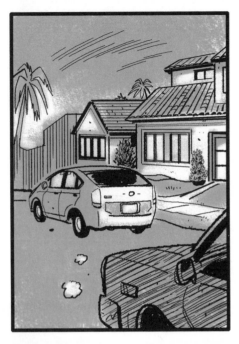

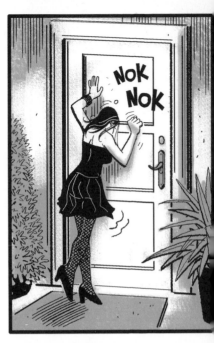

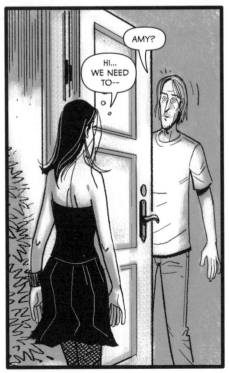

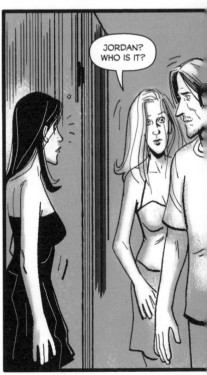

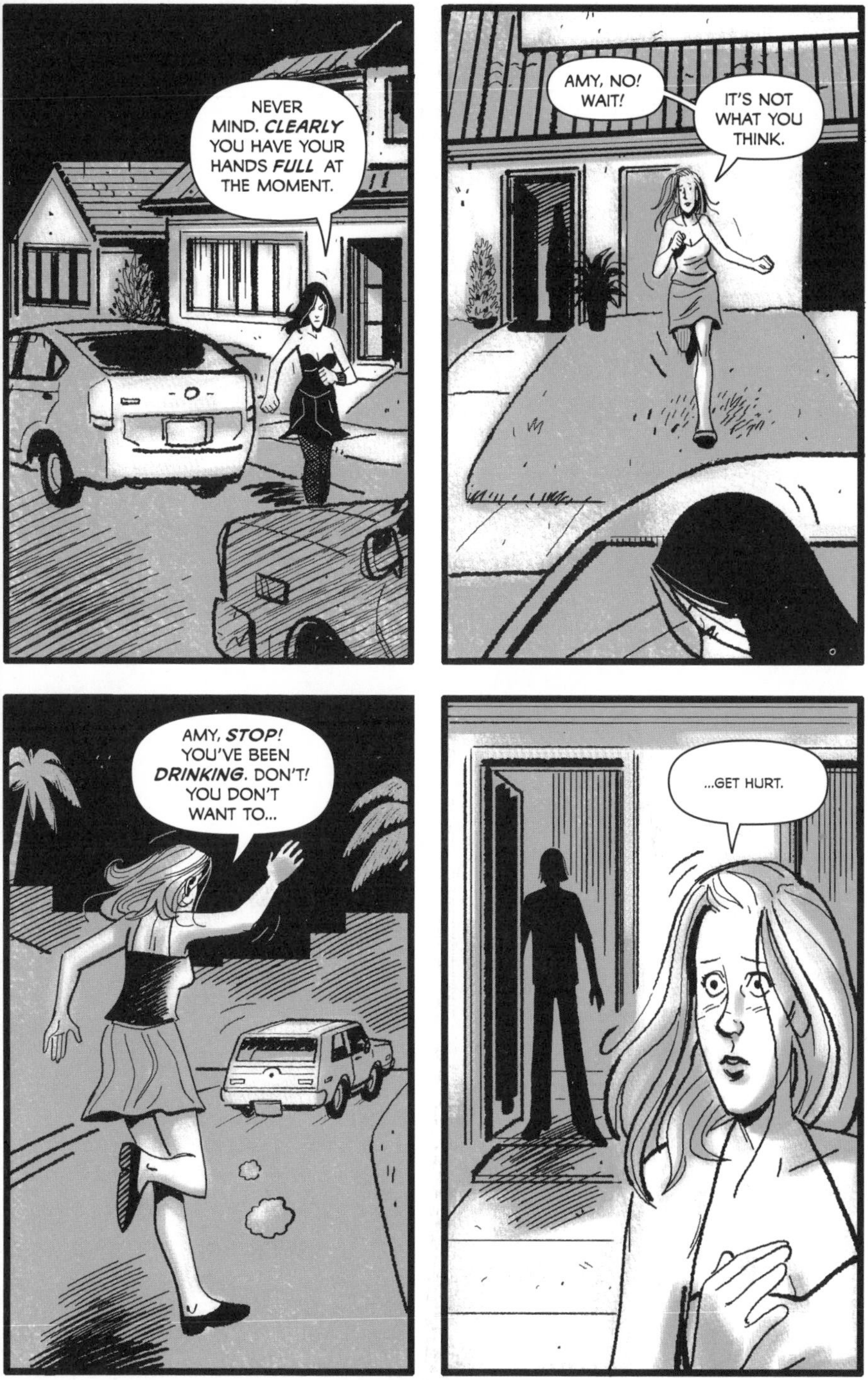
NEVER MIND. CLEARLY YOU HAVE YOUR HANDS FULL AT THE MOMENT.
AMY, NO! WAIT!
IT'S NOT WHAT YOU THINK.
AMY, STOP! YOU'VE BEEN DRINKING. DON'T! YOU DON'T WANT TO...
...GET HURT.

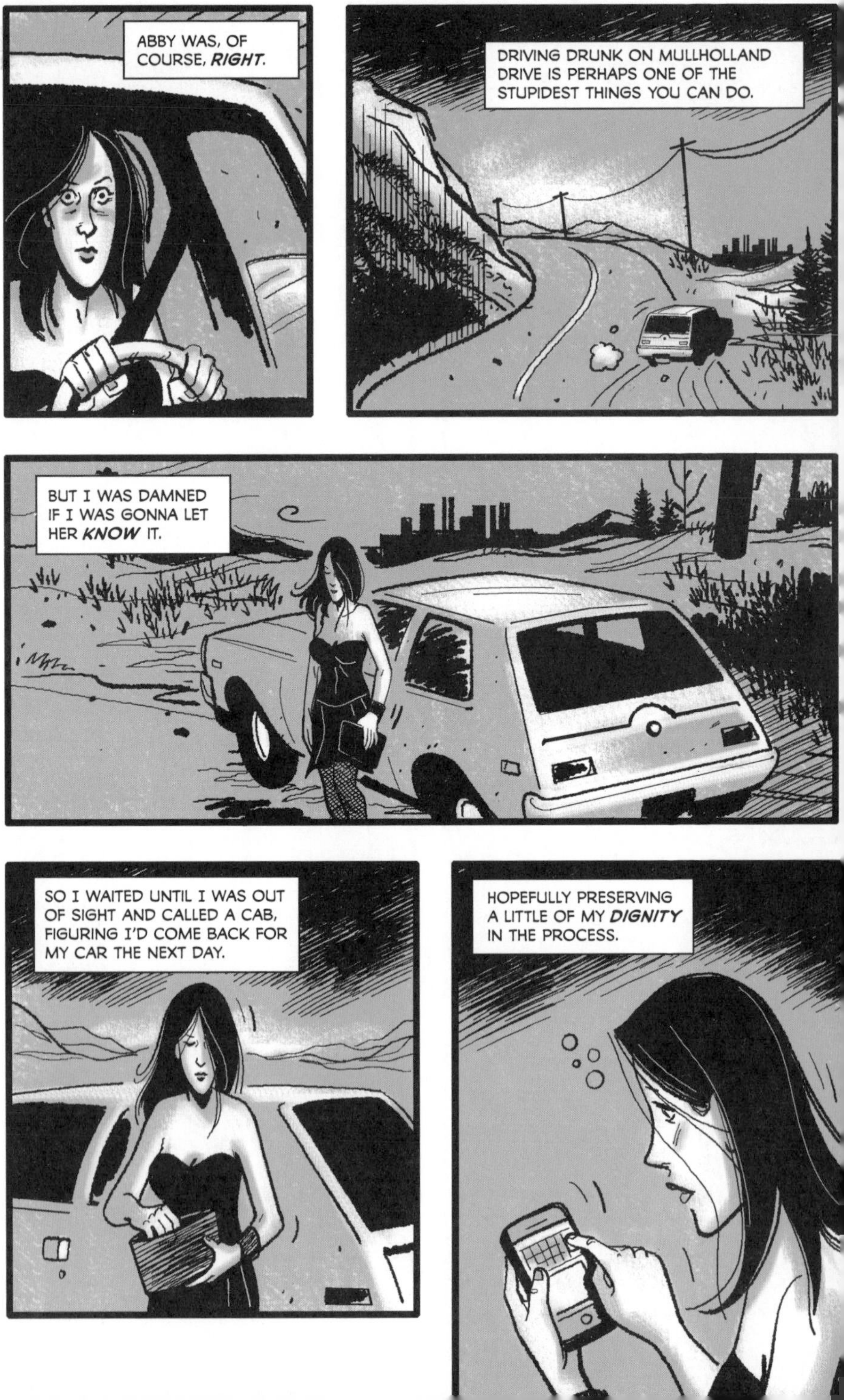

ABBY WAS, OF COURSE, ***RIGHT***.
DRIVING DRUNK ON MULLHOLLAND DRIVE IS PERHAPS ONE OF THE STUPIDEST THINGS YOU CAN DO.
BUT I WAS DAMNED IF I WAS GONNA LET HER ***KNOW*** IT.
SO I WAITED UNTIL I WAS OUT OF SIGHT AND CALLED A CAB, FIGURING I'D COME BACK FOR MY CAR THE NEXT DAY.
HOPEFULLY PRESERVING A LITTLE OF MY ***DIGNITY*** IN THE PROCESS.

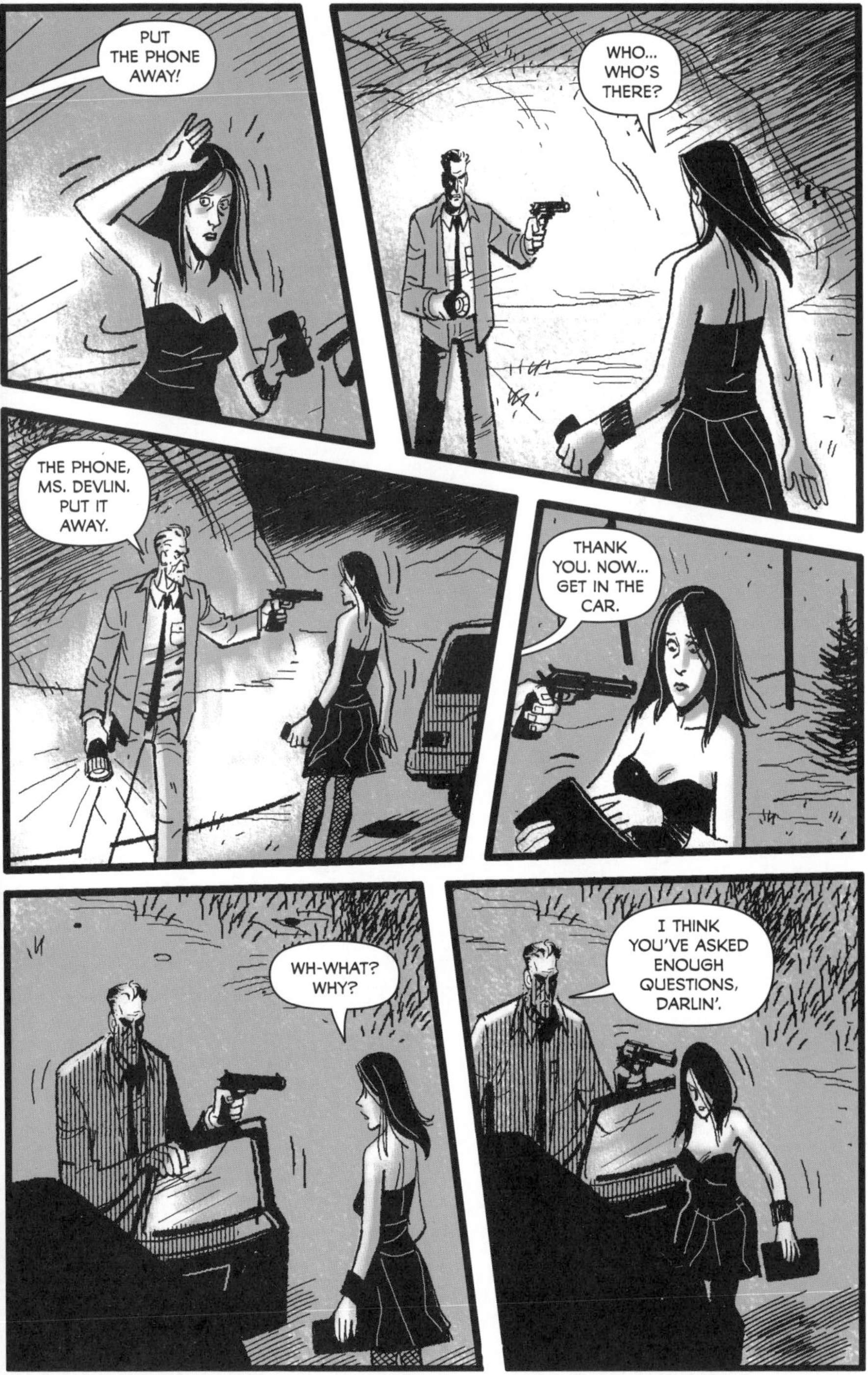
PUT THE PHONE AWAY!
WHO... WHO'S THERE?
THE PHONE, MS. DEVLIN. PUT IT AWAY.
THANK YOU. NOW... GET IN THE CAR.
WH-WHAT? WHY?
I THINK YOU'VE ASKED ENOUGH QUESTIONS, DARLIN'.

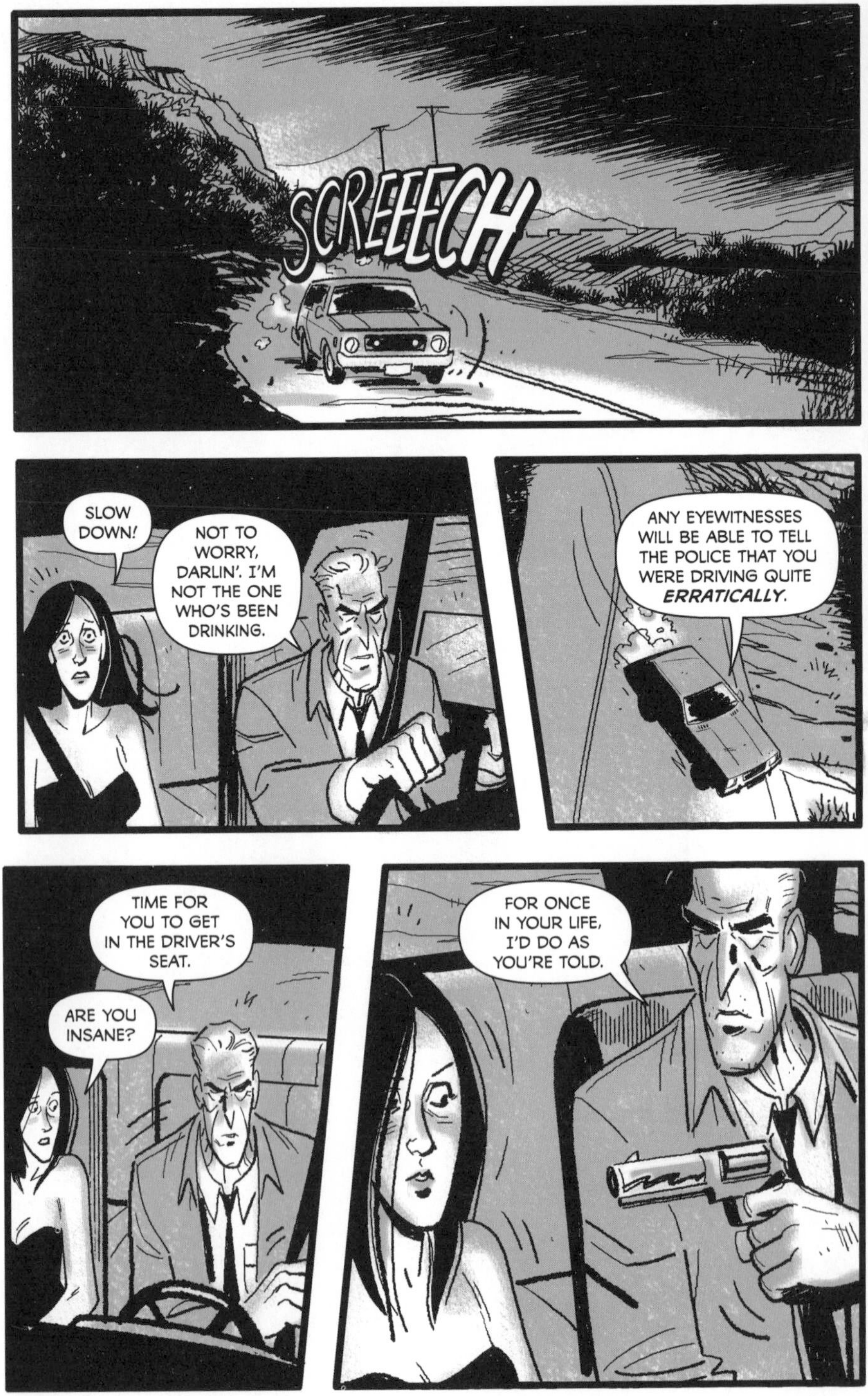
SCREEECH
SLOW DOWN!
NOT TO WORRY, DARLIN'. I'M NOT THE ONE WHO'S BEEN DRINKING.
ANY EYEWITNESSES WILL BE ABLE TO TELL THE POLICE THAT YOU WERE DRIVING QUITE ***ERRATICALLY***.
TIME FOR YOU TO GET IN THE DRIVER'S SEAT.
ARE YOU INSANE?
FOR ONCE IN YOUR LIFE, I'D DO AS YOU'RE TOLD.

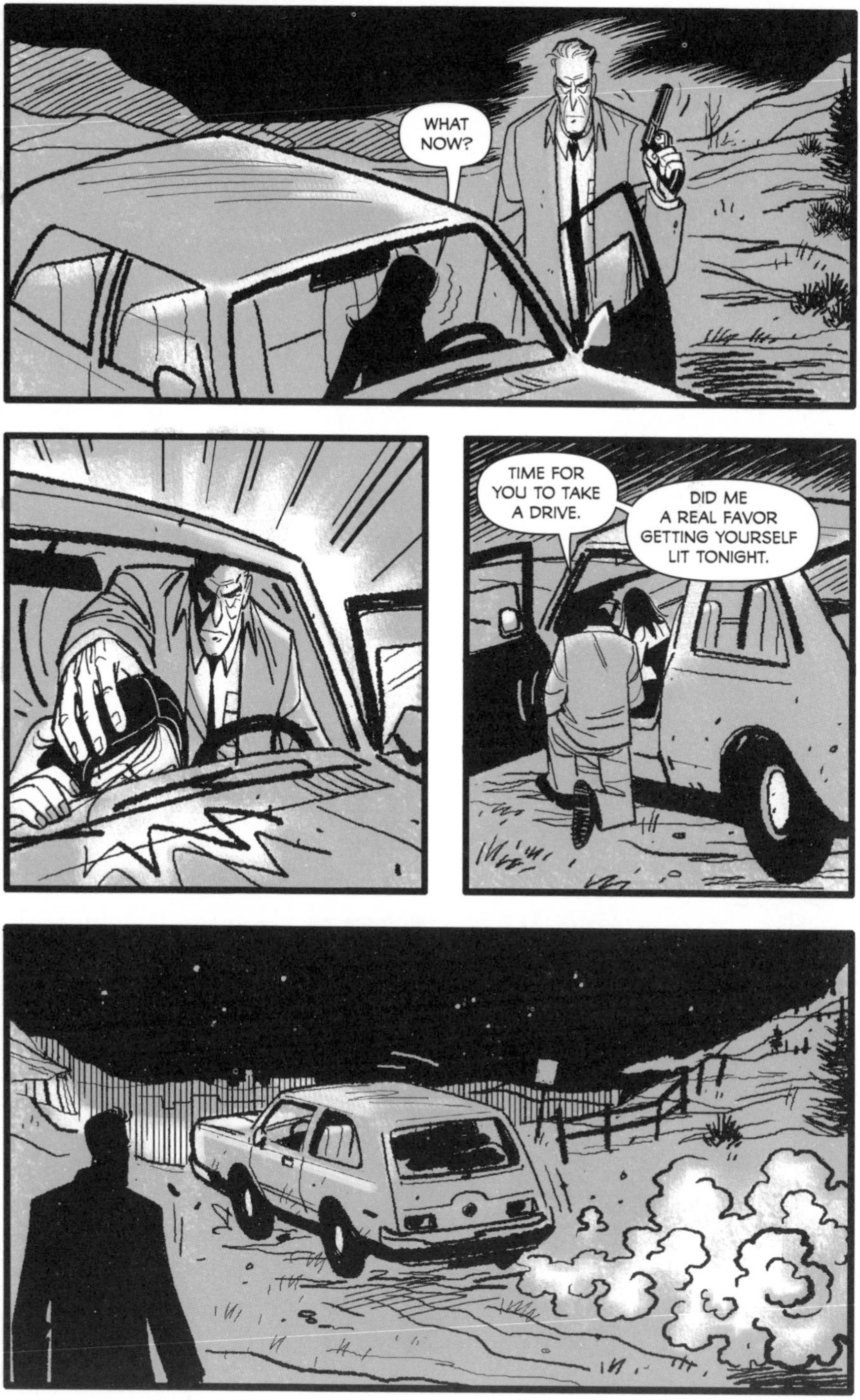
WHAT NOW?
TIME FOR YOU TO TAKE A DRIVE.
DID ME A REAL FAVOR GETTING YOURSELF LIT TONIGHT.

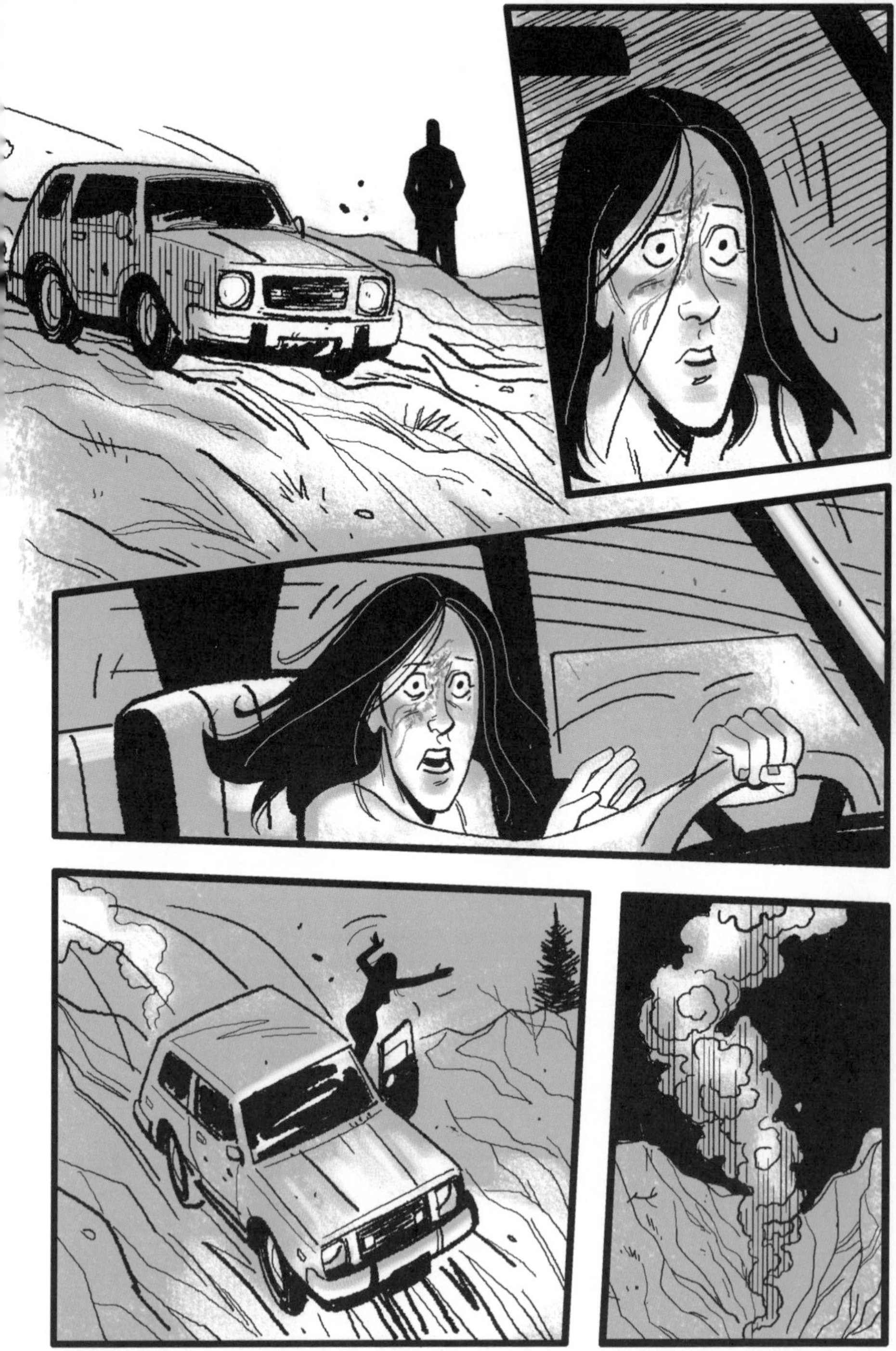

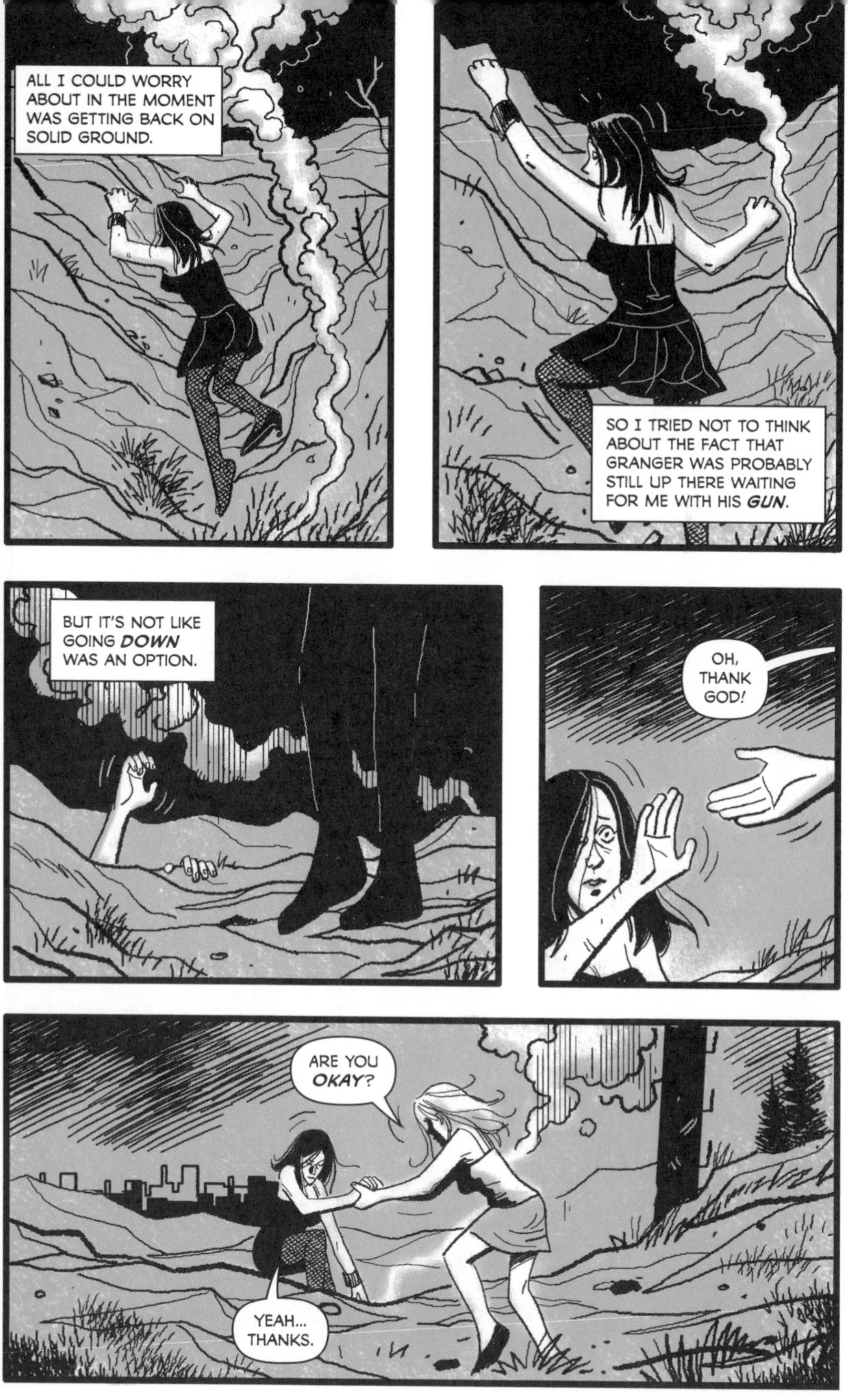
ALL I COULD WORRY ABOUT IN THE MOMENT WAS GETTING BACK ON SOLID GROUND.
SO I TRIED NOT TO THINK ABOUT THE FACT THAT GRANGER WAS PROBABLY STILL UP THERE WAITING FOR ME WITH HIS *GUN*.
BUT IT'S NOT LIKE GOING *DOWN* WAS AN OPTION.
OH, THANK GOD!
ARE YOU *OKAY*?
YEAH... THANKS.

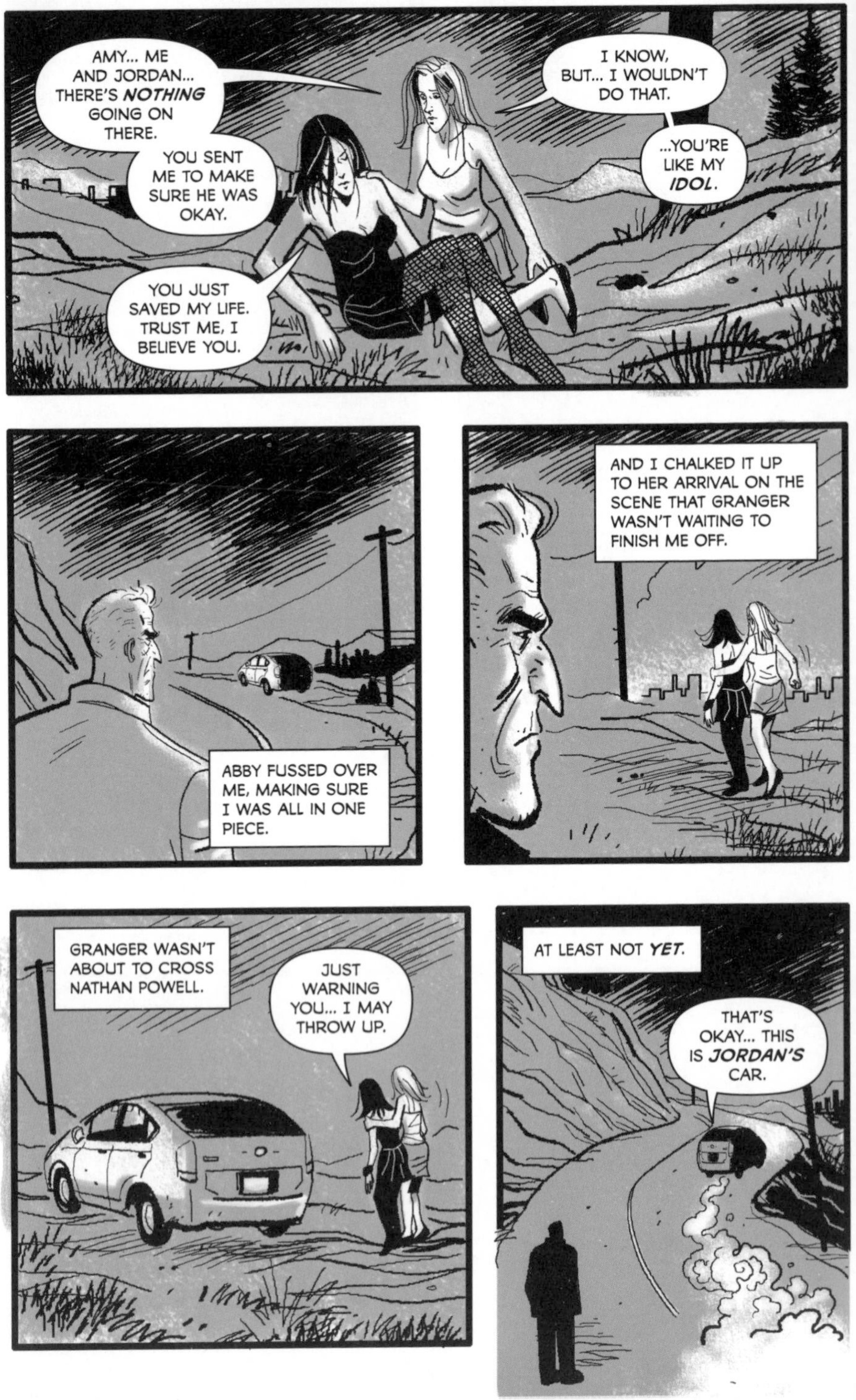
AMY... ME AND JORDAN... THERE'S *NOTHING* GOING ON THERE.
YOU SENT ME TO MAKE SURE HE WAS OKAY.
I KNOW, BUT... I WOULDN'T DO THAT.
...YOU'RE LIKE MY *IDOL*.
YOU JUST SAVED MY LIFE. TRUST ME, I BELIEVE YOU.
ABBY FUSSED OVER ME, MAKING SURE I WAS ALL IN ONE PIECE.
AND I CHALKED IT UP TO HER ARRIVAL ON THE SCENE THAT GRANGER WASN'T WAITING TO FINISH ME OFF.
GRANGER WASN'T ABOUT TO CROSS NATHAN POWELL.
JUST WARNING YOU... I MAY THROW UP.
AT LEAST NOT *YET*.
THAT'S OKAY... THIS IS *JORDAN'S* CAR.

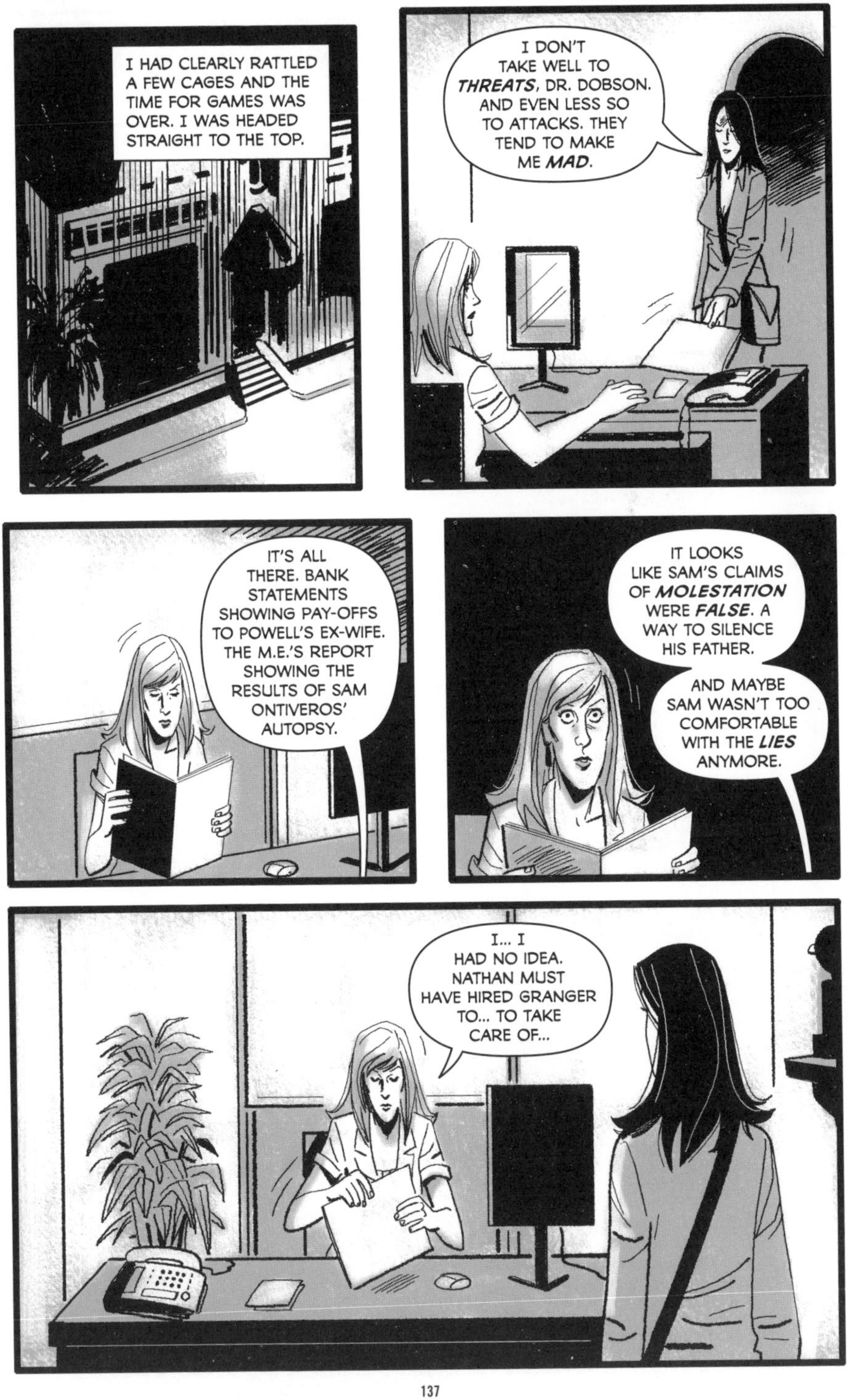
I HAD CLEARLY RATTLED A FEW CAGES AND THE TIME FOR GAMES WAS OVER. I WAS HEADED STRAIGHT TO THE TOP.
I DON'T TAKE WELL TO *THREATS*, DR. DOBSON. AND EVEN LESS SO TO ATTACKS. THEY TEND TO MAKE ME *MAD*.
IT'S ALL THERE. BANK STATEMENTS SHOWING PAY-OFFS TO POWELL'S EX-WIFE. THE M.E.'S REPORT SHOWING THE RESULTS OF SAM ONTIVEROS' AUTOPSY.
IT LOOKS LIKE SAM'S CLAIMS OF *MOLESTATION* WERE *FALSE*. A WAY TO SILENCE HIS FATHER.
AND MAYBE SAM WASN'T TOO COMFORTABLE WITH THE *LIES* ANYMORE.
I... I HAD NO IDEA. NATHAN MUST HAVE HIRED GRANGER TO... TO TAKE CARE OF...

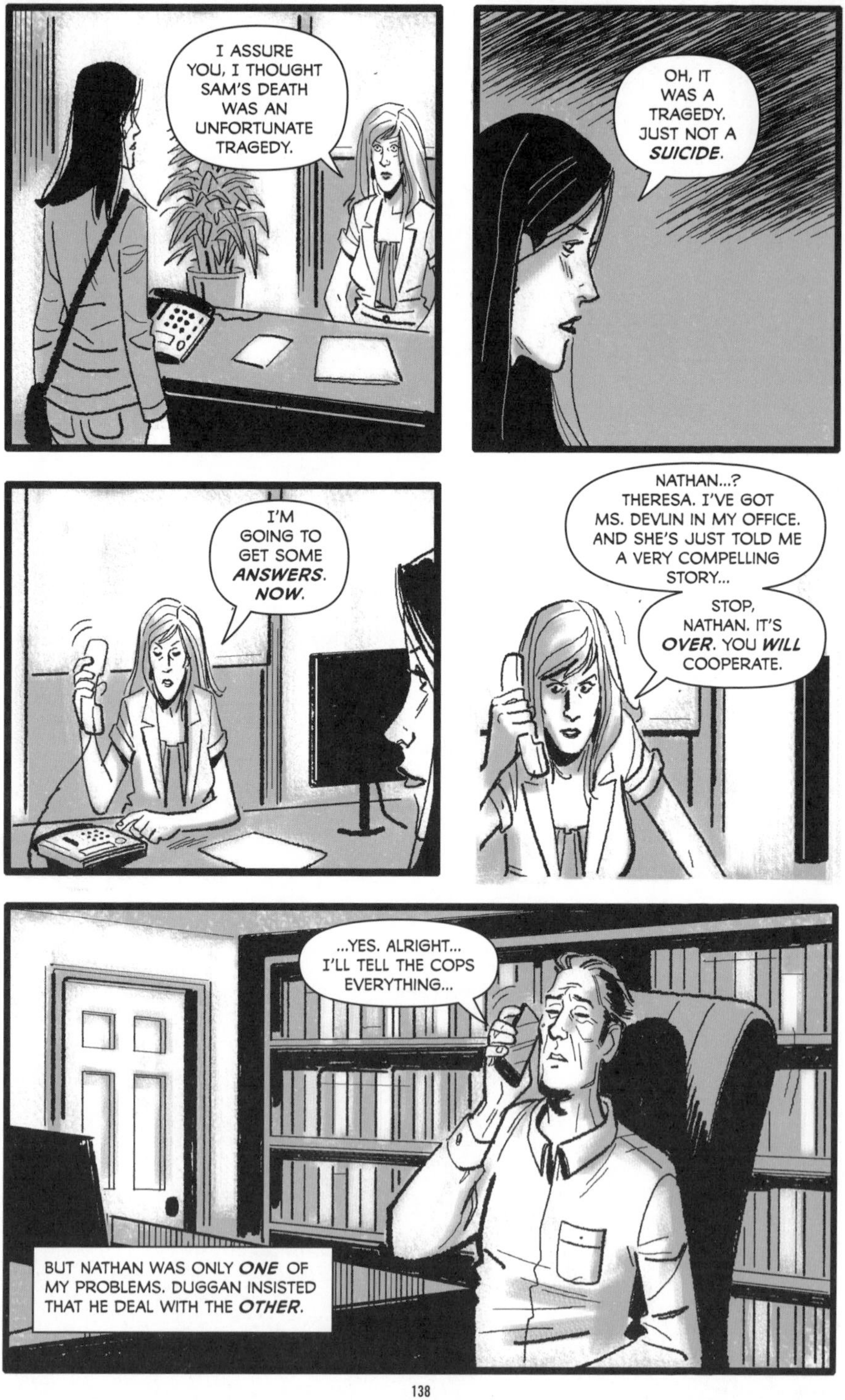
I ASSURE YOU, I THOUGHT SAM'S DEATH WAS AN UNFORTUNATE TRAGEDY.
OH, IT WAS A TRAGEDY. JUST NOT A *SUICIDE*.
I'M GOING TO GET SOME *ANSWERS*. *NOW*.
NATHAN...? THERESA. I'VE GOT MS. DEVLIN IN MY OFFICE. AND SHE'S JUST TOLD ME A VERY COMPELLING STORY...
STOP, NATHAN. IT'S *OVER*. YOU *WILL* COOPERATE.
...YES. ALRIGHT... I'LL TELL THE COPS EVERYTHING...
BUT NATHAN WAS ONLY *ONE* OF MY PROBLEMS. DUGGAN INSISTED THAT HE DEAL WITH THE *OTHER*.

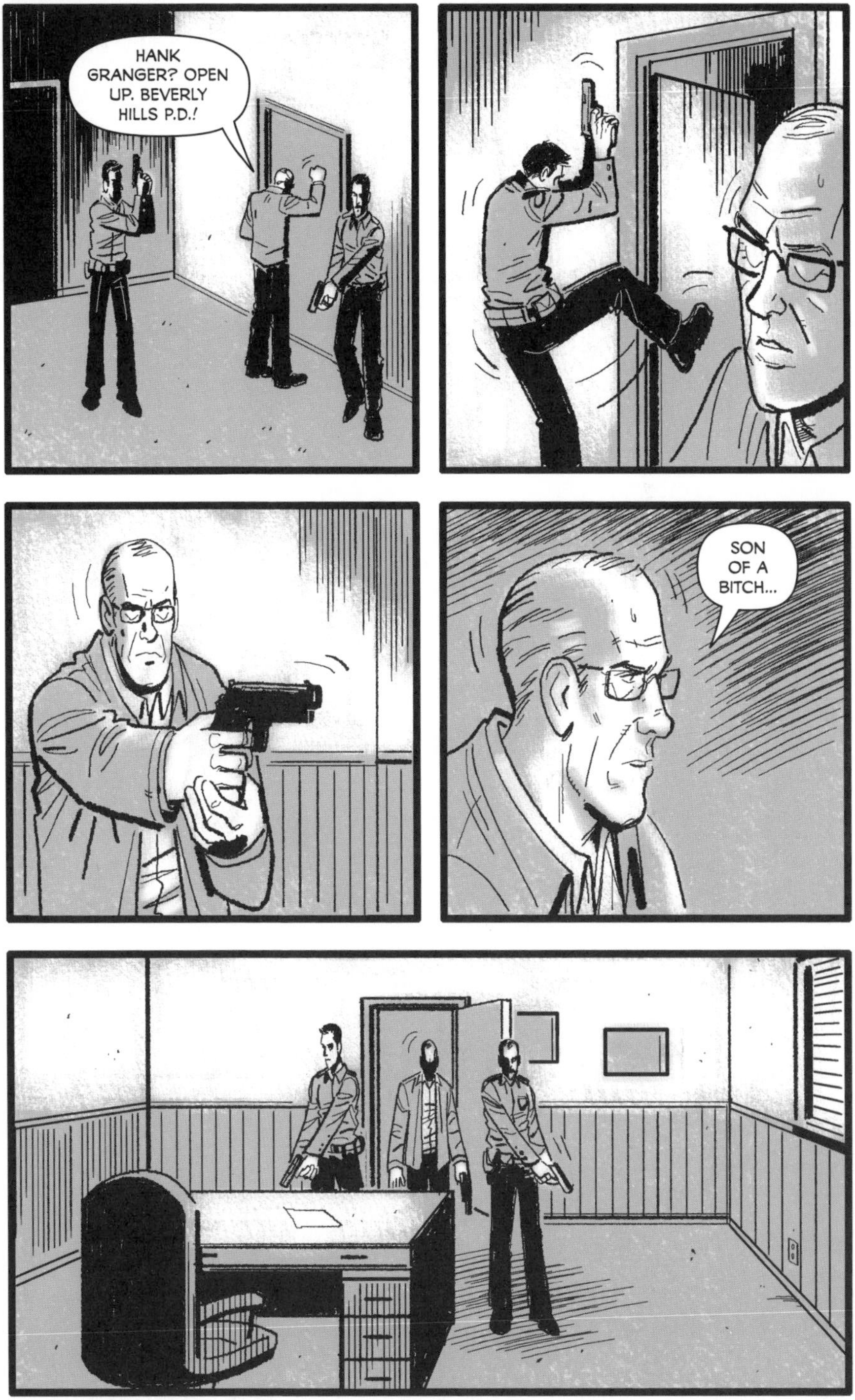
HANK GRANGER? OPEN UP. BEVERLY HILLS P.D.!
SON OF A BITCH...

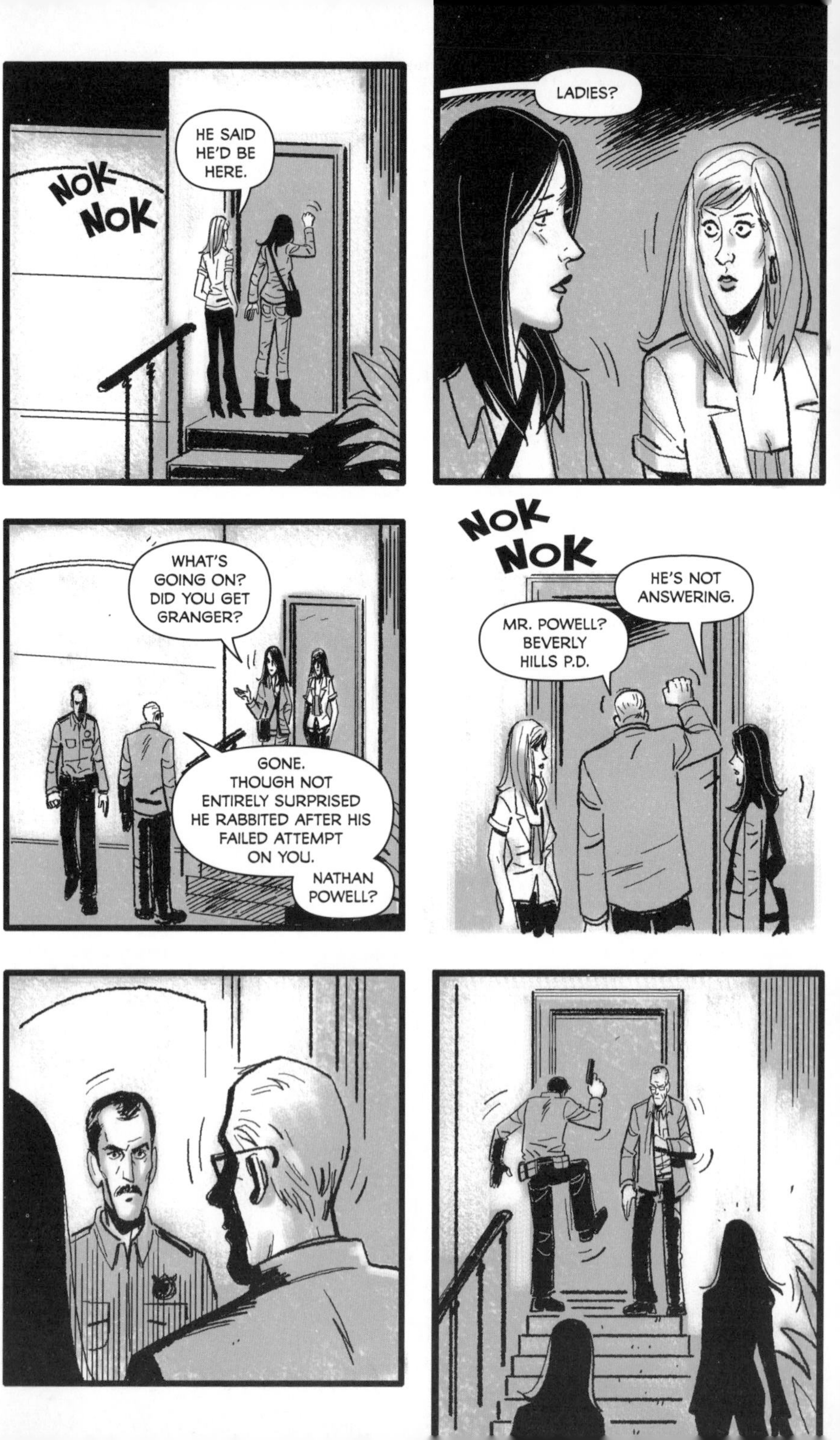
NOK NOK
HE SAID HE'D BE HERE.
LADIES?
WHAT'S GOING ON? DID YOU GET GRANGER?
GONE. THOUGH NOT ENTIRELY SURPRISED HE RABBITED AFTER HIS FAILED ATTEMPT ON YOU.
NATHAN POWELL?
NOK NOK
HE'S NOT ANSWERING.
MR. POWELL? BEVERLY HILLS P.D.

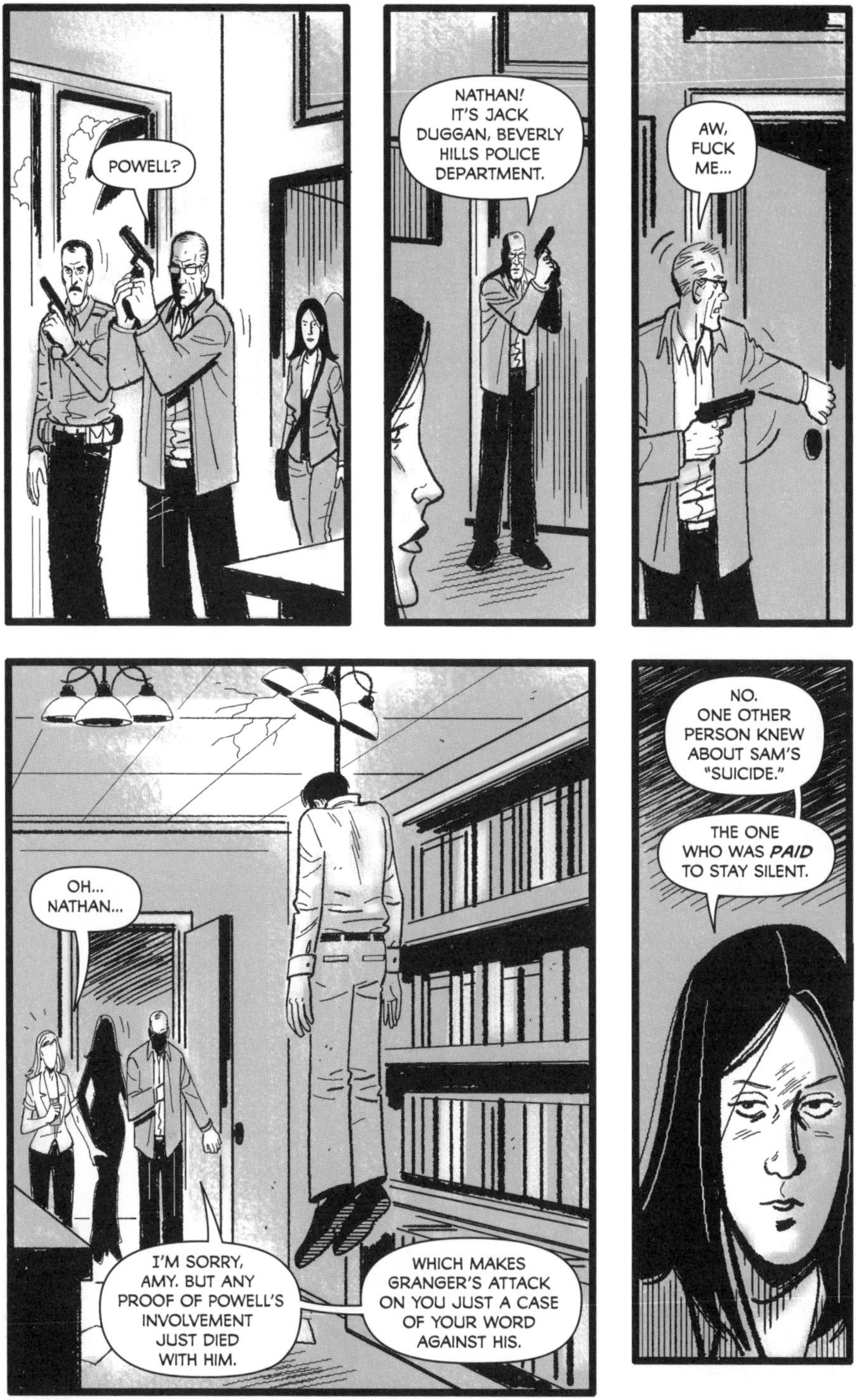
POWELL?
NATHAN! IT'S JACK DUGGAN, BEVERLY HILLS POLICE DEPARTMENT.
AW, FUCK ME...
OH... NATHAN...
I'M SORRY, AMY. BUT ANY PROOF OF POWELL'S INVOLVEMENT JUST DIED WITH HIM.
WHICH MAKES GRANGER'S ATTACK ON YOU JUST A CASE OF YOUR WORD AGAINST HIS.
NO. ONE OTHER PERSON KNEW ABOUT SAM'S "SUICIDE."
THE ONE WHO WAS ***PAID*** TO STAY SILENT.

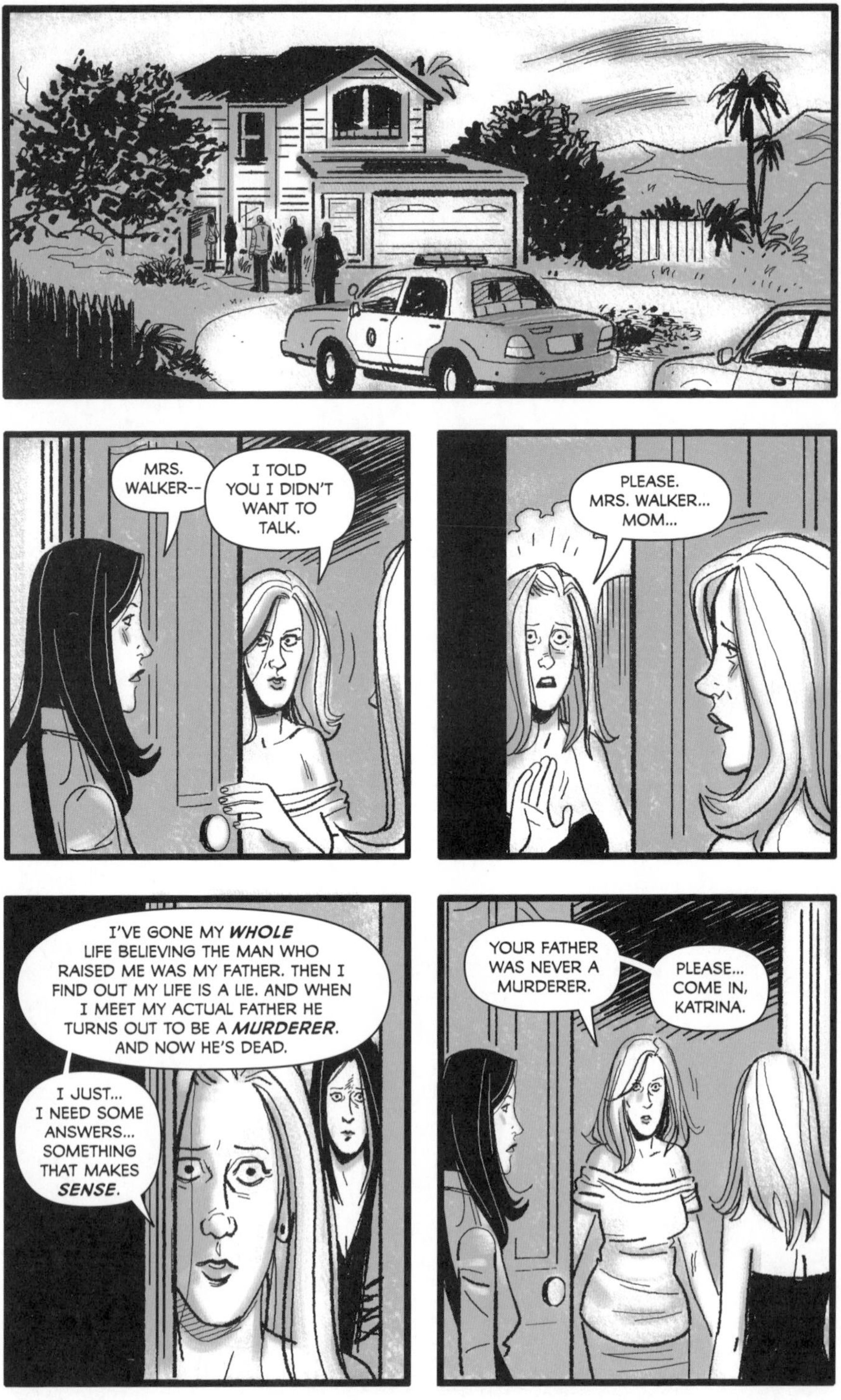
MRS. WALKER--
I TOLD YOU I DIDN'T WANT TO TALK.
PLEASE. MRS. WALKER... MOM...
I'VE GONE MY ***WHOLE*** LIFE BELIEVING THE MAN WHO RAISED ME WAS MY FATHER. THEN I FIND OUT MY LIFE IS A LIE. AND WHEN I MEET MY ACTUAL FATHER HE TURNS OUT TO BE A ***MURDERER***. AND NOW HE'S DEAD.
I JUST... I NEED SOME ANSWERS... SOMETHING THAT MAKES ***SENSE***.
YOUR FATHER WAS NEVER A MURDERER.
PLEASE... COME IN, KATRINA.

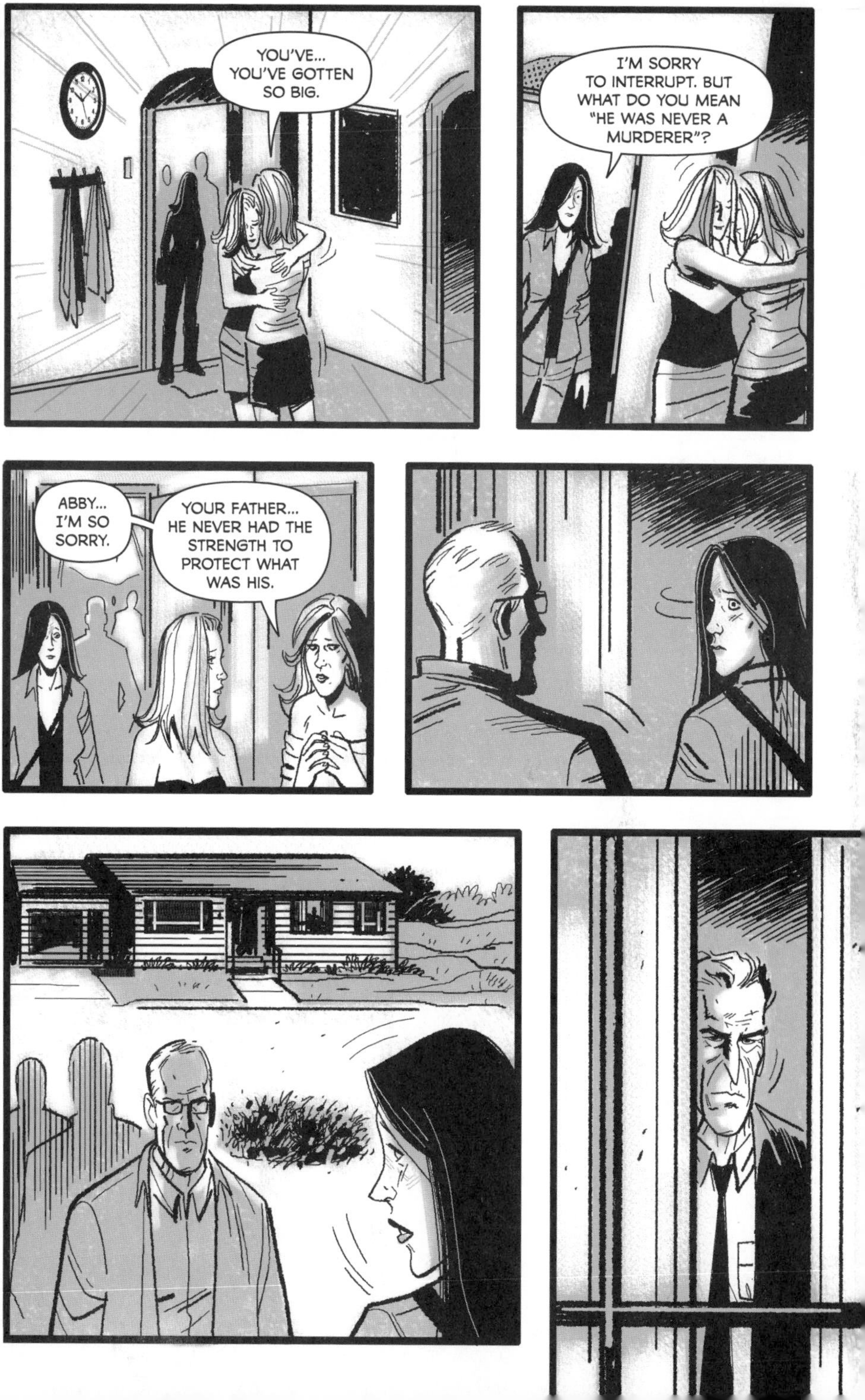
YOU'VE... YOU'VE GOTTEN SO BIG.
I'M SORRY TO INTERRUPT. BUT WHAT DO YOU MEAN "HE WAS NEVER A MURDERER"?
ABBY... I'M SO SORRY.
YOUR FATHER... HE NEVER HAD THE STRENGTH TO PROTECT WHAT WAS HIS.

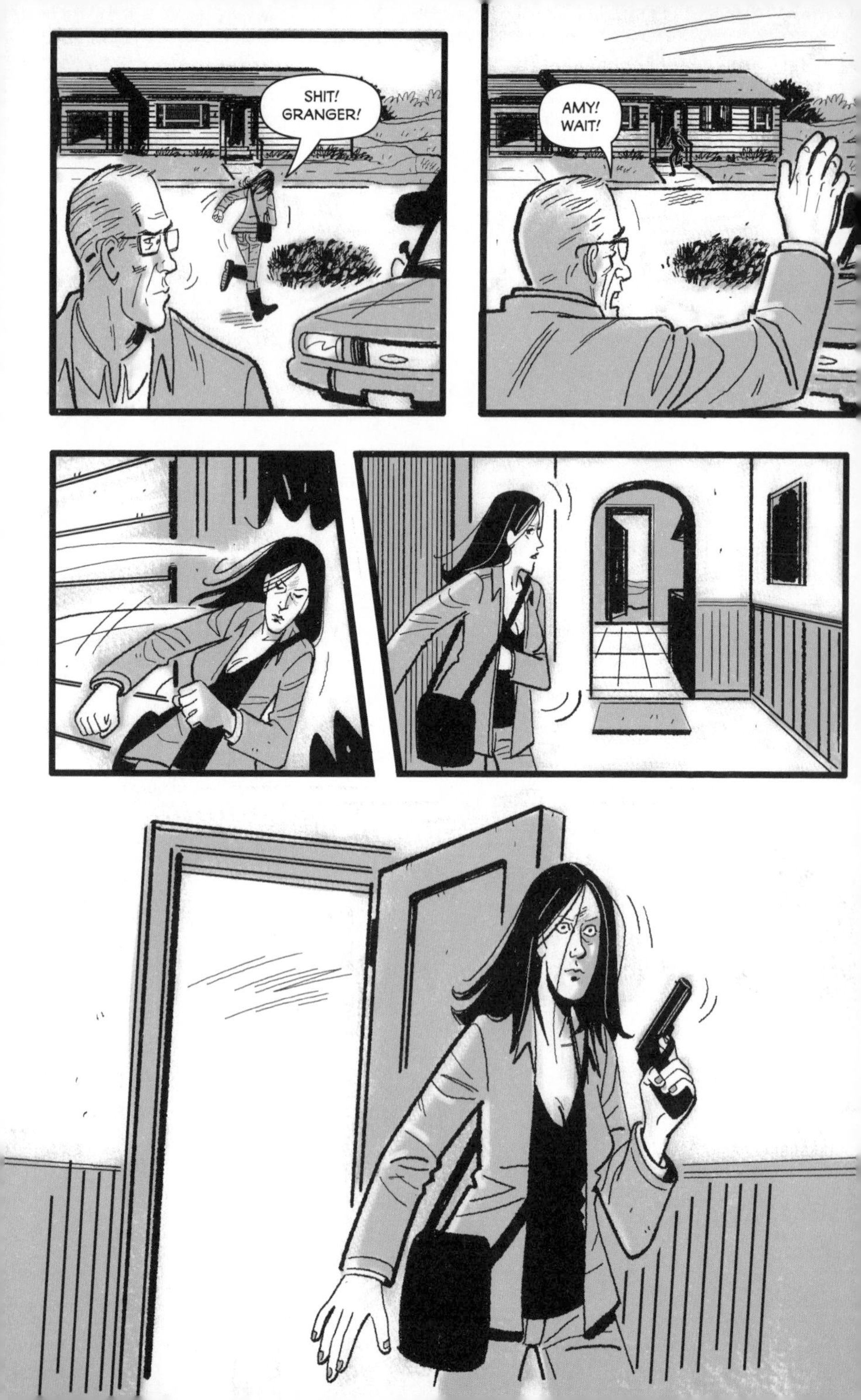
SHIT! GRANGER!
AMY! WAIT!

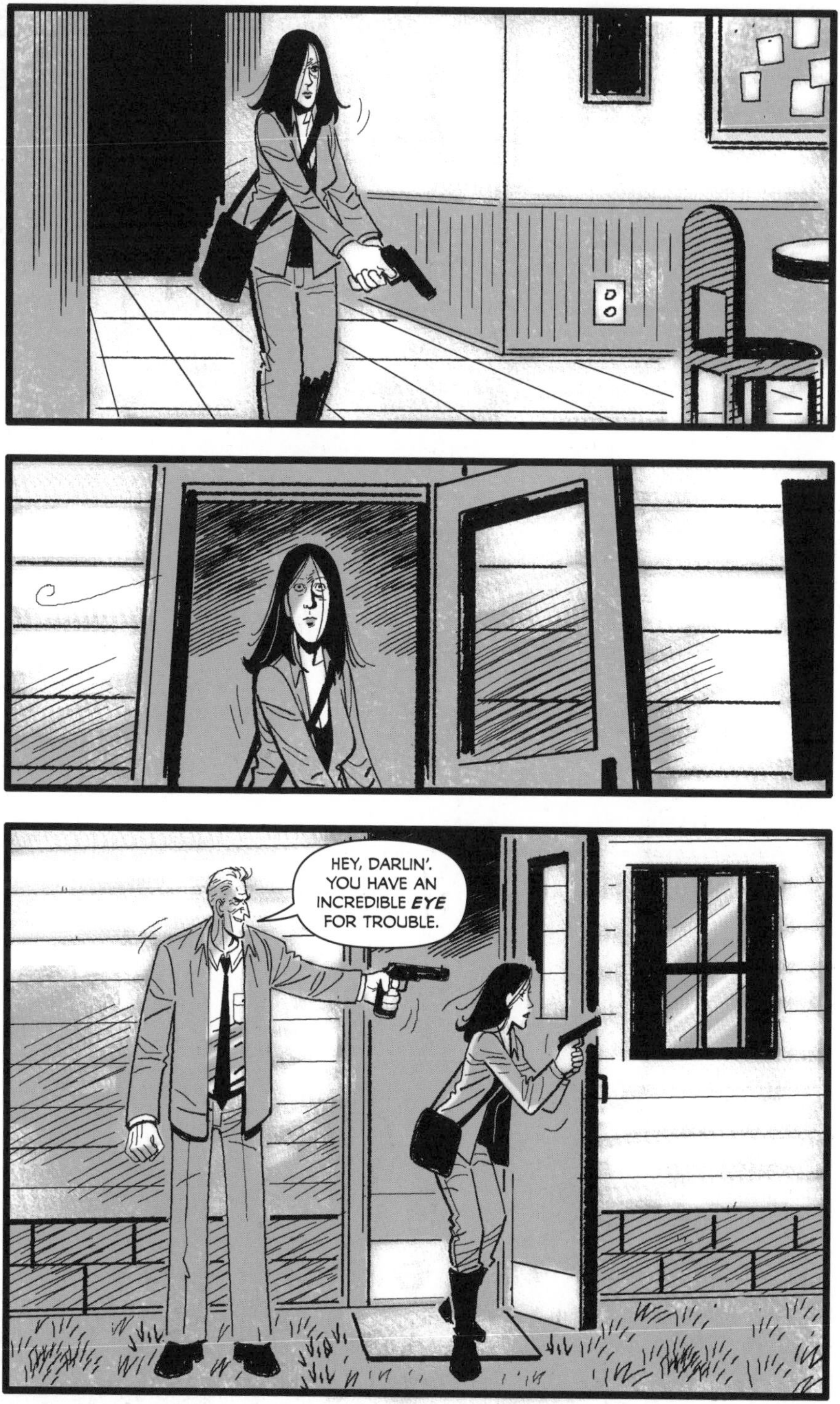
HEY, DARLIN'. YOU HAVE AN INCREDIBLE *EYE* FOR TROUBLE.

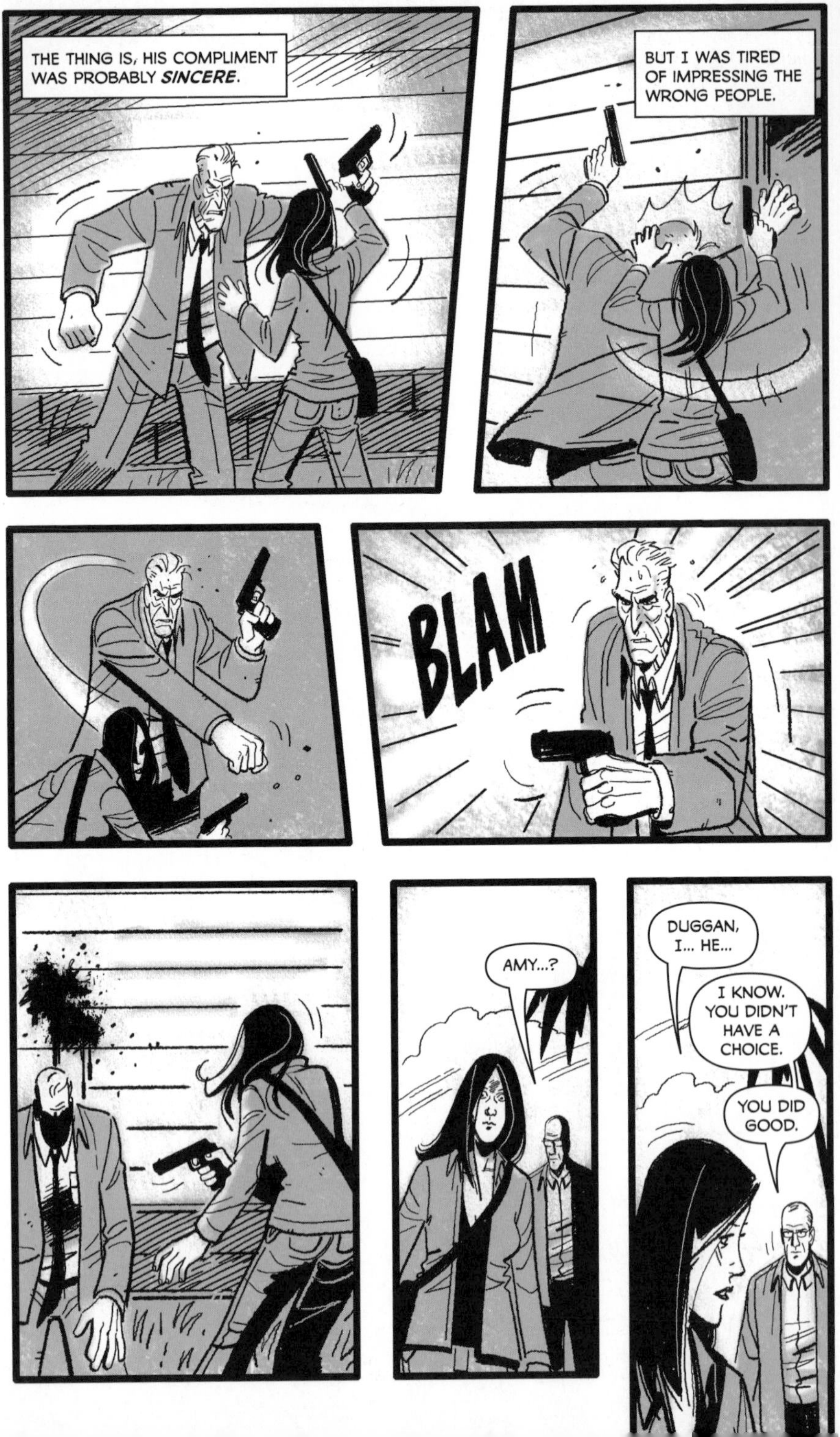

THE THING IS, HIS COMPLIMENT WAS PROBABLY *SINCERE*.
BUT I WAS TIRED OF IMPRESSING THE WRONG PEOPLE.
BLAM
AMY...?
DUGGAN, I... HE...
I KNOW. YOU DIDN'T HAVE A CHOICE.
YOU DID GOOD.

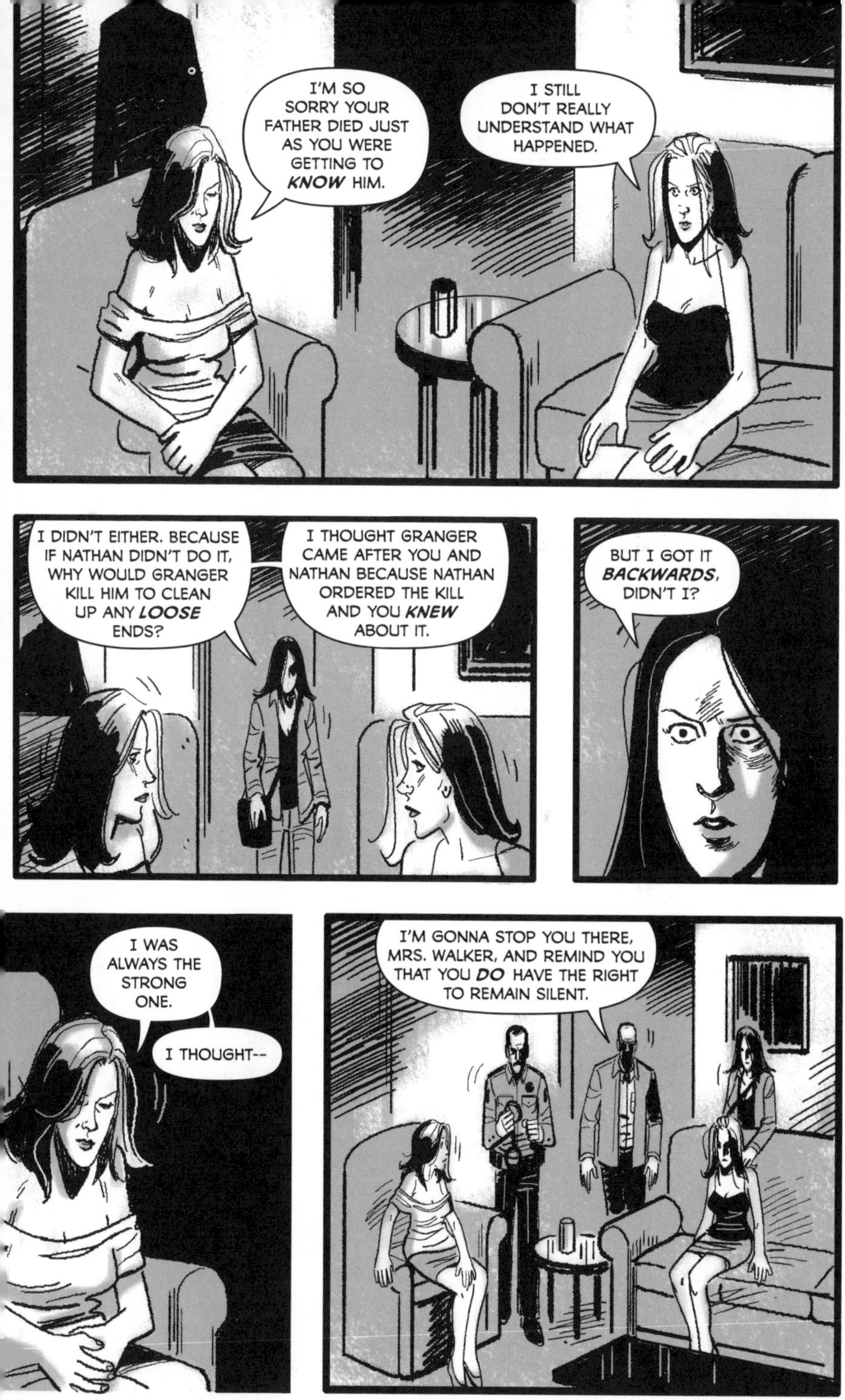
I'M SO SORRY YOUR FATHER DIED JUST AS YOU WERE GETTING TO *KNOW* HIM.
I STILL DON'T REALLY UNDERSTAND WHAT HAPPENED.
I DIDN'T EITHER. BECAUSE IF NATHAN DIDN'T DO IT, WHY WOULD GRANGER KILL HIM TO CLEAN UP ANY *LOOSE* ENDS?
I THOUGHT GRANGER CAME AFTER YOU AND NATHAN BECAUSE NATHAN ORDERED THE KILL AND YOU *KNEW* ABOUT IT.
BUT I GOT IT *BACKWARDS*, DIDN'T I?
I WAS ALWAYS THE STRONG ONE.
I THOUGHT--
I'M GONNA STOP YOU THERE, MRS. WALKER, AND REMIND YOU THAT YOU *DO* HAVE THE RIGHT TO REMAIN SILENT.

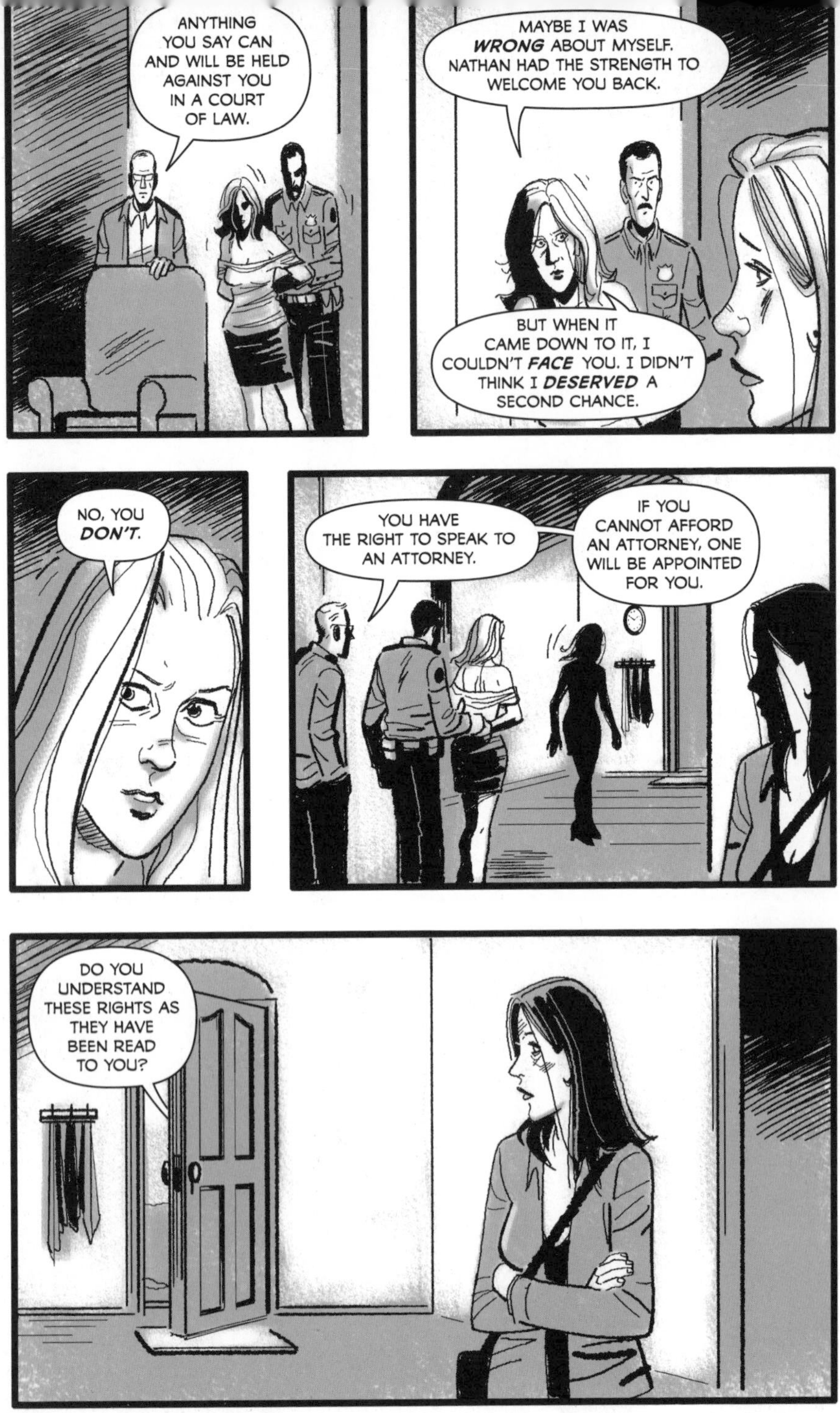
ANYTHING YOU SAY CAN AND WILL BE HELD AGAINST YOU IN A COURT OF LAW.
MAYBE I WAS **WRONG** ABOUT MYSELF. NATHAN HAD THE STRENGTH TO WELCOME YOU BACK.
BUT WHEN IT CAME DOWN TO IT, I COULDN'T **FACE** YOU. I DIDN'T THINK I **DESERVED** A SECOND CHANCE.
NO, YOU **DON'T**.
YOU HAVE THE RIGHT TO SPEAK TO AN ATTORNEY.
IF YOU CANNOT AFFORD AN ATTORNEY, ONE WILL BE APPOINTED FOR YOU.
DO YOU UNDERSTAND THESE RIGHTS AS THEY HAVE BEEN READ TO YOU?

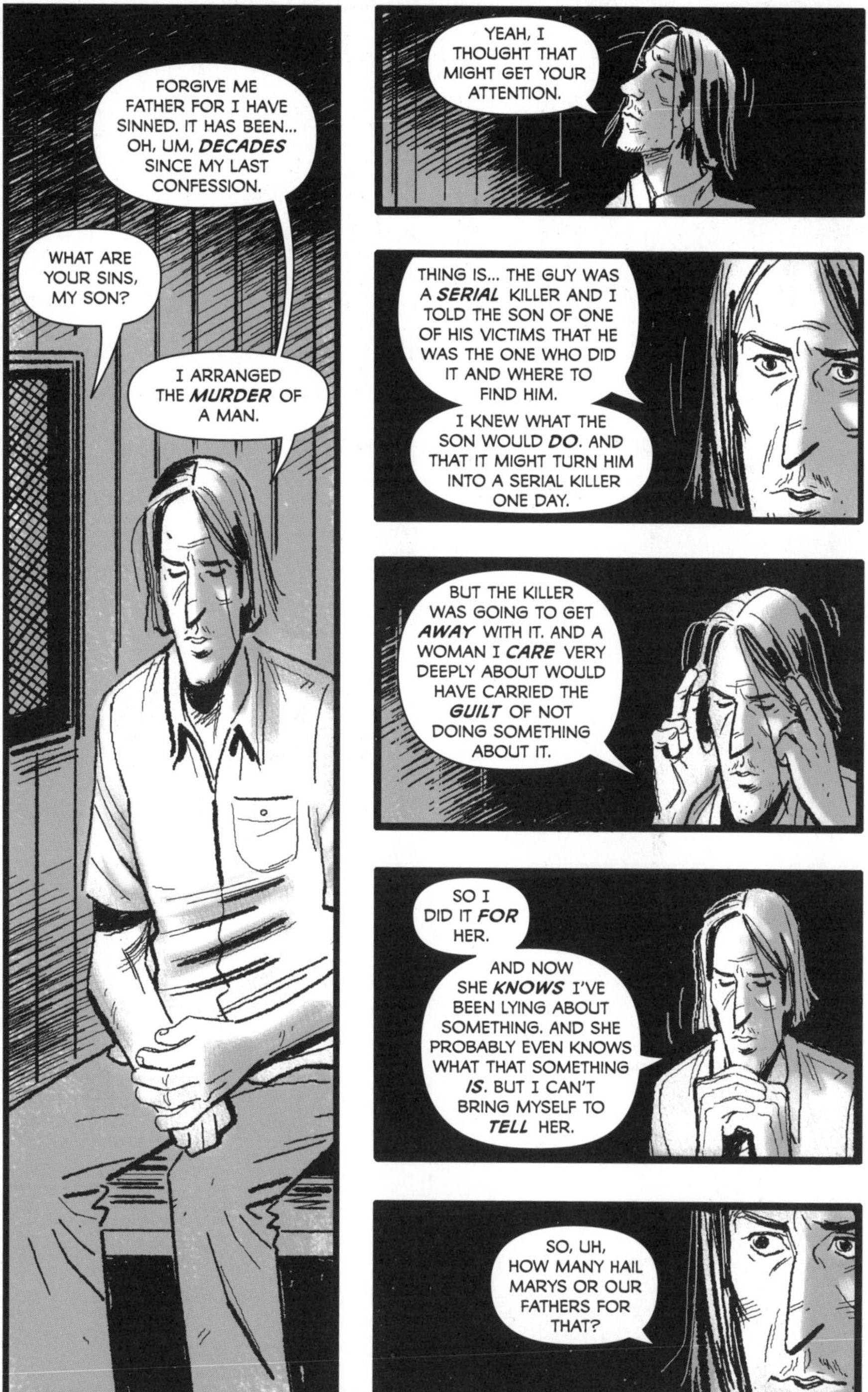
FORGIVE ME FATHER FOR I HAVE SINNED. IT HAS BEEN... OH, UM, ***DECADES*** SINCE MY LAST CONFESSION.
WHAT ARE YOUR SINS, MY SON?
I ARRANGED THE ***MURDER*** OF A MAN.
YEAH, I THOUGHT THAT MIGHT GET YOUR ATTENTION.
THING IS... THE GUY WAS A ***SERIAL*** KILLER AND I TOLD THE SON OF ONE OF HIS VICTIMS THAT HE WAS THE ONE WHO DID IT AND WHERE TO FIND HIM.
I KNEW WHAT THE SON WOULD ***DO***. AND THAT IT MIGHT TURN HIM INTO A SERIAL KILLER ONE DAY.
BUT THE KILLER WAS GOING TO GET ***AWAY*** WITH IT. AND A WOMAN I ***CARE*** VERY DEEPLY ABOUT WOULD HAVE CARRIED THE ***GUILT*** OF NOT DOING SOMETHING ABOUT IT.
SO I DID IT ***FOR*** HER.
AND NOW SHE ***KNOWS*** I'VE BEEN LYING ABOUT SOMETHING. AND SHE PROBABLY EVEN KNOWS WHAT THAT SOMETHING ***IS***. BUT I CAN'T BRING MYSELF TO ***TELL*** HER.
SO, UH, HOW MANY HAIL MARYS OR OUR FATHERS FOR THAT?

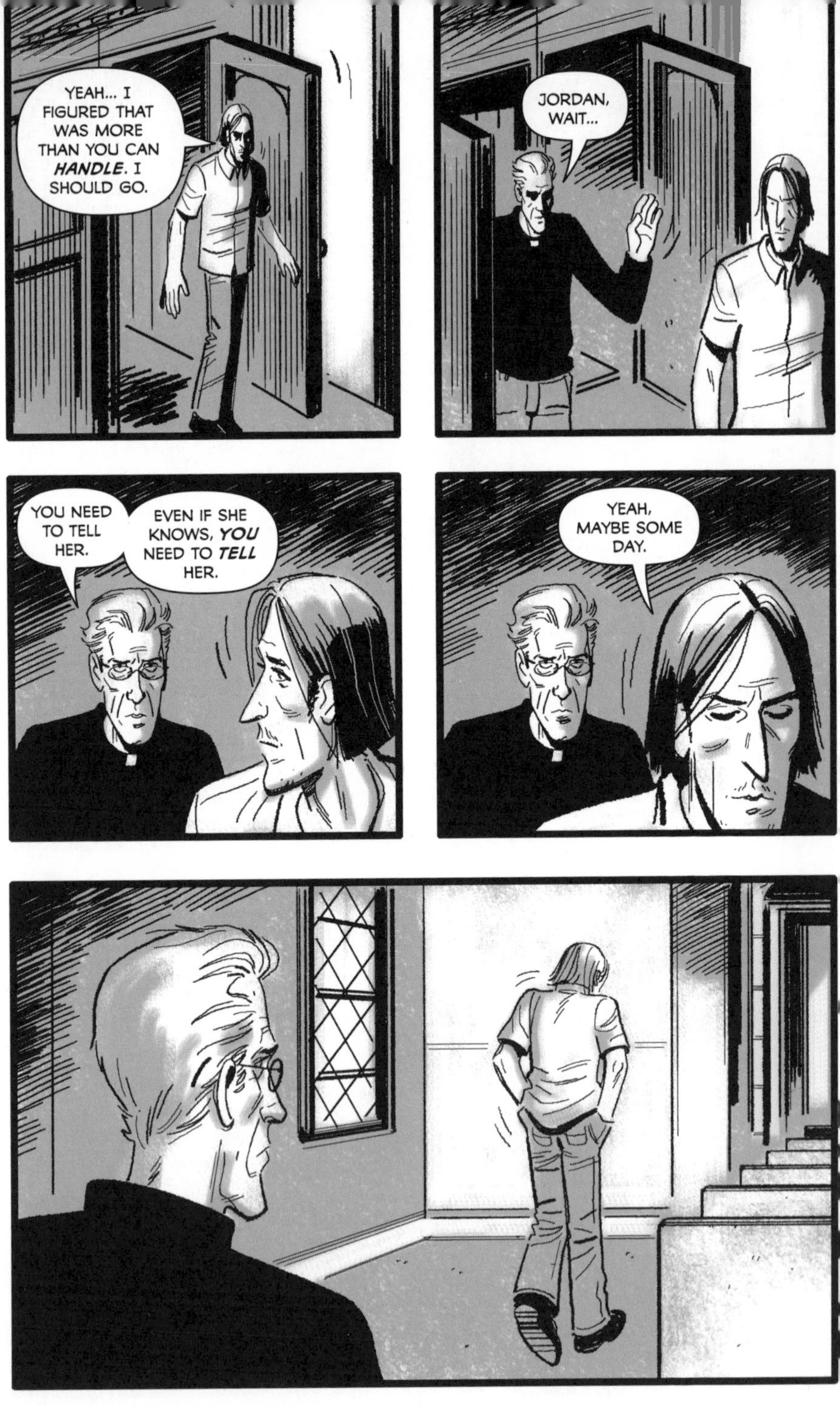
YEAH... I FIGURED THAT WAS MORE THAN YOU CAN HANDLE. I SHOULD GO.
JORDAN, WAIT...
YOU NEED TO TELL HER.
EVEN IF SHE KNOWS, YOU NEED TO TELL HER.
YEAH, MAYBE SOME DAY.

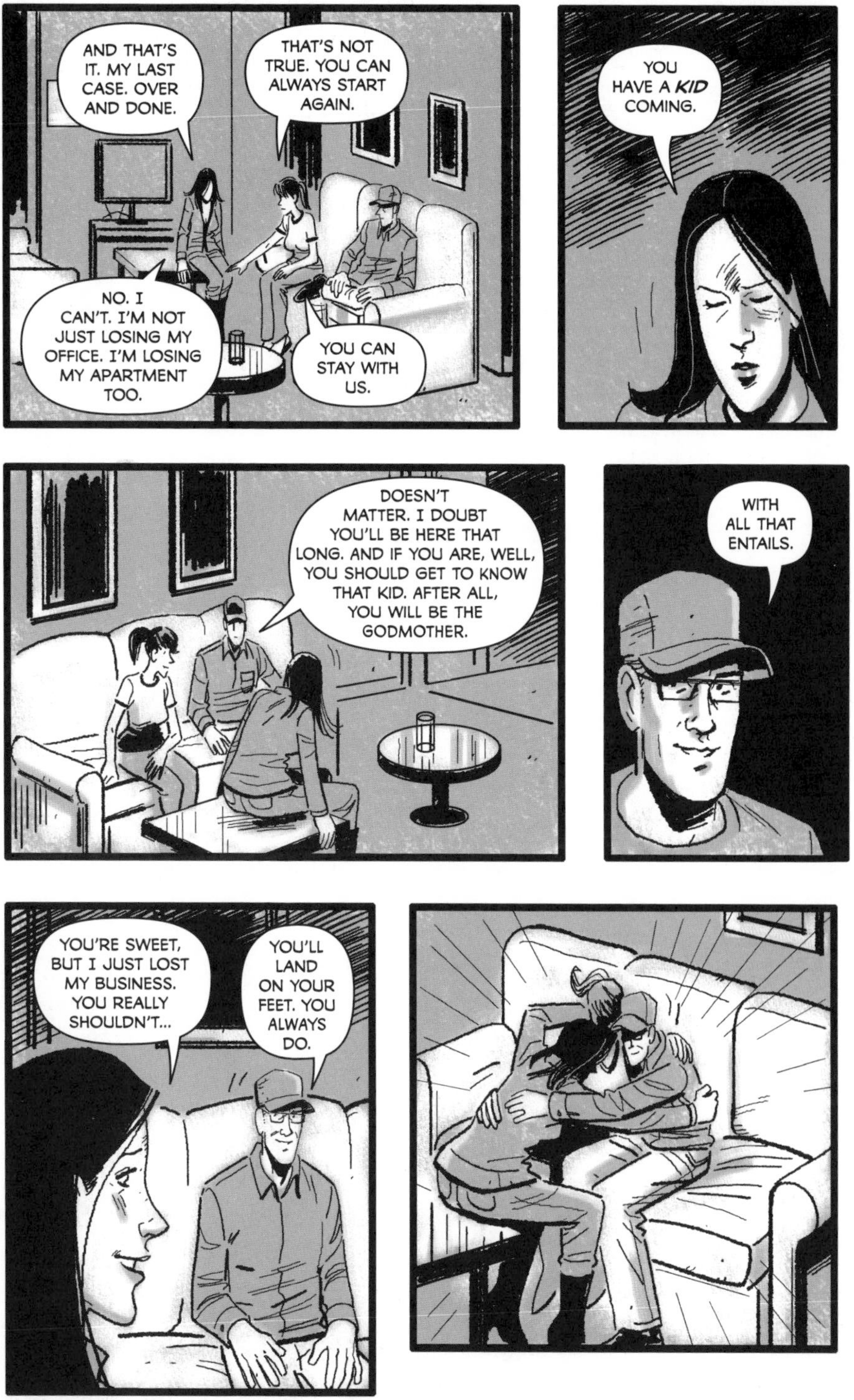

AND THAT'S IT. MY LAST CASE. OVER AND DONE.
THAT'S NOT TRUE. YOU CAN ALWAYS START AGAIN.
NO. I CAN'T. I'M NOT JUST LOSING MY OFFICE. I'M LOSING MY APARTMENT TOO.
YOU CAN STAY WITH US.
YOU HAVE A *KID* COMING.
DOESN'T MATTER. I DOUBT YOU'LL BE HERE THAT LONG. AND IF YOU ARE, WELL, YOU SHOULD GET TO KNOW THAT KID. AFTER ALL, YOU WILL BE THE GODMOTHER.
WITH ALL THAT ENTAILS.
YOU'RE SWEET, BUT I JUST LOST MY BUSINESS. YOU REALLY SHOULDN'T...
YOU'LL LAND ON YOUR FEET. YOU ALWAYS DO.

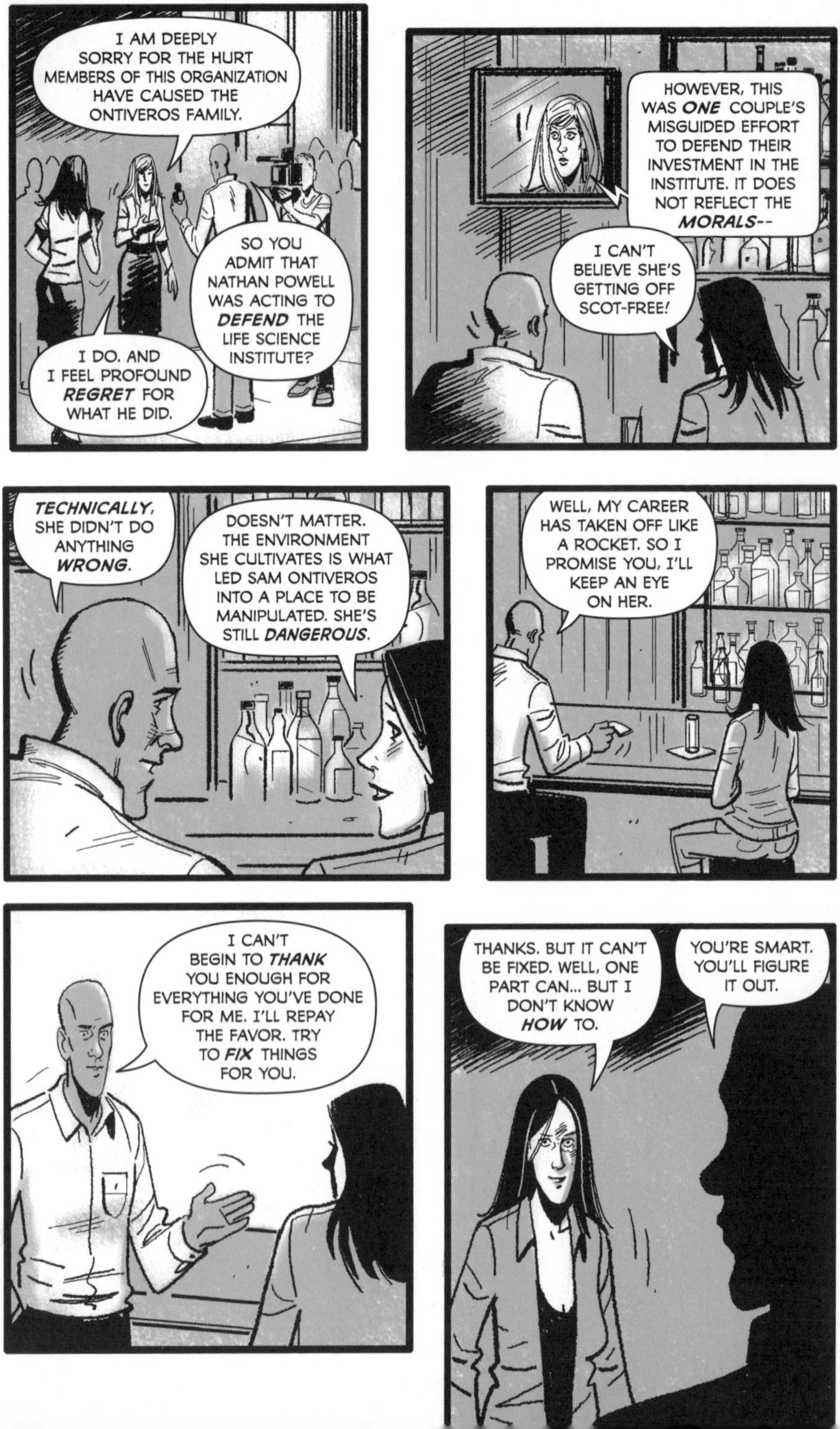
I AM DEEPLY SORRY FOR THE HURT MEMBERS OF THIS ORGANIZATION HAVE CAUSED THE ONTIVEROS FAMILY.
SO YOU ADMIT THAT NATHAN POWELL WAS ACTING TO DEFEND THE LIFE SCIENCE INSTITUTE?
I DO. AND I FEEL PROFOUND REGRET FOR WHAT HE DID.
HOWEVER, THIS WAS ONE COUPLE'S MISGUIDED EFFORT TO DEFEND THEIR INVESTMENT IN THE INSTITUTE. IT DOES NOT REFLECT THE MORALS--
I CAN'T BELIEVE SHE'S GETTING OFF SCOT-FREE!
TECHNICALLY, SHE DIDN'T DO ANYTHING WRONG.
DOESN'T MATTER. THE ENVIRONMENT SHE CULTIVATES IS WHAT LED SAM ONTIVEROS INTO A PLACE TO BE MANIPULATED. SHE'S STILL DANGEROUS.
WELL, MY CAREER HAS TAKEN OFF LIKE A ROCKET. SO I PROMISE YOU, I'LL KEEP AN EYE ON HER.
I CAN'T BEGIN TO THANK YOU ENOUGH FOR EVERYTHING YOU'VE DONE FOR ME. I'LL REPAY THE FAVOR. TRY TO FIX THINGS FOR YOU.
THANKS. BUT IT CAN'T BE FIXED. WELL, ONE PART CAN... BUT I DON'T KNOW HOW TO.
YOU'RE SMART. YOU'LL FIGURE IT OUT.

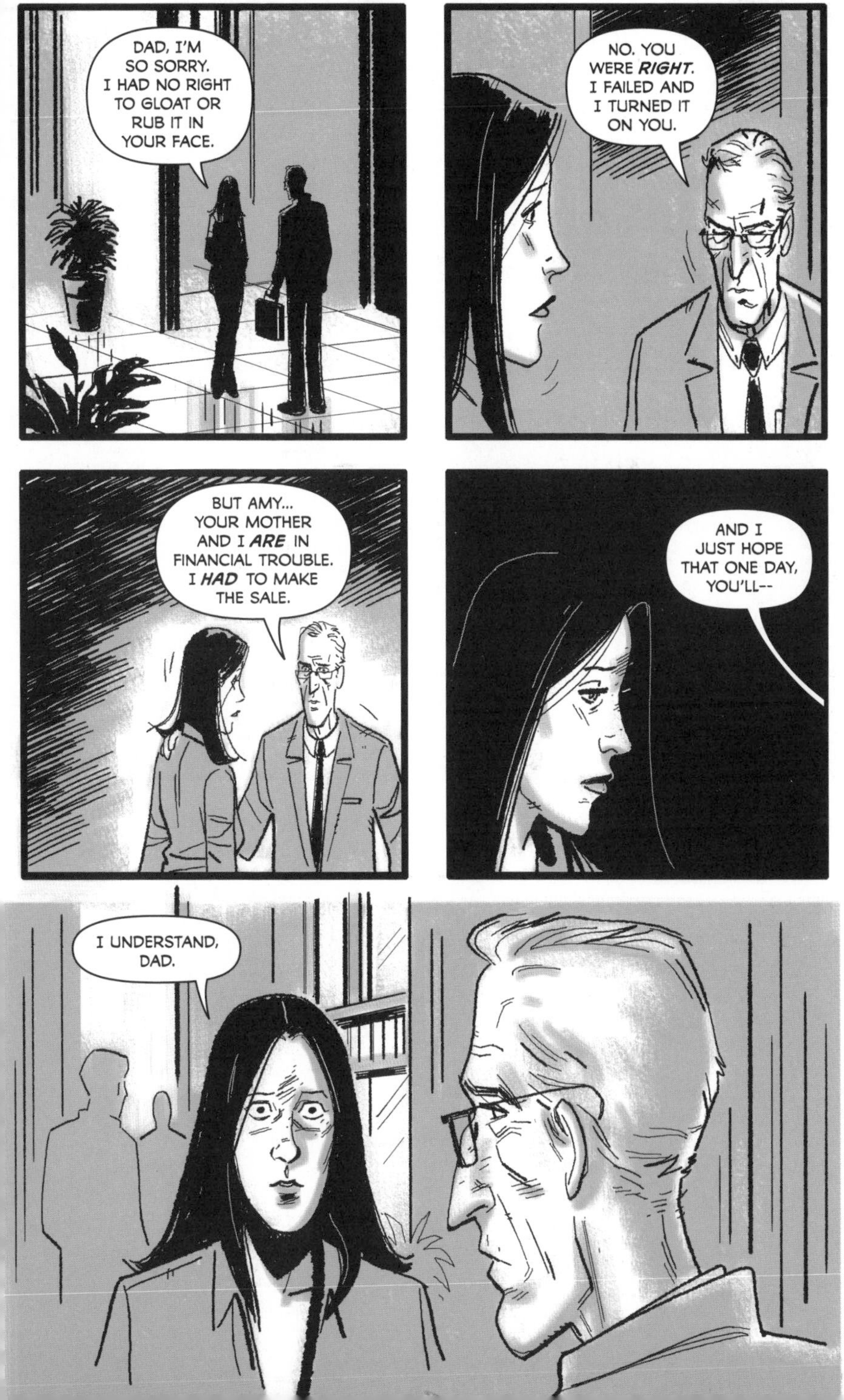
DAD, I'M SO SORRY. I HAD NO RIGHT TO GLOAT OR RUB IT IN YOUR FACE.
NO. YOU WERE ***RIGHT***. I FAILED AND I TURNED IT ON YOU.
BUT AMY... YOUR MOTHER AND I ***ARE*** IN FINANCIAL TROUBLE. I ***HAD*** TO MAKE THE SALE.
AND I JUST HOPE THAT ONE DAY, YOU'LL--
I UNDERSTAND, DAD.

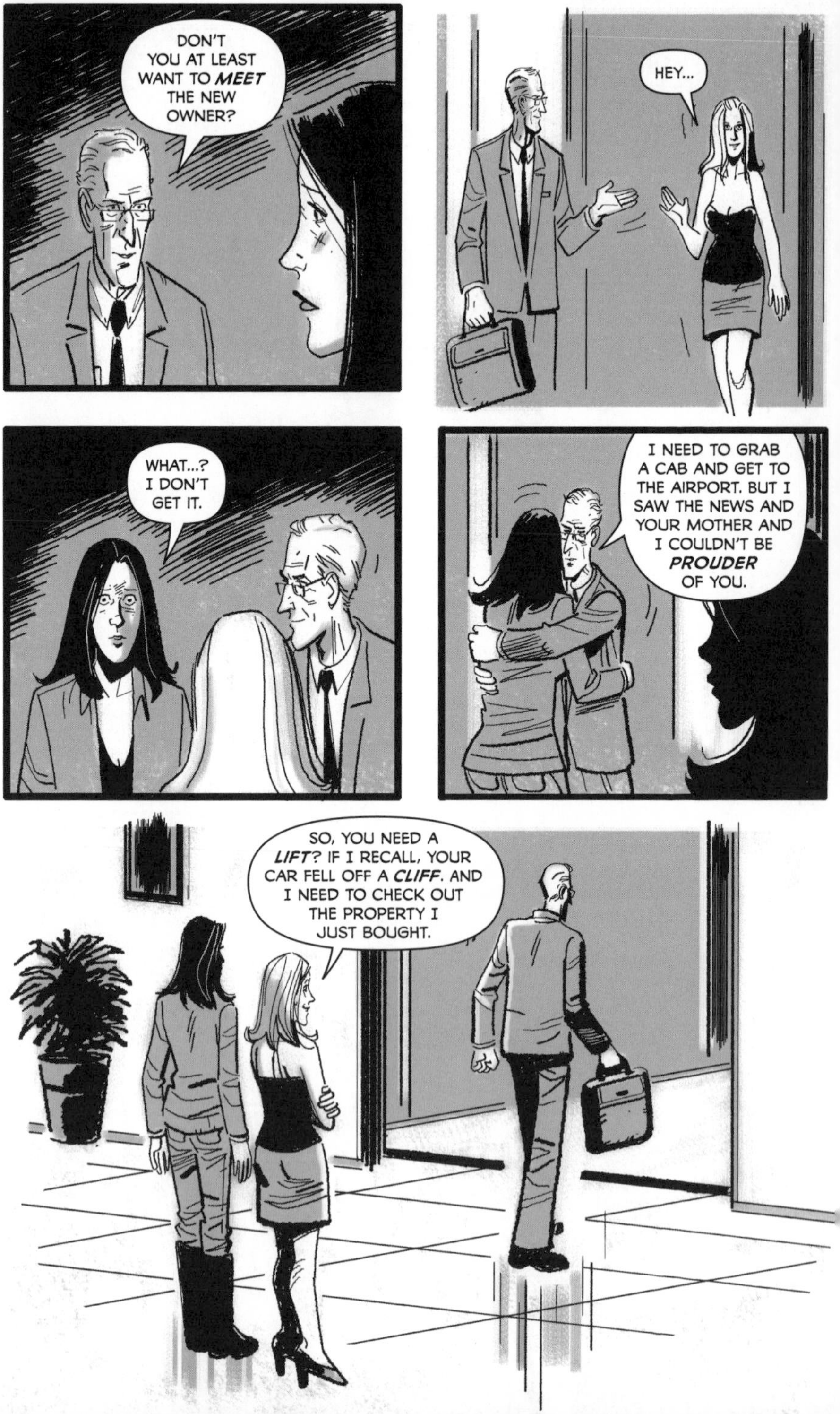
DON'T YOU AT LEAST WANT TO *MEET* THE NEW OWNER?
HEY...
WHAT...? I DON'T GET IT.
I NEED TO GRAB A CAB AND GET TO THE AIRPORT. BUT I SAW THE NEWS AND YOUR MOTHER AND I COULDN'T BE *PROUDER* OF YOU.
SO, YOU NEED A *LIFT*? IF I RECALL, YOUR CAR FELL OFF A *CLIFF*. AND I NEED TO CHECK OUT THE PROPERTY I JUST BOUGHT.

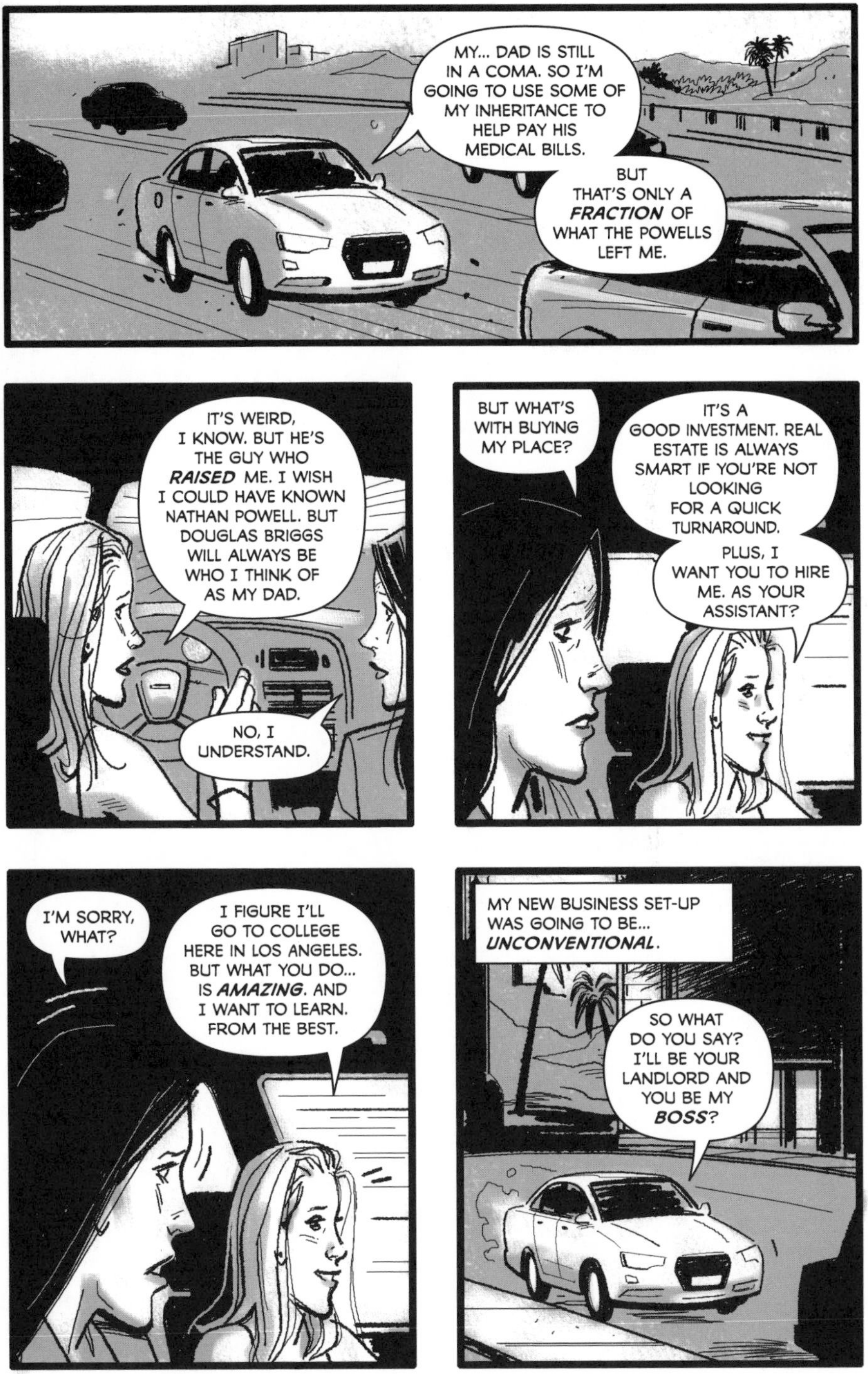
MY... DAD IS STILL IN A COMA. SO I'M GOING TO USE SOME OF MY INHERITANCE TO HELP PAY HIS MEDICAL BILLS.
BUT THAT'S ONLY A *FRACTION* OF WHAT THE POWELLS LEFT ME.
IT'S WEIRD, I KNOW. BUT HE'S THE GUY WHO *RAISED* ME. I WISH I COULD HAVE KNOWN NATHAN POWELL. BUT DOUGLAS BRIGGS WILL ALWAYS BE WHO I THINK OF AS MY DAD.
NO, I UNDERSTAND.
BUT WHAT'S WITH BUYING MY PLACE?
IT'S A GOOD INVESTMENT. REAL ESTATE IS ALWAYS SMART IF YOU'RE NOT LOOKING FOR A QUICK TURNAROUND.
PLUS, I WANT YOU TO HIRE ME. AS YOUR ASSISTANT?
I'M SORRY, WHAT?
I FIGURE I'LL GO TO COLLEGE HERE IN LOS ANGELES. BUT WHAT YOU DO... IS *AMAZING*. AND I WANT TO LEARN. FROM THE BEST.
MY NEW BUSINESS SET-UP WAS GOING TO BE... *UNCONVENTIONAL*.
SO WHAT DO YOU SAY? I'LL BE YOUR LANDLORD AND YOU BE MY *BOSS*?

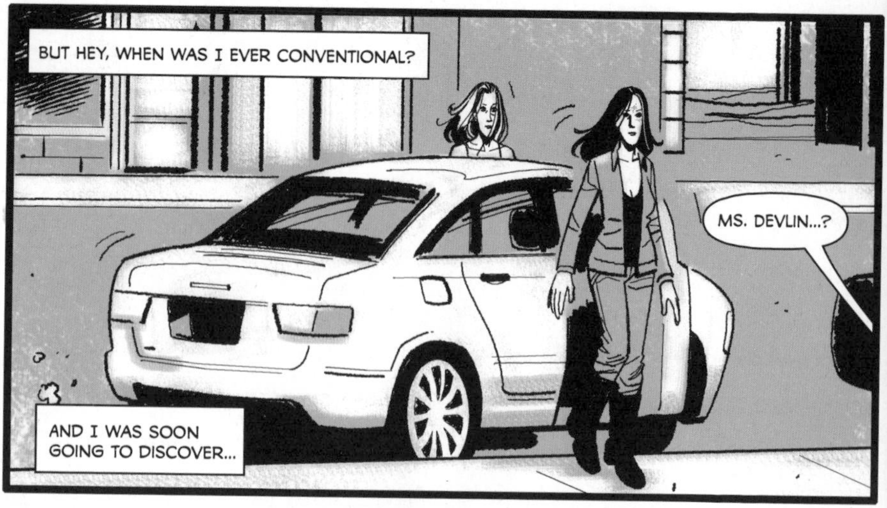
BUT HEY, WHEN WAS I EVER CONVENTIONAL?
MS. DEVLIN...?
AND I WAS SOON GOING TO DISCOVER...

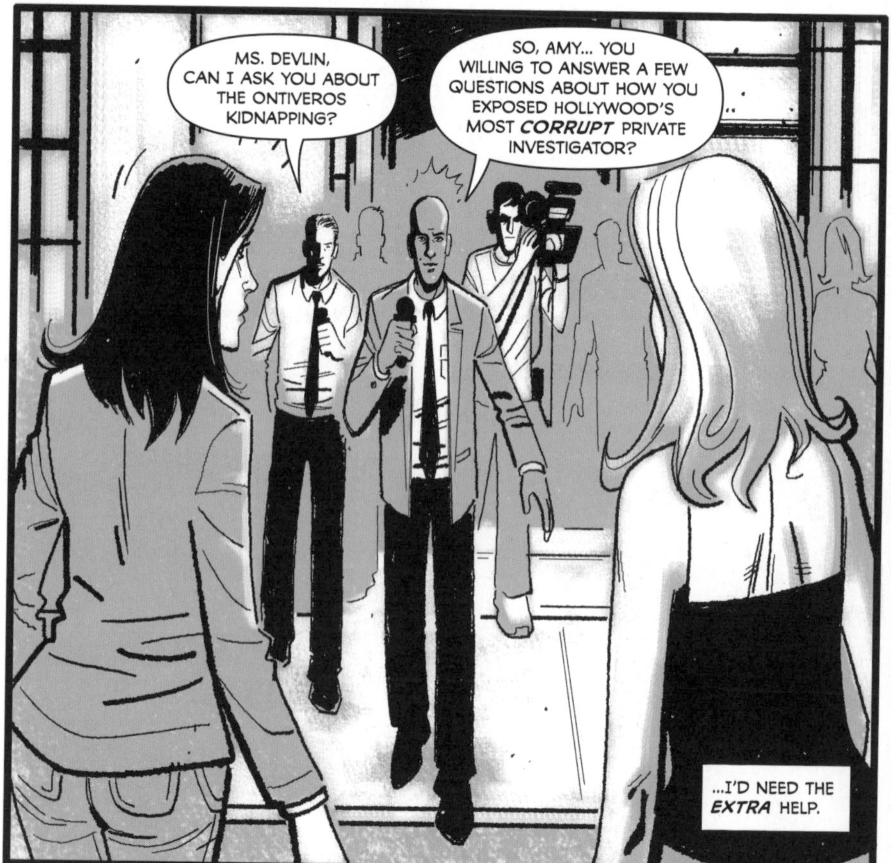
MS. DEVLIN, CAN I ASK YOU ABOUT THE ONTIVEROS KIDNAPPING?
SO, AMY... YOU WILLING TO ANSWER A FEW QUESTIONS ABOUT HOW YOU EXPOSED HOLLYWOOD'S MOST *CORRUPT* PRIVATE INVESTIGATOR?
...I'D NEED THE *EXTRA* HELP.

NUNZIO DEFILIPPIS & CHRISTINA WEIR are a writing team who have worked in comics, television, film and video games. Trained as screenwriters (DeFilippis at USC's Screenwriting Program and Weir at Emerson College's Television Program), they spent two seasons on the staff of HBO's *Arliss* before turning their attention to comics. In comics, they have written a wide array of genres, including such stories as *Maria's Wedding*, *The Tomb*, *Play Ball*, *Frenemy Of The State*, *Bad Medicine* and *The Avalon Chronicles* for Oni Press. Their superhero comic credits include *New Mutants*, *New X-Men*, *Adventures Of Superman*, *Checkmate* and *Batman Confidential*. They have also worked in the field of manga, adapting numerous series from Del Rey, and creating four Original English Language Manga series for Seven Seas Entertainment: *Destiny's Hand*, *Amazing Agent Luna*, its spinoff *Amazing Agent Jennifer*, and the modern horror romance *Dracula Everlasting*. They are also entering the world of prose fiction and have written a novel.

Lost and Found is their third Amy Devlin mystery (following *Past Lies* and *All Saints Day*). They are hard at work on her next case.

T.J. KIRSCH is a cartoonist and illustrator living in upstate New York. A Kubert School graduate, his work has been published by Oni Press, Archie Comics, Top Shelf 2.0, and various anthologies. He is also the co-creator of *She Died In Terrebonne: A Sam Kimimura Mystery* with writer Kevin Church, as well as a frequent contributor to Jonathan Baylis' autobiographical comic series *So Buttons*. More work can be found at www.tjkirsch.com.

This is his first full length graphic novel.

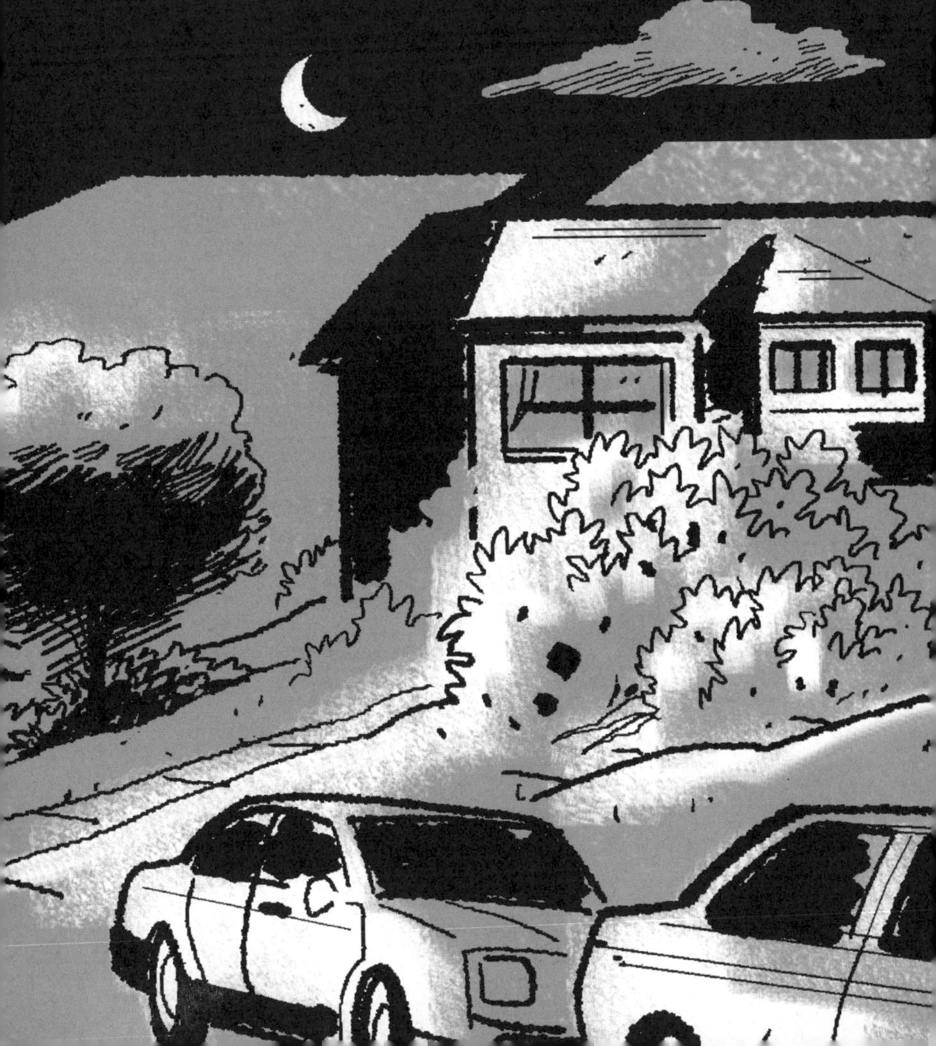